THE CROSS IN THE SKY

The life and adventures of Charles 'Moth' Eaton
Soldier – Pioneer aviator – Pathfinder for global peacekeeping

Charles Stuart Eaton

Foreword by Dick Smith AC

Retrospective by Air Commodore Mark Lax OAM, CSC, PhD (Retd.)

First Published in 2021 by Echo Books

Echo Books is an imprint of Superscript Publishing Pty Ltd, ABN 76 644 812 395

Registered Office: Suite 401, 140 Bourke St, Melbourne, VIC, 3000

www.echobooks.com.au

Copyright © Charles Stuart Eaton

Creator: Eaton, Charles Stuart author.

Title: The Cross in the Sky: The life and adventures of Charles 'Moth' Eaton
Soldier—Pioneer aviator—Pathfinder for global peacekeeping

ISBN: 978-0-6488546-2-3 (softcover)

 A catalogue record for this book is available from the National Library of Australia

Book layout and design by Peter Gamble, Canberra.
Set in Garamond Premier Pro Display, 12/15 and Trajan Pro.
Back cover image: *'On patrol' Over the Line: France, 17 June 1918.*
www.echobooks.com.au

CONTENTS

Dedication		v
Foreword–Dick Smith AC		vii
Prologue		xi
1	Lambs to the Slaughter, 1915	1
2	The Third Wave: Loos, 1915	9
3	That Minenwerfer Hour: Vimy Ridge, 1916	15
4	Flaming Coffins and the Silent Raid, 1917	23
5	Jump or Burn, 1918	31
6	An Undesirable in Festung Neun, 1918	39
7	Flying High, 1919	51
8	Tribal Protector, 1921	61
9	Fear, 1922	69
10	One Royal Salute and a Close Call, 1927	83
11	A Call to the Rescue, 1929	93
12	The Cross in the Sky, 1929	111
13	Facts From Fiction, 1929	127
14	Kookaburra Postscript	137
15	Flying the Rails, 1929	145
16	'A Miracle'—Finding Lasseter's Golden Quest II, 1931	157
17	Intermezzo, 1931–1939	167

18 Moth Eaton's Flying Circus, 1939–1940	183
19 Confrontations, 1939–40	195
20 War Games, 1941	201
21 Training the Empire, 1942	215
22 'The River War'— West Papua, 1943	221
23 One Wing, a Broken Pipe and a Prayer, 1943–44	229
24 A Knight with Swords, 1944	243
25 'The Hitch-Hiking Consul': Our Man in Timor, 1946	259
26 Oil on Troubled Waters, 1947	269
27 The Pathfinder, 1947	279
28 In the Line of Fire, 1947	291
29 A Diplomatic Missionary, 1948–51	305
30 Twilight: Moth's Last Flight, 1952–81	321
In Retrospect: Air Commodore Mark Lax OAM CSM PhD	333
Family Background	337
Last Word: Author's Notation and Acknowledgements	343
Endnotes	348
Abbreviations	355
References–Bibliography	357
Illustrations	371

Lieutenant Keith Anderson's grave in the desert. Sergeant Eric Douglas (left) and Flight Lieutenant Charles 'Moth' Eaton (right)

DEDICATION

'Ft. Lt. Eaton first saw the cloud and pointed it out to me ... it was quite eerie.'
Sergeant Eric Douglas,
29 April 1929

'For knowledge cannot be gotten from ghosts and spirits, cannot be had by analogy, cannot be found out by calculation.
It must be obtained from people, people who know the conditions of the enemy.'[1]

The Cross in the Sky is dedicated to reconnaissance personnel of all nations who served their country in war and peace. Their dangerous and lonely missions rarely led to public glory or popular acclaim, but without the information they collected the security of their respective countries would have been diminished. Also remembered, with pride and honour, are Keith Vincent Anderson and Henry Smith 'Bobby' Hitchock, who laid down their lives for their friends.[2]

'Aerobatics.' Flight Lieutenant Charles Eaton left and Major Hereward de Havilland in the front cockpit. Circa 1934.

Foreword — Dick Smith AC

'My obsession—for that is what it became—the finding of the Kookaburra. The fact is, I wanted to solve a mystery ... it was a chilling experience to stare down at that appalling waste; and which they had tried to cross in their tiny old-fashioned and patched-up mono-plane.'

Dick Smith, 1980

My association with Charles Eaton began with my ambition to locate the remains of the monoplane *Kookaburra*, which had disappeared in the Tanami Desert of Central Australia in April 1929. Pilot Keith Anderson, together with his mechanic Bobby Hitchcock, had been searching for Australia's hero, Charles Kingsford Smith, and his aircraft *Southern Cross*, and been reported missing. The saga of the search for the *Kookaburra* and its tragic consequences, the torturous deaths of the two lost aviators, is firmly embedded in aviation folklore. Charles commanded the month-long search but unfortunately the two aviators perished of thirst before the lost aircraft was located. Immediately after burying Anderson, an exceptional natural phenomenon was seen by Charles and other members of the expedition; that incident provides the title of this book.

The Kookaburra affair also triggered Charles' long association with Australia's north, including leading the successful search for lost members of the second Lasseter Expedition in 1931. The numerous Territorial memorials and place-names in Charles Eaton's honour testify to his status as a pioneer aviator of northern Australia.

After successfully finding the sad remains of the Kookaburra on my third attempt in August 1978, I decided to visit the extraordinary Charles 'Moth' Eaton. I found Moth and his wife Beatrice in a retirement home in the Melbourne suburb of Frankston. Even at this stage, now well into his eighties, he was dynamic and had the eyes of a true adventurer. His memories of locating the *Kookaburra* with his ground party and burying the aviators' bodies were clear and evoked strong emotions. In those days, travelling deep into the Australian deserts on horseback had risks of its own; in Moth's case it resulted in 11 of his party's 26 horses dying of thirst.

A group picture of London schoolboys taken in 1910 shows a 14-year old Charles looking away and gazing into the distance towards the adventures of his dreams. For the next 40 years he fulfilled those dreams in a manner beyond which he, or anyone else, could ever have imagined. Moth was the ultimate survivor after serving with the 'Colours' every day of both world wars; first as a trench bomber, as a reconnaissance pilot in, and over, the bloody fields of France and when dodging bullets from German guards when escaping from the notorious Festung Neun fortress during World War I. His life of adventure and danger continued in India, the deserts of Central Australia and during World War II, when he experienced some 'close calls'.

This extraordinary account by his son, Charles Stuart, evokes an image of a man totally dedicated to duty and service, first to Great Britain and, later, to his adopted country—Australia. The story is told through sequential vignettes, themselves an illustration of the tumultuous events of the last century coupled with a portrayal of the units and personalities with whom Moth served.

Moth mentions in his brief personal notes that '*autobiographies are usually dull and uninteresting*' but added that his intention was to give to the younger generation a grasp of what could happen to '*all who have inherited a spirit of travel and adventure*'.

Although Moth is well known in Australian aviation circles, I was surprised to learn that he was an initiator of military monitors in the early days of the United Nations. His contribution to world peacekeeping in 1947 should be recognised as the major achievement of his life.

Perhaps no better accolade for Charles Eaton can be given than by one who served with him in the 30-day drama that dominated the Australian media and polarised the nation. Sergeant Eric Douglas, a pilot in the search for the *Kookaburra* who accompanied Eaton on the horrendous ground expedition, wrote in 1954:

> Flight Lt. Eaton, upon whom most of the responsibility had fallen, had proved equal to the task and had proved to be an outstanding leader. He had been in the forefront of all flying operations and ground work and had spent long hours in arranging requirements and making dispatches to the Air Board.
>
> Undoubtedly his personal example and courage displayed had been followed by his officers and men and never at any time was there the slightest dissention among the members of the search party. For his great efforts he was awarded the decoration of the Air Force Cross.

Charles Stuart Eaton has spent hundreds of hours accumulating supporting archival records and cataloguing his father's unique photographic collection to strengthen the story and to learn about his father's and his compatriots' lives. The result is a fascinating and important biography of one of our most deserving Australian flyers and diplomats of the 20th Century.

Dick Smith

Sydney, 2019

Sergeant Eric Douglas, April 1929

The stranded Western Widgeon monoplane, Kookaburra, mid-afternoon on 28 April 1929. In the right foreground, the grave of Henry 'Bobby' Hitchcock and in the mid-foreground, the hole dug by the two aviators in their fruitless search for water.

PROLOGUE

Deserts are pitiless places. What the desert claims, the desert will likely keep. Such a place—the remote and trackless Tanami Desert of Australia's Central Australia—had claimed the lives of Keith Anderson and 'Bobby' Hitchcock at some time in the days before the search party could find them.

With a modest burial service and final goodbyes offered, the bodies of the two perished aviators were finally committed to the infinite solitude of the Tanami's sands. Dusk was approaching when Flight Lieutenant Charles Eaton gave the order for the search party to return the 25 miles to their camp and water. As the small party trudged away from the *Kookaburra* and the graves of his two fellow aviators, Eaton looked skywards and was struck by the sight of high cirrus clouds scribing the sign of a cross in an otherwise cloudless sky. Such a vision was almost too much to bear, even for a man of his faint religious conviction. He later described it as '*a perfect cross*', while his companion, Sergeant Eric Douglas, thought it uncannily '*eerie*'.

The sensational story of the disappearance of the *Southern Cross* and Australia's hero Sir Charles Kingsford Smith and his crew, the subsequent forced-landing of the *Kookaburra*, the progress of the Eaton Expedition's search and the horrendous deaths of Anderson and Hitchcock dominated Australia's media for months and launched a controversy that continues to the present. At the official inquiry into the so called 'Coffee Royal Affair', Eaton's evidence exonerated Sir Charles of any impropriety.

The month-long saga introduced Charles Eaton to the Northern Territory, where he was to make a significant contribution, first by establishing and then participating in the aerial defence of northern Australia and West Papua. Following World War II, he was delegated to establish Australia's diplomatic relations with both East Timor and an emergent Indonesia. In September 1947, he became the pathfinder for United Nations peacekeeping.

THE WESTERN FRONT 1914–1918

Images: Australian War Memorial and the Charles Eaton Collection

Private Charles Eaton's War on the Western Front: 1915-1918

1. 25 May, 1915. — Givenchy - First direct action, bombing the Prussian Guards' trenches.
2. 18 Sept. — Loos - Escorting gas to 'The Line'.
3. 25 Sept. — Loos - 'Over the Top' in the third wave against the Bavarians.
4. 27 Sept. — Loos - Burying the dead after Loos
5. December — Hohenzollen Redoubt - Holding 'The Line' captured by the 15th Scottish.
6. 4 January, 1916. — Loos Sector - Relieving the French 18 Division.
7. March — Vimy Ridge - Manning 'The Line'.
8. 21 May — Vimy Ridge - 'That Minerwefer Hour'. Assault by the German 5th Foot Guards. Company retreated.
9. 24 May — Company regained their trenches.
10. July 1916 – February 1917. — Somme battlefield - Company transferred to IV Corps. Attached as mobile support troops, trench bombers, trench raiding and reconnaissance, plugging the line.
11. February-April 1917 — Somme battlefield. Scouting the withdrawal of the German Army, reconnoitre the Somme river crossing for IV Corps. Transferred to Royal Flying Corps for training and the defence of London.
12. May 1918 — Joined 206 Squadron, Alquines in France.
13. June 23 — Jointly claimed a Fokker Dr I.
14. June 24 — Unsuccessfully claimed a Albatross Vee Strutter.
15. June 26 — Shot down by German aircraft.
16. June 29 — Lestrem. Crash landed, in the forward German trench line.
17. July — Solitary confinement in Lille Civil Goal after failed escape attempt. Transferred to Stalag Karlsrule in Germany.

Leonard Keyworth, VC, second left, after his investure with the Victoria Cross in 1915. The insignia of the Pascal Lamb can be seen on the soldiers' caps.

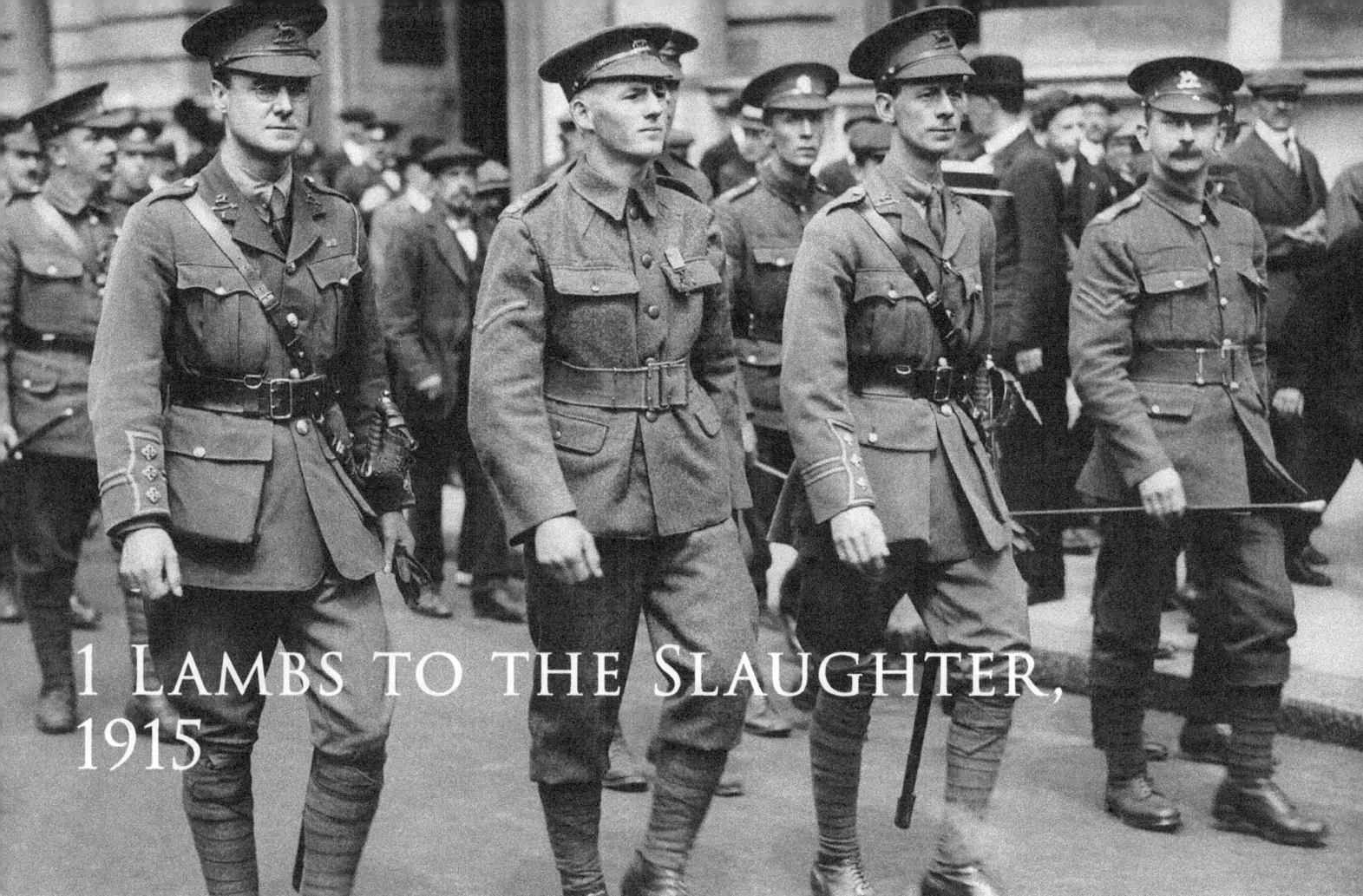

1 Lambs to the Slaughter, 1915

Of course, the usual experiences which have so often been told regarding the trench warfare in Europe, the usual excitement, followed by periods of dull monotony —all this until 1917.

Charles Eaton, 1953

Charles Eaton enlisted as a Territorial private soldier in 1912, initially training as an infantryman with the Queen's West Surrey Regiment, popularly known as 'The Lambs'.[1] He subsequently served as a soldier and then aviator throughout the entirety of both world wars. During his 25 months in 'The Line'[2] on the Western Front, Charles experienced the *'usual excitement'* faced by most frontline soldiers of all armies.

Charles served in France from 1915 to 1917 with 47 (Territorial) London Division and, later, with a specialist mobile battalion of the British Army's IV Corps. Although he played only a minor role in many fierce encounters that sometimes involved hundreds of thousands of belligerent soldiers, Charles' participation must have moulded his character and resilience. It must have shaped the tenacity that helped him overcome the many adversities and challenges he faced throughout his life.³

In August 1914 the division's units, which were partially armed and equipped, began intensive training. Charles transferred to the division's Cyclist Company which, together with C Squadron King Edward's Horse, formed the division's mounted troops. By the outbreak of war, many infantry battalions had cyclist units as mobile support troops. The cyclists were employed as trench bombers, filled the gap when infantry units were over-run and investigated 'green fields beyond'—enemy trench reconnaissance or 'trench raiding'. When in reserve, cyclists became despatch riders, undertook guard duties and buried the fallen.

While Charles was still stationed in England, in France the French Army had checked the German advance on the Marne and the British Expeditionary Force (BEF) had halted the Germans' assault at Ypres. Early in March 1915, the BEF launched a misconceived attack at Neuve Chapelle with heavy losses. To strengthen the depleted divisions of the BEF, 47 Division was ordered to France to join I Corps under General Douglas Haig.

Charles and his comrades-in-arms travelled by train from Watford to Southampton on the cold wet morning of 14 March 1915. At 7 pm that evening they embarked on the SS *Copenhagen*. Few soldiers slept due to cold, sea sickness and anticipation of what the company's history termed their *'Great Adventure'*. On disembarking at the French port of Le Havre the following morning, the young raw soldiers were introduced to *'French cobbles, bullybif, bisque and jig-a-jig'*.

On 19 March the company, commanded by Captain HC Leman, rode to Bourecq as mechanical cavalry, wearing shaggy grey or piebald goatskin coats. The unit's historian wrote that they looked more like a *'wild west show'* than regular soldiers, causing much merriment to other formations. Due to the BEF's shortage of rifles⁴, the company were initially issued with

The Young Lamb: Private Charles Eaton, Regt No. 357, 1914.

The cyclists were employed as trench bombers, filled the gap when infantry units were over-run and investigated 'green fields beyond'—enemy trench reconnaissance or 'trench raiding'. When in reserve, cyclists became despatch riders, undertook guard duties and buried the fallen.

bayonets only. They relieved the Meerut Indian Division, which was holding The Line at Festubert. Indian *sepoys*[5] had fiercely contested the German advance during the winter of 1914–15, with Naik (Corporal) Dawan Singh Negi of the 39 Garhwal Rifles winning the Victoria Cross (VC) for exemplary bravery.

In *No Man's Land*, Sargent Stadler of the Lambs recorded that where the Indians had attacked, there had been a terrible slaughter: '*There were dozens of dead in all sorts of frightful attitudes and conditions.*' Charles mentioned his high regard for the Indian soldiers, who fought so far from their homes in bitterly cold conditions. From his contacts with the Meerut soldiers, he gained a taste for Indian cuisine. Only five years later he participated in the first aerial survey of India and acquired a harmonious relationship with the indigenous pre-Aryan peoples of Orissa's hill tracts—and a lifelong fascination for wildlife and orchids.

The cyclists received their first casualties while guarding the breastworks. Initially there were no trenches at Festubert; the war of the static trenches for the troops began a few weeks later. The company's War Diary recorded that the cyclists carried out every conceivable purpose and, more than once, took their turn most efficiently in the trenches. Charles wrote a field service postcard to his family: '*I am quite well,*' and '*I have received your letter.*' Nothing else was added to the pre-typed script; all replies paid by the sender. He was worried about his family's concerns for his safety as the division had already been heavily shelled, with 320 men killed or wounded. The BEF's—and the division's—trench warfare was about to begin in earnest. A new trench line, named the 'Scottish Trench', was constructed at the nearby village of Givenchy. The trench was to be the jumping-off point for the division's first planned offensive and the final action of the wider battle of Festubert. More than 2000 sandbags, 30 scaling ladders and 800 hand grenades strengthened the trench.

Captain Dunn described Givenchy in an infantryman's language:

> The Givenchy sector was in front of the village of the same name. It had a dry sticky trench system running northwards to 'The Warren' where the ground fell sharply, thence the line ran north to Festubert. Here, too the Germans had advantage of elevation. No-man's-land was more than

Sargent Stadler of the Lambs recorded that where the Indians had attacked, there had been a terrible slaughter

Charles wrote a field service postcard to his family: 'I am quite well,' and 'I have received your letter.'

300 yards wide on the right: at The Warren, a rectangular projection in the German system narrowed it to 100 yards, and mine craters nearly filled the space, reducing the distance between the opposing bombing posts to 25 yards. Craters along most of the front were mostly German-blown; they were of great tactical value in defence.

On 25 May the brigade's commander, bestowed with the potpourri of a moniker, Brigadier-General The Honourable Charles Strathavon Heathcote-Drummond-Willoughby, or more simply dubbed 'Charlie', issued the following instructions:

> The Brigade will attack the enemy's trench and breastwork lying East of GIVENCHY from the B3 Section at 6.30 p.m. today. Objective—The Line I8–J 11. This objective when gained will be at once consolidated and connected with our present line by a defensive right flank 18–12–14. The left flank will maintain (in) touch with the 140th Infantry Brigade and be prepared to connect with the Canadian Division attack. The 140th and 141st Brigades will maintain their present ground and assist the attack by fire.

Two brigades were to attack the German line known as 'S Bend' with the First Canadian Division. The bend in the trench system was clearly the rectangular projection referred to by Captain Dunn. The offensive was to start at 6.30 pm; the main attack was to be by 142 Infantry Brigade, which included 24 and 22 Lamb battalions. The artillery barrage was to begin at 2 pm, with 10 minutes of shrapnel followed by half an hour of high explosive shelling; this pattern was to be used until 6.25 pm. A French battery that strengthened the division's artillery was commanded by an aggressive officer who ordered '*Arroser les Boches. Tuez les Boches, et encore tuez les Boches!*' ('Spray the Huns. Kill the Huns, and again kill the Huns!'). Each soldier was issued with 200 rounds of ammunition with another 300 rounds in reserve. Apart from rifles and ammunition, every man was to carry his knapsack, two sandbags, respirator, a full water bottle and a day's food ration; each unit carried 20 blankets for the wounded. Regimental aid posts were allocated for each battalion and directions given for the evacuation of the wounded, but no mention was made about the disposal of the dead. The divisional ambulances were to assemble at the aptly named 'Harley Street'.

A French battery that strengthened the division's artillery was commanded by an aggressive officer who ordered 'Arroser les Boches. Tuez les Boches, et encore tuez les Boches!'

The attack began on time. Charles and 'Charlie' Napier—his school friend, mentor and now corporal—were part of the trench bombing party of 75. Trench bombers carried no rifles; they were armed with bombs and daggers: '*The almost private weapon, made of iron, certainly brought forth many sarcastic remarks in contempt for those that thought of it.*'[6] By 1 am, after capturing 20 Germans, heavy losses amongst the bombers necessitated the abandonment of trenches I.2 to I.9. The Germans had counter-attacked with bombing and sustained rifle fire from the right flank. At 3.30 am, D Company and two other platoons were withdrawn to their original jump-off point, the Scottish Trench. Unfortunately, a number of D Company soldiers who had joined the attack by mistake now lay dead or wounded or were missing in the tangle of abandoned trenches. Dawn saw the loss of communications between the remaining occupied trenches. Runners ran back to the Scottish Trench for assistance to evacuate the hundreds of wounded and attempt to extricate the dead.

Sargent Stadler explains:
> Givenchy was a death trap. There was a network of trenches named after all the thoroughfares around Whitehall; enemy bombardments were frequent and heavy. We were warned that the enemy were using flamethrowers; this last piece of information was not very comforting.

Brigadier Charlie reported on the appalling congestion in the communication trench, where parties carrying ammunition and bombs were attempting to avoid the wounded and dead. Enemy shelling recommenced at 7.30 am from the right flank, causing more casualties. All officers of 23 Battalion were now dead or wounded and there were barely enough men to hold the forward trench. Lieutenant Chance, a young subaltern, lay mortally wounded in open ground but ordered his men not to rescue him as it would be suicide to try. Orders were to hold the front, so Captain Millner volunteered to crawl to the forward position to direct the disorientated survivors who by now had suffered 13 hours of murderous combat and were holed up in half-made trenches. Although brigade headquarters understood that the forward trench was about to be abandoned, the front somehow held under Millner's firm leadership.

Trench bombers carried no rifles; they were armed with bombs and daggers.

Givenchy was a death trap.

The exhausted Lambs, including the wounded, dug in and managed to hold their tenuous positions. Millner reported that the Germans had also suffered heavy losses in their counter-attacks. At 11 am, D Company and a section of their fellow Lambs of 22 Battalion relieved 24 Battalion. Although German shelling continued throughout the afternoon, no more enemy counter-attacks were mounted; by 5 am the following day, all was quiet apart from spasmodic and random sniping.

Meanwhile, the cyclists not in the bombing party had the unenviable job of collecting stragglers and then identifying and burying the dead. The casualties suffered by 24 Battalion over 24 hours included 408 killed, wounded or missing—about 40 per cent of total strength. 22 Battalion got off more lightly with only two killed, two missing and 73 wounded. Death was no respecter of rank; 141 Brigade Commander, General Nugent, died by a sniper's bullet.

Brigadier Charlie acknowledged the cyclists' trench bombing efforts:

> The 24th Battalion (by runner) sent me a message (timed 8.40 pm) saying they were unable to advance with A., B. and C. Companies which were now about I.4, but were endeavouring to consolidate, and required bombs in large quantities. I sent him up bombs and shortly afterwards a party of Divisional Cyclist Co. who had been trained as bombers under 2nd Lieut. K. G. GUNN arrived at my headquarters and I sent them up to report to Colonel Simpson. This party did exceptionally good work.

Following the battle, Charles' mate Charlie Napier received the Distinguished Conduct Medal (DCM) and another Lamb, Lance-Corporal Leonard Keyworth, the Victoria Cross. Keyworth stood fully exposed for two hours tossing about 150 bombs at the Germans only a few yards away. Sadly, he died of wounds at Loos later in the year. 24 Battalion's commander complimented the bombers and highlighted the casualty rate of almost 80 per cent:

> I should like to draw attention to the good work done by the bombers both of this Battalion and the Divisional Cyclist Company. The bombers went into action 75 strong and came out numbering 17.

Leonard Keyworth, Charlie Napier and Charles Eaton were among the 17 bombers who survived. The brigade's fighting strength had been reduced to a third after 24 hours of combat. Eaton never referred to any particular incident of his army service between 1914 and 1917, except to say, *'One never could escape the filth, the dirt and the mud,'* and to praise the Indian soldiers.

'One never could escape the filth, the dirt and the mud,'

The details of the Givenchy trench attack and the Loos incident (Vignette 2), *'firing over the bodies of his dead comrades,'* were related by Beatrice Eaton.[7] Perhaps these horrific experiences were a factor in Charles' total refrain from discussing death.

The young Lambs, the majority from Surrey or South London, had experienced enemy shelling for the first time only weeks previously. In the broad scale of WWI, the attack on Givenchy's trenches represented only a minor skirmish and was a secondary and final component of the Battle of Festubert, *'where the British went over the top in ordered massed ranks and died the same way—mowed down by a scythe of lead costing over 10,000 casualties'*.

Charles was initiated into bloody combat at Givenchy; thereafter, he mentioned Givenchy perhaps only two or three times, rather distantly and never in detail. The one-line quote from Eaton's notes, written in 1953, is the only recorded memorandum he made after 25 months as a frontline soldier on the Western Front during WWI:

Lance Corporal Leonard Keyworth (centre) being chaired by fellow 'Lambs' after being decorated with the Victoria Cross following the night action of 25–26 May, 1915; Givenchy, Artois France. An estimated one third of those pictured in this photograph who served in France lost their lives.
(Courtesy: Surrey Military Museum)

Of course, the usual experiences which have so often been told regarding the trench warfare in Europe, the usual excitement, followed by periods of dull monotony—all this until 1917.

Postscript

Lance Corporal Lenard Keyworth, VC—Citation:

> For most conspicuous bravery at Givenchy on the night of 25–26th May, 1915. After the assault on the German position by the 24th Battalion, London Regt, efforts were made by that Unit to follow up their success by a bomb attack, during the progress of which 58 men out of a total 75 became casualties. During this very fierce encounter Lance-Corporal Keyworth stood fully exposed for 2 hours on the top of the enemy's parapet, and threw about 150 bombs amongst the Germans, who were only a few yards away.[8]

Charles Napier, DCM—Citation:

> For conspicuous gallantry on the 25th and 26th May 1915, at Givenchy. After the withdrawal of a bombing party, and having become separated from it, he remained in the trenches with a Serjeant and some men of another Battalion, and greatly assisted this small party by the use of his bombs in retaining possession of a captured trench.

On 24 February 1916 Charles Napier also received the *Médaille Militaire* from France *'in recognition of distinguished service during the campaign'*.

The 47 London Division advancing through the gas barrage, Loos, 25 September 1915. Charles was in the third wave. (Source: Public Domain)

Charles 'Charlie' Napier with parents, 1918

2 THE THIRD WAVE: LOOS, 1915

When a platoon commander of the platoon ahead of the poet Robert Graves jumped out of his trench and called 'forward', not a man moved. The commander berated his troops 'you bloody cowards, are you leaving me to go alone'. His sergeant, himself badly wounded, replied 'Not cowards Sir. Willing enough. But they're all dead.' As they climbed their ladders after the whistles blew, an observant German machine gunner caught them all.

Graves, R, 1957

The BEF's commander, Field Marshal Sir John French, decided to support the French Army in Artois Province. French preferred to tackle Aubers Ridge or Messines but France's General 'Papa' Joffre influenced the British to capture Loos instead. In late September, to support their allies, the BEF's First Army made plans to attack at Loos. A coal mining and farming town, Loos (officially Loos-en-Gohelle) is a commune in the Nord-Pas-de-Calais region of France. By the end of WWI, not a single building or tree survived.

The plan was for 12 divisions to capture the German fortifications and encircle the enemy defenders. Located on the extreme right of the proposed attack, Charles' division was the only Territorial unit that participated but had the critical role of capturing the defence system on the Lens–Bethune road. Some of the mounted troops stayed in reserve and others were given special duties to accompany the infantry in the attack. Charles and his unit had the dubious honour of ferrying *'the heavy, filthy'* gas cylinders to The Line; the first occasion gas was used in the history of the British Army.

Four days of artillery bombardment preceded the offensive, scheduled for 25 September. At 5.45 am on a warm, dry autumn morning, 951 British guns lit up the morning sky and demolished part of the front German line 100 to 500 yards distant. At 6 am, more than 150 tons of gas were expelled towards the enemy lines, some of which drifted back into their own trenches. When officers' whistles blew 30 minutes later, some 75,000 men climbed out of the trenches in staged waves in a bloody frontal assault. One Middlesex unit had to advance earlier, driven out of their trenches by their own gas.

Poet Robert Graves witnessed the total annihilation of an adjoining platoon as they lumbered out of their trench line. Liddall Hart records the ineptitude of a divisional commander after a junior officer cancelled the attack due to gas blowback:

> [General] Horne replied with an order 'the programme must continue whatever the conditions'. As a result of this obstinacy, many of the infantry were poisoned by their own gas. Those who were able to advance were soon stopped then slaughtered by German machine gunners. Nevertheless, Horne ordered a fresh assault, which was only abandoned after his Brigade commanders had protested against the 'useless sacrifice of life'.

A section of the cyclists may have formed a part of the third wave; family anecdotal evidence tells of Charles and his comrades being pinned down in open No Man's Land by concentrated enemy fire and barbed wire. Charles continued firing his rifle at German soldiers he could see standing on parapets; for protection he used 'human sandbags'—the bodies of British dead from the first and second waves. In similar circumstances at Ypres, the hard-pressed Liverpool Regiment built a wall of German dead as protective cover. Years later, Bea Eaton recalled that the first day of Loos had been the most horrendous day of her husband's life.[1]

Charles and his unit had the dubious honour of ferrying 'the heavy, filthy' gas cylinders to The Line; the first occasion gas was used in the history of the British Army.

Charles' 47 Division encountered substantial barbed-wire defences, resulting in hundreds of soldiers hanging on the wire either dead or wounded; an event that sparked Charles' life-long abhorrence of barbed wire. Corporal Moylan, who went over the top at the same time as Charles, gives a vivid image:

> In an attack, the whole thing seems a bit like a dream. It doesn't take as long as you think. Crossing No Man's Land. There were a lot of our dead in No Man's Land as we crossed and more at the places where they'd arrived at the wire and it wasn't cut. Then they were sitting ducks. We just went through the gaps in the wire but we weren't in the first wave luckily.

Sargent Stadler, a fellow Lamb, wrote that he stood on the brink of hell:

> Around me I saw piles of barb wire torn in heaps, unexploded shells, dead and dying, there was Bomber Miller dead, another tearing at the soil in his death agony.

On the stalled left flank, the British suffered crippling losses before the undamaged wire defences, as confirmed by German witnesses:

> We had a wonderful view. The English attacked in whole hosts and with great dash. Our men fired standing up as fast as they could pull the triggers. No Englishman got through the wire entanglement and the ground in front was covered in bodies.

However, 15 (Scottish) Division battered and bayoneted through the German line, causing panic at the German headquarters. The success of the Scots came at a huge cost, with more than 6000 casualties in two days. In General Capper's words before he was himself killed, the Scots had *'done the impossible by completely breaking the German lines of defence'*. Capper commanded 7 Division at Loos; armed only with a bayonet, he was cut down going forward with his soldiers.

Acts of bravery on both sides were common. Piper Laidlaw of 15 (Scottish) Division saw from his trench the appalling confusion caused by blowback gas and uncut barbed wire. Without orders, he leapt over the parapet and marched up and down in open No Man's Land, piping his compatriots on with stirring Scottish airs. Severely wounded in both legs,

'Around me I saw piles of barb wire torn in heaps, unexploded shells, dead and dying, there was Bomber Miller dead, another tearing at the soil in his death agony.'

Laidlaw continued to play the pipes while prostrate on the killing fields, thereby winning the Victoria Cross.

In one extraordinary incident, 17-year-old *lycee* student Mademoiselle Emilienne Moreau became involved in battle after her house became a first-aid post for wounded British soldiers. As the enemy attacked, she borrowed a pistol from a wounded officer and shot a number of German soldiers dead. In his despatches, General Haig termed Emilienne the 'Joan of Arc of Loos'. She was awarded the Military Medal (MM) by King George V and the *Croix de Guerre* by the French Government. Emilienne later became a decorated resistance fighter in World War II.

At about the same time, elsewhere on The Line, two runners with the Bavarians—one Corporal Hitler and one unnamed—risked their lives to find out what was happening to their endangered compatriots and returned 'by the skin of their teeth' to report the worst; their unit was cut off. Hitler ran to inform the hard-pressed Bavarians that a British attack was imminent and survived the deadly barrage once more.

Eventually, frontal attacks over open ground ceased and Loos became a series of trench hand-bomb fights; another Givenchy, but on a grander scale. By 5 October, Charles' company returned to their old job of trench bombers in support of IV Corps.

Conceivably, if Field Marshal French had committed British reserves 24 hours earlier and 47 Division had continued their advance and routed the Bavarians, world history may have taken a different turn. Loos damaged French's career; his replacement as commander of the BEF was a Scot, Douglas Haig.

In *Loos 1915*, historian Trainor wrote:

> However, no one could deny that a grand opportunity had been lost. [Field Marshal] French had started out with a triumph, turned it into a stalemate, and ended up with a disaster. British casualties totalled 2,013 officers and 48,367 men. No fewer than 28 battalion commanders died at Loos.

An observation officer, Richard Hilton, confirmed Trainor's opinion:

> *A great deal of nonsense has been written about Loos. The real tragedy of that battle was its nearness to complete success. Most of us who reached the crest of Hill 70, and survived, were firmly convinced that we had broken through on that Sunday, 25th September 1915. There seemed to be nothing ahead of us, but an unoccupied and incomplete trench system.*

Some historians estimate the British casualties at the five-day battle as more than 60,000 killed, missing, wounded or taken prisoner. The parallel French offensive in Champagne was an even bigger disaster, with the loss of over 100,000 *poilu*.[2] German losses were fewer, with 19,836 casualties and another 3153 taken prisoner.

Charles was one of the many casualties of Loos, receiving a wound to his left calf that required a field dressing. A six-inch pencil-line scar was a life-long memento of the battle and the only physical injury he received in two world wars. Charles was yet to survive protracted action on the Somme front in 1916–17, being shot at by German guards after escaping from *Festung Nuen,* at least eight aeroplane crashes caused by German and Japanese action or engine failures, and an ambush by vigilantes in Indonesia's war of independence.

By all accounts, the Battle of Loos was his darkest hour. In retirement, when the word Loos was mentioned on a news documentary, Charles sat back in his lounge chair, face in the air, and mumbled *Looooooooz* as if the word had no ending.

British cyclists passing through the ruined village of Brie following the German withdrawal to the Hindenburg Line, Somme 1917.
Q1868: Lt Ernest Brook
(Courtesy Imperial War Museum)

3 That Minenwerfer Hour: Vimy Ridge, 1916

70,000 shells delivered by 80 German batteries on a 1,800 yard front in four horrendous hours.[1]

In November 1915, after two months in The Line, Charles' unit was relieved; they had taken part in wide-ranging and diverse *'excitements'* that included delivering chlorine gas, the Loos assault, trench-bombing, burying the dead and night raids on enemy positions. The cyclists were rested at Sailly-Labourne for a pre-Christmas dinner and then issued with sheepskins, jerkins and frost-bite grease. On their return to the trenches, they would face their twin enemies, 'Jack Frost' and the German Army.

In mid-December, the company manned the Hohenzollern Redoubt that British IV Corps had captured. They found the trenches almost uninhabitable, not least because they first needed to remove bodies that protruded from the mud and the debris of war. Many British soldiers had become accustomed to trenches that perhaps resembled the cave-dwellings of early man.

New Year 1916 saw Charles' company, acting as infantry, relieving the French 18 Division on Vimy Ridge, adjacent to the Loos sector. The British line was extended by 20 miles, thereby releasing the French 10 Army to relieve pressure on Verdun. Vimy Ridge was aptly named 'The Windy Corner of the Western Front'. The cyclists' unit history reported the trenches, evacuated by their French allies, were *'atrocious'*. The continuous fortified front trench system shown on army maps did not exist. Historians of WW1 wrote that The Line was at times unfit for use, with non-existent drainage and sanitary arrangements, with unburied bodies and the flotsam and jetsam of battle strewn everywhere:

> The trenches were described by the incoming troops as merely shell holes joined up ... hastily organised positions in 'mine craters' ... the front trenches can only be reached at night over the open, and with great difficulty ... The wire, where any existed, was 'weak and thin' ... Dug-outs were 'small damp and bad' ... To sum up, the ground might be sufficiently organised for the launching of an offensive, but offered only precious tenure as a defensive line.²

Since the catastrophic battles of the 1915 Champagne campaign, the Allies and Germans had operated a passive 'live and let live' approach. The company enjoyed this unofficial armistice. The enemy exposed themselves freely and even made efforts of friendly conversation. One thoughtful German unit sent a copy of *The Times* to their opposing trench line. This approach ended with aggressive reconnaissance raids of enemy trenches by the cyclists; the raiding parties soon discovered that the enemy had taken advantage of the phoney peace to activate deep mining.

As specialist troops, the company's duties included raiding enemy positions. With blackened faces, they raided German positions to capture prisoners, identify enemy units, collect *'loot and enemy novelties'* and see no mining was being carried out. On one occasion, sappers accompanied the trench raiders

The cyclists' unit history reported the trenches, evacuated by their French allies, were 'atrocious'.

With blackened faces, they raided German positions to capture prisoners, identify enemy units, collect 'loot and enemy novelties' and see no mining was being carried out.

with explosives to blow the enemy trench. On another raid, the cyclists were met with artillery, trench-mortar and machine gun fire. In this incident, only a few raiders managed to get close to their objective, throw their bombs and quickly depart. These raids were fraught with danger, as Maude's 47 Division history noted:

> Undoubtedly many such enterprises were spoiled by the fact the Boche frequently overheard our telephone conversations on his listening sets. Many months later, we learnt from a captured document that he had on one occasion heard our Town Mayor of Villers-au-Bois announce to a frontline battalion that he would have billets ready for them after their relief that evening.

Secret Operation Order 36 exemplified the responsibilities the raiding parties were expected to carry out:

1. GENERAL

It is proposed to conduct a minor operation against the German trenches in M26.c at a date to be notified later. The operation will be divided into two enterprises, one known as 'THE MISSION', and the other known as 'THE HARVEST PARTY'.

2. OBJECTIVES

    (a)   To obtain prisoners and identifications.
    (b)   To kill Germans.
    (c)   To obtain information
    (d)   To obtain loot and enemy novelties.
    (e)   To ascertain whether mining works are in progress.
    (f)   To ascertain whether gas is installed.
    (g)   To destroy M.G. (Machine Gun) emplacements.

When on raiding operations, the raiders carried no equipment except for their own helmet, gas mask, rifle and bayonet, one clip of ammunition in the magazine, five spare clips, two bombs and a wire cutter. All hands and faces were blackened with charcoal and Vaseline. They were banned from carrying any identification marks, personal papers or letters. Once the raid had met its objective, officers usually sounded horns and fired coloured rockets to signify a hasty withdrawal with prisoners and loot. If they captured prisoners, they were not to converse; if captured themselves, they were to give their rank and number only. Throughout his life, Charles never kept a personal diary; when asked why, he said his training stipulated that he *'should have nothing on me in case of capture or death'*. This practice was confirmed by Private P Osmet, reminiscing about his participation at the Battle of Loos:

> I regret that I am not able to give you any letters or diaries, in the first place we have little time to write letters and anything written about the battle would be censored ... As for keeping diaries by other ranks would have been death or any other less punishment as may be inflicted upon you by a General Court Martial as read out to all troops regularly before the outbreak of war.³

After another change of trenches, Charles and his company found their new accommodation, 'Ersatz Alley', chaotic. During April and May, the company reconstructed trenches, dug dugouts and made their position as strong as possible, interrupted by the occasional trench raid. Their enemy was well entrenched in another village, also called Givenchy. Although the cyclists were adaptable multi-disciplined troops, they were never used as miners. At one stage, more than 10 tunnelling companies were undermining the German trenches. Once a mine was exploded, there was much machine-gunning and hand bombing by both sides, but virtually no frontal attacks with rifle and bayonet.

In the late afternoon of 3 May, four mines were 'fired' by British sappers directly in front of the cyclist's trenches at Ersatz Alley, causing three massive craters. Charles' 142 Brigade seized these craters—named after unit commanders Momber, Love and Kennedy—as the rims proved to be ideal observation posts.

On 21 May, 140 and 142 brigades experienced what the company's history termed *That Minenwerfer Hour*—70,000 shells delivered by 80 German batteries on an 1800-yard front in four horrendous hours. 140 Brigade's front was almost obliterated and the trench garrisons suffered terrible casualties.

Throughout his life, Charles never kept a personal diary; when asked why, he said his training stipulated that he 'should have nothing on me in case of capture or death'.

As the German barrage lifted at 7.35 pm, a German mine exploded. A minute later, the German assault commenced, led by the 9, 86 and 163 Reserve regiments and 5 Foot Guard Regiment. The Germans smashed through 140 Brigade's defence almost unhindered; only halted by their own barrage. Many British soldiers in the forward trenches and dugouts were captured, many while dazed and shocked from the explosion.

On the right of the German advance, where the cyclist company was manning Ersatz Alley, 141 Brigade had more success in holding the enemy's advance. Reinforcements, including engineers and support troops, were hurriedly organised to help the cyclists, who withdrew some 300 yards from their forward observation trench. Throughout his long life, Charles never mentioned the *Minenwerfer* barrage or his company's retreat; it was either a horrendous or humiliating experience for him, or perhaps a combination of both.

The German attack came to a halt after gaining 1000 yards at the deepest penetration over a 1500-yard front. A minor counter-attack by units of the division commenced at 2 am the next day but only managed to recapture the original support lines. Another counter-attack was attempted in the evening of 23 May but enemy artillery destroyed the cramped jumping-off trenches. One officer protested that it would be murder to continue after one of his platoons had been reduced to half; messages were sent to recall the advancing columns of the division, but the order was never received. German machine guns swept no-man's-land and the cyclist runners found nothing but dead and wounded soldiers. Although 24 Battalion recaptured their original trenches, they soon lost them again. The next day, in conjunction with two cavalry brigades, the cyclists attacked and cut off German rear-guard infantry as they fell back to their original trenches.

Between 21 and 24 May, 2107 men of 47 Division were killed, wounded or missing. The divisional hospital, three miles behind The Line, treated more than 1500 wounded men. The division was then relieved by 2 Division on the night of 25 May. The battle ended as a stalemate, with no side claiming success. The division moved on to Villers au Bois then to Hermin for a well-deserved rest.

On 1 July 1916, after 18 months' service, the company was officially separated from 47 Division; it was reinvented as C Company of IV Corps Cyclist Battalion. On that day, the British Fourth Army, commanded by General Rawlinson, went on the offensive in the Somme Valley. Although some ground was captured, the losses were catastrophic; more than 19,000 men were killed in the first 24 hours and the objective of a decisive breakthrough of the German line utterly failed. IV Corps were not involved in that disastrous bloodbath.

Charles' last action with the company was pursuing the German strategic withdrawal to the Hindenburg Line between 25 February and 5 April 1917. The rationale behind the German plan was to shorten their defences by 20 miles, thus releasing an extra 13 divisions for reserve duties. In conjunction with regular cavalry, the cyclists were to observe and harass the rear-guard of the German retreat. They were the first to witness the massive destruction caused by the retreating Germans; a slash and burn tactic reminiscent of General Sherman's infamous march through Georgia during the American Civil War. Villages were laid to waste, bridges destroyed, and booby traps laid. The cyclists came across graffiti on the rubble of the 15th century Péronne Town Hall: *'Nicht argren, nur wundern'* ('Don't get angry, simply wonder').

Mid-March saw Charles based at Rosières, where he clashed with both the *Uhlans*[4] and mounted *Jägers*.[5] His unit pushed forward, accompanied by cavalry, to engage the enemy rear-guard. The battalion's War Diary records:

> 8/3/1917. 10.15 am. Touch was obtained with the enemy at DRESLINCOURT WOOD, & our own patrols were fired on from windows of houses at the village of POTTE. From tracks on the road it was evident that enemy cyclists had occupied the villages & endeavoured to delay our advance along roads, while his cavalry occupied woods & high ground generally & observed our advance. Little opposition was offered.

The cyclists occupied small villages until they came to Potte, where a C Company patrol had been fired upon a few hours before. It was here they exchanged fire with their German cyclist counterparts. A Lewis gun team joined their force and they took Nesle by noon; another village cleared

The cyclists came across graffiti on the rubble of the 15th century Péronne Town Hall.

of the enemy. Together with King Edward's Horse, C Company patrols pushed ahead to reconnoitre the crossings over the Somme River. By mid-afternoon the patrols reported that all crossings had been destroyed by the withdrawing Germans. The next day, again accompanied by cavalry, they entered Béthencourt Village, still burning after the enemy's sabotage. By noon C Company were the first across the Somme River, establishing a bridgehead crossing for both the cavalry and the main body of IV Corps. The utterly exhausted cyclists returned to devastated Béthencourt where, somehow, they managed to find billets for the night. Similar pursuits continued to the last days of March when they experienced:

> ... true open warfare, the first perhaps, that British troops on the Western Front had seen since 1914 ... a fluid programme, artillery moving across country by daylight and being in action from three positions within 24 hours, open flanks, and a speed bewildering by recent standards.[6]

On April's Fools Day 1917, C Company patrols were ordered to Bois de Savvy to seize the town. It was here the cyclists bid farewell to the *Uhlans* and where Charles and Charlie Napier also said their goodbyes to their fellow comrades. Charlie, who had applied to join the Royal Flying Corps (RFC), had told Charles he was not going leave him in France and pressured him to also apply for the fledgling air force. Both were accepted. Charles wrote of his departure to England with obvious relief: '*I was posted to the Royal Flying Corps and with very great pleasure left my Infantry Regiment to train as a pilot in England.*'

Postscript

The Lamb battalions of the Queens Regiment lost more than 8000 men, killed in action in WWI, 31 per cent of total enlistment. Both Victoria Crosses won by soldiers of the 47 Division were won by Lambs; Leonard Keyworth at Givenchy and Jack Harvey during the final advance in September 1918. Viscount Esher wrote in the division's history:

> The 46th and 47th were the first two Territorial Divisions to fight in France. No divisions throughout the war have a more brilliant record.

Charles wrote of his departure to England with obvious relief.

The Territorial force stood in 1915 between the dead Regular Army and the living Kitchener Armies that fought the battle of the Somme and enabled the war to be ultimately won.

Little did Lance Corporal Eaton, now aged 21, imagine that his trench raiding excursions during WWI would provide the stimulus for many years of reconnaissance as an aviator in India, the deserts of Australia and the south-west Pacific before and during WWII. It must have provided him with the aptitude to initiate the first deployment of United Nations peacekeeping observers when investigating the Netherlands–Indonesian conflict in September 1947.

Pearson's crash. Aircraft of Lt Lester Pearson, Charles fellow trainee pilot and later Prime Minister of Canada. Hendon, England 1917.

4 Flaming Coffins and the Silent Raid, 1917

How many old pilots remember the period of training at Oxford, followed by the flying training at one of the schools near London? I qualified for my Royal Aero Club Certificate after a total of 4 hours 25 minutes dual and solo flying on Farman aeroplanes. Without further ado, I graduated on a Martin Light Scout and received my Graduation Certificate as a pilot of the Royal Flying Corps with the total of 18 hours flying.

Charles Eaton, 1953

In May 1917, together with his comrade Charlie Napier, Charles transferred to the Royal Flying Corps (RFC) from France. He wrote of *'very great pleasure'* at their departure from The Line, indicating their relief to leave the horrors of trench warfare they had endured continuously since March 1915.

British strategic doctrine in WWI called for significant numerical superiority in the air, as soon as possible. Because of the high casualties for much of the war, RFC pilots had the minimum training needed to get them airborne. Pilots either learned fast or faced almost certain injury or death. At some stages of the war the average life span of a new RFC pilot was measured in weeks, especially in the more vulnerable and slower reconnaissance aircraft.

When on frontline patrol, RFC 'sorties' were of three to eight aircraft, while German flights of ten or more were common. Although the British flew more flights[1], the Germans seldom fought at a numerical disadvantage.

Charles was introduced to the RFC at Winchester on 14 May 1917 when he started training at Oxford's Air Training School. Soon after his first solo flight another trainee crashed into his aircraft as he was landing, severing his two top wings. Tragically, his fellow trainee was killed; Charles was not injured but was severely shaken. He was taken to the mess by his South African instructor, Captain Edwin Emmett, fortified with whiskey and instructed to take off again in a new aircraft. In some training units this was routine practice to ensure new pilots kept their nerve. Captain Emmett had served in East Africa before transferring to the School of Aerial Fighting in the United Kingdom. Many years later, Charles spoke of how Captain Emmett's tutorship saved his life during a serious misadventure while testing a new Australian aircraft (Vignette 10).

Charles was not alone. Historian Michael Skeete wrote that the RFC had a *'shockingly casual'* attitude towards training pilots. Skeete recorded there were at least two dozen aircraft crashes a day by RFC cadets, many fatal. He stressed the emotional effects this had on the trainees and how training deaths shocked cadets. Some 2670 trainee pilots and observers were killed while training in WWI—

Charles's trainer aircraft, a Maurice Farman Shorthorn A2225. Trainees dubbed the plane 'Rumpety' due to the noise the under-carriage made on landing and taxiing.

Lost my two wings' —BE 2e aircraft, 11 August 1917.

almost 30 per cent of all RFC/RAF mortalities during the war. One RFC cadet summed up his feelings: *'We boys do not talk about death except very privately and quietly, in twos and threes, and then in almost an impersonal manner.'*

Ivo Agnew, a young Tasmanian ex-army gunner who trained as a pilot in 1916, crashed on a golf course and was pulled out of his aircraft by a golfer. Agnew noted: *'A chap gets a bit nervy when he goes up solo for the first few times and a lot of chaps lose their heads when they begin to come down.'* Agnew became the first battle casualty of the Australian Flying Corps (AFC) in France when taken prisoner in October 1917.

Charles, perhaps influenced by having witnessed death in the thousands in The Line, maintained an eerie silence on the subject of death, including those who died in battle, while training and in aerial combat.

After finishing his training, Charlie Napier returned to France as a fighter pilot with 20 Squadron and later 48 Squadron. On 4 August, Charles was transferred to a training squadron and, five weeks later, to 19 (Reserve) Squadron, a Home Defence detachment at Hounslow near Croydon, quite close to his home and family.

Not all Eaton's flying activity was mundane training. He relates:

> After this period I was posted to a Defence of London Squadron and endeavoured to chase the odd Zeppelin which made its way over England at night time. Although several chases were made the nearest approach to a Zeppelin was to see the big ship in the beam of a searchlight at a distance of about 5 miles.

German airships and Gotha heavy bombers dropped more than 280 tons of bombs over Britain during the war, killing some 1413 people and injuring 3408, mostly civilians. In *The Zeppelin Fighters,* Whitehouse wrote that Winston Churchill, then First Lord of the Admiralty, penned a memorandum in September 1914 saying the United Kingdom needed air defences from aerial attack. This was before the first bomb had fallen and shows Churchill's *'remarkable anticipation of the problem'.* The first aircraft in Home Defence were from the Royal Naval Air Service (RNAS), but some RFC pilots originally assigned to France stayed in southern England specifically for the defence of London.

Field Marshal French was now Commander Home Forces, including all RFC units. In January 1918 French directed that only one RFC squadron was to be allotted for the immediate protection of London. The squadron's three flights were dispersed at three different aerodromes within London. Only 64 anti-aircraft guns, backed up by searchlights, were allocated for London's defence. Another eight squadrons stationed around London's periphery were supported by 249 guns and 323 searchlights.

Air-to-air contacts against both Gotha bombers and Zeppelin airships by some 24 regular squadrons were recorded. In addition, unlisted training and reserve units made sorties in DH-4 two-seater fighter-bombers. The DH-4, which went into service in early 1917, was nicknamed 'The Flaming Coffin' because the fuel tank was located between the pilot and his observer/air gunner.

Charles may have also chased the odd Zeppelin while serving with 19 Squadron. Mitchell Williamson, who researched Charles' RFC service, suggests his first brush with a Zeppelin was on the night of 24 September 1917,

The DH-4, which went into service in early 1917, was nicknamed 'The Flaming Coffin'.

'The Flaming Coffin.' Eaton's aircraft DH-4 A7422.

when 37 RFC aircraft were used. New Zealander WW Cook, in a BE-2c of 76 Squadron, reported two airships were held by searchlights but escaped into thick cloud.

Another likely contact was during the massive Zeppelin raid of 19 October. Dubbed the 'Silent Raid' because the airships could not be heard due to their high altitude and could not be seen as the ground searchlights were turned off, 11 Zeppelins dropped 273 bombs, killing 36 civilians and injuring 55 in the Midlands, East Counties and London.[2] Unfortunately for the airships, which were flying up to 19,000 feet, a deep depression with strong gale-force winds moved over the British Isles; many of the Zeppelins released their bombs at random and attempted to return to their home bases in the Baltic. Around 11.30 pm, four of the airships flew to London, close to Hounslow where 19 Squadron was based.

Of the 73 Home Defence aircraft despatched that night, none could reach the required altitude. Fortunately, the bad weather dispersed the Zeppelins, saving many lives—and London—from serious damage. Because of the gales and crew exhaustion, many of the airships floundered in France and their crews were captured; LZ-50 drifted to a watery grave in the Mediterranean. The DH-4 pictured above was flown by Charles and was probably the aircraft in which he chased a Zeppelin. Charles said he could never get sufficient height to close in on the airships. This ceiling factor was confirmed by *Oberleutnant* Friemel in LZ-52; when a RFC BE-2c aircraft pursued his airship, he reported, '*The pilot could not gain enough altitude to make an attack.*'

By the end of November 1917, Charles was posted to 110 Squadron in Norfolk with the rank of Second Lieutenant. By Christmas he was flying with 9 Squadron in Norwich. In March 1918, he attended the 4 School of Air Gunnery and the 1 School of Navigation and Bombing, where he joined up with Second Lieutenant Ernest Wilfred Tatnall, or 'Tat', who was to become his observer/air gunner. They were both instructed in aerial photography for reconnaissance work.

The basic principle of vertical aerial photography was to fly level and straight at a constant height to secure the desired overlap of each photograph. Simple box cameras were initially used, but by 1915 more sophisticated equipment had been developed. By 1916 the RFC was producing about 1000 negatives a day, completely changing the tactics of warfare; army photographic analysts could assess troop positions and movements and locate ammunition stores and trench construction. To comprehend the extent of the use of aerial photography, in mid-1918 the French Air Force delivered to Allied Command more than 56,000 negatives taken over a four-day period.

Charles's introduction to photography must have had a major impact on him; although he never kept a diary and his personal notes were miserly, he recorded on camera the many events of his personal and service life.[3]

One RFC officer, John Slessor, later Marshal of the RAF, summed up the RFC's role:

> In the great, grim siege that was the Western Front the R.F.C. was an ancillary of great and increasing importance—but an ancillary. Its prime job remained reconnaissance and observation for the guns and that it did, on the whole, extremely well, undeterred by heavy losses.

'*The pilot could not gain enough altitude to make an attack.*'

Although Charles never kept a diary and his personal notes were miserly, he recorded on camera the many events of his personal and service life.

'Oops!' Training with the RFC, England 1917.

Postscript

Soon Charles would experience the first of many dramatic incidents as an aviator that would continue for the next three decades, both in war and peace. In war he chased Zeppelins, destroyed two enemy aircraft, was shot down, ploughed into the German front trench line, had numerous crash landings and was severely *'shot-up'* in a Beaufighter by Japanese *ack ack* over the island of Timor in 1944. In peacetime, he had the satisfaction of flying the British Prime Minister and a future American President to the Paris Peace Conference. His greatest thrill, however, would be flying in the spectacular Himalayas while carrying out the first aerial survey of India in early 1920. The awe of that spectacular panorama remained embedded in his memory for the rest of his life.

'On patrol' Nord-Pas de Calais, France, 17 June 1918. The photograph was taken from Eaton's DH 9 aircraft, above left.

5 Jump or Burn, 1918

Whether I was on the German or British side I did not know until I found the aeroplane surrounded by bursting ack-ack, and in front of me I could see the Forest of Nieppe which I knew was on the British side.

Charles Eaton: 5.17 pm German Time, 29 June, 1918

We Haven't Got a Hope in the Morning

*When you soar in the air in a Sopwith Scout,
And you're scrapping with a Hun and your gun cuts out.
Well, you stuff down the nose till your plugs fall out,
'Cos you haven't got a hope in the morning.*

Royal Flying Corps Ditty

On 21 March 1918, boosted by numerous divisions transferred from the Eastern Front following the collapse of Russia, the Germans launched 'Operation Michael', which virtually annihilated General Gough's British Fifth Army. German General Ludendorff's objective was to open a gap between French and British forces and seize the English Channel ports.

During the first two weeks of the assault, the Allies suffered more than 255,000 casualties. The failure of the BEF to stop the Germans resulted in Gough's dismissal. Another consequence of the British collapse was the appointment of French General Foch as overall Allied commander. In the middle of the crisis the RFC separated from the Army, becoming an independent entity on 1 April. This new Royal Air Force (RAF) contributed significantly to slowing the German offensive. Charles automatically became an inaugural member of the RAF and was transferred to France to join the fray.

As the Germans continued shattering the British line, the dependence on air reconnaissance came to the fore. On 12 April, the RAF flew more missions and dropped more bombs than on any other day during the war. During the eight weeks of Operation Michael, more than 400 aircrew from Britain and its dominions were killed and more than 1000 aircraft lost. On 5 May Charles' comrade-in-arms and mentor, Charlie Napier, aged 25, was killed in aerial combat over Lamotte with his observer, 22-year-old Patrick Murphy. Charlie had shot down nine enemy aircraft and was decorated with the Military Cross, adding to the decorations he had won with The Lambs in France. Having no known graves, Napier and Murphy are honoured on the RFC Memorial at Arras.

It was into this forbidding holocaust that Temporary Lieutenant Charles Eaton and his observer, Second Lieutenant Ernest Tatnall, were posted to 206 Squadron, formerly 6 Squadron RNAS, based at Flez/Bray Dunes in northern France. Charles records:

> Then once again to France, this time in De Havilland aircraft and attached to a General Headquarters Squadron. My work was chiefly long range reconnaissance and bombing.

The squadron's responsibilities were to reconnoitre The Line between 10 miles north of Ypres in Belgium and the Nieppe Forest, a distance of 30 miles. 206 Squadron formed part of 11 Wing, commanded by South African, Lieutenant-Colonel Hesperus Andrias Van Ryneveld, originally of the

The young RAF airman.

'Then once again to France, this time in De Havilland aircraft and attached to a General Headquarters Squadron. My work was chiefly long range reconnaissance and bombing.'

Loyal North Lancashire Regiment. Well-known fighter aces in the wing's fighter squadrons included Canadian 'Billy' Bishop, Irishman 'Mick' Mannock and Australian 'Harry' Cobby.[1] It is probable that Cobby and Charles met at this time; 25 years later, Cobby was to become Eaton's commanding officer. The two would later front a court of inquiry following a Royal Australian Air Force (RAAF) command conflict in West Papua during WWII.

The wing was a mixed unit that included Canadians, South Africans, Australians, a Rhodesian, a Sikh and five United States Army pilots. Although 206 Squadron was initially formed as a day bomber unit, photographing enemy positions became its most vital duty; it became the reconnaissance squadron of the British Second Army. RAF reports state the aircraft maintenance of 206 Squadron was of the highest order and the squadron had one of the finest reputations in France; it was regarded as the leading squadron of its type. The squadron's War Diary confirmed its effectiveness:

> It is believed that the casualties suffered by this Squadron have been far lighter than other D.H.9 formations and this, in spite of the fact that reconnaissance and photographic work was continually carried on, invariably without escort. This is largely due to the excellent work of the Flight Commanders, the capability of all pilots and the very efficient manner in which the machines have been looked after by the mechanics.

Early June saw the squadron return to its former base at Alquines. On 7 June 11 Wing flew 19 reconnaissance missions and 15 contact and counter-contact patrols, firing 30,980 rounds of ammunition. Of more than 100 enemy artillery batteries engaged, 13 were neutralised. The wing's aircraft took 1385 photographs of enemy positions and dropped 34 tons of bombs. Charles and Tat, flying DH-9 C6240 at 14,000 feet, had their first success in aerial combat; together with Captain Stevens in DH-9 C1181 and his observer Lieutenant Christian, they shot down and 'claimed' a Fokker Dr.I.

The War Diary reported:

> Triplane was one of formation of 4 E.A. (Enemy Aircraft) which dived over the objective. Fire was concentrated on one E.A. which came within

50 yards of the formation, 100 rounds being fired at it by 2nd Lt. Tatnall and 200 rounds by Lt. Christian, who saw E.A. dive, and burst into flames. Confirmation by other observers, one of whom saw E.A. crash and continued burning at sheet 36.m.6.d.4.4.

Tat and Charles' claim to the Fokker had been confirmed by Flight Commander Captain INC Clarke, an Australian who had a distinguished career with the RNAS. Clarke was well known for his aggressive leadership and teaching methods. Blandford wrote: *'It was to him that we were indebted for our exceptional high standard of formation flying and formation tactics.'* After two years' active service, Clarke was posted back to England to 1 (Communication) Squadron, meeting up again with Charles in May 1919. He returned to Australia to become an original member of the RAAF. In a twist of destiny, he resigned his commission to re-join the RAF at the same time Charles joined Australia's fledgling air force in 1925.

'It was to him that we were indebted for our exceptional high standard of formation flying and formation tactics.'

Cloud often prevented clear observation, preventing claims being made. For example, the following day, when Charles and Tat, flying DH-9 C1181, claimed an Albatros Vee-Strutter that was driven down out of control just west of Comines at 2.55 pm, their claim was disallowed. They had been a 'tail-end Charlie' flying at 14,000 feet after a bombing sortie when the fight occurred. The incident is recorded in *Combats in the Air*:

> DH9 C1181 was the last machine over the objective and just after leaving Comines was attacked by one enemy aircraft which with four other enemy aircraft climbed up under the formation. About 100 rounds were fired at it by 2/Lt Tatnall at 300/200 yards range and the enemy aircraft thereupon went down in a spin for 3,000 ft, emitting a cloud of smoke. It was still spinning and leaving a trail of smoke when lost in cloud.

DH-9 bomber raids and reconnaissance flights in general, and 'tail-end Charlies' in particular, were vulnerable without fighter escort. As the commander of one DH-9 wing commented, when arguing for greater coverage of fighter escorts for his bombers:

Then the lowest height at which it was considered safe for these DH9As to cross the lines was considered to be 12,000 ft, which meant with their heavy weight of bombs meant a long, cold climb and a strong chance of engine trouble developing. That was a miserable way to start a bombing raid. I soon discovered however, the Huns were being chased up by their own headquarters and were told to stop these raids at all costs, so that they soon found it worth their while to have a second Squadron of assailants ready to deal with the unprotected DH9As. The bombers suffered losses accordingly, and generally cherished a grievance against their escort for letting them down.

Accordingly, during May and June 206 Squadron suffered losses, with many young pilots losing their short lives flying the slow and vulnerable DH-9s. At times, the average life of a pilot on the Western Front was between three and six weeks. Fatalities included Raymond Berridge, 19, Bertram Dunford, 19, William Cutmore, 18, Fredrick Taylor, 19, Albert Slinger, 19, Arthur Steele, 19, Fabian Reeves, 21, and, going down in the same aircraft, Athol Howell-Jones and Francis Reddy, both 18. *Knights of the Air* reported that the French air arm suffered 77 per cent casualties throughout WWI. In his book, *Sagittarius Rising*, Cecil Lewis wrote that he reported for active duty in France at 18. When asked by an officer how much flying experience he had, his answer was:

'Fourteen hours, Sir'. The officer's reply: 'Fourteen! It's absolutely disgraceful to send pilots overseas with so little flying. You don't stand a chance ... Another fifty hours and you might be quite decent; but fourteen! My God, it's murder.'

'Another fifty hours and you might be quite decent; but fourteen! My God, it's murder.'

Despite the high casualties, morale was usually high in most RFC squadrons. As Peter Gunn observed, *'In the evening they drank and rollicked with mirth in the mess because the next morning they may be lying injured or dead in the muddy fields of France.'* Charles was an old boy of 22 when he almost met a similar fate twice within three days. He was fortunate to have accumulated flying hours and experience while serving in Home Defence for six months.

Charles and Tat had their first close call flying DH-9 D2783 on a familiarisation patrol of their own front line on 26 June 1918. Their aircraft was machine-gunned by an enemy plane and they crashed at Estrée Blanche. Although the plane was a complete write-off, Charles and Tat were unhurt. By coincidence, another Eaton, Lt EC Eaton of 65 Squadron, was killed on the same day. It is unknown if Charles' damaged aircraft was on fire but evidently he and Tat did not have to make the horrendous decision to 'jump or burn' as described by Captain Marrow of 62 Squadron. As parachutes were not issued to RFC/RAF aircrews in WWI, pilots had to decide what Marrow dramatically witnessed:

> I was flying the same time as Lt AB Cort and 2nd/Lt Mitchell who were in the same machine and they went down in flames above 10,000 ft N of Albert in the morning and they pulled the machine on its back and fell out. It was an air fight and they were shot in the air. Wouldn't like their relatives to be told this ... It's too horrible.[2]

Harry Cobby witnessed a similar incident involving a German aviator. After shooting down an Albatros he wrote:

> The machine went badly out of control, the pilot must have been seriously wounded for he tried to regain several times. He presently went into a side-slip and his left-hand wing collapsed and presumably went down with his aircraft ... Watson must have shot one of the observers while he was going on his parachute, and severed the cord in some way or another as he parted company with his chute. It wasn't pleasant to see him finish the last couple of thousand feet by himself.

Mick Mannock, the RFC's highest-scoring ace, had nightmares about burning aircraft; once, when on leave, he burst into tears after relating his experiences of aircrew being immolated in their cockpits. He kept a loaded revolver *'to finish myself as soon as I see the first sign of flames'*.

Wind direction was another major factor for pilots, with winds on the Western Front normally blowing from west to east. Inexperienced pilots frequently found themselves deep in German territory after a dogfight and had difficulty returning to their lines, particularly if they were shot up or had engine failure. On the other hand, Germans in similar situations could land just about anywhere in friendly territory.

He kept a loaded revolver 'to finish myself as soon as I see the first sign of flames'.

In the last week of June, Baron von Richthofen's famous *Jagdgeschwader 1*, now commanded by Wilhelm Reinhard and later by Herman Goering, visited the front line patrolled by 206 Squadron. Conceivably, it may have been one of the 'Flying Circus' fighters that claimed Charles on 26 June, as they had clashed with the squadron's aircraft during that period. In later life, Charles casually mentioned to his younger son, Charles Stuart, that he '*mixed it with the Circus*'. Young Charles did not fully believe it until 1 January 2005, when he read 206 Squadron's history—24 years after his father's death!

On 29 June 1918, Van Ryneveld issued his routine daily orders, announcing that two renowned fighter pilots of the wing, Major Bishop and Major Mannock, had been decorated by King George V. The War Diary reported that 30 reconnaissance, five contact, and counter-attack patrols were made on that day and 30 tons of bombs dropped. That same day, 13 months after starting his flying training, Charles was ordered to fly on a lone special mission over an enemy aerodrome at Tournay on the Belgian–French border. His aircraft, DH-9 C1177, had been written off twice already, but was considered expendable for reconnaissance flights. The aircraft had previously crashed with 98 Squadron and been repaired on 30 April. It was returned to a RAF repair park in May and, after renovations, reissued to 206 Squadron. This practice was not unlike the Royal Navy's practice of obtaining aircraft write-offs from the Western Front and somehow launching them from ships' decks to scout the seas around the fleet. Once the pilot's mission was completed, he would land his plane in the water, as close to a navy ship as possible, jump out and either swim as best he could or wait for a ship's lighter to haul him aboard.

Charles' aircraft developed engine trouble over the target, forcing him to turn back. It is unknown if wind was a factor in his predicament, but after flying due west he could clearly see the Forest of Nieppe about 800 yards away. Charles explains in his notes:

> After carrying out a special reconnaissance of the Tournay aerodrome in France,[3] I had engine failure and immediately turned for home. The day stands out in particular. It was clear over the target and as I approached

the lines the cloud base obscured the ground at 3,000 feet. On entering the clouds, still making west, they were about 1,500 feet thick and on coming out I found that I was right on top of the end trench lines.

He knew the forest was within the British lines, but the aircraft was losing altitude fast and enemy anti-aircraft fire was bursting around his aircraft. In later life he recalled: *'The ack ack was getting higher and higher and we were getting lower and lower.'* The RAF War Diary recorded that, on 29 June 1918, five aircrew were killed, six wounded and five missing in action, including Charles and Tat. 11 Wing Routine Orders bluntly noted:

T. Lt. C. Eaton, RAF. Flying Officer, who is missing, is struck off the strength of No. 206 Squadron with effect from 29-6-18.

Ernest Tatnall, left, and Charles in Stalag Karlsruhe, July 1918.

'The ack ack was getting higher and higher and we were getting lower and lower.'

6 - An Undesirable in Festung Neun, 1918

Festung Neun was considered the ultimate depository for incorrigibles and undesirables.[1]

Nihil Nos Effugit: Naught Escapes Us
(Motto of 206 Squadron, RAF)

Charles and Tat were part of 206 Squadron 11 Wing when, on a special mission over enemy territory on 29 June, they experienced engine trouble and were forced to plough into the front German trench line. Charles describes what happened next:

> The plane turned over and I was thrown out. My Observer was under the wreckage and while attempting to get him out some men came running towards the crash. Immediately they were called upon to assist and did so—

and it was not until we dragged the Observer from the wreckage that I had another shock in finding that my helpers were Germans! The Observer was not badly injured and we were then taken into the trenches, when it was found that we had come down 800 yards from the British front line and just behind the German first line of trenches.

To be a prisoner is a most depressing shock, a feeling which only those who have experienced such an event can ever know. However, that was that, and we were immediately taken to the rear and to an advanced German aerodrome. There we were questioned by a German flying officer and our hurts attended to, given some food and placed in a hut under guard. While we sat in the hut, my Observer and I, the usual feeling of the newly captured prisoners came on us and, of course, we determined to try to get to our own lines at the first opportunity. We were given beds to lie on, and that evening we found the guards not perturbed or very attentive and during the night, we made our first attempt to get away. We certainly got out of the hut, but without getting away from the vicinity of the aerodrome, we were again captured by German guards.

After this little episode, my Observer and I were separated and I was placed in the Lille civil gaol to cool my heels. An experience which cannot be forgotten was the small cell about 10 feet square with nothing to do all day and given the bare necessities of life. This for about a week, when I was told that I had been court-martialled and sentenced for the escape attempt.

During his week's solitary confinement in the Lille Civil Goal, Charles survived on *'brown bread with a little beet top soup and water'*. He was transferred to Stalag Karlsruhe in the state of Baden-Württemberg, near the French–German border; fittingly the city's name translates as 'Charles' repose'. On 11 July the British War Office informed Charles' parents, William and Maude Eaton, that their only son was missing-in-action. Four weeks later, the War Office went further, listing him as having died on 3 August. A few weeks after that, Charles' fiancée, Bea Godfrey, received a Red Cross postcard mailed from Germany saying he was alive, uninjured and in good spirits. Furthermore, he was delighted to be reunited with Tat in Karlsruhe, a clearing station for prisoners-of-war.

During his week's solitary confinement in the Lille Civil Goal, Charles survived on 'brown bread with a little beet top soup and water'.

One prisoner describes his experiences at Karlsruhe:

> There is a hotel there to which all prisoners are at first taken. My own experience is very similar to what always happens. I was first locked in a small room alone. Soon a very plausible German interpreter (officer) came and made himself pleasant. He explained that he had to interrogate us simply for form's sake and because 'the camp commander is rather a fussy old man'. I adopted the attitude, which I always found completely successful, namely, to tell him my name, rank and regiment (R.F.C.). That I am honour bound to give nothing more—'do you expect me to break my honour?' This invariably shuts them up.[2]

Karlsruhe's food rations in June–July 1918 were determined by the chronic food shortages in the German population. Charles and Tat, who arrived at Karlsruhe in early July, would have enjoyed the following rations menu, issued during the previous fortnight, 23–29 June:

DATE	7 am	Noon	5.30 pm
23/6	bread/coffee	potato/gravy	barley soup
24/6	bread/coffee/jam	macaroni/turnip soup	slam soup
25/6	bread/coffee	macaroni/barley soup	slam soup
26/6	bread/coffee/butter	macaroni/barley soup	canary soup
27/6	bread/coffee	macaroni/barley soup	slam soup
28/6	bread/coffee	carrot soup	potato soup
29/6	bread/coffee	sago	potato soup

Tea was served 2.30 pm daily

Unlike his first week in solitary confinement in Lille, his morale had improved, as a postcard from Karlsruhe to his sisters indicated. He appeared not unduly distressed and his reported demise was not mentioned, if indeed he was aware of that event.[3]

Absender Lt C Eaton RAF
Offiziers Kriegsgefangenenlager Karlsruhe
                                                            29th of July 1918

Dearest Marie and Connie

How are things I am very fit and going on fine, am looking forward very much for your letters. I sent Ma a card on the 21st have also sent some photos along which I think are pretty good. Shall be able to send a letter to Mother at the beginning of the month. Had a hot bath today very nice too, have been able to get a change of under clothing. How's school and biz are you on holidays yet?

Fondest love to all, Charles

Following Charles' interrogation concerning his crash, capture and escape, he was court martialled and classified as a *unerwuenscht*—an undesirable. He was transferred to a punishment establishment, Festung Neun, at Ingolstadt on the Danube. Tat, who was considered less responsible for their escape, was sent elsewhere. Tat and Charles were separated once more and, despite efforts to make contact, were destined never to meet again.

Ingolstadt is an ancient fortress city in central Bavaria. The picturesque town was first mentioned in 806 by Charlemagne and became famous as a centre of anatomical studies and classic Gothic buildings. The German War Ministry ordered that Festung Neun be used for prisoners classified as 'undesirable aliens'. Many were sentenced to hard labour; in Charles' case, to work in salt mines close to Festung Neun. Charles explains his arrival at Festung Neun with some panache.

> From this time I was taken through the routine prison camps, of which so much has been written, to a prison camp called 'Fort Neun' at Ingolstadt, on the Danube near the border of Austria. Here I was to do my term of imprisonment. Fort Neun was an amazing camp and books have been written on it. A South African and myself were the only British prisoners, the majority of the others being French, Belgian and Russian; all prisoners serving a length of imprisonment for various crimes they were alleged to have committed. There is no doubt that some of the cases were very tough, some of whom had escaped up to 8 or 9 times, were serving years of imprisonment, as decided by the court-martialling Germans.

Following Charles' interrogation concerning his crash, capture and escape, he was court martialled and classified as a unerwuenscht—*an undesirable.*

> The camp was very picturesque. It was an old fort surrounded by a moat. Prisoners lived down in the dungeons and were allowed on the ramparts during the day time. Escape from such a place was most difficult, although weird and wild escapes had been made from the camp at odd intervals.

Of the estimated 192,000 British prisoners-of-war in WWI only 86, or 0.16 per cent were imprisoned in Ingolstadt's forts together with prisoners of non-Anglo-Saxon backgrounds.

Festung Neun was cold, overrun with insects and always damp, perhaps due to the moat. The officers' living quarters were poorly illuminated gun casemates, a reason why internment in Ingolstadt was feared. The casemates measured 12 by 6 metres and generally accommodated six to seven officers—authentic medieval dungeons! Older officers were supplied with mattresses while their younger comrades were given bedding of sacks, sea-grass and hay. A meagre ration of coal was given to each casemate only between December 1 and May 1. Fortunately for Charles, he was interned in the summer; during winter, the cold was almost unbearable and prisoners were forced to scavenge anything that burnt. While conditions at Festung Neun must have been unpleasant, Charles wrote to his younger sister in high spirits, noting he was even playing tennis when not mining salt:

> Lt C Eaton (1315) Offiziers Kriegsgefangenenlager Ingolstadt Fort IX
>
> 8th September 1918
>
> My Dearest Connie
>
> Well how are things going, quite strong I hope, trust you are keeping yourself very fit. Have you been playing tennis much? I have started again on a hard court. No luck yet with regard the post, but I hope every day for letters. Am quite O.K. here I am swatting French now and am picking it up fine I have a special tutor you see. Just going to lunch now, chicken and rice (?) not bad.
>
> Bye Bye be good Charlie

A former inmate of Festung Neun was a young French officer, Captain Charles de Gaulle, who had perfected his German. He had escaped a number of times but was always recaptured, allegedly due to his conspicuous height. De Gaulle described another prisoner as a handsome, stocky, insolent young

Russian called Tukhachevsky. Tukhachevsky eventually became a Marshal of the Red Army. Known as the 'Red Bonaparte', he was arrested and executed by Stalin in 1937 as a counter-revolutionary. Another inmate, Georges Catroux, was sentenced to death years later *in absentia* by the Vichy Government; he was to become the Governor-General of Algeria.

Charles became particularly friendly with Belgian flying ace Edmond 'The Flying Judge' Thieffry, a lawyer in civilian life. He had 10 enemy aircraft destroyed to his credit and was now Charles' French tutor. The two men kept in contact after the war until Thieffry was killed in an aircraft crash in Africa aged 36. Edmond Thieffry has a Metro train station in suburban Brussels named in his honour.

Each fortress guard was equipped with a loaded rifle and three belts of ammunition. However, arms were used only if a prisoner tried to escape and resistance could only be suppressed by the bullet. According to Commandant Peters, only two prisoner deaths were attributed to gunfire. Some forts, such as Festung Neun, had moats, which made it even more difficult to escape. The Germans also used guard dogs to intimidate would-be escapees.

Only a few weeks after his arrival at Festung Neun, Charles and the only other 'Empire' prisoner in the fortress, a South African, narrowly avoided becoming the third and fourth fatalities while making a dramatic attempt to escape and return to duty. Charles explains how they intended to break out of the prison:

> The South African and myself got our heads together and decided on a plan in which we asked the senior officer of the camp, a Frenchman, to assist us. I think he thought the plan mad but, however, he agreed to do what he could and one afternoon, for our benefit, a fight commenced between the French and Belgians up on the ramparts.
>
> The guards, both on the ramparts and round outside the moat, immediately had their attention drawn to the scrap. At this period the South African and myself slipped into the moat and made for the bullrushes in a channel from the moat leading to the Danube. We both had heavy packs on without very many clothes.

> I made the bullrushes all right and was there unseen, but unfortunately the South African could not swim too well and went down to the bottom of the moat. However, he managed to get rid of his pack and came up with a bit of a splash. Then the shots started to fly. He was not hit but was immediately recaptured.
>
> I stayed in the bullrushes and was there until dark, and my escape had still not been found out. After dark a way was made along the channel until a safe position was reached, then I dressed myself from the clothes in my pack and made my way. I managed to get across the Danube and was out for a few days but again recaptured through the efforts of a farmer while I was endeavouring to get food. Again returned to Ingolstadt in the charge of the German police and again court-martialled and this time sent from Ingolstadt to Holzminden, near the Dutch frontier. The journey was not very pleasant and after one or two exciting incidents I arrived at Holzmiden, and again in the cells.

'Then the shots started to fly. He was not hit but was immediately recaptured.'

During his few days at large, a famished Charles ate raw turnips dug from a field and stole a chicken, which he was prepared to eat raw. The bird made a loud racket while being strangled, which led to Charles' capture by the fowl's owner. Unfortunately for posterity, Charles did not enlarge on *'the one or two exciting incidences'* surrounding his escape. He was court-martialled once more, resulting in his transfer by train to another infamous prison, Holzminden in Lower Saxony, to serve his six-month sentence in solitary confinement.

Tongue-in-cheek, Charles penned a postcard to his school friend, Jack Warden, referring to his change of location and to his dark, gloomy, solitary-confinement cell.

Offizier-Gefangenenlager Holzminden

28th September 1918

Dear old Jack,
Been changing my address lately and no new letters yet. How goes it old bean absolutely OK I hope and Gertie Al too. Am looking forward to a letter from you, how do you like the blue sky ... by gum I envy you. Am quite OK and fit. Best of luck
Your old pal Charlie

Holzminden had been opened as an *Offizier Gefangenen Lager* for British officers in September 1917. It was the largest camp in Germany, holding 600–700 officers and 150 orderlies. Historian Hansen wrote that Holzminden was a 'black hole' jam-packed with incorrigible escapees, who dubbed it 'Hellsminden'. Although heavily guarded, the camp was the scene of the famous 'Tunnellers of Holzminden' affair, in which 29 prisoners escaped through a tunnel in 1918. Unfortunately, the majority were soon recaptured and subsequently court-martialled. Only 10 of the escapees made it back to the United Kingdom.

As was routine with all new prisoners, Charles was paraded on arrival and given a vigorous personal search. Any files, saws, maps of Germany, compasses, travelling bags, mufti clothing, torches, and sundry tools that could aid an escapee were strictly forbidden and, if found, were immediately confiscated. A senior British officer reported that the accommodation buildings were crowded and summarised the restrictions of Stalag Holzminden:

> The whole attitude of General von Haenisch, the Commanding General, appears to be hostile to British prisoners-of-war. Other matters in which the orders of the Commanding General are partly or wholly responsible for the unpleasant conditions in the camp are:
>
> 1) His appointment of Hauptmann Niemeyer as Commandant after the latter's actions at Ströhen were well known and had been condemned by the Kriegsministerium.
>
> 2) The method of awarding punishments.
>
> 3) Bad service of letters.
>
> 4) Severe orders about censorship of parcels and tins, which have led to constant thefts.
>
> I have no hesitation in saying Hauptmann Niemeyer is temperamentally absolutely unsuitable to command a camp or unit of any kind. He gets wildly excited over trifling matters, loses his head, and uses language to prisoners, irrespective of rank, which proves him totally unsuited for his position. (He speaks fluent American).

Hauptmann Niemeyer, known to all prisoners as 'Milwaukee Bill', had been censured at Stalag Ströhen by his own commander for conduct unbecoming an officer. He was notorious for flourishing his revolver and constantly threatening prisoners with it. One prisoner recalls that Niemeyer had spent 17 years in America and was fond of greeting new prisoners *'in broad Yank language and told us, that he was always glad to see any Englishman, that he had been great friends with the English himself before the war, and that he hoped to be so again. But in the meanwhile war is war'*. Milwaukee Bill's antagonism to some prisoners was well known. Leefe Robinson VC, in the solitary cells at the same time as Charles, had his detention increased on any pretence. According to Hansen, Robinson, who shot down the first Zeppelin over England, was given excessive punishment, allegedly to avenge the death of the Zeppelin's commander, Wilhelm Schramm, who was Milwaukee Bill's hero. On a more compassionate note, an Australian pilot had a torrid love affair with a *fräulein* from Holzminden's administration office. It is not known if either were apprehended and punished for fraternisation.

Lieutenant Ortweiller, who had also been at Karlsruhe, was transferred to Holzminden. He was a recipient of particularly harsh treatment due to his Germanic name. Ortweiller pointed out that although food parcels were sent from the British Red Cross, there was an iniquitous practice of profiteering by charging prisoners for food:

> In most camps an officer is not required to take the German food, and then he need not pay for it; here (in Holzminden) we were compelled to pay for it whether we took it or not; as a matter of fact, if on any particular day the officers had all required German food, there would have been no coffee at all and not enough food for one-fifth of the officers. There were about 600 officers there. Each officer pays 2 marks per day for German food; he pays that whether or not he actually takes the food. Food for 400 was not provided; consequently, the commandant would make 800 marks a day.

The prison food was all slopped together in pails. One Royal Marine officer said, *'We never touched it.'* Hanson noted, *'They called it soup—water with a few vegetables thrown in and on Sunday a bit of horse flesh.'* No English food

'They called it soup—water with a few vegetables thrown in and on Sunday a bit of horse flesh.'

was allowed. Often the guards woke prisoners in the detention cells with rifle butts shouting *'raus raus'* ('wake up, wake up'). Prisoners in the detention cells had to have a fellow inmate on the outside bring them food, toiletries and mail. As there were only two shower rooms for up to 700 inmates, those in the solitary cells had to be taken in relays, by their minders, twice a week. Even lukewarm water was a rarity.

When describing Holzminden, Hansen the historian wrote of the hardships that solitary remand prisoners faced:

> They were incarcerated in long, narrow cells, eight feet high and six feet wide by fifteen feet long, with one small barred window high in the outer wall, at ground level. The only furniture was a small table, a stool, a tin basin, a jug for water and a bare-boarded bed—although some prisoners were allowed to take their matresses to the cells with them. The cells were dark, poorly ventilated, freezing cold in winter and suffocating in summer, and there the captives remained, sometimes without exercises, without light ... often deprived of the opportunity of washing, reading, writing or smoking ...

As there were no toilets in the detention cells, prisoners from the outside were delegated to accompany the detainees for their toilet visits. A bucket was kept in the cell to serve as a urinal. Hansen writes of one British orderly who incurred the wrath of Milwaukee Bill. After requesting a toilet visit, he was told, *'You can shit where you like. You can shit yourself. You can shit the bloody bed but you will not go to the latrine tonight.'*

Charles was held in cold, damp cells; he had no opportunity to play tennis or see the blue skies he hankered for. Throughout his life, Charles never mentioned Holzminden, except to say that he was incarcerated in a cell near Leefe Robinson and that he was released by his fellow prisoners.

By October 1918, the German Army was exhausted. Historian Ian Kershaw wrote that desertions and those shirking frontline duty were estimated to be close to a million. In the first week of November, Charles was still confined to his cell when sailors of the German Navy mutinied and refused

'You can shit where you like. You can shit yourself. You can shit the bloody bed but you will not go to the latrine tonight.'

to sail on a proposed 'Death Cruise' against the Royal Navy. Agitated sailors commandeered a train and embarked for Berlin. The Ministry of Defence countermanded orders to the German Air Force, which was about to bomb the mutineers *en route* to the city. Holzminden's guards reported mass civil unrest throughout Germany, caused by starvation and war fatigue; even cats and dogs were being eaten. This situation affected the camp's guards, many of whom just melted away.

During that last chaotic week of WWI, after Charles was released by his fellow prisoners, he immediately headed west on an open road for neutral Holland. Once again he was able to see the blue skies. He allegedly learnt of the Armistice when he reached the German–Dutch border. Charles was repatriated to England on 14 December. After more than three and a half years of war; he had no more than a minor wound from Loos, a few scratches after crashing on the German side of The Line and a bruised ego on being captured.

Postscript

In later life, Charles never wrote or voiced animosity towards his German captors, despite being held in two of the three most notorious internment establishments in Germany, except to say that he missed *'the blue sky'* and *'was not too keen on digging salt'*.[4] He remarked that he had broken their rules by escaping and had accepted their punishment without question. Unlike others, who may have been justifiably upset about prison conditions, Charles may have felt that however bad the circumstances, it must have been seventh heaven compared with the slaughter of his comrades in Givenchy's trenches, the suicidal frontal attack at Loos, the stench of unburied bodies in the sodden trenches of the 1915–16 winter and that horrific *Minenwerfer Hour* on Vimy Ridge.

Perhaps at the end of WWI, Charles thought that his life of *'excitements'* was over; in reality, they were just beginning.

*Aerial Survey of India,
28 Squadron RAF ground party
en route to Murree (now Pakistan),
April 1920.*

7 Flying High, 1919

An aerial mail and passenger service was instituted in the latter part of 1918 for the purpose of providing a rapid means of communication between London and Paris for the convenience of the Government and of the Headquarters staff of the Air Ministry.[1]

The world's first official airmail service was a flight from Allahabad to Hyderabad in India in 1911 by Henri Pepuet. In the same year, Gustav Hamel flew 23 pounds of Coronation Mail in a Blériot aircraft to Windsor Castle at a top speed of 55 miles per hour. However, it was the RAF's 86 Communications Wing that launched the world's first international mail and passenger flights with a regular twice-daily London–Paris return service in November 1918. After the Armistice, flights were also made from London to Germany and Belgium, but 90 per cent of all flights were London to Paris, primarily ferrying delegates to the Paris Peace Conference.

The Paris Peace Conference, held at the Château de Versailles, was inaugurated by French President Poincaré on 11 January 1919—the same auspicious day that Charles and Bea were married in London. The conference, which aimed to settle outstanding issues of the Great War, was attended by 27 nations, including the United Kingdom and all British dominions, together with India. After four months of negotiations, a treaty was presented to Germany on 7 May. The conference's 52 committees then deliberated on outstanding questions that included Germany's reparations, the future boundaries of Europe, the German colonies and the fragmentation of the Ottoman Empire.

Following Charles' repatriation from Holland to England in December 1918, and after accumulated home leave that included his wedding, he was posted to 29 Squadron in February 1919. Some months later he was posted to No. 1 (Communications) Squadron[2], stationed at Buc near Paris, accompanied by his new wife. In his succinct manner, Charles briefly described his participation in aviation history as a pilot on the world's first international air service and his participation in the most celebrated international political conference yet conducted:

> I had not been in England very long and was on leave when I was offered a job on the first London–Paris air service which was then being undertaken by the Royal Air Force in flying the delegates of the peace conference between London and Paris. This was a job full of interest. We were stationed at a place called Buc in the vicinity of Versailles, and usually our work consisted of one trip a day, either to London or from London to Paris, always with two most interesting persons, high delegates of the peace conference, and this work went on until the completion of the peace conference towards the end of 1919, when the Squadron was disbanded and the work taken over by the Instone Airline prior to the formation of Imperial Airways.

This period proved one of the most enjoyable times for Charles and Bea. They let their hair down after four years of war, making the most of their time in 'gay Paree' bolstered by a higher salary. During visits to the Folies Bergère and Moulin Rouge, they were enchanted with the legendry songstress, Mistinguett.

The British Air Ministry had converted 13 'Flaming Coffin' DH-4 aircraft into passenger aircraft by remodelling the rear open observer's seat into an enclosed cabin that allowed two passengers to sit face to face. The pilot was up front in the open cockpit with no way of communicating with his passengers. Charles' first flight in DH-4A F5759 carried only mail bags—nine British and one American. The flight departed from Hounslow at 10.15 am and arrived in Paris at 2 pm French time, a distance of 205 miles. Charles later graduated to ferrying various military and civil delegates to the Conference.

While his social life was exciting, he also had some exhilarating dramas during his flying duties. Flying DH-4A F5759 from Paris to London in thick weather, Charles and his passenger, CM Reys, made a forced landing with engine trouble at Marden in Kent. After repairs, Charles managed to get his aircraft in the air and followed the railway line to London. Nearing Godstone in Surrey, his engine finally ceased, forcing him to crash-land heavily; neither Charles nor his passenger was injured. Charles enjoyed his duties, especially the return flights to England when his aircraft carried *'wine, perfume and politicians in that order of priority'.* The Director-General of the American Relief Administration, later President Herbert Hoover, flew at least once with Charles. On another occasion, Prime Minister Lloyd George may have been surprised to know that he was sitting on a case of Dom Perignon that Charles was carrying back for his family and friends.

Charles enjoyed his duties, especially the return flights to England when his aircraft carried 'wine, perfume and politicians in that order of priority'.

Converted DH4 F 5764, Eaton's aircraft that crashed at Darlington en route to Newcastle, 4 August 1919.

In mid-1919, Great Britain experienced industrial unrest sparked by Ernest Bevin's stand in court for the Dockers Union, primarily over working conditions and wages.³ The police and prison officers went on strike on 1 August in protest against the new Police Commissioner's policy that the police could not join unions. In Liverpool, almost half the police force refused to go on duty and the army had to quell riots. On 4 August Charles was ordered to fly anti-strike leaflets to Newcastle in DH-4A 5764. His participation in the strike came to an abrupt and inglorious end when his aircraft crashed at Darlington, well short of his destination. He had now written off five planes since graduating as a pilot, with more to come.

Charles had another forced landing on 18 August in DH-4A 8040 at St Cloud in France. While crashes and forced landings were common, with one pilot claiming 17 forced landings in open fields on a single Paris–London flight, there were surprisingly few fatalities. During the 744 direct London–Paris flights, three pilots and one passenger died. From the beginning of the wing's operations in 1918 to the end of August 1919, the service carried 934 passengers and 1028 mailbags and despatches. The majority of the 32 aircraft were DH-4s, including 13 converted DH-4As, Handley Pages and Martinsydes. On the completion of the conference, the London–Paris RAF air service was transferred to Instone Air Line, thus becoming Britain's first international commercial airline. 86 Wing was disbanded in September 1919.

One Instone pilot, Captain Shaw, took off in bad weather from Paris and headed into turbulent clouds. In the open cockpit of his DH-4A, he had no way of knowing how his passengers fared. He made plans to make an emergency landing to off-load his two passengers onto a train for London but this proved impossible so he flew on, fighting his way through blinding rain.

Shaw wrote:
> Once or twice I gave passing thought to what was going on in the cabin behind me, for there was no means of communication, and after doing half a turn of a spin over Westerham I wondered if it mattered anyway.

'Once or twice I gave passing thought to what was going on in the cabin behind me, ... I wondered if it mattered anyway.'

On landing at Hounslow (now Heathrow), Shaw was amazed to see his passengers in high spirits and thanking him for a magnificent display of stunting. One had hit his head on the cabin roof with such force only the rim of his bowler hat remained. The other passenger, an Irish priest, gripped an almost empty brandy bottle, which he passed to the pilot in appreciation of either the aerobatics or their safe arrival.

On 11 November 1919, the first anniversary of the Armistice, Charles commanded a draft of airmen to RAF Headquarters in Cairo. Bea and their new baby, Aileen, remained in London ready to join him at a later stage. After a month in Egypt, Charles sailed for Berbera in the Somaliland Protectorate, where he off-loaded two DH-9As that had been converted to flying ambulances. A few weeks previously, a flight of eight DH-9As had been ferried to Somaliland by the HMS *Ark Royal* to support the King's African Rifles, the Camel Corps and local Somali militia to capture a religious fanatic, Mohammed bin Abdullah Hussan, who had declared a *jihad,* or holy war, against all infidels in the Protectorate.

Charles sailed from Somaliland to Bombay in January 1920 to join 114 Squadron, soon re-designated as 28 Squadron. Six of the eight RAF squadrons in India were employed on reconnaissance, cooperating with ground troops in the volatile North-West Frontier, and two were for scouting. On his arrival, Charles was confirmed as Flying Officer Number 11469. Some of the RAF squadrons were equipped with Bristol-F2b fighters. Together with the Indian Army, they were to support British India's pacification policy on the North-West Frontier. The squadrons were to restrain the tribesmen from their perennial inter-tribal feuds and looting on both sides of the Afghanistan–India border, the 'Durand Line'. RAF intervention fell into three categories: direct attacks on aggressive tribesmen, bombing hostile villages and air blockades. RAF commanders encouraged regular patrols so aircrews could familiarise themselves with the frontier's physical environment and, specifically, assist army intelligence:

Detailed topographical intelligence of the areas and villages occupied by the tribes and their sections, including particulars of cultivated areas, water supplies and watering points, the position of caves and other likely places of refuge, religious centres and buildings. Economic intelligence, such as the pastoral and agricultural proclivities of the tribesmen, their means of existence and sources of supply, their methods of grain storage and the structure of their buildings. Intelligence relating to personalities, such as the names and habitations of the principal leaders, their chief supporters ... likely to offer the most stubborn resistance ... and those likely to be well disposed.[4]

So enduring was the reputation of the Afghan Frontier that many young air cadets looked upon transfer to India with trepidation. RAF regulations emphasised that air crews should negotiate their own terms of release should they be captured; leaflets dropped over tribal areas stated that tribal chiefs were held responsible for any mistreatment of RAF aircrew.

A popular belief was that redheads were preferred as pilots on frontier patrols; in case of emergency landing amongst the frontier tribes, they normally escaped the attention of tribal women for mutilation. A Gurkha officer, William Slim, later Governor-General of Australia, commanded ground patrols at the same time as Charles was patrolling the skies above. Slim reported that when one of his supply convoys was cut off by tribesmen, soldiers who were not immediately slaughtered were handed over to the tribal females for torture and castration. Flight Lieutenant 'Tony' Dudgeon of 28 Squadron said, *'There is an apocryphal story about an air-gunner who was shot down, way back in the Bristol Fighter days, who had red hair and was immediately put to stud!'*[5] A young Royal Australian Air Force (RAAF) cadet in the 1930s, Rollo Kingsford Smith, relates a mess song of the time that advised how to neutralise the advances of the Pathan ladies: *'If your engine cuts over the Khyber Pass, you can shove your Lewis gun right up your arse.'* Charles' hair was a light brown; he never mentioned whether he had to face a comparable situation.

First aerial survey of India, 1920. Officers of 28 Squadron RAF Ambala, Punjab. Charles is at the far right, back row.

28 Squadron undertook the first aerial survey of the Indian sub-continent from bases in Ambala, Agra and Maree. The survey flights used topographical methods that pinpointed physical features such as hills, townships, villages, roads and railways that could be used for air navigation purposes. When surveying, aircraft had to take account of wind, the correct use of compasses and rudder control. While stationed at Ambala in the Punjab, Charles found he could only climb to a maximum of 15,000 feet and therefore had to fly abreast of the Himalayan mountains near Ambala.

Charles described his feelings in the peacetime environment of a new exciting country:

> Peacetime service in India is an ideal training for the outdoor man—hard work and hard sport—and during my short service life the formation of a peacetime Air Force in India made training and work exceptionally hard and interesting. To prove the value of an air force in peacetime, my unit took on the job of an aerial survey of uncharted country, a most

'Peacetime service in India is an ideal training for the outdoor man—hard work and hard sport—and during my short service life the formation of a peacetime Air Force in India made training and work exceptionally hard and interesting.'

interesting job, done in conjunction with the Imperial Survey Service. The sport chiefly was riding and shooting, and every minute of time was taken up with either work, tennis, golf, riding or shooting. Ambala is a usual military and civil township of India. The bungalows, hotels and club were comfortable and jolly.

At Agra, a few hundred miles south of Ambala, the centre of our air survey activities, I enjoyed living near the beauty of the Taj Mahal of which so much has been written, and more still to ride out early in the morning, usually by a tonga to the River Jumna, taking snap shots at odd jackals along the track, and then when the sun was up to stalk the wily crocodiles, called by the locals the smugger, sunning themselves along the banks of the river. The Jumna at Agra is wide with sandy shores and high banks. Stalking along under cover of the bank one can hear crocodiles bellowing as they swim on the surface of deep pools after sun up and as the sun gets higher in the sky and the air warmer, out of the water they come to bask on the sand or mud. This is the time for a shot but a most careful approach must be made. The crocodile, like all wild beasts, will take fright and be off for cover into the water at the slightest sound or movement that is unusual.

On 18 March 1920 Bea and five-month-old Aileen sailed from England to Bombay on the British India SS *Chyebassa* with 45 other passengers. On the completion of the aerial survey, Charles resigned his short-service commission on 23 July 1920, bringing eight years' service with the Lambs, RFC and RAF to an end. He accepted an appointment with the Imperial Forest Service (IFS) in the eastern province of Orissa. He explained his thoughts when transferring to life as a servant of the Raj[6]:

> The old adage of a rolling stone is perfectly true but who wants to become mossy? Early in 1920, I decided to leave that very fine Service, the R.A.F. purely because of some adventuresome urge and as a young man to be offered an appointment in the Imperial Forest Service of India comprised all sorts of dreams of travel and jungle life. Now looking back, would I do the same again—yes, without any doubt at all. My wife and young daughter had arrived in India a short while before I resigned my

'The old adage of a rolling stone is perfectly true but who wants to become mossy?'

commission and, as it was the summer in India, the hot season, I had sent them to Dalhousie, which is 5,000 feet up in the Himalayas, on the border of Kashmir.

There I went for a short holiday before proceeding to my new appointment some 1,500 miles to the South. Thus from July, 1920, I was to be out of the Service but at the same time to have three years of most interesting adventure in the Indian jungle.

*These good people.
Khond villagers in
Orissa, 1920.*

8 Tribal Protector, 1921

'They grow their crops and glean the jungle of nature's produce for their isolated but happy existence; life is far from dull for these good people.'

Charles Eaton, 1953

From aerial surveying in northern India, Charles' *excitement* was in the Province of Orissa, which borders the Bay of Bengal and is renowned for its extensive natural forests and wildlife.

As an officer with the Indian Forestry Service, Charles and Bea's new home was in the town of Sambalpur, on the banks on the Mahanadi River some 200 miles west of the Bay of Bengal. In 1878, the British Raj gazetted the jungles of Sambalpur as Forest Reserve, creating them from jungles and hill tracts that had been seemingly in no-one's permanent possession. The first forestry officers were appointed in 1887. One officer, Dewar, reported in 1902 that although the Sambalpur district abounded with wild game, encroaching cultivation restricted their grazing grounds, so posing a threat to the district's wildlife.

In 1920 Charles found the hill-tract jungles of central India a fascinating land *'where the tribesmen lived in their small, clean, well-kept villages, people of charm and friendliness, with a fine sense of intelligence—and good humour'*. He was describing the tribal Khonds, a Dravidian people who formed the majority of the population of southern India. The Khonds, indigenous to Orissa, believed the world began as one great bare plain. After their deity, Bhagavan, created life, he took hairs from his body and scattered them around the earth, turning them into trees; hence the large forests of Orissa. British colonial officers remarked in the 1850s that the Khonds considered the only honourable occupations were cultivating, hunting and warfare. The Khonds' bond with their land was more than economic; it centred on a series of sacred rites for agricultural activities directed to the mythical female, Nirantali. Their most significant ritual, until the British banned it in the mid-19th century, was *'mariah'* or human sacrifice.

Charles described his impressions of Sambapur and Orissa Province:

Sambalpur, a small township, is the centre of the local administration of the province of Orissa. The town is on the banks of the Mahanadi River that runs through Sambapur and after a few hundred miles enters the sea. In the dry season, the Mahanadi is only half a mile wide and is spanned by a bridge of boats which is laid down after the waters go down after the monsoon and taken up before the monsoon is due to break. In monsoon weather, the river becomes three miles wide and is a raging torrent. Travel along the river in normal circumstances is made on large rafts that carry not only personnel, but bullocks as well. At one part of the river, above Sambalpur, travel is not possible except by dugout canoes. Five miles of rapids exist and to go through these in a small dugout canoe with an Indian kneeling ahead with a pole to guide between the rocks, is the most thrilling experience I have had.

The European section of the town was along the small hill rising to a few hundred feet about two miles from the bazaar centre of the town. Bungalows

In 1920 Charles found the hill-tract jungles of central India a fascinating land.

'Five miles of rapids exist and to go through these in a small dugout canoe with an Indian kneeling ahead with a pole to guide between the rocks, is the most thrilling experience I have had.'

were scattered along the hill, with the administrative centre near the usual club house on the edge of the town. The house we took over was on top of the hill, built of concrete with a porch, two-storied bedrooms and a flat roof for sleeping out at night. Servants' quarters were separate, with garage and stables attached. The household establishment was fairly considerable and supplied the servants for looking after the house and for touring. For three to four months of the year, all Government officials are at their residences. This is during the rainy period, when touring cannot be undertaken. The other part of the year is spent by all officials out on tour around the district they manage. The usual number of officials at such a station is the commissioner, the policeman, the railway man and the forest officer.

At the station, one's life is mostly concerned with administration and preparation of budgets for the ensuing tours. Apart from work, the few European members of the community meet each evening at the station clubhouse for sport, tennis and golf, afterwards a game of cards and then usually each evening all dined together at anyone's bungalow. To newcomers it is a little bit surprising, particularly for ladies, to be asked out for a dinner party and then to find their own silver, glass or cutlery in front of them without any previous knowledge. This is a general understanding between the bearers and anything wanted for a dinner party is arranged between them. How many come to dinner is not the worry of the lady of the house, as regards general dinner service.

Charles' responsibilities included supervising the forests bordering the Mahanadi River, with regular inspections during the dry season from November to May. The term 'tour' meant the inspection of all forest-related activities:

> Duties on the tour consisted of general forest management, the correct carrying out of working plans, marking of timber for cutting, correct cutting for regeneration, road aligning, minor bridge buildings, forest sales, dealing with forest offences, fire protection and fathering of the general jungle population.

For a forestry officer, travelling in the jungle was a complicated affair; transport was by horse or elephant and the officer was accompanied by his clerk,

Charles Eaton as a Forestry Officer, Indian Forestry Service in Orissa, 1922.

bearer, or *major domo*, cooks and attendants for the horses and elephants. An important member of the touring party was always the *shikari*, or hunter, whose job was to supply fresh game and control any animals causing property damage or loss of life. Charles wrote scantily about his roles in the Great War yet opens up with relish when describing his life with the people and wildlife of Orissa. He explains his long treks into the tribal areas:

> For a young man keen on his work, could a more interesting life ever be imagined, particularly when India was still Kipling's India. Preparation for a tour was quite considerable. For our journeys, which extended up to four or five months without returning to the station or seeing another white person and no further supplies than we took out, about six buffalo carts were needed. Two carried the tents, one tent to each cart, but the tent was quite a decent one or two sections with a small bathroom attachment; the other carts were laden with general supplies for the trip. Fresh meat, of course, had to be hunted and shot. Two bullocks drew each cart and the rate of progress would be about two miles an hour. Experience showed that it was necessary not to have all types of things in one cart, but to separate one's stock.

'For a young man keen on his work, could a more interesting life ever be imagined, particularly when India was still Kipling's India.'

Tribal Protector, 1921

Overturning carts in gullies and by wild animals frightening the bullocks could not be called a common occurrence, but did happen on occasions, and should a case of beer be in one cart it would be most unfortunate. My area of responsibility comprised about 40,000 square miles of forest spread over a large area of country.

To get around one had to be continually on the move and the usual period at any one camp was only three or four days. After our first camp was struck, the other camp cart with bedding gear went on eight or ten miles to erect the next camp; then when this was occupied the old camp was taken up and leaped-fogged on to a distance of eight or ten miles from the new camp. This was the method of travel in carrying out one's duties. The forests of the area throughout were mostly of sal, *Shorea robusta*, with an undergrowth of bamboos. In various forest areas companies were logging and generally, bamboos were cut and sold by the forest people. A remarkable feature of this country was the number of forest villages, which were established by the Khonds. These were villages where the Government had given the villages the right of possession of parts of the forest area for cultivation, where, at the same time, adult males were enlisted for any forest employment and as forest guards near their village. In addition, throughout the area were scattered forest bungalows where the travelling forest officer, as a change from living in camp, could live in a small bungalow suitably appointed and with some degree of civilization. The jungles of Orissa are the most primitive in India and from Sambalpur there is a distance of many miles before a railway or town.

The Khond villages were scattered throughout the area, which was under my control. These villages varied in size with between fifty to two hundred houses in each. Usually the villages were situated in open areas in the general forest region. They consisted of small mud huts with a surrounding mud wall for protection against the intrusion of marauding wild animals. The villagers lived by cultivation of small areas of rice, sugar, etc., and the grazing of a few cattle and goats. Most Khond men carry spears, bows and arrows and in the cultivated areas, tall bamboo towers were built, again for the protection of their crops from animal intrusion. At night-time, these towers were manned by the sentries with tom-toms that could be heard throughout the night in an endeavour to deter elephants and deer.

'At night-time, these towers were manned by the sentries with tom-toms that could be heard throughout the night in an endeavour to deter elephants and deer.'

The cattle were rounded up and put each night in a compound, again guarded as a precaution from the depredations of tiger and leopard. The general customs of the villagers can be described as tilling the soil and the bartering of goods between their village and others; the method of trade was purely by barter with a system of shell coinage. Some of the young men worked in the forest areas while the old men and the women gathered forest fruits, such as mohul and mangoes. The older men and women vied with each other to get to the various fruit trees of the jungle as early as possible and it was generally on these occasions that human casualties occurred from animals, particularly bears. These animals were sometimes coming to feed whilst the Khonds were collecting their fruit and, unless a young man accompanied the older villagers, they were often badly mauled during their food seeking expeditions. On such occasions, they are often attacked and taken by a tiger.

'On such occasions, they are often attacked and taken by a tiger.'

Our camps were generally pitched in prepared previously used sites within easy distance of villages and barter was then made with the Khonds for chicken, milk and the payment made by tobacco and Indian currency. Life in camp began at daybreak when, after a light breakfast, one proceeded on the job of forest inspection returning to camp at about mid-day for lunch. After lunch, interviews would take place with forest guards and any disputes settled. In the late afternoon, there was generally a walk with a gun to obtain fresh game such as jungle fowl, duck and pigeon. Dinner in the evening was usually fairly late and had by a campfire. It is usually cool in the jungle at night, and dinner consisted of various courses which the Indian cooks are so good at providing. Being out on tour for months at a time, dress for dinner was very varied. Sometimes just a shirt and shorts and on some occasions, dinner dress as a reminder that one still belonged to a civilisation.

During my absence on morning inspections, Bea used to be visited by very shy jungle women, many having never seen a white woman before. It was a wife's duty, through an interpreter, to go into their troubles, look at their babies and try to give the right medicine for any ailment. Often when I came home, I found her garlanded with flowers and with gifts of sweetmeats wrapped in leaves of colour. It is an unwritten law that if a garland is received and placed round one's neck it cannot be taken off until sundown.

In sharp contrast to his life of the previous eight years, primarily waging war, Charles now found himself in a more gratifying role as a mentor to friendly forest folk. He was also soon embroiled in the internal politics of the Raj. The policy outlined by the Conservator of Forests was to encourage the jungle peoples to be brought under the protection of the Forest Department rather than being administered directly by the Indian Civil Service. The department needed the cooperation of the Khonds for the upkeep and maintainance of the forests—any action detrimental to their welfare would be unwelcome. The Forest Department considered it could effectively cooperate with the Khonds to preserve the forest areas for which it was responsible. Another, and more commerically sophisticated people, the Aryan Oriya, were dispossesing the indigenous people of their land through questionable loans and land deals. In an interesting interchange of paternalistic colonialism, the Forest Department did its utmost to take control of the Khonds from a reluctant civil service. Within weeks of Charles joining the department in Orissa, his superior, F Trafford, approached the civil service's Orissa Commissioner stating his department's case:

> I enclose a copy of a letter dated the 4th September 1920, from the Divisional Forest Officer which, read with the Conservator's letters sets out the case fully from his department's point of view. The advantages which are claimed for the proposal, briefly stated, are:
>
> (i) The value of the forests would be enhanced.
>
> (ii) Government will be relieved from the long standing difficulty of collecting rents in the area as the Department will pay the demand.
>
> (iii) The Khonds will benefit materially by getting forest land free for rice and will gain valued privileges in grazing and use of forest produce while the Department will be able to prevent more successfully the abuses of privileges.
>
> (iv) They are out of touch with the Civil authorities and benefit by using a department which can maintain more intimate and personal touch with their needs; emigration will be discouraged.

(v) The Khonds are already dependent for their livelihood on the work supplied by the Forest Department, and the arrangement will enable the Department to control adequately the labour which it requires. The present arrangement gives no control.

The hidden message in paragraph four implied that the department was worried about the influx of non-Khond immigrants such as land-hungry Aryan Oriya settlers. To voice this concern was perhaps not politically correct at a time when the Indian National Congress was agitating for political power throughout the sub-continent.

Charles relished his role as a protector of the Khonds and voiced concerns for their welfare throughout the rest of his life. Indeed, the influence of the philosophies of the then Governor of Orissa, Lord Satyendra Sinha, whose approach to self-government and independence was pragmatic and based on legal constitutional progression, was to make a positive impact on Charles. Sinha's values were to serve Charles well in early September 1947, when he was mediating in the Indonesian–Netherlands crisis.

Postscript

Ninety years on, Charles would not have been surprised to learn that *The Guardian Weekly* reported in 2013 that Orissa's tribal land rights, as protected by the Indian Forestry Service, were to be amended, with major infrastructural projects to be exempt from obtaining consent for forest clearance from tribal communities. Those servants of the Raj, Satyendra Sinha, Trafford and Eaton, all guardians of the tribal peoples, would have been concerned that their attempts to protect and conserve the Khond's land rights had been nullified for consumerism's insatiable appetite.

Matty, Aileen's pet tiger, Orissa 1922.

9 Fear, 1922

I awoke petrified with fear; my hair standing on end. This was the actual feeling and I could not move. I wanted to grip my rifle still resting in my hands, but I could not do so, I was incapable of any movement.

Charles Eaton, 1953

The various sub-groups of Khonds retained a rich heritage of colourful myths that described their mystical, celestial, plant and animal worlds. Reflecting on his life with the Khonds 33 years later, Charles wrote with empathy for their way of life:

> Religious, birth and marriage festivals which are so well and diligently prepared, are enjoyed by every man, woman and child, with a fervour and pleasure above comparison with the artificial world of cinema, radio and TV. Without shops, the bargaining instinct of women and the business instinct of men are well catered for by the simple, time-taking method of intense and exciting bartering of goods between both the village communities themselves and the communities of other villages. For the

young men, full of vigour, their main excitement is the continual battle against the jungle animal life. The forests of Orissa abound with game—elephant, bison, sambur (forest deer), cheetah, tiger, leopard, wild dog and bear the commonest of all. It was very rare that out in camp that one did not have contact with some type of animal.

They grow their crops and glean the jungle of nature's produce for their isolated but happy existence; life is far from dull for these good people.

At such a place, it is rather extraordinary to discover the type of pets that exist. In one bungalow there may be a young bear ambling around the place, in another a leopard, and another, a tiger. We finished up with a young tiger cub that went 6'3", which caused quite a lot of excitement to visitors. However, he was quite a good sport and a companion to my dogs until he got too big. A worthwhile trick to play on visitors was at dinnertime for the bearer to give the young tiger, which had not been seen before, a piece of meat just outside the room, and then endeavour to take it away. The growling that ensued, as can be imagined, caused considerable excitement until the beast appeared. A young tiger cub is most playful but very clumsy and when having a game, over goes the furniture and sometimes down come the curtains.

All travel in the jungle was on horseback and in between travelling and camps, some quite exciting incidents occurred to us. On most occasions when we were on the move and going to a new camp, I would proceed on my work from the old camp and arrive at midday or later on at the new camp site. Bea had to travel on her own with the *ayah* (nursemaid), two servants with my young daughter carried on what is called a *doolie* by four carriers. The *doolie* is a kind of stretcher with a sun-protection covering and mounted on poles. As can be imagined, the young white child also came in for lots of attention and, as she had very fair hair, intense admiration from the tribal women. I think the fact of having Aileen with us had a great effect on Bea's undoubted popularity amongst the forest women. The *doolie* became part of the general convoy of my bullock carts in the moves to the new camps and helped to make up quite a little cavalcade. On the other hand, Bea travelled by herself on horse with her *chuprassi*, or steward, who carried her gun.

'For the young men, full of vigour, their main excitement is the continual battle against the jungle animal life.'

On one occasion, she was travelling along a jungle track when her steward pointed out a tree, which was full of green pigeons. This bird is beautiful, of good size and very good eating. Bea dismounted and after tying up the horse went and shot a few pigeons when the *chuprassi* became quite excited and with a shout of *bhag* (tiger). Not making head or tail of this, Bea got on her horse and was somewhat bewildered by the *chuprassi* still shouting *bhag, bhag*! However, the position rather clarified itself when the horse took fright and, just before her horse bolted, Bea saw a tiger on the edge of the jungle and away she and the horse went right past the tiger. The horse had a start of 2–300 hundred yards leaving the tiger behind. My wife reached the camp O.K., but in a somewhat frightened condition.

Of course, a tale like this must have its shooting yarns. It is the convention of the jungle that a wounded animal must be followed up and killed. This is not only dangerous but a very tiring procedure in some cases. The first leopard I got was a magnificent beast. It had killed a village cow and I was asked by the villages to shoot it. I was taken by the *shikari* along a track to where the dead cow was. I waited in a clump of bushes in the late afternoon and I had only been there about five minutes when along came the leopard to continue his feast. My shot entered just behind the shoulder but did not kill the leopard and he made off. The villagers, hearing the shot, came out to see a dead beast but found it was still alive and wounded. Instead of waiting for the wound to stiffen, I immediately followed up his blood tracks with the *shikari* and a number of Khonds with spears. I had not gone more than a quarter of a mile before there was a rustle in the undergrowth. I knelt down and waited. There was a growling and a rush in front of the leopard and he came straight for me. On his last jump, I got him with my .405 Winchester in the throat that turned him over in the air and he died at my feet—a very lucky shot for me.

Christmas 1920 saw Charles, Bea, 18-month-old Aileen and her *ayah* camping in the jungle near Maghapal. Accompanying the party was Charles' bearer, Pathan Din, who had become a key link between the Eaton family and the people of India. Charles said their time in Orissa would have been difficult without Pathan Din; in later life, he always mentioned his name with respect and admiration.

'The horse had a start of 2–300 hundred yards leaving the tiger behind. My wife reached the camp O.K., but in a somewhat frightened condition.'

Charles' guide and teacher, Pathan Din, and wife. Orissa, 1922

Their campsite was close to a Khond village and Charles set out on his routine forestry duties on Christmas Day. On returning to camp, he was surprised and delighted that the villagers, knowing it was the *ghorah log puja,* or a European religious festival, had come to visit Bea and Aileen. They had decorated the site with bamboo and decorative leaves, presented gifts to the family with specially made sweetmeats packed in artistic little containers made of leaves. They also garlanded Bea and Aileen with strings of beautiful tropical flowers—a truly festive atmosphere. The villagers had made the same traditional offerings as they would do to their own, thus accepting the Eaton family as part of their community.

However, this blissful atmosphere dramatically changed the following day, Boxing Day, when Charles wrote, '*An unfortunate incident occurred to mar our happy camp*'.

'An unfortunate incident occurred to mar our happy camp'.

An old man out collecting fruit had been attacked and mauled by a bear. His cries had brought other villagers in the vicinity to the rescue and after the bear had been driven off, the old man was carried back to the village and to our camp with terrible lacerations to his arms and face. With our first aid kit, Bea got to work; washed, sewed and dressed his wounds as best she could without experience. It was a very upsetting episode. However, the villagers seemed pleased and even admired the heavily bandaged victim, and the old man, after I had given him a tot of brandy, was very stoic about it. Except for further dressings that we gave him, the patient did not receive any other medical attention, which in any case was not available.

Although the climate is hot, the bear, known as the sloth bear, seems to thrive in the jungles of the low hills with their rocky outcrops. With his stiff, thick black hairy coat and a white V vest, he, in a squatting posture, is almost indistinguishable from a large boulder: nature's camouflage. The sloth is a big fellow, on his hind legs stands up to six feet, and must weigh over 300 pounds. His chief annoyance to the villagers is the scrumming of fruit and root crops. A vegetarian in principle, although I have actually seen a bear sample, with gusto, a portion of raw dead meat, the remains of a tiger's kill. Bears, like most other jungle animals, usually feed morning and evening but it is in early morning when contact is generally made between villagers and bears.

The villagers collect fruit from the jungle, particularly the fruit from the *mohul* tree that is also greatly favoured by bears.[1] Should a bear happen to be feeding in the vicinity he does not like being disturbed. The bear is cunning and, should it see the intruders are well armed with spears and axes as the villagers usually are, it will make off and seldom attack, particularly when weapons and shouts are brandished at him. However, should the intruder be an old man or woman, his resentment may result in a terrible mauling, for his cruel claws are two inches long.

It was late morning, after the injured man had been attended to, that I went with my gun and men of the village, armed with their spears and axes, to the scene of the attack. We then scouted around and found the tracks of two bears in company. The jungle in this vicinity was open with much litter on the ground, particularly old and broken bamboo stems. This made the stalking of the bears with any degree of stealth impossible. The particular area was only a small pocket of jungle, about three or four hundred acres.

We decided not to try to track down the two bears, as this would probably frighten them back to the main jungle. It was arranged to beat out the area, while I waited at a point along the creek where the bears would probably emerge to escape to the main jungle. The area was ideal for this and simple arrangements were put in hand to carry out the beat in the afternoon. It was in the cool of the afternoon when the village headman reported to me that all was ready and, with my wife, I set out from camp for a short walk to the jungle area. The male population of the village, some forty odd men, followed us and youths armed with spears and axes, and carrying tom-toms and other noise-making implements.

On reaching the jungle, a main party strung themselves out at intervals along the edge nearest the village. With the headman and six other villagers, my wife and I proceeded to the dry creek. We positioned ourselves on the far bank behind some bushes, from where we could clearly see a pathway through the jungle on the opposite side of the creek.

Three men stationed themselves at intervals, in trees, on each flank of the path along the edge of the jungle where it joined the creek. Their job was to clap their hands if they saw the bears approaching to cross the creek or in any other place than opposite to me. A moving animal, if not unduly

'The male population of the village, some forty odd men, followed us and youths armed with spears and axes, and carrying tom-toms and other noise-making implements.'

frightened, can be turned by this ruse. All this was done as quietly as possible, and then off went the headman to join and lead the main party. In a few minutes, a distant din of shouting, tom toms, and other weird noises commenced. The beat was underway. My wife and I were kneeling down on the alert with eyes fixed along the jungle path opposite, which we could follow in sight for a few hundred yards. I had told Bea that if the bears appeared she was to take the first shot, but not until a bear had cleared the jungle and was on the edge of the creek bed, where it would probably pause before crossing, at a distance of 30 to 40 yards from our position.

Charles wanted Bea to take the first shot to bolster her confidence after an alarming incident with a bear soon after they had arrived in Orissa. Bea, raised in suburban London, had no experience with guns but soon became an apt pupil. One day, while she was waiting to shoot jungle fowl flushed out by the villagers, a fully mature bear broke cover and appeared only 30 yards directly in front of her. She was *'surprised and with a certain amount of shock, sighted her gun and pulled the trigger'.* The bear must have received a prickling sensation as the number four birdshot peppered his thick hide. Bea kept pulling what she thought was the second trigger, but nothing happened. Standing a few hundred yards away, Charles also had only birdshot loaded; he rushed towards the bear shouting as hard as he could, which had the desired effect. The bear made off without attacking Bea. Although frightened, she appeared to take the close encounter outwardly calmly. She could not have fired a second time because she had been continuing to pull the first trigger of her double-barrelled shotgun! Perhaps it was fortunate she had not fired the second shot, as the bear may not have been very pleased with yet another peppering.

Returning to the hunt for the two bears that mauled the old man, Charles continues:

> The noise was increasing as the line of beaters approached. A few jungle fowl flew out and then there was a rush and a scurry as some wild pigs broke cover and dashed across the creek on our side. A few minutes passed and then along the jungle path opposite we could see two bears, one just behind the other, slowly ambling in their ungainly gait towards us. They were in

She was 'surprised and with a certain amount of shock, sighted her gun and pulled the trigger'.

no great hurry and could not see us, concealed as we were in the bushes. I raised my hand to restrain Bea from shooting too soon. In a few seconds, they reached the creek bank, and the front bear, which I thought was the mother bear, paused. I lowered my hand and gripped my rifle. Bea fired, hit the front bear and the unbelievable happened.

The bear was slightly wounded and its immediate reaction was one of savage annoyance. Thinking she had been struck by her mate behind, she turned on him in a fierce attack. The other, taken by surprise, went down underneath after the initial attack. I restrained my wife from taking a second shot and we watched in amazement. The bears locked together, clawing, biting and emitting unearthly growls as they rolled down the bank to the creek bed continuing their fight. Only once did they separate and stand up, then within a second were at each other again, tooth and claw.

All the time, the gap of a few yards between us was closing and into the mass of seething furious fur, I fired my .405 Winchester. The result certainly stopped the fight. Both bears flew apart, each in the opposite direction along the creek and into the jungle. Their departure was so quick and surprising that I did not have a chance of another fleeting shot.

From the time of the first shot and during the fight, the beaters who were closing in were shouting and making a terrific din with everything they had. It was a very eerie few minutes for us. We stepped out of the bushes in the creek bed, where the beaters emerging from the jungle soon joined us. The men who had been in the trees on the flanks of the pathway had also seen the fight; gesticulating in excitement and showing lumps of fur and blood, they explained to the other astonished beaters what had happened. Excitement was at its highest when two of the men went up to the path and, with great gusto, re-enacted the scene from the first shot, to the amusement and laughter of all, including ourselves.

After a degree of calmness returned, we found from tracks that both bears had been wounded. I sent my wife back to camp with the majority of the beaters who were anxious to return to tell their women-folk about the extraordinary fight. With the headman and two or three other stalwarts, I started to track down the wounded bears. The first bear we went after had entered the main jungle not far from the scene of the fight. It was easy to see

'I lowered my hand and gripped my rifle. Bea fired, hit the front bear and the unbelievable happened.'

from blood marks on leaves that he had been badly hit, however, it was nearly a mile before we came on him. He was lying down and as we came close, he moved off growling. I carefully stalked on to sight him and in quick time, he came at me, in an upright position, through the low brush. There was no great rush and in an outstretched position to grab me, his white V vest was like a bulls-eye target approaching, making the shot to kill him a simple one.

The bear was the male and it was my bullet that had wounded him to end the fight; therefore, it had been the inconsiderate female that had turned on the male and started the combat. We then went back and started tracking the second bear, which had gone deeper into the jungle than the first. The final stalk was more or less a repetition of the first and I killed it with a single shot. It was a female and the bullet from my wife's gun had hit its shoulder. Additional men were called up from the village and both bears were carried into camp on poles just after darkness had set in. The villagers were jubilant that the two kills had been made and pleased with the distribution of bear meat. I must say, we too enjoyed, the following day, a real bear steak. It was a great thrill we had, about a year afterwards when we were again passing the village, to see the old man proudly displaying his well-healed scars. He treated my wife as a queen.

When a medical officer in WWI, Lord Moran wrote that fear is the response to the instinct of self-preservation and is only exceptional when it is out of proportion to the extent of danger. It is unknown what the effects of fear had on Charles during his many *excitements* in the Great War. He never spoke of, or recorded, his feelings about fear except on two specific occasions. The first was in the jungles of Orissa, and the second when testing an aircraft that had become uncontrollable in flight. Charles recalls his first acknowledged encounter with fear many years after the event:

> It falls to the lot of all human beings to make acquaintance with degrees of fear throughout their lifetime, and how well we remember the scares and frights we have endured and how well we remember for our lifetime reactions to some particular frightening incident. My biggest fright occurred many years ago, but when I think over the incident, it seems as if it happened only a short time ago, and I can still remember every detail.

'It was a great thrill we had, about a year afterwards when we were again passing the village, to see the old man proudly displaying his well-healed scars. He treated my wife as a queen.'

'My biggest fright occurred many years ago, but when I think over the incident, it seems as if it happened only a short time ago, and I can still remember every detail.'

Charles was fascinated with tigers. The Bodos, a tribe of central India, believed that the tiger was originally a man who became mad, attacked people and bit them. The Bodos' demi-god, Maraprabhu, drew lines across the madman's body with a red-hot scythe then chased him into the jungle where he turned into a tiger. Government reports from the Sambalpur district in the 1920s said tigers were numerous but numbers had decreased because of human population pressures. Tigers were mainly found in the jungle hill tracts bordering the district and moved to adjacent districts when disturbed by woodcutters. Charles wrote of the mystique of tigers:

> The tiger, I consider is the most magnificent animal in the world. He is a solitary beast and lives on his own, except during mating time, and he also stays with the tigress to help feed any young cubs. His camouflage in the jungle is perfect; he is very wary, shrewd and a most difficult target unless one takes part in a big jungle shoot by beating and on elephants. Being on my own, I had considerable time to study the habits of this magnificent animal. He lives on sambar and cheetal, the common deer of the Indian jungle. A tiger will take native cattle when he is lazy or when he is getting old. Tigers attack humans only if they are injured and cannot go after their natural game, or when old and decrepit. It is a fact that a tigress will sometimes take to man-eating for a period after she has had cubs. The Khond villages always looked to the Forestry Officer on tour to get any tigers that are in the vicinity and annoying them by taking their cattle or killing their people. Annoying to the tiger, and helpful for the hunter, are the monkeys of the forest. They loathe the tiger and shout and screech at them as they pass by.
>
> I was camped near a small jungle village and since early morning had ridden some distance inspecting the alignment of a new road and other forest work. After a rather tiring day, I had returned in the afternoon to my camp. The day had been hot and I was relaxing in my tent and having afternoon tea when a commotion announced the arrival of several excitable Khonds outside my tent. The village chief, with his headmen, was there asking to see me immediately. After the paying of the customary compliments, I was told by the chief that in broad daylight a tiger had come out of the jungle. When close to the village, it had killed and carried away a cow.

'The tiger, I consider is the most magnificent animal in the world.'

Of course it had to be the beast, would I come at once and kill the tiger. Taking my gun, and together with my *shikari* I walked with the chief and his men to the scene of the kill and there found every man, woman and child of the village awaiting my arrival. They all were in a state of excitement and were examining the pugmarks of the tiger. From their chatter and gestures, obviously each was making their claims as to the age, size, and sex of the tiger. Although not an expert on tigers I had had some experience and dealings with them, and it was easy to see that this particular tiger was a large one. After killing the cow, it had dragged the dead animal about a quarter of a mile to the edge of the jungle and then disappeared with his kill out of sight. The jungle in the area was more or less a bamboo forest, the clumps of bamboo growing close together with trees scarcely interspersed; the track the tiger had made in dragging his kill was easily discernible.

By this time, the afternoon was well on the wane and I agreed with my *shikari's* opinion that it was too late to make arrangements for the erection of a *machan*, or platform, in a tree to sit up for the tiger. I decided to track the tiger to his kill alone with the hope that I would get a shot at him on the kill or, if not, when he returned to his kill at dusk, a favourite time.

After telling the villagers to return to their homes and not to make too much noise, I proceeded cautiously along the drag track the tiger had made. I was careful in making as little noise as possible, and crawled slowly under the low bamboo. It seemed to me a very long way before I reached the kill. Actually, it was only about half a mile, and when I did come on to it, the tiger had gone. It had eaten very little of the cow and I felt certain that, unless I had frightened it away on my careful approach, the tiger would return at dusk which by now, was not too far off.

Tigers, except when they are wounded or are man-eaters, are usually very timid beasts, easily frightened by strange noises. This is one of the reasons why they are so difficult to bag. To see and not be seen is probably the best axiom in tiger shooting, but this is a lot easier said than done. It is the main reason why a *machan* in a tree, to wait over a kill, is a successful method of shooting of tigers.

The partly eaten cow had been left on the top of the bank of a *nulla* or stream, which was dry, although at some places water holes remained. By his pugmarks, it seemed that the tiger had gone down stream along the top of the bank and under cover of the jungle for a drink. The kill was against a clump of bamboo and in a clear position. Another bamboo clump about twenty yards away offered an ideal position for me if I could only conceal myself in it. I carefully pushed the bamboo aside and successfully wedged myself inside. I was in quite an easy posture, half-sitting on young bamboo without any of my limbs feeling uncomfortable or cramped. My rifle, a trusty .405 Winchester, I pointed between two bamboo stems directly onto the kill and between the bamboo stems I could see quite a distance of the approach to the kill from both up and down the bank of the stream.

Feeling very pleased in anticipation of bagging the tiger, I awaited and hoped for its early arrival. After about thirty minutes or so, I began to get rather drowsy after my exertions of the day, but only realised this when from some distance away I heard the screeching of monkeys, a sure sign the tiger was on the move. Monkeys hate tigers, and vent their hatred in no uncertain terms whenever they see their dreaded enemy. Monkeys are such tasty morsels for tigers should they relax their artfulness, and are caught on the ground. The noise immediately alerted me, and I waited with rather intense expectation. With nothing happening after ten minutes or so, and the noise from the monkeys having ceased, my nerves relaxed. As I did not have a torch affixed to my rifle, I began to think that if the tiger did not appear very soon it would be too dark to shoot and I had better make my way back to the village.

I remember I was again becoming drowsy, but would wait on a little bit longer as I could still see the kill. I remembered still seeing its outline as it became practically dark and then I unwittingly and unforgivably fell asleep with my rifle still in my hands, cocked and pointed at the target area. It must have been about an hour afterwards that the tiger came in a circuitous route towards his kill and he came alongside my clump of bamboo, and either saw or smelt me, or both. The tiger's reaction was one of annoyance, and he opened his mouth and let out an ear-splitting roar. I awoke petrified with fear; my hair standing on end.

This was the actual feeling and I could not move. I wanted to grip my rifle still resting in my hands, but I could not do so, I was incapable of any movement. The tiger was standing a foot or so away, with a few bamboo stems separating us; breathing hard and uttering snarls. His close presence completely overawed me, and it seemed minutes rather than seconds before he leaped on his kill and with another roar, went off with it down the *nulla*. As the tiger leaped on to his kill my nervous reactions came good, and enabled me to grip my rifle and raise it to my shoulder, but it was both too late and too dark to shoot.

With my senses fully active again, I sat quietly and nervously for a few minutes. Hearing the tiger dragging away the kill, I thought what an utter fool I had been and kept feeling my hair that I swear had been on end. I have been told this is a physical impossibility. After a short time, I got out of the bamboo clump and made my way very warily to the edge of the jungle where my *shikari*, the village chief, and his men carrying torches met me. They had heard the tiger roar and as they had not heard a rifle shot they feared for my life. I then had to make appropriate explanations and excuses, as I could not let them know I had so stupidly gone to sleep. When I got back to my camp, even after two or three good pegs of whisky it was a long time before I could go to sleep again.

The following morning I went with the *shikari* to the previous night's scene and found that the tiger had taken his kill nearly a mile down the bed of the *nulla* to a water hole and there had his feed. Very little remained of the dead cow, and although we tried to track the tiger we failed to catch up with him and the cause of my greatest fright got well away and in fact was not heard of again in that particular locality. Although I am certain that the tiger did not go off with more than one per cent of the fright he gave me.

The tiger that had sniffed Charles must have taken heed of the mythical Kittung's advice to tigers to '*only eat men sometimes*'.

In early 1922, two serious incidents occurred in the Eaton family. Aileen was diagnosed with a serious fever; what fever she had will never be known, but the doctor pronounced there was nothing more he could do for the young girl. Christian graveyards throughout India were littered with children of the Raj.

The tiger that had sniffed Charles must have taken heed of the mythical Kittung's advice to tigers to 'only eat men sometimes'.

Aileen's *ayah* suggested they give the young girl alcohol. A conservative, Charles was unreceptive to this idea but when he saw Aileen slowly sinking, he agreed that the *ayah* treat Aileen with brandy. He later recorded: *'It was a miracle. Suddenly a flush came to her plaster-white cheeks; the brandy kick-started Aileen and she eventually fully recovered.'*

The second setback was that Bea suffered a severe attack of malaria that permanently deafened one ear and partly affected the other. Her doctor's advice was that they leave India. This suggestion was much against their wishes as they had become closely associated with life in the forests, the people of Orissa and the social activities of the Raj. Young Aileen's understanding of the local dialect was so advanced that she acted as interpreter between her mother and the many hawkers and villagers that came regularly to the Eaton's household.

The family needed to make the painful decision of what to do and where to go next. Charles did not want to return to England, where he felt that there was nothing for him. Before the war, he had planned to go to Australia as a 'jackeroo'—a trainee on a cattle station. He had received this idea from his father's connections in the London meat trade. He had met many Australian soldiers and airmen during the Great War and had taken them home when stationed in England during the summer of 1917. Fortunately, his superior was sympathetic to Eaton's predicament so he arranged a forestry position for him in Queensland, Australia. In mid-1922, the family said goodbye to their many friends in Orissa, presented their pet tiger, Matty, to the Calcutta Zoo and set out for Australia on the passenger steamer SS *Ormonde,* bound for Melbourne.

'It was a miracle. Suddenly a flush came to her plaster-white cheeks.'

Charles Kingsford Smith and Charles Ulm in the Southern Cross flying over Melbourne University after their historic Trans Pacific flight, escorted by the RAAF's 'Flight of Honour', 1928. Flt Lt Charles Eaton RAAF, Flight Commander.

10 One Royal Salute and a Close Call, 1927

After two or three turns, normal procedure was adopted for the aeroplane to come out of a spin, but it refused to do so. Douglas and I considered the end had come.

Charles Eaton, 1953

The Eaton family arrived in Melbourne from India on the SS *Ormonde* in June 1922. Charles caught up with Squadron Leader Clarke, formerly a flight commander with 206 Squadron RAF in France, now with the Royal Australian Air Force (RAAF), who introduced him to Victoria's famous ales and the legendary painting of *Chloe* in the saloon bar of the Young and Jackson Hotel in central Melbourne. Clarke encouraged Charles to join Australia's new air force there and then but, although tempted, Charles did not wish to break his commitment to the Queensland Government.

A few days later the family travelled north to Brisbane then to the Atherton Tablelands in far north Queensland, where Charles took up his appointment with the Queensland Forestry Service. The Eaton family lived on the Atherton Tablelands for the next three years, adjusting to living under conditions that were in sharp contrast to their large colonial bungalow in Orissa with four household staff and gardeners.

Charles described his life in Queensland:

> For three years I carried out various forest duties on the Atherton Tableland. In those days, the Tableland was not as nowadays, no made roads or tobacco growing, but it was a wonderful district with a temperate climate with very fine people. It is doubtful if any other part of Australia is endowed with natural rich deep chocolate soil and bountiful vegetation. The forest is dense with stands of larger trees and dense undergrowth with stands of maple, cedar, bull-oak, walnut, and kauri pine. Those were the days, too, of the old bullock teams and the bullockies, with their wonderful vocabulary. Much of the good timber country had been selected, the timber removed, the scrub cleared and burnt then sowed with grass, usually paspalam, to make maize and dairy farms. At that time, strenuous efforts started for forest conservation and timber surveys were carried out. Attempts at natural regeneration of the principal native species of timber trees and artificial plantings of those same species commenced. How different the fauna of this country was to India. In the Upper Barron River platypus were plentiful. Life amongst the North Queensland people was very pleasant but a wandering urge got the upper hand.

'Those were the days, too, of the old bullock teams and the bullockies, with their wonderful vocabulary.'

One weekend Bea, having purchased their traditional English fare of fish and chips, noticed an advertisement for RAAF flying instructors in the newspaper wrappings. As the paper was three months old, Charles thought it would be too late, but Bea insisted he apply. Months passed without a reply, so they presumed the position was filled. Then, *'out of thin air'*, Charles received a telegram requesting him to report immediately to RAAF headquarters in Melbourne. With some misgivings, as the family loved the beauty of the Atherton Tablelands and the friendliness of its people, he resigned from the

Charles and daughter Aileen, Queensland Forestry Department quarters, Atherton Tablelands, 1924.

Queensland Forestry Service. The family travelled to Melbourne by train via Brisbane and Sydney; a journey covering almost the entire length of Australia's east coast. They thought it *'not a very pleasant journey'*.

The RAAF had been established on 31 March 1921. Many of the officers had served in WWI. The service comprised 21 officers and 130 non-commissioned airmen, many of whom went on to achieve high rank in WWII. They included Richard 'Dickie' Williams, the first Chief of the Air Staff, George Jones, Adrian 'King' Cole, Frank Lukis, 'Harry' Cobby, 'Bill' Bostock and 'Frank' McNamara VC. These airmen formed the core foundation of the RAAF, which was to become an effective arm of Australia's armed forces. Over the next 20 years, Charles was to form professional and personal relationships with many of these RAAF pioneers.

On 14 August 1925 Charles was confirmed as Flying Officer Number 24 and given a short service commission. Charles wrote:

> Point Cook was my first destination and as I had not flown for five years, I was required to undertake a refresher course. This I accomplished and

They thought it 'not a very pleasant journey'.

began my service as a short service commissioned Flying Officer as an instructor. At that time, the Air Force expanded which required more flying instructors, hence the reason for my appointment. It was my lot for the next seven years to train pilots for the Royal Air Force, Royal Australian Air Force, and the Citizen Air Force. Flying instruction is a most interesting but tedious work, except for various incidents that happened during my years as a flying instructor. The type of planes used for training was Avros and De Havillands.

Following RAF training practice, trainees attended courses in flying instruction, formation flying, reconnaissance, gunnery and the recently introduced parachute jumping. One cadet, Richard Kingsland, remarked on the variety of cadets who enrolled at Number 1 Flying Training School (FTS) at Point Cook:

> ... came in different sizes, shapes, types, mentality, and attitudes—with a great *esprit de corps*—very proud of being cadets. We wore our white bands around our caps, and were noticeable if we were away from our station and wearing cadet uniforms and very thrilled to be in this game of flying. There was about 30–35 on my course.[1]

Flying Training School instructors, from left, Fred Stevens, Norman Evans and Charles, Point Cook.

Kingsland wrote in 2007 that he remembered Charles as *'not flaunting his WWI record or his seniority. His identifier was always the PIPE'.*

Only four months after their arrival at Point Cook, on 23 December 1925, Bea and Charles celebrated the birth of a son, Peter Charles Godfrey. Another daughter, Irene, had been born in 1924 but died in infancy. Brian John was born in 1930 but also died soon after birth; the deaths of these two children were never mentioned. The couple lost so many friends and relatives in WWI they perhaps suppressed and restricted their memories of those killed as a healing measure. For example, Charles never discussed the death of his close friend and mentor Charlie Napier, killed in 1918. Both were only sons, and Napier had been an elder-brother model; his early and heroic death must have weighed heavily on Charles' mind.

Charles' reputation as an instructor was classed as A3 in efficiency. Many officers who achieved high rank in the RAAF in WWII and senior positions in civil aviation passed through his strict training regime. He was gratified when his students received the Sword of Honour for topping his course. Air Commodore 'Bull' Garing, who was later to command the air support for the Australian Army's victory at Milne Bay in Papua in 1942, was one of his early students. Aubrey Koch, later a senior pilot for Qantas, was a student at Point Cook in the late 1920s. He told Charles years later, when reminiscing at the local Returned Services League (RSL) club, *'Thank God I was not in your class. We could hear you shouting instructions from the ground at your poor* [airborne] *students.'*

Charles' propensity to brush with danger continued in Australia and, although he emerged uninjured, others were not so lucky. One such tragic accident occurred during a RAAF flypast to honour the state visit of the Duke of York, later King George VI, to Melbourne on 21 April 1927. George Jones[2] was commanding the formation of seven DH-9As with Charles as deputy commander. The aircraft had been flying in close formation for more than two hours at about 100 mph. As the flypast began its final approach towards Government House, witnesses noted that Number Six,

'His identifier was always the PIPE'.

'Thank God I was not in your class. We could hear you shouting instructions from the ground at your poor [airborne] students.'

piloted by Flying Officer Vince Thornton and with photographer Sergeant Bert Hay as passenger, was lagging behind. Charles was flying starboard immediately behind Jones with Air Craftsman Class 1 (AC1) 'Joe' Rhyder as his observer.

Jones, unaware of Thornton's problem, began his dive followed by the rest of the flight. He led the Royal Salute across the gates of Government House at 500 feet. After reaching the bottom of their salute, all aircraft put on full power to gain ceiling. Witnesses saw Thornton's plane crash into Number Four, Flying Officer Ron Dines' aircraft, which was flying immediately behind Charles. The impact smashed Dines' port wing and his aircraft began plunging to the ground. Thornton's plane burst into flames and spun into Dines' aircraft—killing all four crew members of the two aircraft. The collision occurred just as the Duke began reviewing the RAAF Guard of Honour under Squadron Leader Harry Cobby. The Duke allegedly commented to Cobby, *'Two poor buggers gone,'* but the *Melbourne Age* quoted the Duke as saying, *'I fear there has been a fatal crash.'*

The following day the two Melbourne papers graphically reported the tragedy:

> There was a crack like a pistol shot and spectators were horrified to see two aeroplanes falling in a trail of smoke ... hundreds of women screaming and fainting as they saw the planes disappear. Suddenly, there was a shriek; followed by terrified cries from numbers of women ... both aeroplanes appeared to mingle in a sickening medley of rending, crashing noises. For an instant, the two wrecked aeroplanes clung together, tumbling all ways as they fell and crumpled up so that the wing of one and the tail of the other were seen to fall away.

The RAAF convened a court of inquiry that called seven witnesses, including Jones and two other surviving pilots, but not Charles. Historian Mark Lax wrote that the result of the investigation was not well received: *'It was poorly constructed, poorly researched and the findings were totally inconclusive.'* Another inquiry summoned Charles, but again there was mixed and unclear evidence.

'It was poorly constructed, poorly researched and the findings were totally inconclusive.'

One Royal Salute and a Close Call, 1927

Squadron Leader Cole, who had been at Government House, thought Thornton had not been paying sufficient attention in keeping station, while Charles stated the two aircraft behind him had been *'staggering'*. The two inquiries found the crews were medically fit, the two machines were airworthy and there was no evidence of mechanical failure. In the inquiry's opinion, specific regulations for the difficult manoeuvre been had not been practised sufficiently. Thornton may have altered his aircraft's position so his passenger, the photographer, could take photographs. The inquiry concluded that Thornton committed an *'error of judgment'* relative to his position with Dines. Charles never spoke of, or recorded, what was the RAAF's first mid-air collision. If he had opinions to the contrary, he took them to the grave. The distressed Duke of York planted a tree in Melbourne as a memorial to the four deceased airmen.

Since 1925, there had been 15 fatalities through aircraft accidents in the RAAF. Prompted by the 'Royal Salute' incident, Air Marshal Salmond of the RAF was commissioned by the Australian Government in 1928 to inspect and report on the RAAF's establishment, equipment and aircraft. One of his conclusions was that the RAAF's aircraft were obsolete and a drawback to the efficiency of the service. The following year, Charles was to prove the Air Marshal's conclusion in a most dramatic fashion. The Salmond Report also made recommendations for expanding the air force but pointed out there was no requirement for a permanent air base at Port Darwin, Australia's most northern military base. Contrary to this advice, 11 years later Charles commanded a new squadron of six Avro Anson bombers and a flight of Wirraway fighter-bombers to be based in Darwin to provide air protection for the entire north-west of Australia.

Another almost fatal incident for Eaton, which occurred at Point Cook, was his second self-acknowledged brush with fear. He wrote of the incident:

> In (1929) a new type of training aircraft was built in the Commonwealth, its name being the Warrigal I. I remember, to this day, the aircraft arriving at Point Cook and being extensively examined by the Chief of the Air Staff. He asked me what I thought of it and I told him that I would tell him after test flying it.

I took off with Sgt. Douglas in the back seat of the aircraft and flew around until a height of 2,000 feet, threw a loop or so and then tried the aircraft in a spin. After two or three turns, normal procedure was adopted for the aeroplane to come out of a spin, but it refused to do so, and both Douglas and I considered the end had come. Remembering my old RFC instructor's advice at the last minute, I put the engine on while in the spin and the slipstream over the tail pulled me out of the spin and I just managed to clear the ground coming out of the dive. It was a very near go and it was discovered that the aeroplane was short in the tail, so that the rear controls would not operate when it was in a spin. It was only the fact of putting air over the tail by putting the engine on that I was lucky enough to get out of it.

Charles had ordered Eric Douglas to parachute as the Warrigal was spinning out of control to what Eaton expected would be their instant deaths. Eric opted to stay with the aircraft and his pilot. Historian Christopher Clark confirmed that '*Eaton and Douglas were two very alarmed and shaken airmen*'. Colleague 'Paddy' Heffernan thought the Warrigal was '*under powered and overweight*'. The Warrigal was written off months later in a crash landing; a young cadet, Valston Hancock[3], wrote that many of the RAAF's pilots '*sighed with relief*'.

It was the practice of officers at Laverton to fly to country towns throughout Victoria to present addresses on Anzac Day. On one such occasion, Charles flew to Hamilton in western Victoria. He was met at the town's landing strip by a taxi, taken into the town to give his speech, entertained for luncheon by the returned servicemen and returned to his aircraft by the same taxi. The driver politely asked Charles if he would take him on a short joy ride. After a short flight over Hamilton, the passenger shook his pilot's hand in appreciation and introduced himself as Reginald Ansett.[4] Charles forgot the incident but some years later, on 17 February 1936, received an invitation to fly on the inaugural Melbourne to Adelaide flight of Ansett Airways.

In the early morning of 12 April 1929, Charles received a telephone call from the Chief of Staff, Air Commodore Williams. The instructions he was given were to dramatically change the course of his life.

One Royal Salute and a Close Call, 1927

Aileen (aged 10), Charles (aged 34) and Peter Eaton (aged 3), Point Lonsdale, Victoria, 1929.

*The wreckage of Charles' aircraft, DH-9A A1-1.
The aircraft's Liberty engine is now displayed at the
Tennant Creek Airport as a National Trust memorial to
'Pioneer Aviator Group Captain Charles 'Moth' Eaton OBE AFC MID
Commander-Knight of the Oranje Nassau with Swords'.*

11 A Call to the Rescue, 1929

The story of the crash landing of Charles Kingsford Smith's Southern Cross in March 1929 and the subsequent deaths of Keith Anderson and Bobby Hitchcock while searching for the lost plane is a classic drama of pioneering aviation. It is a tale of intrigue, rivalries, accusation and counter-accusation, of yellow journalism and the attempted character assassination of a national hero, of the risks taken by the early pilots, and of the harsh, destructive power of the Australian desert.[1]

Charles was gazetted as a flight lieutenant with a permanent commission with the RAAF in February 1928. In April the following year, a sequence of events instigated by the disappearance of the Fokker monoplane *Southern Cross* propelled him from an unknown officer of modest rank to national attention in what became known as the 'Coffee Royal Affair'.

Aviators Charles Kingsford Smith and Charles Ulm were piloting the *Southern Cross* on the second half of a circumnavigation of the world from London. After leaving Sydney on 30 March 1929 for Wyndham in Western Australia, more than 2000 miles distance, the *Southern Cross* sent a single message that the aircraft was in trouble.

Kingsford Smith's biographer, Davis, wrote:

> His first signal that he was about to make a forced landing dismayed the public, but the total radio silence that followed created a wave of despondency. As days followed without news, it was thought the dense mangroves and alligator infested swamps of the North-West had swallowed Australia's idol. Then rumour followed rumour. All that was known for certain was that the Southern Cross had either crashed in desolate country or had overshot the coast and had been lost at sea.

There was a loud clamour in the Australian media for their rescue. Captain Leslie 'Les' Holden, a pioneer New Guinea aviator and WWI veteran, formed a Citizen's Committee in Sydney to organise and fund his proposed aerial search in DH-61 *Canberra*. Independently of the Citizen's Committee, Sydney victualler John Cantor financially backed a one-time business associate of Kingsford Smith's, Keith Vincent Anderson, to find the *Southern Cross*.

'Then rumour followed rumour. All that was known for certain was that the Southern Cross had either crashed in desolate country or had overshot the coast and had been lost at sea.'

THE SEACH FOR THE WESTLAND WIDGEON *KOOKABURRA*, CENTRAL AUSTRALIA 1929

Unbeknownst to the world, Kingsford Smith, Ulm and their crew had managed to make a forced landing 218 miles south-west of Wyndham near the Glenelg River just as the engines, starved of fuel, first coughed. They had sandwiches, baby food, Coffee Royal and a flask of brandy—and found fresh water close by. The air searches became a nationwide drama. Because of a misinterpretation of the agreement between Cantor and Anderson, people concluded the disappearance had been a publicity stunt instigated for Kingsford Smith's benefit. The resulting controversy and malicious recriminations against Australia's hero, Kingsford Smith, continue to the present day.

Born in Western Australia, Anderson learnt to fly during WWI and served in France with 73 Squadron RFC. While he suffered no physical injuries, according to historian Ian Mackersey he paid a *'heavy psychological price'*. In March 1924, Anderson teamed up with Kingsford Smith to run a road haulage business in Western Australia to raise finance to purchase an aircraft for a trans-Pacific crossing. Mackersey described the partners: *'Smithy was a happy go lucky, well-organised, jovial sort of bloke—Anderson was a real dreamer: slow, careless, and almost helpless.'* They disposed of the business in 1926 to finance the proposed trans-Pacific flight. Unfortunately, the partnership did not last. A disillusioned Anderson withdrew. Kingsford Smith, with new partner Charles Ulm, went on to achieve glory by flying the Pacific a few months later.

Keith Anderson left Sydney at 7 am on 7 April for Wyndham in his Westland Widgeon monoplane *Kookaburra* accompanied by Gallipoli veteran, mechanic Henry Smith 'Bobby' Hitchcock. He planned to fly to Alice Springs, then across the inhospitable and partly unexplored Tanami Desert to Wyndham. Sergeant Eric Douglas described Anderson's flight path: *'This direct route meant flying over at least 400 miles of an unmapped, waterless, uninhabited, and almost featureless desert.'* A defective lock-nut necessitated a forced landing in South Australia but the *Kookaburra* arrived in Alice Springs at 7 pm on 9 April. The Government Resident in Alice Springs reported that the *Kookaburra*, overloaded with fuel, left Alice Springs early the next day.

'This direct route meant flying over at least 400 miles of an unmapped, waterless, uninhabited, and almost featureless desert.'

It then disappeared. Anderson's decision not to follow the overland telegraph line was to have tragic consequences.

Contrary to the outcry over its poor response following the disappearance of the *Southern Cross*, the Government mobilised quickly. The clamour included the Footscray City Council attacking the RAAF as incompetent:

> After the disappearance of the aviators, the country had learnt with a shock that there was not in the Air Force a machine that would prove airworthy in the long search flight. Coupled with this shameful lack of efficiency the department made no adequate move to rescue the airmen, and thereby brought upon itself the indignation of the public. Cr. O'Toole: The name Air Force is a misnomer. When Parliament re-opens, there will be a scathing denunciation by certain members of the lack of 'force' in this country's Air Force.

Early on 12 April, two days after the *Kookaburra* went missing, Air Commodore Williams issued instructions to Charles to command two DH-9As of 1 Squadron and proceed immediately to Central Australia. Charles wrote 25 years later: *'Our Air Force was in a difficult position, possessing only old aircraft of First World War vintage which were exclusively used for training and entirely unsuitable for long desert search flights.'* However, orders are orders—maps and a list of petrol and oil depots *en route* were issued before take-off.

That afternoon the two DH-9As—A1-1 with Charles as pilot and Corporal Phillip Sullivan as aero-fitter, and A1-7 with Flying Officer Andrew Gerrand as pilot and Sergeant John Campbell as aero-fitter—flew to Mildura in northern Victoria, completing the 330-mile journey by 6.30 pm. Charles and Sullivan had both had served in the same regiment, The Lambs, in WW1 but in different battalions. The aircraft carried generators, petrol pumps, two wheels, control and aileron wires, skids and a propeller. They also carried the normal equipment set out in Air Force Orders for cross-country flights: food, water, sleeping bags, binoculars and a Colt revolver. Special containers filled with food and water that could be dropped by parachute were attached to bomb racks. Perhaps Charles did not realise it, but this unexpected

'The name Air Force is a misnomer. When Parliament re-opens, there will be a scathing denunciation by certain members of the lack of "force" in this country's Air Force.'

RAAF DH-9As, A 1-1 and A 1-7, en route to Central Australia to search for the Kookaburra, April 1929.

challenge offered an opportunity to test his leadership qualities, flying skills and organisational ability under conditions that would include scorching temperatures, mechanical breakdowns, logistical problems and the real possibility of perishing.

Explorer Michael Terry wrote that Russia had its Urals; early America, its California; Arabia, its Mecca and North Australia, its Tanami Desert. The Tanami is a peneplain of about 71,000 square miles (184,000 square kilometres)—almost the size of England and Scotland combined. The nomadic Wallamulla tribe sparsely populated the desert around its fringes. In summer, the country is saturated with heat and light, with day temperatures consistently over 100° Fahrenheit (38° Celsius). The vegetation is primarily low spinifex scrub, so provides little shade. Although the land is virtually waterless, the name Tanami is derived from the local indigenous name, 'tan-ar-me' or 'never dry', so named for two rock holes that contain permanent water just three miles from the Tanami gold fields. It was into this forbidding environment that Anderson and Hitchcock had flown from Alice Springs and, days later, the RAAF expedition to find them.

As Charles and his crew embarked on the rescue mission on 12 April, Captain Holden discovered the missing *Southern Cross*. His radio operator, Stannage, flashed the news nationwide: '*Found. All Safe.*' Unknown to Kingsford Smith, Charles and the rest of Australia, Anderson and Hitchcock must have been close to death or already dead.

Unknown to Kingsford Smith, Charles and the rest of Australia, Anderson and Hitchcock must have been close to death or already dead.

At Mildura, the two over-loaded RAAF aircraft had to be re-packed; A1-1 was tail heavy. The two planes flew the 800 miles to Maree in South Australia, arriving at 2.30 pm on 13 April. On re-fuelling and carrying out the maintenance of spark plugs and distributors, the crew encountered their first problem—A1-1's leaking fuel tank. Due to the urgency of his mission, Charles decided to continue with the leak only partially repaired. They left Maree just after noon the next day, cruising at 4000 feet; that altitude provided adequate visibility and the engines benefited from the cooler airflow. Soon after leaving, Charles noticed an unpleasant smell in the cockpit. The petrol tank seam had fractured again and was leaking badly. The aircraft reached Oodnadatta at 3 pm. In 1929, Oodnadatta consisted of several shops, a general store, about ten houses and a hotel. The 'aerodrome' was nothing more than a rough paddock littered with old tins and rubbish and surrounded by Afghan camel pens. After landing, they taxied up the town's main street to the sole garage. The top wing was removed, *'with the help of the whole township ... which were not many'*. The repairs on the fuel tank continued until after midnight.

After landing, they taxied up the town's main street to the sole garage.

A1-1 was finally ready for flight by 3 pm on 16 April, but a puncture to A1-7 caused a further delay. When the two aircraft reached Alice Springs, 300 miles to the north and late in the afternoon, they were warmly greeted by Government Resident John Cawood. Alice Springs was the capital of

'The whole town' helping DH-9 A1-1 under repair at Oodnadatta's only garage, 14 April 1929.

Central Australia, with only a few hundred inhabitants. The airmen found the aerodrome to have a good one-way strip with adequate approaches apart from a precipitous range of hills about one mile to the south. The weather was dry and cloudless with daytime temperatures hot, averaging 40° Celsius, but cooler at night. This weather pattern prevailed for the next two weeks; with no rain, flying visibility remained fine.

Charles described his impressions of 'The Alice', writing in 1953:

> 'The Alice' as it was so affectionately known by the residents of Alice Springs was, and still is, a most interesting place. In 1929 the railway from Adelaide had not reached there, and situated as it is just north of the MacDonnell Ranges with their wonderful colourings at dawn and sunset, it possessed an exclusive atmosphere of charm and the real Australian outback, good natured and helpful residents.

Charles sought witnesses to the movements of the *Kookaburra* after it left Alice Springs on 10 April. The post office and overland telegraph facilities were put at his disposal and he was able to contact Barrow Creek, Tennant Creek, Newcastle Waters and Darwin regarding any news that would help the search. Charles cabled the Air Board on 16 April:

> ANDERSON LAST SEEN ON 10/4/29 ABOUT 0900 HOURS AT POINT 20 MILES N.W. OF RYANS WELL 90 MILES FROM ALICE SPRINGS TRAVELLING IN WESTERLY DIRECTION STOP HAVE ESTABLISHED HIS PROPOSED ROUTE WAS RYANS WELL LANDER CREEK SALT LAKE LAT 20 LONG 131 APPROX TANAMI HALLS CREEK WYNDHAM STOP ENDURANCE APPROX 10 HOURS POSSIBILITY LIMITED TO 8 HOURS ON ACCOUNT OF OIL RESERVE NOT FUNCTIONING. STOP MY PROPOSAL TWO NINE AYES SEARCH THIS ROUTE FROM ALICE SPRINGS AND TWO MORE NINE AYES OR AND HOLDEN SEARCH REMAINDER OF ROUTE FROM WAVE HILL STOP FOR NEXT THREE DAYS PROPOSE SEARCHING ROUTE AND W OF TELEGRAPH LINE FOR 200 MILES FROM ALICE SPRINGS WHEN I SHOULD PROCEED WITH MY MACHINES TO WAVE HILL ON ARRIVAL OF TWO MORE NINE AYES STOP NOT IN TOUCH WITH HOLDEN YET SUGGEST HE SEARCHES IMMEDIATELY FROM WYNDHAM OR WAVE HILL STOP FIRST PATROL BOTH MACHINES LEAVE ALICE SPRINGS 0700 HOURS 17/4/29 FOR LANDER CREEK DISTRICT STOP.

'Anderson last seen on 10/4/29 about 0900 hours at point 20 miles N.W. of Ryans Well 90 miles from Alice Springs travelling in westerly direction.'

The next morning Eaton and Gerrand carried out the first patrol, pursuing a course Anderson may have taken. The planes' maximum range was fully tested during the 8 am to 1.30 pm flight. It was A1-7's turn for trouble when a broken valve spring and carbon brush had to be replaced before they could fly.

That evening they heard the good news that Captain Holden and the *Canberra* had arrived at Wyndham to join the search for the *Kookaburra*. Their second patrol left Alice Springs at 8.30 am the next morning and returned just after 1 pm. Although A1-7's engine cut out above the aerodrome, Gerrand skilfully landed the plane without mishap. With no trace of the missing aircraft, it became apparent a new base was needed to increase the range of the search.

Due to the deteriorating condition of both aircraft, Charles had cabled the Air Board requesting three more DH-9As. They left Laverton on 17 April under the command of Flying Officer Leo Ryan: A1-5 with Leo Ryan as pilot and Corporal Doug Endean as wireless operator/mechanic; A1-20 with Sergeant Eric Douglas as pilot and Leading Air Craftsman WJ Smith as aero-rigger; and A1-28 with Flying Officer 'Max' Allen as pilot and Air Craftsman First Class George Allen as aero-fitter. Corporal NR Cottee left for Alice Springs by train carrying equipment and spares for the DH-9As. Only A1-5 was fitted with a wireless but it could not be used effectively. The three aircraft had no aeronautical charts but the pilots made sketches while flying, marking relevant distances and features on a standard atlas map of Australia.

Douglas recorded a near disaster which exemplified the flying conditions of those early aviators:

> All went well; about three hours later we sighted Hawker approx. six miles away on our left and shortly afterwards we saw the north south railway line. We then turned to the north and set a course to Maree that was to take us more or less over the railway line. About half an hour later, a fierce dust storm was sighted rolling in from ahead and to the left.
>
> We increased speed and passed just in front of it. Several minutes later, the country astern was blotted out by a thick dust haze, which extended from ground level up to about 6,000 feet. It appeared that this dust had

originated at Lake Torrens many miles to the north west of us. By this time, the Flinders Range was showing up to the right and it could be seen extending away to the north east as a very extensive mountain range.

By map reading, it was obvious that our ground speed was decreasing and it was apparent we were now fighting a strong north-west wind, which had commenced to worry us at Hawker. We were aware this could prove serious with our depleting fuel. The DH-9 had a fuel endurance of 4¾ to 5½ hours depending upon the speed selected and already we had been airborne 4 ¾ hours with 90 miles to cover.

As we were pushing on at our maximum cruising speed of 110 to 115 miles per hour it was evident we would be cutting things fine. When our flying time reached 5 ¾ hours, all eyes were anxiously peering ahead for sight for Maree. At last, the settlement could be seen just where the railway line turned abruptly to the west and in a few minutes we were throttling off to make a landing straight ahead into a strong ground wind on an old oval situated about 500 yards from the Maree Hotel.

A check revealed that we were all down to our last few gallons of petrol; in fact, one machine only had 2 gallons. The DH-9 had a large fuel tank in the fuselage situated between the engine and the pilot in addition to a small fuel tank of 8 gallons capacity known as the gravity tank, which was located on the top wing, thus when the main tank became nearly empty the pilot turned on the petrol cock of the gravity tank. We then knew that he had about 20 minutes of safe flying left. In this flight from Mildura to Maree, we all turned on our gravity tanks when about 20 minutes flying time from Maree.

Luck had averted a major catastrophe. However, Leo Ryan hit a camel pen on landing at Oodnadatta, damaging the tail-skid.

The next day, 19 April, Charles and Gerrand flew from Alice Springs, trying to reach Lander Station. As the last station before meeting the true Tanami Desert, it was important to know if they had seen the *Kookaburra*. It proved impossible to reach the station from Alice Springs so the crew identified a site at Ryan's Well that could be easily turned into a suitable landing strip, thereby extending their aircrafts' range by 100 miles and allowing them to reach Lander Station and further north. Returning to Alice Springs, they arranged to ferry fuel to the new strip under the supervision of Campbell and an Aboriginal policeman.

Ryan's flight landed at Alice Springs late that day. According to Douglas, Charles gave them *a hearty welcome and was very pleased to see us and that our three aircraft were serviceable*. He gave an account of the search's progress and explained the plan to move the search north to Wave Hill cattle station, past Tennant Creek. The Minister of Defence, who now realised the precarious state of the aircraft, had asked Qantas for an aircraft to support the search. Captain Lester Brain in *Atalanta*, a Qantas DH-50 aircraft, was to join the search, operating from Wave Hill. Charles was to use the Tennant Creek Telegraph Station as a temporary base and ordered 1200 gallons of petrol be delivered to Wave Hill.

Charles now had five DH-9As plus the *Atalanta* and the *Canberra* to find the missing *Kookaburra*. The DH-9As were to fly north to meet Captain Brain and Captain Holden after the three newly arrived aircraft had their engines checked after flying from Laverton, Victoria. Douglas, a vigilant diarist, recorded that the overhaul proved difficult as the flight's workshop tools had been thrown overboard by the pilot of the leading aircraft near Oodnadatta. When requested to explain his actions the pilot replied, *'Don't bother with those things, when your engine stops you stop.'* The aero-fitters took a poor view of that decision.

Later that day Charles received a reply from the Air Board:

CONCUR YOUR PROPOSALS KEEP US POSTED BEFOREHAND CHANGE DISPOSITIONS AND PROPOSED ACTIVITIES ALL YOUR MACHINES STOP ENSURE NO AIRCRAFT SEARCHES ALONE STOP REALISE DIFFICULTIES AND APPRECIATE YOUR EXCELLENT WORK ENSURE YOU GET SUFFICIENT REST STOP HAVE INFORMED HOLDEN MOOLA BOOLA SUPPLIES DIVERTED FLORA DOWNS AND CONSIDER THAT HE SHOULD ASCERTAIN EARLIEST POSSIBLE FROM TANAMI DISTRICT WHETHER ANY INFORMATION ANDERSON STOP QANTAS MACHINE LEFT BRISBANE TODAY FITTING EXTRA PETROL TANK LONGREACH ALSO REPORTED FITTED WTH WIRELESS AND EXPECTED ARRIVE WAVE HILL SUNDAY TWENTY FIRST WILL CONFIRM THIS LATER AIR BOARD STOP

Charles thanked the Air Board for co-opting the two modern aircraft, *Atalanta* and *Canberra*. The older DH-9As could not operate for any length of time under 3000 feet due to the intense heat; in short, the air force's aircraft were beginning to fall to pieces. While in The Alice, the crews stayed at the Stuart Arms Hotel, where excellent service was provided despite the outlandish hours the airmen kept. Douglas wrote of the riotous behaviour of railway fitters who had just returned to town after months in the wilderness laying the overland railway tracks:

> We did not get much sleep that night due to the continual noise of the plate layers 'binge' which was highlighted by bottles and 'bodies' crashing through windows of the Hotel at regular intervals. They were in such numbers it was not possible for the few police to control them without resort to violence.

The next day, 20 April, A1-5 and A1-28 left Alice Springs for Tennant Creek Telegraph Station, arriving at 3.30 pm. Charles gave instructions for A1-28 to follow the overland telegraph line and A1-5 to fly 20 miles to the west but to remain in sight of each other. As a safety precaution, he insisted that four aircraft would always fly in pairs, thus allowing the fifth DH-9A time for repairs and maintenance. There was no sign of the lost airmen on the flight to the telegraph station.

Meanwhile, A1-7 and A1-20 made their last patrol from Alice Springs but were delayed by a puncture to A1-7; punctures were now a daily event. After refuelling at Ryan's Well, they proceeded to the Lander River, which proved easy to follow as '*a long white ribbon in an otherwise featureless country*'. The planes circled over Lander Station homestead and dropped a message, with a reply code, requesting information about the lost aircraft. The answer was a white sheet in the form of an arrow pointing in a north-westerly direction; Gerry Gerrand thought this must refer to the direction of the *Kookaburra*'s flight path, so he landed on a small open patch near the homestead. Eric Douglas was quite alarmed to watch Gerrand's aircraft swerve suddenly towards the trees and end up tilted on its left wing; a tyre had blown on landing!

Douglas decided to help, but to avoid the danger of a collision found another clearing. Although it had a landing run of 350 yards, it was surrounded by termite mounds. After one abortive attempt, Douglas made, '*a heavy landing which pulled me up a few yards short of the ant hills*'. The pilots interviewed the station owner, Mr Morton, who confirmed an aircraft, which he believed to be the *Kookaburra*, had flown overhead at 11 am on 10 April. The two crews changed the blown tyre by manually tilting A1-7 on its right wing. It was impossible to return all the way to Alice Springs that day with their news, so the planes spent the evening at Ryan's Well, which they reached just on twilight. After a meal of tinned beef and Horlick's milk tablets, they slept in the open in their flying suits using their parachute packs as pillows. Douglas remarked, '*By midnight the cold became intense so we made up a fire with mulga scrub and lay close to it and dozed.*'

Back in Alice Springs, Charles managed to contact Ryan at the telegraph station, who said some Aboriginal men had reported smoke west of Powell's Creek. Ryan said Allen's A1-28 was unserviceable and could not take any further part in the search and one of the bearings of his engine was giving trouble and the sump oil had high quantities of white metal. Charles instructed Ryan not to proceed alone to try and locate the *Kookaburra*, but to endeavour to repair A1-28. Arriving only two days before from Victoria, the condition of the three support aircraft was now no better than the original two. Charles suggested Ryan investigate the origin of the smoke with Captain Brain in the DH-50, which was due to arrive in Tennant Creek the following day.

A1-7 and A1-20 returned to Alice Springs from Ryan's Well early on 21 April; Charles had been alarmed at their disappearance for more than 24 hours and was relieved to see them. From the evidence, and the signs of smoke reported by Ryan, it was concluded that Anderson had crossed the river near Lander Station homestead. This made further patrols from Ryan's Well ineffective, so Charles ordered the search be based at Wave Hill Station, north of the Tanami.

After one abortive attempt, Douglas made, 'a heavy landing which pulled me up a few yards short of the ant hills'.

The three aircraft still at Alice Springs were to refuel at Ryan's Well and Tennant Creek *en route* to Newcastle Waters to meet Captain Brain. Charles instructed that each plane fly independently by following the telegraph line. In the event of a forced landing, they were to cut the telegraph line, which would bring assistance. Douglas landed at Ryan's Well first, quickly refuelled and took off. Before heading north for Tennant Creek, he circled the landing strip to ensure the safe landing of the other two aircraft. He saw A1-1 swerve sharply at the end of its landing run; Douglas immediately landed again to assist. Charles' aircraft had run into patch of soft black earth, or *gilgai,* and was bogged up to the axle. It was extracted from the quagmire through engine power and the manual efforts of all three crews. Another three punctures had to be repaired and, to cap it all, A1-1's throttle jammed. By mid-afternoon, when the plane was serviceable, Charles and Sullivan departed for Tennant Creek. Due to a cross wind, Douglas took off just above stalling speed, barely missing the mulga scrub. Douglas knew he'd made a mistake when taking off but by skilful flying, he leap-frogged over the scrub, briefly touched down again on a small clearing then just managed to obtain sufficient lift and air speed to get airborne.

The three aircraft flew parallel, five miles apart, towards Tennant Creek Telegraph Station. They investigated smoke from a scrub fire some 30 miles west of Renner Springs but found no evidence of the *Kookaburra*. After two hours, and only 20 miles south of Tennant Creek, Charles noticed his engine's thermometer fluctuating between 185° F and 205° F. The Liberty engine boiled and partly seized but continued to fire intermittently. Flying at 5000 feet, Charles throttled his aircraft down to 1000 rpm and brought it down to 2000 feet. He hoped this might help cool the engine and, as a precaution, shut off the petrol cock. Eric Douglas had noticed white smoke belching from A1-1 and, flying closer, saw a white substance oozing from the aircraft's engine; the pistons were melting.

Douglas wrote:
> Flight Lt. Eaton pointed forward and put the nose of his aircraft down indicating his engine had failed and that he intended to make a forced

landing. I dived down close to the ground from an altitude of 3,000 feet and picked out the most likely looking place for a crash landing close to the telegraph line, as there was no area within his gliding distance that would afford a safe landing. I then opened full up and climbed steeply and met Flight Lt. Charles's aircraft at about 800 feet. I indicated to him what appeared the best place to put his aircraft down. He waved and manoeuvred his plane so that on flattening out it would carry him on to some low mulga scrub near the telegraph line.

The next thing I saw was a cloud of red dust that obscured his aircraft as it ploughed along over the scrub and ground. A few seconds later, we observed F/L Eaton and Sullivan standing beside the wreck and waving to indicate they were uninjured which was a great relief to us.

Charles was more economical with his words:

As there was no clear space in the vicinity I was forced to crash the machine in the best possible manner among the trees alongside the overland telegraph line about eight miles from Tennant Creek ... It was a good crash, the trees stripped my wings and pulled me up, and the fuselage just flopped on the ground.

'The next thing I saw was a cloud of red dust that obscured his aircraft as it ploughed along over the scrub and ground.'

'It was a good crash, the trees stripped my wings and pulled me up, and the fuselage just flopped on the ground.'

The Kookaburra photographed in the Tanami Desert from the air by Captain Lester Brain, 21 April 1929.

Charles instructed that all salvageable instruments be removed from the wreck of A1-1. The aircraft's aero-fitter, Phillip Sullivan, inspected the engine and concluded the piston of the third right cylinder had seized and melted, causing the flames. His opinion was that excessive atmospheric heat caused the meltdown. Thus ended the life of the Royal Australian Air Force's first formally registered aircraft, nine-year-old DH-9A A1-1.

They then walked to the telegraph line, cut it to attract attention, and began walking north along the line carrying their parachutes. They were found by the station's two linesmen only four miles from the telegraph station. Meanwhile, the other two aircraft had landed safely at the telegraph station. On arrival at the telegraph station Charles learnt that Captain Brain had sighted the *Kookaburra*. He had been flying direct to Wave Hill in the *Atalanta* and investigated the smoke reported by the Aboriginals and Leo Ryan. By heading south, he found the lost aircraft some 80 miles north-west of Powell's Creek.

Brain graphically described what he saw:

> Coming lower we could see the figure of a man lying in the shadow of the starboard wing, and circling again and again at a height of 15 ft we were able to see that he was black in the face, feet and arms, and this together with the parched appearance of the skin led me to conclude that he had been dead for some days. I endeavoured to decide which of the pair this was, but it was difficult in view of the high speed necessary for our machine that was heavily loaded, and the body being in the shadow. However, from the dark appearance of the hair, the size of the figure etc. it looked most like Anderson.

Douglas later commented, *'Ryan unfortunately lost the honour of sighting the Kookaburra first.'* Charles had been justified in refusing permission for Ryan to investigate alone and risk his own death and that of his auto-fitter.

Charles arranged to meet Captain Brain at Newcastle Waters the following day to discuss the next stage of the search—to determine the fate of the second aviator. Before leaving Tennant Creek, Douglas prepared parachutes in case they were required to get to the plane: *'F/L Eaton had*

'Ryan unfortunately lost the honour of sighting the Kookaburra first.'

insisted that the first man to make the jump would be himself. The Air Board approved that A1-1 be written-off but for Eaton to seriously consider the risks before making a parachute jump. Maintenance on A1-5, A1-7 and A1-20 continued until 2 am so all were ready to fly to Newcastle Waters at daylight. Max Allen and aero-fitters Sullivan, Smith and George Allen were left in Tennant Creek with instructions from Eaton to make every effort to get A1-28 serviceable.

In the early morning of 22 April, Charles flew with Douglas in A1-20 and all three aircraft landed at Newcastle Waters at 9.30 am to meet Captain Brain. He had revisited the *Kookaburra* and gave the position of the grounded aircraft as 80 miles east-south-east of Wave Hill Station. Charles decided to visit the site by air that afternoon with the *Atalanta*, A1-5, A1-7 and A1-20. Flying over the stranded plane, they observed the body under the wing but no evidence of the second airman; there were indications of an open grave alongside the starboard wing. The fire that Ryan had reported on 20 April, which had led Brain to the *Kookaburra* the next day, was still burning and now covered about 100 square miles. Charles concluded it would be difficult to look for the second body from the air, particularly as the DH-9As' engines continued to boil at low altitude. All four planes flew on to Wave Hill Station, arriving at six that evening. The smoke from the fire had been seen from Wave Hill for some days but no connection to the lost *Kookaburra* had been made as seasonal scrub fires were normal.

Eaton cabled the Air Board:

> MACHINES A1 7 AND A1 5 A 1200 DH-50 ARRIVED WAVE HILL 1800 HOURS STOP ANDERSONS PLANE UNDAMAGED FROM APPEARANCE FORCED DOWN WITH ENGINE TROUBLE RUNWAY IS CLEARED FOR A TAKE OFF STOP MACHINES SEARCHED NEAR PLANE FOR ONE HOUR ONE MAN DEAD UNDER THE WINGS AND FROM APPEARANCES ONE MAN PARTLY BURIED BY PLANE STOP IMPOSSIBLE TO LAND NEARBY WITHOUT DAMAGING MACHINES STOP NO PARTY HAS BEEN SENT OUT FROM HERE BUT ARRANGING FOR EITHER CAR OR PACK HORSES WITH TRACKER TO PROCEED BY TOMORROW MORNING INTEND ACCOMPANYING PARTY WITH DOUGLAS TO BURY VICTIMS AND IF POSSIBLE FLY KOOKABURRA

'Searched near plane for one hour one man dead under the wings and from appearances one man partly buried by plane.'

BACK TO WAVE HILL STOP DO NOT CONSIDER IT NECESSARY FOR ATALANTA AND CANBERRA TO REMAIN STOP IMPOSSIBLE FOR NINE AYES TO SEARCH LOW DOWN DUE TO HEAT IF THE OCCUPANT NOT AT MACHINE IT MOST IMPROBABLE HE COULD BE FOUND BY AIR OWING TO NATURE OF COUNTRY STOP FIRE STARTED BY ANDERSON CAN NOW BE SEEN SIXTY MILES FROM AIR STOP INTEND USING NINE AYES TO COOPERATE WITH MY GROUND PARTY STOP ALLEN AND A1 28 AT TENNANT CREEK AWAITING MY INSTRUCTIONS STOP EATON

Charles was grateful to Captain Brain for his successful participation in the search and requested he remain another day at Wave Hill before returning to Queensland. Just five minutes before Brain departed, Captain Holden arrived in the *Canberra*. Charles thanked him also and said it was unnecessary for him to remain as he had three serviceable DH-9As to provide air support for the proposed ground party. Now the missing plane had been located, Charles' next mission was to reach the *Kookaburra* in the shortest possible time. As only one body had been seen, there was a remote chance the second aviator may be still alive.

Wave Hill stockmen; Daylight Parunja Janama, Sambo Brisbane Jangurra and Alec Jupurrula and the Expedition's horses at Wave Hill Station, 23 April 1929.

12 THE CROSS IN THE SKY, 1929

It was just about two hours since we reached the site and when we were preparing to leave that we saw it ... high up ... right above the Kookaburra, in an otherwise clear sky, a PERFECT CROSS formed by what may have been streaky cirrus cloud. We did not say much to each other but I think we all thought a lot as we made our weary return journey.

Charles Eaton, 1953

In 1929 Wave Hill was one of the largest cattle stations in Australia, covering some 8000 square miles. With its smooth surface and long east–west runway, the station's airstrip proved suitable for the aircraft seeking to retrieve the *Kookaburra* and its crew, Keith Anderson and Bobby Hitchcock.

On his arrival at the station, Charles began organising a ground party to reach the ill-fated aeroplane. Station manager A McGuggan informed Charles that no suitable vehicle was available but pack and saddle horses would be provided. Gerrand flew north to Victoria River Downs Station to parachute a message to the manager, 'Alf' Martin, inquiring about procuring suitable motorised transport. Martin signalled that a car would arrive at Wave Hill that afternoon. He was widely known as 'Hell-fire Alf' because of his habit of driving irrespective of the state of the road or his passengers' nerves.

By coincidence, Alex Moray, the station's pastoral inspector, arrived on one of his periodic visits. Moray placed the station's facilities at the RAAF's disposal and offered to accompany Charles and his party with his Buick Roadster. Significantly, he offered the services of three experienced Aboriginal stockmen to direct the expedition over country that had never been traversed by white men. Charles readily agreed:

> I decided to accept this very generous offer and on the arrival of Mr Martin from Victoria Downs, explained the position to him. He realised this fully and after offering such aid and advice as he could give, returned to Victoria Downs that evening.

Charles selected Eric Douglas to accompany the party as he would be able to check the *Kookaburra's* engine and fuselage if, and when, they reached it. He discussed with Ryan and Gerrand how they could support the party by air. Their aircraft were to make daily flights from Wave Hill, drop urgent supplies, scout for surface water, receive urgent requests from the ground and guide the party to the lost plane. A series of 22 signals were devised, including 'drop drinking water from air', 'O.K.', 'can't find second body' and 'how far from water'. Charles stipulated that the DH-9As were to operate in pairs while the third was serviced and maintained. Ryan was to cable the expedition's progress to the Air Board.

On the afternoon of 23 April, all RAAF ranks and Wave Hill employees prepared the Buick and pack horses. The three stockmen, led by Parunja Janama, left at 8 pm with 26 pack and saddle horses for Junjamimji, a watering hole some 20 miles south of Wave Hill, where they were to wait for the Buick. Janama, a Gurindji man, spoke English well.

Twelve days after leaving Laverton, Charles, Moray and Douglas set out in the Buick at 9.30 am to reach Junjamimji. They drove through rocky country until 3 pm when driving became difficult due to soft sand and anthills. On the way, they had three punctures and the engine was constantly boiling because

A series of 22 signals were devised, including 'drop drinking water from air', 'O.K.', 'can't find second body' and 'how far from water'.

the Buick was largely restricted to second gear. At 4.30 pm, when the two DH-9As flew overhead, Charles signalled 'O.K.' and indicated for them to return the following morning. That evening set the scene for the coming days. The party fed on the cold salted beef, damper[1] and black tea that was to be their only sustenance. Day temperatures consistently rose above 100° F but nights were cold; the stockmen cleverly made fires that burnt all night.

Although Douglas managed to repair the Buick, the next morning it soon came to a halt with two flat tyres and radiator problems. A1-5 and A1-20 arrived and, on seeing the Buick's predicament, the pilots landed on a clay pan. Charles rode to meet them, requesting the crews to obtain soldering iron and food supplies. Ryan informed the expedition that a water hole was about half a mile away. He directed the ground party to the pool by circling his aircraft over it; this muddy billabong was to be the party's lifeline in the days ahead.[2]

The aircraft soon returned, dropping the rations and solder. Although Douglas tried to repair the radiator, the Buick had to be abandoned. At 5 pm they continued by horse, travelling past dusk before camping at the billabong. The delays caused by the Buick meant they had only travelled 12 miles in two days. Douglas wrote of his preference for horses versus the Buick:

Charles, left, and Alex Moray with the abandoned Buick, April 1929.

I was given a sturdy pony named 'Daisy' and found the saddle a good place after the immense danger of being scalped by the scrub when crouching in the car. F/L Eaton was quite an experienced horseman while I had sufficient experience to enable me to jog along.

Next morning, 25 April, after replenishing water bags and watering the horses, they made an early start while Alec Jupurrula returned to the Buick with four horses and provisions. Charles describes their journey:

That evening we camped at the last known water hole nearest to the *Kookaburra* and at dawn the following morning set out on our journey, pushing our way through waterless desert country, covered with low thick brush, every leaf covered black with flies, the only life seen in this country, no animals, no birds. The journey was a nightmare, as the horses pushed through the scrub; myriads of flies rose and settled on horses and man alike: they would not be brushed off, and we were just covered in a sticky mess. After 24 hours, it seemed impossible to go further, the horses having no water were giving trouble.

'After 24 hours, it seemed impossible to go further, the horses having no water were giving trouble.'

A1-7 indicated the general direction of the *Kookaburra*; Eaton signalled Gerrand that more rations were required later that day. After three days free from malfunctions, two of the planes had problems: A1-5 had broken a tailskid on its last landing; and A1-20's petrol pump had seized, its engine boiled and oil pressure fluctuated. The aircraft could not be flown with safety. Charles later wrote that delays to repair of A1-5's tailskid were owing to the inferior nature of the tools available. He did not refer to the tools that had been thrown overboard when Ryan's flight was approaching Oodnadatta.

The party continued through terrain with a firm surface covered with stunted tree growth, spinifex and anthills. A1-5 and A1-7 returned in the afternoon and dropped supplies. The pilots pointed to a possible water source two miles away that had been seen *en route* to Wave Hill. Janama was sent to find the water but was unable to locate it. The horse party continued until 7.30 pm; Charles calculated they had made 25 miles that day and were perhaps only five miles from the *Kookaburra*. He also noted that the fire started by the lost aviators had burnt itself out. The fire had burnt an area of 300 square miles; it had certainly been the right signal!

The Cross in the Sky, 1929

Eric Douglas was impressed with the bush craft of Jangurra, a Yanyuwa tribesman from Borroloola near the Gulf of Carpentaria who had been given the English name 'Brisbane':

> We were now in country never before traversed by white man and I was riding in the company of Jangurra and found his knowledge of tracking and bush craft fascinating as he explained it to me in his halting English. He could pick most of the horses by name by looking at their hoof marks. He tried to teach me how to track the horses even when the hoof marks were obliterated by moving over hard ground. This he did by reading signs on freshly broken branches and leaves but it was too tiring to follow continuously—we had perpetual thirst which only black tea could quench.

The next two days would prove frustrating. Janama and Jangurra were sent ahead to scout for any sign of the *Kookaburra* but, although they climbed the rare 20-foot tall trees, found nothing. The Tanami was indeed flat, confirming what Kelly later recorded in 2003 as *'Not even a bump disturbed the horizon. From east to west was an unbroken sea of scrub.'* Due to the poor state of the horses, having had no water for 24 hours, Charles called a halt. Unknown to the ground party, the pilots could not take-off; A1-5 had fractured a shock absorber and, adhering to Eaton's strict orders, Gerrand could only wait until the aircraft was repaired. The ground party waited until 2.30 pm before turning back on their tracks to eventually find the elusive water well. The well proved to be a double-tiered sinkhole some 80 feet deep and, to their utter disappointment, completely dry. The sinkhole was on the Dream Time trail of Jurntakal, the giant death adder. Due to the critical condition of the horses, Charles sent them back with Jangurra and Janama to the billabong for water, both for the horses and the search party.

> Myself, Sgt. Douglas and Mr Moray remained in camp at the sinkhole. The horses left at 1900 hours and reached water at approximately 0500 the following morning, the horses having been 45 hours and travelling a distance of about 75 miles without water.

Sergeant Douglas arose sometime after midnight for a call of nature and fell into the sinkhole's orifice, by a miracle landing on a small ledge not far

'This he did by reading signs on freshly broken branches and leaves but it was too tiring to follow continuously—we had perpetual thirst which only black tea could quench.'

from the rim. By the clever use of a pen knife, he managed to cut hand grips and extradited himself from the sinkhole. He was too embarrassed to inform his companions of the mishap. If he had fallen the full 80 odd feet, the result may have had serious consequences for the party.

The expedition's leader was anxious about the scarcity of water, the deteriorating condition of the horses working in such high temperatures, and the stress on Douglas, Moray and himself. The two Aboriginal stockmen appeared quite comfortable and unconcerned, even after their epic return journey to the billabong. Charles was determined to reach the *Kookaburra* at all costs to complete their mission and, above all, solve the mystery of the second aviator.

Eighteen days after leaving Laverton, on 29 April, Janama guided the white men and nine horses in the direction indicated by the RAAF aircraft. As a precaution, Charles ordered the remaining horses to stay at the sinkhole under the care of Jangurra. Once again, A1-5 and A1-7 left Wave Hill late, this time because of a puncture and the refitting of a generator to A1-5. Finding the party ten miles from the sinkhole, they flew in circuits, guiding the four men to the *Kookaburra* through the flat, sandy desert with its thick low scrub and not more than 150 yards visibility from horseback and 50 yards at ground level. At midday, Moray warned Eaton of the danger:

> ... owing to the arduous nature of the journey in that type of country, Mr Moray informed me that he did not think it possible to go any further and still return safely to water. I halted the party and after signalling to the aircraft, received a message that our destination was only ½ mile further on. We again proceeded and arrived at the *Kookaburra* at 1330 hours. Owing to the time the D.H.9As had been flying this day I decided to instruct them to return to WAVE HILL immediately. The D.H.9As returned to WAVE HILL after a 4½ hours patrol.

The men must have had mixed emotions on reaching the *Kookaburra* and its tragic outcome. The body under the wing was dressed in only a shirt and underpants, but was identified as Hitchcock because of a bandaged

'Owing to the arduous nature of the journey in that type of country, Mr Moray informed me that he did not think it possible to go any further and still return safely to water.'

leg; Sister Inglis of the Alice Springs Hospital had treated the infection. Although the Air Board had suggested the bodies be carried to Wave Hill, Charles had been authorised to bury them if he thought otherwise. Given the condition of the horses and the body's advanced state of decomposition, Charles considered it better to bury Hitchcock immediately. Moray read The Lord's Prayer and the men buried Henry Smith 'Bobby' Hitchcock where he was found—under the starboard wing—with a rough cross of desert timber placed at the grave head.

Eaton and Moray at the burial of Hitchcock 2.30 pm 29 April, 1929.

There was no sign of Keith Anderson. The 'open grave' seen from the air by the RAAF crew and Captain Brain proved to be a shallow hole dug by the airmen in a futile attempt to obtain subterranean water. Janama stressed the necessity for the party to return to water immediately, otherwise they '*could end up like the body under the wing*'. However, Charles would not order a return until Anderson was found: '*Otherwise the whole of Australia would think I had left Anderson alive to die alone in the desert.*'

'Otherwise the whole of Australia would think I had left Anderson alive to die alone in the desert.'

Janama continued the search and returned after finding Anderson's body in spinifex scrub, about 400 yards south-west of the stranded aircraft.

Charles explained:

> We proceeded to the spot, following Lieut. Anderson's path as indicated by the tracker. At a point on this track, an air cushion and two bottles of petrol were found. After collecting papers and other personal effects, we buried the body at 1630 hours. Owing to the entire absence of water, no wild animal or bird life was discovered after leaving the water hole in the creek. The bodies had not been touched by rodents, dingoes or crows.

Janama described how Anderson had sat under some scrub then shed his coat and flying helmet, aircraft log, watch and scarf. After a while, Anderson got to his feet and, according to Janama, *'the white man was very sick'*. He had started to wander, deranged with thirst, and divested himself of all clothing. Eventually he fell to the ground but continued to advance by crawling in the sand until his merciful death. At 4.30 pm, gallant Keith Vincent Anderson, aged just 32, was laid to rest in the infinite loneliness of the Tanami.

The papers Charles found near his body confirmed his identity; later, they would prove to be the crucial evidence that cleared Kingsford Smith's name of any impropriety in the Coffee Royal Affair. The horrendous manner by which both men had perished was much on the minds of all four men. Charles concluded the aviators had eaten at least one meal but two packets of biscuits were found in the cockpit. They had taken only two bottles of water, the absolute minimum amount for a single day in those scorching temperatures. The stranded aviators had opened the compass to retrieve methylated spirits, which they mixed with oil, petrol and their own urine to drink.

Anderson had kept a diary describing their predicament by writing on the plane's rudder.[3] It poignantly described their last hours.

'Owing to the entire absence of water, no wild animal or bird life was discovered after leaving the water hole in the creek.'

After a while, Anderson got to his feet and, according to Janama, 'the white man was very sick'.

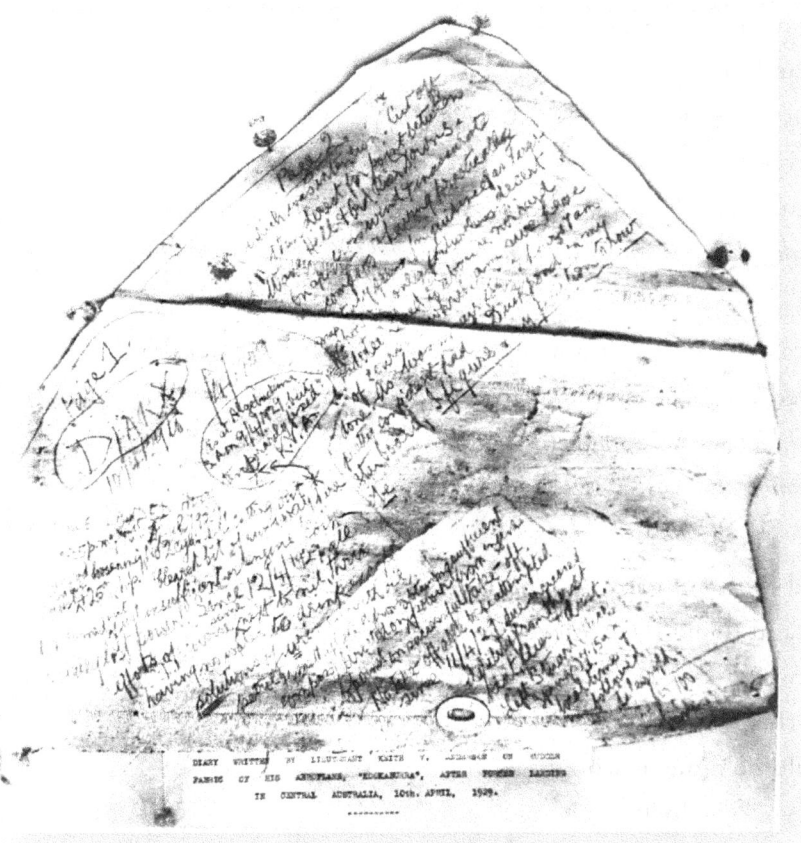

The rudder diary which the rescue team cut out as evidence.

The following is a transcript of the diary:

Diary 10/4/29 to /4/29

Force landed here 2.35 pm 10th April 1929 thru' push rod loosening No 2 cylinder cutting out (as at Algebucking S.A. on 9/4/1929, but temporarily fixed. K.V.A.) exhaust valve & 25% .hp. Cleared bit of runway here which turned out just insufficient of engine coincidently lost power. Since 12/4/1929 all efforts, of course same next to nil, thru having no water to drink except solutions of urine (with oil, petrol, methylate from compass) directed on obtaining sufficient power from engine to permit on successful take-off. No take-off able to be attempted since 11/4/29 due to increased debility from thirst, heat, flies & dust. Left Stuart [Alice Springs] 7.15 am local time and followed telegraph for 100 miles which was intention. Cut off then direct for point between Wave Hill & Ord River Downs. On a/c cross wind & inaccurate compass & having practically only sun for guidance as large map showed only featureless desert determined to above or nor'ward of course, which am sure have done. As was in air 7 hours & am pretty confident had 'Duckpond' on my starboard. I figure my position now to be …'

Hitchcock and Anderson had carried no axe or any suitable tool, but had tried to clear a runway of 160 yards with their hands. From the wheel tracks, four or five attempts had been made to take off but the runway was insufficient. Charles wrote that the two aviators had done everything possible to clear a path, *'but it was a physically impossible task, and they both may have perished within 48 hours of the time that they forced landed and so ended their gallant attempt on the search for Smith and Ulm.'*

Douglas found the *Kookaburra* was serviceable. The condition of the engine was good, well serviced and, when fired on full throttle, *' ... was functioning perfectly. The aileron, elevator and rudder controls, and tail-plane actuating gear quite normal. Apart from a few small rips, the body work was normal but one tyre was punctured.'*

The loose lock-nut of the push rod that had caused the forced landing had been repaired by Hitchcock. Charles and Douglas noticed the compass had been removed and found it a few yards from the machine. The men debated the possibilities of Charles flying the *Kookaburra* back to Wave Hill and although they agreed it could be done, it would take a full day to clear a suitable runway and fix the tyre. The lock-nut would be suspect in flight and could not be completely rectified until a full engine overhaul.

The party retrieved all the personal articles they could salvage and Charles compiled a detailed inventory that included maps, newspaper cuttings of the disappearance of the *Southern Cross*, a driving licence, spectacles, a lottery ticket and personal clothing. A Bible resting on the plane's wing contained photographs of an unidentified child and a young woman with thick dark hair. Charles also removed the control column from the pilot's cockpit and had photographs taken of the stranded plane and the two graves. As the rescue party and their horses were now at their physical limit, Charles ordered their return to the sinkhole. They left the *Kookaburra* and the two brave aviators in the solitude of the Tanami.

'It was a physically impossible task, and they both may have perished within 48 hours of the time that they forced landed and so ended their gallant attempt on the search for Smith and Ulm.'

The Cross in the Sky, 1929

As they were leaving, Charles, an outwardly non-religious person, observed what he described 25 years later:

> It was just about two hours since we reached the site and when we were preparing to leave that we saw it ... high up ... right above the Kookaburra, in an otherwise clear sky, a PERFECT CROSS formed by what may have been streaky cirrus cloud. We did not say much to each other but I think we all thought a lot as we made our weary return journey.

Douglas wrote of the same phenomena in 1958: *'Lt. Eaton first saw the cloud and pointed it out to me ... it was quite eerie.'* At nightfall, they stopped for the usual cold tea and salt beef and Moray asked Janama if he could lead the party to the sinkhole. Janama led the group with only starlight for visibility.

Douglas noted in his diary:

> I was at a loss to discover how Janama managed to lead us in a direct line through the scrub without once faltering or deviating from his course. Without his assistance, we could not have risked a night march even with the aid of Mr Moray's hand compass. Jangurra was not the least bit excited at our arrival. He acted just as if he fully expected us to show up when we did.

Jangurra had spent the night guarding the horses at the sinkhole; a number were wandering off to seek water in spite of their hobbles. One had disappeared in the night, presumed demented by thirst, and was never found. The rescue party arrived at the sinkhole at 10 pm. Three more horses perished. As for the burial party, all three white men were exhausted, their condition bluntly summed up by Charles: *'All of us were in a sorry state.'*

After a night's rest, they left at 9 am to find water as soon as possible. A1-5 and A1-7 found the ground party a half a mile from the sinkhole; supplies were dropped and Charles signalled to the pilots that both Anderson and Hitchcock had been buried. The horses, faced with the possibility of perishing, needed no urging as they were heading for water.

'We did not say much to each other but I think we all thought a lot as we made our weary return journey.'

'All of us were in a sorry state.'

Charles explained:

> As it was imperative to get the horses to water without delay no further information was given. The DH-9a has returned to WAVE HILL at 1010 hours ... The ground party proceeded to water, which was reached at 1330 hours, nine of the horses having completed a distance of 90 miles and all the horses having been without water for about 50 hours. The ground party had their first wash here since leaving WAVE HILL. It was observed that the water, owing to use and evaporation, was becoming rapidly depleted. As I considered it most desirable to return to WAVE HILL as soon as possible to give the Air Board full details, we again pushed on at 1610. The vicinity of the car was reached at 1900 hours. We could not find the car that night and camped. The day's trip totalled 32 miles.

They rested at the almost dry billabong for a few hours before making an effort to reach the Buick before nightfall. However, exhausted from the previous days' efforts, they managed only a few miles before camping. Janama and Jangurra led them to Alec and the Buick at 9 am. Douglas repaired the vehicle and they arrived at Wave Hill Station late in the afternoon, followed by the three stockmen and the surviving horses. After being warmly welcomed by McGuggan, Charles immediately signalled the Air Board, outlining the expedition's activities and the burials of Anderson and Hitchcock.

The stockmen and remaining horses returned to the station that evening, thus ending the air search and ground party objectives to find the *Kookaburra* and confirm the fate of its crew. Janama and some of the surviving horses had travelled 265 miles during the week. The efforts of the stockmen and their ability to track and guide the party through featureless desert ensured the success of the party's mission. Sadly, 11 of the original 26 horses had perished from thirst or lost their way. By fate and good fortune, the six members of the expedition, all from vastly diverse backgrounds, complemented each other by contributing their particular skills and experience to reach the *Kookaburra* and return without serious

'The ground party proceeded to water, which was reached at 1330 hours, nine of the horses having completed a distance of 90 miles and all the horses having been without water for about 50 hours.'

mishap. Charles, new not only to the desert but also to Australia, readily took advice from the competent bushman Alex Moray and his skilled trackers. Charles stressed that without Janama, the dash to the *Kookaburra* on 29 April and subsequent night march to the sink hole might have ended in disaster. He added that Eric Douglas proved to be a strong and worthy companion who gave effective support throughout the rescue attempt.

Before flying back to Victoria, the RAAF search detachment needed to service and repair the remaining DH-9As. Work began on the three aircraft at Wave Hill by draining radiators, maintaining the rigging and bracing wires and repairing the many holes in the machines' fabric. Charles ordered a 'general stand down' for all RAAF personnel; for the crews of A1-1 and A1-7 this was their first full day's rest since the search had begun 22 days previously. They were in good spirits; Douglas sent a telegram to his wife Bessie in Melbourne on 3 May: *'Having a rest after a hard trip into the desert ... very hot ... all ok ... having a great time here ... Eric 11.30 am.'*

The aircraft were ready for the long return flight to Laverton by 7 May. However, as Charles was taking off from Wave Hill in A1-20, with Douglas as co-pilot, the throttle jammed, the pistons misfired and the engine caught fire. Although the fire was quickly extinguished, Douglas considered the aircraft un-repairable and it became another write-off. Charles and Douglas in A1-5 and Gerrand and Campbell in A1-7 eventually took off for Tennant Creek on 8 May but not before cannibalising A1-20's propeller and tyres. Eaton instructed Ryan and Endean to stay another day at Wave Hill to salvage what they could from A1-20 and destroy it before travelling to Darwin by road and then by ship to Melbourne; a real 'Cook's Tour'.

On arriving in Tennant Creek, Charles found Max Allen and the aerofitters still trying to repair A1-28. When Charles tested A1-28 in the air he found it had undue vibration of the engine and a distinct internal knock. He had no alternative but to write-off yet another aircraft as he considered the risk of A1-28's engine ceasing in flight would pose a serious risk to the lives of the crew. A1-28's pilot and the aero-fitters travelled by mail truck to Alice Springs, by truck and train to South Australia and then on to Melbourne. Corporal Cottee, stationed in Alice Springs for over two weeks, was instructed to return to Victoria with the balance of the unused spares.

The flight home was marred by the usual problems that caused delays and illness. Douglas remarked on the resilience of their leader who, during a forced stopover and while suffering from acute dysentery, agreed to address the small community of Hawker on the rescue. They finally returned home to Laverton exactly one calendar month after the search began, on 12 May. The five DH-9As had flown 238½ hours on the search; Gerrand flying 89 nine hours, Eaton 58, Ryan 45 and Douglas 25.

Before leaving Wave Hill, Charles had received a cable from the Air Board congratulating the RAAF detachment:

> REFERENCE YOUR WIRES OF 2ND. MAY MINISTER VERY PLEASED WITH YOUR WORK STOP AIR BOARD SENDS (SIC) YOURSELF AND REMAINDER OF THE PARTY ON YOUR EFFORTS AND EXCELLENCE OF ALL REPORTS STOP BOARD PROPOSES YOU RETURN AS SOON AS POSSIBLE STOP WOULD LIKE YOUR VIEWS AND RECOMMENDATIONS ON THIS BEARING IN MIND SERVICEABILITY MACHINES AND PROPOSED ROUTE STOP AIR BOARD.

Minister very pleased with your work stop Air Board sends (sic) yourself and remainder of the party on your efforts and excellence of all reports.

The miracle of the RAAF's expedition was that none of the 11 personnel involved were killed or injured. All suffered some degree of dysentery and three also suffered from fever. The efforts of the RAAF personnel who participated in the search were recognised in Charles' official report:

> It must be stated that the entire personnel of my detachment performed their duties with utmost zeal, endeavour and willingness, which was at least equal to the highest traditions of the A.F.C. during the War. At times work on the machines proceeded throughout the night until early morning to enable the machines to be fit for flying. Remarkable energy, skill, and enthusiasm were displayed by all ranks to accomplish the mission of the

detachment successfully. Pilots displayed great skill on all occasions and always carried out their duties in the manner of greatly experienced pilots.

Under these circumstances, it is most difficult to mention particular names, but I wish to bring forward to the special notice of the Air Board the names of the following Officer and Airman for their consistent and splendid work throughout the entire trip, F/O Gerrand and Sgt. Douglas. On account of special conditions the nature of the work of the detachment and the fact that no tropical kit was issued, the uniforms worn by personnel were ruined and several articles of clothing had to be purchased privately. It is desired that a special allowance be made by the Air Board to cover this.

In 1975, in correspondence with the Australian Broadcasting Commission (ABC) Charles, then aged 80, stressed the contribution of all involved: *'I would appreciate if my part be played down, as the whole affair was a team effort.'*

Two heroes: Henry Smith 'Bobby' Hitchcock and Keith Vincent Anderson beside the Kookaburra, 1929.

13 Facts From Fiction, 1929

A hoof mark in the centre of a continent ... this was the target of the Thornycroft expedition. Somewhere in the wilderness were the horses' tracks of Lieutenant Eaton's party.[1]

The sensational story of the *Southern Cross*, the subsequent disappearance of the *Kookaburra*, the progress of the search and the horrendous deaths of Anderson and Hitchcock dominated Australia's media. Sales of one Sydney newspaper jumped 25 per cent above its previous record after publishing faked photographs displaying the stranded *Kookaburra*.

The incident generated the Coffee Royal Affair, where accusations were made against Australia's hero, Charles Kingsford Smith. Stories circulated that Kingsford Smith and a Sydney businessman, John Cantor, had colluded to stage a search as a publicity stunt to enable Kingsford Smith to fund his world circumnavigation flight. Cantor was alleged to have given Anderson sealed orders, presumably the location of the *Southern Cross,* before he left Sydney. The matter was exacerbated by the rumour that Kingsford Smith said after his forced landing, *'Well mates, we may be lost but at least we have Coffee Royal to drink'*.

The headlines were strident:

> The Sacrifice! Why Was it Necessary For Anderson to Have Crashed as He Did? Answers Must Be Found.

The media were loud in their criticism of the affair and aired rumours that the whole event was a farce—a publicity stunt that misfired. However, there were alternative viewpoints, with one article, titled *Tragic Folly,* stating that the hearsay about the affair was just media sensationalism. One historian later wrote: *'Journalism in Australia had sunk to its lowest ebb.'*[2] Prime Minister Stanley Bruce ordered a public investigation to establish what had happened and to learn lessons. The cost of the search had been more than £30,000, a large sum in a world depression, and three RAAF aircraft written off.

The Government and the RAAF had received poignant messages immediately after the *Kookaburra* had been found. As late as 30 April, the RAAF had received a telegram from Bobby Hitchcock's family stating that he was living with an Aboriginal group. Anderson's fiancée, 'Bon' Hillard, contacted the Minister of Defence expressing alarm that the aviators were presumed dead without confirmation by a qualified doctor. The town clerk of Blayney in NSW requested the return of a leather jacket loaned to Keith Anderson by a 'Mr Jackson'. Charles formally replied that the jacket was so badly soiled it was irrecoverable.

Anderson and Hitchcock had become national heroes. The Minister for Home Affairs, the Hon. Charles Abbott, chartered the *Canberra* to undertake a whirlwind air tour of the Northern Territory. Prime Minister Bruce announced the Government would finance an expedition to recover the bodies for reburial with national honours. Thornycroft Australia offered to provide one of their new A3 three-ton trucks, free of charge, for what was to become the 'Thornycroft Expedition'.

'Why Was it Necessary For Anderson to Have Crashed as He Did? Answers Must Be Found.'

'Journalism in Australia had sunk to its lowest ebb.'

The expedition planned to leave Wave Hill loaded with sufficient provisions and fuel to reach the *Kookaburra* and return. After exhuming the bodies, the party was to attempt to tow the stranded aircraft back to Alice Springs. Charles was expected to return to Central Australia in a RAAF aircraft to guide the land party to the *Kookaburra,* but that proposal came to nothing. The Thornycroft truck was transported to Alice Springs by train to join the expedition's appointed leader, Constable George Murray. The nine-man party included a reporter from Sydney's Guardian newspaper, William Berg, and four Aboriginal trackers who joined the party at Newcastle Waters: Bob Janagala, 'Tommy' Midjana Jampijinpa, 'Hughie' Jampijinpa and 'Jack' Jarramirnti Jangari.

The original route was altered in favour of a shorter route due west of Newcastle Waters. Constable Murray planned to drive his own Model T Ford behind the Thornycroft. The expedition took five days to travel the 510 miles to Newcastle Waters from Alice Springs. Leaving Newcastle Waters on 6 June, the party turned west into the desert on an unidentified route.

Berg wrote of the journey:

> We owed our success, perhaps our lives, to the fact that we had with us the greatest pathfinders in the world ... Perhaps in the days of their glory they would have been king, priest, hunter and warrior.
>
> The two vehicles found the going rough through thick scrub; much of the journey had to be in low gear, but the two vehicles stood the test admirably. On occasions, the scrub was so thick they had to double back on their own tracks with Berg, rather poetically, describing the country's vegetation:
>
> For a week we had pushed on through six-foot scrub of turpentine and turkey bush. All we could see was the eternal wall of green, relieved with the yellow turpentine blossoms, and beneath our wheels the red sand, brownish spinifex, and blue and white daisies.

For five days, the trackers scouted ahead seeking the Eaton Expedition's horse tracks. Berg stated that if they missed those hoof prints, the expedition would continue westward aimlessly. Then, on 11 June, those *'wizards of the desert'* found the trail. The hoof-prints were so faint it made the white members of the party *'go cold to think what might have happened if the blacks had not been with us'.*³ The discontented trackers, perhaps due to Constable's Murray's reputation following the infamous Coniston Massacre of 1928, attempted to return to Newcastle Waters. Constable Murray drew his revolver, which kept them quiet, but they remained quite unfriendly for some time.

On 13 June, the party finally reached the *Kookaburra*. Berg wrote of his impressions of the lonely grave and of the aircraft: *'… somehow, the beauty and grace of this man-made machine struck us poignantly as we saw her there, marooned in the pitiless waste of primeval nature.'* They found the graves a *'pathetic imitation of the neat mounds of a civilized burial'.* The two bodies were exhumed and placed in lead-lined coffins.

They found the graves a 'pathetic imitation of the neat mounds of a civilized burial'.

Thorneycroft Expedition with burial caskets on the lorry at the site of the Kookaburra, June 1929. (Courtesy of Mr Dick Smith)

Attempts to clear a runway came to nothing and, after a day at the site, the recovery party retraced its journey. They first drained 18 gallons of petrol from the *Kookaburra* as their own stocks were low. The intention to tow the *Kookaburra* behind the truck proved impractical. The trackers, who had not known the prime reason for the expedition, became very superstitious after the exhumations and slept between two fires and closer to Murray's camp than normal. Davis wrote that the trackers would, on their return home, no doubt tell their fellow tribesmen *'horrifying stories about white men disturbing graves'.*

By the time the Thornycroft Expedition returned to Alice Springs, it must have travelled well over 1000 miles. Apart from punctures, both the truck and the Ford stood up to the challenge. Following a sombre farewell function at Alice Springs, Anderson's body went by rail to Sydney and Hitchcock's to Perth; the expedition's members returned to their homes.

On 9 May 1929, Commonwealth Gazette 45 proclaimed that an official Air Inquiry Committee, under the chairmanship of Brigadier-General Lachlan Chisholm Wilson, would investigate and report into:

1. The disappearance of the *Southern Cross* that left Sydney on 31 March 1929.
2. Why that aircraft was not located until 12 April 1929.
3. The forced landing of the *Kookaburra* and the subsequent deaths of Keith Anderson and R S Hitchcock.
4. The loss of the RAAF aircraft DH 9a A1-1.
5. Determine what precautionary measures should be taken *'in the interests of pilots, passengers, and crew, and of the community generally.'*

The inquiry began in Sydney on 14 May and held sittings over the next month in Melbourne and Adelaide. The 74 witnesses included a roll-call of elite Australian aviation: Kingsford Smith, Charles Ulm, Les Holden, 'Bertie' Heath, Lester Brain, Norman Brearley and 'Jimmy' Woods. Charles Eaton represented the RAAF.

Sergeant Douglas noted:

> Lt. Charles Eaton was able to present in his evidence papers obtained from Lt. Anderson's body in April. Those papers cleared both Keith Anderson and Charles Kingsford Smith of allegations that the forced landing of the *Southern Cross* was pre-arranged and that Anderson 'was in on the deal' to be the person who was to find the *Southern Cross*. No evidence whatsoever was forthcoming to give any indication that there was any substance of fact to these rumours.

Evidence at the inquiry suggested that a failed applicant for the epic 1928 trans-Pacific flight of the *Southern Cross* might have fabricated malicious rumours for the media. Anderson's backer, John Cantor, declared that he and other concerned Sydney citizens had offered Anderson £500 to help find the *Southern Cross*. As for Kingsford Smith endorsing a promissory note, Cantor said, '*That is a malicious lie. I endorsed the Promissory Note purely as a matter of friendship.*' Charles had found this note with other personal papers neatly bundled together near Anderson's body. He had also cut out the hero's last known written words, the diary on the tail-plane, and presented it as part of his evidence.

In its report, the inquiry committee found there was poor coordination in the initial stages of the search for the *Southern Cross*. For instance, there was confusion by the would-be rescuers whether the *Southern Cross* had passed over Port George or the Drysdale missions. The report highlighted that the radio receiving set of the aircraft had not been converted to a transmitter. The technology was available but the radio operator of the aircraft had been unaware of it. The report said, 'If this knowledge had been in the possession of the wireless operator the position of the *Southern Cross* could have been broadcast on the day following the forced landing.'[4]

The committee concluded that Kingsford Smith should not have continued the flight after losing an aerial. The wireless operator was censured for failing to repair the aircraft's radio transmitter. In addition, the committee questioned the paucity of provisions and said the failure of the crew to use spare engine oil to light a fire was 'inexplicable'. Following exhaustive cross-examinations, the committee found there was no suggestion the disappearance of the *Southern Cross* had been pre-arranged. The committee found the single-engine *Kookaburra* was ill-equipped to undertake such a perilous flight over uninhabited and waterless desert. The decision of Anderson to short-cut over the Tanami Desert, flying with a faulty compass and failing to carry sufficient provisions, cost both his own and Hitchcock's lives.

'That is a malicious lie. I endorsed the Promissory Note purely as a matter of friendship.'

The report on the inquiry concluded:

> The committee considered that the compass was the primary cause of the tragedy but that the *Kookaburra* could have followed the overland telegraph line. In view of the experience of both these aviators in long-distance flights, the committee can only come to the conclusion that Lieutenant Anderson was so anxious to start on the search for his old comrades and friends and so anxious to carry every possible gallon of petrol, that he would not wait to have his compass properly tested and would not carry an extra pound of rations or tools.

Although Kingsford Smith was exonerated, the Coffee Royal Affair continued to haunt him for the rest of his life.

After investigating the loss of DH-9A A1-1, the committee concluded that at 5000 feet, and some 20 miles from Tennant Creek Telegraph Station, the aircraft's engine had over-heated. The pilot, Flight Lieutenant Eaton throttled the aircraft down to 2000 feet but flames appeared from the air intake and the engine seized. The pilot decided to land the machine *'in the best possible manner'* near the overland telegraph line.

The committee said:

> In the circumstances, no blame is to be attached to the personnel of the Air Force or to Flight-Lieutenant Eaton, who is commended for his skill in landing his machine without causing injury to himself or his mechanic.

The report concluded that the DH-9As used by the RAAF were of *'an obsolete pattern'* and totally unsuitable for Australian desert conditions. Captain Brain, in a letter to the Secretary of the Air Board, reiterated the committee's and Eaton's opinion regarding the unsuitability of the DH-9As:

> Knowing the old machines with which they are equipped, the class and amount of country over which they have flown, the severe flying conditions and the spirit displayed by them in their work, I should like to commend the Air Force party engaged on the search to the highest praise and to your special attention.

'No blame is to be attached to the personnel of the Air Force or to Flight-Lieutenant Eaton, who is commended for his skill in landing his machine without causing injury to himself or his mechanic.'

Based on Charles' recommendations, the inquiry proposed precautionary measures for the safety of pilots and passengers, particularly for flights over uninhabited deserts. Those measures included two-way radio sets in every aircraft, comprehensive maps, the demarcation of recognised air routes and the availability of reliable weather reports.

Bobby Hitchcock was laid to rest at Perth's Karrakatta cemetery in a simple and private ceremony on 3 July 1929. Because of his family's religious convictions, Hitchcock was deprived a State funeral. Davis wrote, '*Hitchcock was buried as he had lived for 37 years—quietly and unobtrusively.*' Keith Anderson was reburied with full State and military honours on 6 July in Mosman in Sydney. This was very different from the lonely burial in the desert 12 weeks previously. A Guard of Honour composed of six RAAF officers met Anderson's casket on its arrival in Sydney. Thousands of Sydney citizens filed past his coffin paying their respects and laying flowers. One bouquet read: '*He died in solitude—he has lain in State—may he Rest in Peace.*' Berg described the lying in State:

> The homage shown Anderson was wonderful. For a day, the dead airman lay in state in St Stephen's Church, Phillip Street, and crowds of all types of citizens filed passed in reverence. Keith Anderson was buried on the heights of Mosman, overlooking the harbour, with full military honours, while a squadron of planes circled overhead in the form of a cross. How different from that other grave, in the dust of the desert and the ashes of the spinifex! May he rest in peace.

'Hitchcock was buried as he had lived for 37 years—quietly and unobtrusively.'

Thousands of Sydney citizens filed past his coffin paying their respects and laying flowers.

An estimated 6000 mourners attended Anderson's funeral, including his distressed mother and fiancée Bon Hillard. By public subscription, a plaque was engraved and placed at his gravesite.

Kingsford Smith had been sorely grieved by his friend's death and deeply touched by Anderson's diary etched on the fabric of the *Kookaburra's* tail plane. Kingsford Smith spoke of his friend Anderson:

> To me personally, the last diary of Anderson's approaches in pathos and tragedy the last words of Captain Scott as he lay dying in his tent in the Antarctic.

'To me personally, the last diary of Anderson's approaches in pathos and tragedy the last words of Captain Scott as he lay dying in his tent in the Antarctic.'

*The remains of the Kookaburra
as found by Dick Smith,
49 years later in 1979
(Photo courtesy of Mr Dick Smith)*

14 Kookaburra Postscript

It was a chilling experience to stare down at that appalling waste ... which they had tried to cross in their tiny old-fashioned and patched-up mono-plane.

Dick Smith, 1980

For some 32 years the skeletal remnants of the *Kookaburra* were lost in the endless space of the Tanami. Various attempts were made to locate both the plane and a gold reef reported by Frank Nottle, a member of the Thornycroft party. Nottle had reputedly picked up a rock containing a high analysis of the mineral only 14 miles (22 kilometres) from the abandoned *Kookaburra*.

On 24 July 1961, surveyor Vern O'Brien was examining a pastoral access across the Tanami at 18° south latitude, east of the Wave Hill/Hooker Creek Road. He was in a hurry, towing a disabled Land Rover, and had less than five days to complete his task. On the third day of the survey, an estimated 87 miles from Wave Hill, O'Brien reported: *'When rounding a patch of dense turpentine noticed to the north the wheel of an upturned aircraft which was taken to be identified later as that of Anderson and Hitchcock of 1929.'*

O'Brien, navigating by hand compass only, had reached 132° east longitude. By mere chance, he had stumbled across the wreckage of the aircraft, now reduced by desert fires to a heap of twisted rods and rusty rims. He photographed what remained of the *Kookaburra* and removed the engine identification and instrument panel. Subsequent land and aerial searches to relocate the elusive aircraft were unsuccessful. O'Brien and John Haslett, a dedicated aviation historian, launched one such expedition. Haslett wanted to recover the wreckage and display it within a realistic desert setting as a memorial to the two gallant airmen who had given their lives in their attempt to save others.

This first official search party since the 1929 Thornycroft Expedition proved fruitless. Organised by the Northern Territory Museum and led by its director, Colin Jack Hinton in 1975, the search party also included O'Brien, Haslett and the ABC's David Poynter. The ten-day search by four-wheel drive transport and a helicopter found no evidence of the missing aircraft; even with the helicopter searching from the sky, the Tanami was determined to keep its secret. Hinton later concluded the party had missed its target by a mere 100 yards. The next year, the Administrator of the Northern Territory declared the yet unknown site of the Kookaburra as protected area under the Native and Historic Objects Ordinance and that no parts of the machine were to be removed.

A young and successful Sydney businessman, 'Dick' Smith, was not only passionate about aviation but what he termed: *'My obsession—for that is what it became—the finding of the* Kookaburra *... The fact is that I wanted to solve a mystery.'* Some 48 years after the event, Smith flew his Comanche over the same route Anderson had taken across the desert. From his sophisticated aircraft, Dick Smith voiced his opinion on Anderson's earlier flight: *'It was a chilling experience to stare down at that appalling waste ... which they had tried to cross in their tiny old-fashioned and patched-up mono-plane.'*

Returning by helicopter, Smith conducted an aerial survey. To understand the airmen's difficulties, he landed the helicopter; after only a few steps he was astounded to find he could only see a metre or two. Surrounded by dense turpentine scrub, he was momentarily lost. He realised the appalling conditions the two missing airmen and the Eaton Expedition had faced. Smith returned to Sydney and organised a fully-equipped search expedition.

By mid-1977 Smith had six land vehicles, a helicopter, a Piper aircraft and a road grader at his disposal. His 18-member party included the ABC's David Poynter and a qualified surveyor, Nigel Davis. Smith appreciated that accurate survey work and a systematic ground and air search was the key to success. Based on O'Brien's 1961 sighting and a map of the *Kookaburra's* locality by Eric Douglas, the expedition began its search at 18° south longitude and 132° east latitude; a position they named 'Anderson's Corner'. However, when the helicopter had an accident a few days into the search, Smith abandoned his quest. Before leaving, he laid a plaque at Anderson's Corner to commemorate the attempt of the 'Dick Smith Kookaburra Expedition'.

Not a man to concede defeat, Smith returned to Wave Hill in August the following year. He had learnt of the sinkhole that Charles and his party had used for a base camp in 1929. After some hours flying to the south-east, his wife 'Pip' spotted the sinkhole, which appeared as a great gaping hole; for the first time, Smith had a geographic feature that was an important part of the Eaton expedition. After plotting the probable track of the Thornycroft Expedition, which stated the *Kookaburra* was 23 miles south-east of the sinkhole, Smith resumed his search. In the afternoon of the second day, when his fuel was almost exhausted, he suddenly shouted, '*We found it. We found it.*' There it was, barely visible in turpentine scrub. The date was 31 August 1978, almost 50 years after Anderson's forced landing.

Smith immediately contacted the Government authorities in Darwin but they forbade him from removing the wreckage. He had hoped the *Kookaburra's* remains could be taken to Sydney and displayed in the Charles

In the afternoon of the second day, when his fuel was almost exhausted, he suddenly shouted, 'We found it. We found it.'

Kingsford Smith International Airport. Instead, the aircraft's remains are now displayed at the Central Australian Aviation Museum in Alice Springs. Both John Haslett and Dick Smith returned to the Tanami Desert on separate occasions; the Haslett party held a memorial ceremony and placed a plaque of remembrance at the site.

Biographical sketches

The individuals who played critical roles in the air and ground searches for both the *Southern Cross* and the *Kookaburra* need to be acknowledged.

Andrew 'Gerry' Gerrand, who joined the RAAF in 1927 as a cadet after serving in the Royal Australian Navy, was highly commended by Charles for his participation in the search for the *Kookaburra*. Later in 1929, Gerrand piloted a RAAF Wapiti on a survey flight in Central Australia for the South Australian Geographical Society. He also piloted the race organiser of The Great Air Race, Guy Moore (Vignette 15: Flying the Rails). Gerrand won the speed section in the South Australian Aerial Derby of 1930.

In early 1931, again with Charles, Gerrand flew in the successful search for the lost aircraft the *Golden Quest II* west of Alice Springs (Vignette 16: A Miracle, The Search for the *Golden Quest II*). Gerrand resigned his commission with the RAAF the following year, entered the commercial world of civil aviation and migrated to New Zealand. During WWII, he served first with the Royal New Zealand Air Force and later with the RAF's Transport Command. After the war, he became operations manager for the New Zealand National Airways Corporation and, in 1950, was appointed the De Havilland Company's production manager. Gerrand remained in New Zealand until his death in the 1960s.

Parunja Janama, who almost single-handedly guided the Eaton Expedition to the *Kookaburra*, was known by his descendants as a 'big ceremony man'. He became a well-known leader of the Gurindji in their fight for land rights at Wattie Creek, now reverted to its Gurindji name, Daguragu. He died at Kalkarindji in the mid-1970s.

Lester Brain AFC[1], born in 1903 and educated at Sydney Grammar School, joined the first flying course at Point Cook in January 1923 as one of the first five civilian pilots to be trained by the RAAF. After graduating, he joined Qantas and flew the airline's Queensland routes for several years. In April 1929 he joined Charles' search for the lost *Kookaburra*; he was flying to meet the RAAF expedition when he investigated the smoke from the bush fire reported by Leo Ryan and was the first to sight the lost *Kookaburra*.

As the company's senior pilot in 1934, Brain ferried the first Qantas DH-86, the *Canberra*, from England to Australia. On 10 December 1934, he flew DH-61 *Diana* on the first leg, Brisbane–Darwin, of the Brisbane–Singapore route. In 1937 he went to England to learn to operate flying boats and was involved in the introduction of the Empire Air Mail scheme using the Short Empire machines. When the service opened at Rose Bay in Sydney in 1938, Brain carried letters to the King, the British Prime Minister and the British Postmaster General on the flying boat *Camilla*. In March 1942, Brain was Qantas' operations manager at Broome when Japanese fighters attacked and devastated the port; he was decorated for his bravery. After WWII he became General Manager of Trans Australian Airlines and from March 1955 he was managing director of De Havilland Australia until he retired. Lester Brain died after a car accident at the age of 76 in 1980.

Sergeant Eric Douglas was born at Parkville, Victoria in 1902. He qualified as a mechanical engineer in 1920 and immediately joined the new Australian Army Flying Corps as an air mechanic, becoming its youngest member. When the corps evolved into the RAAF in 1921, Douglas automatically became an original RAAF member. Within seven years he became a flying instructor at Point Cook. In 1929 he proved a talented pilot-engineer when searching for the *Kookaburra* and accompanying Charles on the ground expedition that located the aircraft. Charles' official report stressed Douglas' positive contribution to the air search and the land expedition.

When Sir Douglas Mawson requested a second RAAF pilot for his Antarctic expedition, Charles recommended Eric Douglas. He was to prove an outstanding asset to Mawson's party, not only as a pilot but also for his engineering abilities. Douglas found the American explorer Lincoln Ellsworth and his pilot Hollick-Kenyon when they were lost in the Antarctic. Mawson named two geographic features after him, Douglas Peak and Douglas Bay. He was awarded the rare Polar Medal twice. After serving in WWII as a test pilot and station commander, Douglas retired from the RAAF as a Group Captain in 1948. He then served in the Royal Australian Navy as a senior civilian planner for the navy's new Air Arm. Eric Douglas died in 1970.

Sergeant Eric Douglas with Mawson's expedition. (Photo by Frank Hurley, courtesy of Ms Sally Douglas).

Scottish-born **Alex Moray**, also known as 'Alex' Moray-Lawrence, who organised the trackers from Wave Hill and was an integral part of the success of the expedition, was an important figure in the northern Australian cattle industry. He retired to Longreach in Queensland and reputedly died there in 1950.

Leslie 'Les' Holden, born in 1895 and educated in Sydney, enlisted in the AIF and served at Gallipoli and then in France until he transferred to the AFC in December 1916. After graduating as a pilot, he spent a short time with 57 Squadron RFC before his transfer to 2 Squadron AFC. In 1925, Holden was granted a commission with the Citizen Air Force (CAF) but resigned the following year. Engaged by the Sydney Citizens Relief Committee to search for Kingsford Smith's *Southern Cross,* Holden found the grounded aircraft on 12 April 1929. The Government refused to pay his expenses but he and his crew later received £500 from a special rescue fund. Holden moved to New Guinea in 1931 to start his own air service. He was killed in September 1932 in an aircraft crash at Byron Bay, NSW.

LJ 'Leo' Ryan was born in 1904 and graduated from Duntroon Military College in 1926. The following year he transferred to the RAAF to enter Point Cook's fifth FTS course. On completing his training he joined 1 Squadron, Laverton. In April 1929, with Corporal Douglas Endean as fitter, Ryan flew to Central Australia to join Eaton's flight searching for the missing *Kookaburra*.

Because Ryan had reported excessive levels of white lead in his engine oil, Charles refused permission to investigate the smoke seen west of Powell's Creek without an escort. Colin Owers, writing in 2001, remarked: *'This correct decision robbed the RAAF of the honour of finding the* Kookaburra.' Ryan also flew a back-up Wapiti aircraft as support for the Great Air Race in 1929 (Vignette 15: Flying the Rails, 1929). Only a few months later, aged only 25, he died instantly when his DH-60 Gipsy Moth crashed near Laverton. Charles, writing to an aviation historian in 1975, mentioned *'how the RAAF had lost a fine pilot and prospective leader'*.

Postscript

Timothy Coyle, who studied the navigation aspects of the RAAF's search 77 years after the event, emphasised the danger of remote operations and the need for leadership in such conditions. Perhaps, in the history of aviation, there were never more inappropriate aircraft requisitioned to carry out such a challenging and exhausting mission. While adequate for short-distance reconnaissance sorties during the latter part of WWI, the DH-9As were obsolete by 1929 and were quite unsuitable for the harsh environment of Central Australia. Only two of the original five aircraft that set out on the expedition returned to their home base; the other three are skeletons littering the desert. One RAAF comic suggested at the time that Eaton should be decorated for getting rid of such antiquated machines.

Coyle summarised the RAAF's 1929 search accomplishments:

> In extended and remote operations, such as the *Kookaburra* search pilots had to be constantly aware of their fuel state so as not to risk fuel starvation and a forced landing. In his tactical command and control over the air search assets, including the QANTAS DH-50, Eaton showed a keen regard for the operating conditions faced by the airmen and the limitations of the aircraft by deploying them in two groups. This episode demonstrated the RAAF's capacity to mount and sustain a complex search in isolated regions in support of a national effort that was initiated by the disappearance of the *Southern Cross*.

'This correct decision robbed the RAAF of the honour of finding the Kookaburra.'

'Bung ho! Me and Prudence'.
Charles en route from Sydney to Perth in
The Great Air Race of 1929
in a DH-60M Gipsy Moth (VH-UKC 28),
September 1929.
Pilot Charles (rear cockpit) with passenger Moyle.

15 Flying the Rails, 1929

A memorial occasion in the history of aviation in Australia took place in October 1929 when the so-called 'Great Air Race' between Sydney and Perth was arranged. According to present standards, the race was a simple and minor affair but in those days, with the types of light aircraft that were flying in Australia at that time, the race was quite an event.

Charles Eaton, 1953

Flying in those early days was innately suited to man's natural propensity to compete—to go faster and further than his fellows and break records. Six years after the Wright brothers' first flight in 1903, American Glenn Curtiss won the air speed trophy at the first International Air Meeting or 'Grande Semarine d'Aviation', held in France. In 1919, a United States transcontinental east–west reliability trial proved disastrous, costing nine pilots their lives. Despite the dangers, air racing and pageants became popular worldwide; Australia was no exception. Early aviators such as brothers Ross and Keith Smith, Roscoe Turner, Clyde Pangborne, Charles Scott and Tom Campbell-Black made their names famous in international air races. Aviatrices such as

Amelia Earhart, Thea Rasche and Louise Thaden competed with remarkable success.

Many pilots lost their lives attempting to attain glory. During the 'Dole Derby' from California to Hawai'i in 1927, ten pilots and their observers were lost, with only two of the competing aircraft actually reaching their destination. German aviatrix Thea Rasche, an acquaintance of the Eatons, said of her own participation: *'Flying is more thrilling than loving a man ... and much less dangerous.'*

When Western Australia commemorated its centenary of British settlement in 1929, a Captain Guy Moore of Perth proposed an air race from Sydney to Perth to mark the occasion. The race was to be on a pre-designated route covering 2389 miles, staged over six days in two categories—speed and handicap. All entries were to fly with their maximum weight capacity, which included a passenger or equivalent weight. The major prize was in the handicap section, with £1000, £300 and £100 to the first three places. The aircraft with the overall fastest time was to receive £300 and there were daily section prizes of £50 to pilots recording the fastest handicap time.

Titled 'The Western Australian East–West Air Contest', the race was generally referred to as 'The Great Air Race'. 'Bill' Baker, a historian of the race, wrote that Moore *'set about organising this, what in those days was a stupendous effort'.* Night flying was impossible as there were no navigation lights on outback country airstrips, so accommodation and sustenance for the competitors and their support aircraft were arranged together with fuel, oil and water. The RAAF supplied three Wapiti aircraft to escort the competitors and ensure their safety in case of forced landings. Two of the Wapitis' pilots, Flying Officer Gerry Gerrand and Flying Officer Leo Ryan, had accompanied Charles in the search for the *Kookaburra* earlier in the year.

Once nominations for the race were declared open, the de Havilland Company of Australia requested the RAAF to allow Charles to participate and fly, on their behalf, the first metal Gipsy Moth imported into Australia.

Moore 'set about organising this, what in those days was a stupendous effort'.

Charles writes of his participation:

> Seventeen competitors took part in the race, consisting of many famous old aviators, including Major Hereward de Havilland, a great English pilot and Messrs. P. Knapman, B. Heath, P. Manifold, C. N. McKay, C. D. Pratt, H. C. Miller, L. C. Lee Murray, E. W. Leggatt, E. E. Davies, H. R. Farmer, H. E. Baker, A. A. N. Pentland, W. H. Penny, F. K. Bardsley, A. T. Cunningham and myself. At that time, the first metal Moth had arrived in Australia and Major de Havilland asked me to fly it in the race.

Historian Charles Schaedel noted that Pentland, de Havilland, Davies (the 'Flying Lawyer' from Swan Hill), Eaton, Leggatt, Miller and Pratt were all '*old war dogs*'. The race committee received 24 entries but seven opted out by the starting date. Of the final 17, all carried a passenger except Major Hereward de Havilland, who flew solo for the entire route. He had commanded a squadron in WWI and was the brother of Geoffrey, the aeronautical designer. A renowned stunt flyer, his exhibitions of aerobatics, with Charles generally acting as the enemy, would thrill crowds at air pageants in eastern Australia in the mid-1930s.

Thirteen of the aircraft were manufactured by the de Havilland Company, including Charles' DH-60M, cementing his long association with that company's aircraft. He had first flown a DH-4 'Flying Coffin' against the Zeppelins and a DH-9A during his reconnaissance missions in WWI before training RAAF cadets in DH-9As at Point Cook. All aircraft in the search for the *Kookaburra* and the *Golden Quest II* in the Central Australian deserts were de Havilland aircraft. In the late 1920s, the DH Gipsy Moth appeared as a standard training aircraft for the RAF and, a few years later, the RAAF. Charles received his life-long sobriquet, 'Moth', at this time. Given the honour of flying the first metal Gipsy Moth in Australia, Charles 'Moth' Eaton wore the name bestowed on him with pride for the rest of his life.

The race was to start at Sydney's Mascot Airport on 28 September. Baker described the atmosphere at Mascot as *'a hive of activity with aircraft flying in from interstate, machines being checked and tuned, compasses being adjusted, aircraft being fuelled and oiled, maps and emergency rations being checked and stowed away, etc.'.* Unfortunately, the race was delayed for two days due to bad weather, giving the pilots and their mechanics time to further tune their aircraft to *'squeeze a few extra miles per hour'.*

At 7.30 am Monday 30 September, the 17 aircraft took off from Mascot at intervals of a few minutes. The last entry to the starter's flag was Bert Heath in his fast DH-50, but his engine refused to fire; after a strenuous hour's effort by engineers, he finally took off just after 9 am. Heath, from West Australia, was the outright race favourite as his aircraft enjoyed a speed advantage over all other entrants.

Flying in his DH-60M, dubbed *Prudence*, Charles wrote, *'We all started off from Sydney and flew to Perth by laid down stages, via Adelaide, Ceduna, Forrest, and Kalgoorlie.'* Melbourne's *Age* reported that many of the aircraft were decorated with mascots, with *'the feminine touch being conspicuous'.*

They reached the first staging point, Junee in New South Wales, by mid-morning. Horrie Miller, in G-AUHT, was the first to land, but the fastest time on handicap was Charlie Pratt, in VH-UKX. After lunch, the entrants left for Melbourne in good weather but the going was tough over the Great Dividing Range as all aircraft were flying at low altitude to maximise speed. Unfortunately, Leggatt's Curtiss Meteor lost time with fuel problems. Pentland lost 20 minutes when he flew off course, but finding Bendigo put him back on track. Although Miller was the first to land at Melbourne's Essendon Airport, Pratt took out the first stage's handicap prize. Thousands of spectators watched the entrants arrive in perfect weather, making Essendon Airport *'an ant's nest'* according to the press. Australia had witnessed such an aviation spectacle only once before, when huge crowds had welcomed Kingsford Smith after he had crossed the Pacific the previous year. Baker[1] stated the race's sponsors were elated as Western Australia was getting maximum publicity from the nation's media.

Day two began in heavy weather dominated by high winds. Despite the bad weather, about 7000 people watched the planes depart Melbourne.

The atmosphere at Mascot was 'a hive of activity with aircraft flying in from interstate, machines being checked and tuned, compasses being adjusted, aircraft being fuelled and oiled, maps and emergency rations being checked and stowed away, etc.'.

Many of the aircraft were decorated with mascots, with 'the feminine touch being conspicuous'.

As the aircraft approached Nhill in western Victoria, three entrants landed on greener pastures: Pentland and Leggatt in paddocks and Charles on a golf course. Charles recalled that the few golfers on the fairways emptied their cars' fuel tanks, no doubt with good humour. He lost only 11 minutes on this leg so the transfer of fuel from the cars to *Prudence* must have been carried out in great haste.

Wet weather delayed the start of the leg between Nhill and Adelaide until mid-afternoon. Conditions over the Mallee district of northern Victoria were reputed to be very dusty but Baker records that rainstorms just out of Adelaide *'washed the thick dust from machines and pilots' faces, alike'*. All aircraft reached Adelaide's Parafield airfield later that afternoon; Harry Baker, in his Klemm–L25, was delayed after a forced landing *en route* and disqualified from the main race as he failed to arrive within the scheduled time. However, he was allowed to continue and compete for the daily leg prizes. Charlie Pratt again won the fastest handicap, with Miller and de Havilland running neck and neck for the speed prize. The third day saw the competitors fly over Spencer's Gulf toward the small country town of Kimba. All got off to a good start apart from de Havilland, who lost almost 17 minutes due to engine trouble.

Baker summed up the character of the race when he described the pilots' flying tactics:

> Right throughout the race, four words common in aviation parlance were never applied. These were 'cruise power' and 'safety altitude'! From the drop of the starter's flag at Mascot to the final dash across the finishing line at Perth Oval, all the throttles were kept hard forward and the highest altitude flown above terrain was approximately 100 feet, hedge and fence-hopping was the order and crossing the Spencer's Gulf most pilots kept their eye on the shadow on the water to avoid dipping their wheels in!!

More mishaps occurred. Leggatt had to retire because of fuel blockages in his Curtiss Meteor. Penny's Avro Avian landed with engine trouble and McKay wasted valuable time when he got lost. The unfortunate

Rainstorms just out of Adelaide 'washed the thick dust from machines and pilots' faces, alike'.

Right throughout the race, four words common in aviation parlance were never applied.

'mosquito', Baker's Klemm–L25, made a forced landing and missed the chance of gaining at least a stage prize. Although disqualified and despite numerous emergency landings, the courageous Harry Baker continued the event in his small, underpowered aircraft. By the time the planes arrived in Ceduna on the last leg of the third day, Miller's DH-9 was in the lead in both the speed and handicap sections. De Havilland, Pratt, Heath, Lee Murray, Cunningham, and Farmer were also performing well. On the fourth day, the competitors took off across hundreds of miles of featureless stony country for the diminutive railway settlement of Cook. The transcontinental railway line was 'the iron compass', but many pilots experienced navigation problems by attempting short cuts. Perhaps it was a miracle that all aircraft eventually landed safely at Cook, most with little fuel. Astute pilots 'Flew the Rails'.

After lunch, the competitors flew the next leg to Forrest in Western Australia, the second shortest leg of the race at only 140 miles. Some pilots lost their way. Lee Murray, in his Gipsy Moth, had engine trouble and had to make an emergency landing. In his fast DH-50, Heath allegedly played 'cat and mouse' games with other entrants. Unfortunately for Jerry Pentland, who had an excellent chance to win that stage's speed prize, his passenger, Errol Coote, was sightseeing by putting his head out of the cockpit. Jerry noted something was amiss and yelled to his passenger to *pull his bloody head in*. When the leg's times were calculated he yelled even louder that 'head drag' cost him £50.

Heath broke his propeller on landing at Forrest but managed to borrow another one from the Civil Aviation Authority's DH-50, which was monitoring the race. The Forrest staging airstrip had a larger hanger and comfortable sleeping quarters. After maintenance and repairs, the 14 remaining planes continued to Rawlinna. De Havilland and Miller, who were leading the speed and handicap divisions respectively, now headed the race.

Jerry yelled to his passenger to 'pull his bloody head in'. When the leg's times were calculated he yelled even louder that 'head drag' cost him £50'.

Harry Baker's diary reported that the 225-mile Forrest to Rawlinna leg was the hottest and dustiest stage of the six-day race. Heath got off to a slow start due to the propeller change; perhaps 'bush justice' prevailed given his behaviour the previous day when playing cat and mouse with other competitors. The Flying Lawyer, Charles' life-long friend Edgar Davies, force landed soon after leaving Forrest with engine trouble. Miller's engine overheated because of low flying.

After their scheduled midday stop at Rawlinna the race continued in extreme heat and a strong, dusty north wind to Kalgoorlie, some 225 miles west. Baker's brave Klemm had another unscheduled landing but still kept going. Just before 4 pm, de Havilland landed first, now ahead of Miller in the speed section of the race, with Pratt marginally ahead of Miller in the handicap category. By this time, most of the entrants were feeling the strain, particularly after a day of flying in open cockpits in oppressive heat.

Baker summarised the second last day of the race:

> All the crews were feeling the oppression of the heat and the tension and fatigue of the race; with the final day's racing an emotional aftermath to look forward to the following day, all competitors and escort crews were asleep immediately after the dinner. Only the Official Handicappers burned the midnight oil calculating and re-checking each competitor's actual and corrected times from Sydney to this point.

Early on 5 October, large crowds watched the fatigued aviators take off from the gold-mining town of Kalgoorlie for the final two legs to Perth. The public was excited as the end of the race was close; the media had splashed the progress of the competitors across the nation's front pages. The Melbourne *Age* wrote of the '*Alarming Weather*' and that the race had become a test of the tired airmen's endurance as well as the technical capabilities of their aircraft. Cunningham had an accident taking off, breaking the nose of his passenger, Lennon. The penultimate leg was to the wheat town of Tammin, 250 miles away. Farmer had bad luck in his Sopwith when his engine's cylinders gave trouble and he landed twice, arriving hours after front-runner, Miller.

'All the crews were feeling the oppression of the heat and the tension and fatigue of the race.'

Pratt was a front-runner in the handicap category, so tried to increase speed to keep ahead by flying as low as possible by what the press termed *'just skimming the tree tops'*. However, a sudden gust of wind drove his Moth into a dead tree near the town of Bandee. Although Charles wrote that Pratt *'hit practically the only tree on the Nullarbor Plains and crashed'*, this was perhaps a case of verbal laxity; while Pratt had left that famously treeless plain behind, he had certainly crashed into the only tree in a large wheat field. The impact was heavy, with the aircraft's engine ploughing two feet into the ground. Both Pratt and his passenger, Guthrie, were seriously injured but, fortunately, a farmer named Gigney arrived within 10 minutes and raised the alarm. A doctor arrived about an hour later and the two aviators were taken to Kellerberrin hospital, Pratt in shock and blue with bruises from head to toe and Guthrie in a critical condition with internal injuries. A well-known surgeon, Dr FA Hadley, flew to Kellerberrin from Perth to operate on the two survivors. Due to the medical attention and specialist surgery relatively soon after their crash, both made a gradual but full recovery.

The final leg of the race, Tammin to Perth, was the shortest leg of the race at only 110 miles. The aircraft took off in strong headwinds, with all pilots later complaining of the weather conditions and the very rough ride over the Darling Ranges:

> All pilots spoke of the atrocious weather encountered after leaving Tammin. The wind gusts accompanied by heavy rain, made the last section of the race perfectly abominable. All showed signs of the great stress they had been under. Their faces were badly cut with the wind, and their normal skin showed only under their goggles, giving them a quaint appearance. Some roundly cursed the weather, while others took it philosophically.[2]

Major de Havilland later described the final section as *'rotten'*; the wind blew his goggles off and rain got into his eyes, forcing him off course and to lose time getting back on track. Even the RAAF Wapitis monitoring

Charles refuelling 'Prudence' during the Great Race with Major Hereward de Havilland (far left) and navigator Moyle.

the race took a beating. Flying Officer Gerrand, with the race's organiser Captain Moore as passenger, became disorientated in cloud and made an emergency landing on a field near Toodyay. The experienced Penny said after the race that it was *'the thrill of his life going over the rugged hills,'* though his engine occasionally stuttered and he thought his end had come. Penny added, *'I am going to have a month's holiday now to recover, and then I will fly back.'* Charles was reported in *The West Australian* to have force-landed in a vegetable garden in Chidlow but quickly taken off and resumed his flight to Perth. Journalist Michael Zekulich reported *'He* [Eaton] *was forced to land in*

'I am going to have a month's holiday now to recover, and then I will fly back.'

a cabbage patch at a Chidlow market garden. Undaunted, he borrowed some fuel and took off for his destination, the airport at Maylands.[3]

The official finishing line was at the Perth Oval, where each competitor had to fly over a marked line at 100 feet. They then landed at Maylands Airport which, for the occasion, the Civil Aviation Authority had stipulated no licence was necessary. It was a close, exciting end to the transcontinental race. Bert Heath took line honours, crossing the line at 3 pm, followed within minutes by Lee Murray, Bardsley, Miller, Cunningham and de Havilland. The other entrants, including Charles, filtered in over the next half hour.

De Havilland took out the overall fastest time and collected £300. The handicapping procedures proved so complicated that it was 24 hours before the major prize of £1000 was awarded to Miller (18 hours and 23 minutes). The factors that were considered included weather conditions, model of each aircraft and starting times of each stage. Over 2000 sets of calculations were made to verify Miller's victory.

Charles, who came in at sixth place (22 hours and 20 minutes), was rather economical with his own description of the race:

> The fact that 14 out of the 17 planes entered for the race reached their destination safely after 6 days flying was according to the press of the day, a tribute to the ability of the aviators. The race, a handicap race, was won by H.C. Miller with Major de Havilland making the fastest time. Unfortunately, owing to a shortage of petrol and a forced landing, I lost a considerable amount of time and came in sixth.

The public's heroes were the diminutive Klemm and its pilot, Harry Baker. Although disqualified earlier in the race after making forced landings and experiencing engine trouble, Baker persevered and made it to the finishing line. The police had to restrain the crowd at Maylands from engulfing Baker and his mini aircraft. When interviewed by the press after landing, he remarked, *'They got sarcastic about my little "mosquito", but it got here after all.'* Pentland appealed against de Havilland's fastest time victory as he had

Charles at the end of the 'Great Air Race'

'They got sarcastic about my little "mosquito", but it got here after all.'

changed a propeller at Ceduna; the protest was dismissed. Immediately after the race, Peter Manifold's DH-60G was badly damaged when it was blown by high winds into Charles' metal Gipsy Moth.

Pratt, who was a front-runner up to the second last leg, had had a great chance for the handicap prize before crashing on the last morning of the race. Unlike the catastrophic Dole Derby two years earlier, it was a miracle no one was killed considering the number of engine failures and forced landings, the shocking weather on some of the stages and the 'hell for leather' attitude of the pilots as they pushed their aircraft to the limit. Bill Baker ended his description of the race, aptly summarising it: *'So ended what was, and is still regarded as being the greatest National Air Race in Australia's history.'*

Five years after Australia's Great Air Race, Eaton was to officiate as a race marshal in what was perhaps the most significant international air race ever held—the London to Melbourne Centenary Air Race.

'So ended what was, and is still regarded as being the greatest National Air Race in Australia's history.'

Transporting supplies for the Second Lasseter Expedition and the RAAF search party, Central Australia, January 1931.

Map showing the search for the Golden Quest II

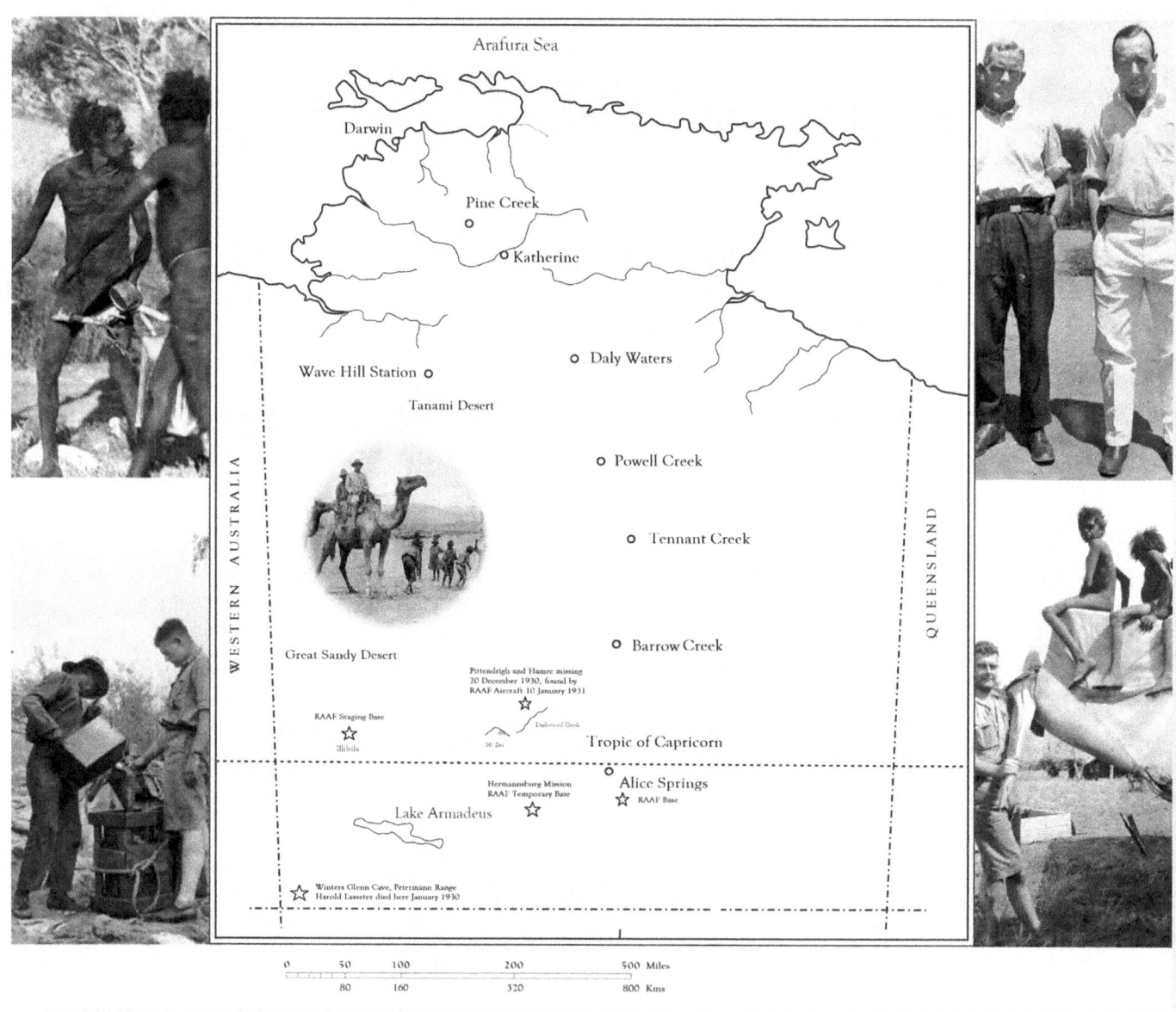

16 'A Miracle'—Finding Lasseter's Golden Quest II, 1931

Missing Fliers Live 21 Days on Water, Grass, and Tadpoles.[1]

A better man than Eaton could not have been commissioned for the search. Cool-headed, and an expert organiser, he demonstrated in no uncertain manner that the Air Board's choice was the best.[2]

Harold 'Possum' Lasseter entered Australian folklore by claiming the discovery of a fabulous gold reef near the Petermann Ranges in the far west of Central Australia during a fossicking expedition prior to World War I. An enterprising bushman, Lasseter claimed the reef was *'greenish, milky quartz four to twelve feet wide, extending above the surface for over ten miles'* and that analysis showed more than three ounces of gold per ton. The fable of 'Lasseter's Lost Reef' is as analogous for Australians as the story of King Solomon's Mines is to the world.

After the Great War Lasseter worked as a bushman, but his passion to rediscover his reef remained unquenched. To further his dream, he approached the Australian Workers Union in Sydney to finance a new expedition to Central Australia. Sufficient finance was raised to incorporate the Centralian Gold Exploration Company, which was to fund 'The Second Lasseter Expedition'. In 1930 the company purchased a Thornycroft truck and a DH-60M Gipsy Moth aeroplane. The expedition was based at Ilbilba, an Aboriginal camping ground consisting of a dozen or so grass huts or *miamia*, 350 miles west of Alice Springs. A primitive landing ground was cleared from the desert scrub.

The expedition's 11-member party soon met with disaster. The Thornycroft could not climb the 40–50 foot sand dunes and the only wireless set was inoperable. There was dissension within the party and it became debatable as to who was the real leader—Fred Blakely, an investor in the expedition who was nicknamed 'The Bicycle Bushman', or Lasseter himself. Thereafter, there were conflicting and confusing reports on the movements and behaviour of the expedition.

What is certain, is that in October 1930 the company's aircraft, *Golden Quest II*, set in train the first Lasseter search when it landed in the desert near Ayers Rock after running out of fuel. The RAAF ordered Charles to search for the plane and its pilot, Eric Coote, with three DH-60G Gipsy Moths but instructions from the Defence Department halted their departure for unexplained reasons. Hearing of the procrastination, Charles Kingsford Smith offered his services to support the RAAF's aircraft. His help was not required and Charles was again ordered to proceed. He was accompanied by Flying Officer Gerrand and Flying Officer Dalton. However, by the time the three aircraft arrived in Alice Springs, Coote had been found alive and the *Golden Quest* intact.

The expedition was a mixed bag with such little bush experience that apparently no one, apart from Lasseter, could even 'cook a damper'. Coupled with the failure of the Thornycroft, the expedition was abandoned. Blakely and the other members of the 'inglorious expedition' returned to Alice Springs in late 1930. Lasseter was left on his own to find his 'mother lode'. He teamed up with a young German dingo-trapper, Paul Johns, but they soon argued. During the ensuing confrontation, Johns pulled a revolver but was quickly disarmed by Lasseter. Lasseter continued alone into the wild desert country but returned to Johns' camp two days later and patched up their altercation. Lasseter told Johns that he had re-discovered his reef and produced bags of rock specimens—but refused to open them. He asked Johns to return to Alice Springs with letters to the Government Resident. Johns gave Lasseter two camels before departing for Alice Springs, where he handed Lasseter's letters to Resident Carrington. Carrington was surprised to read, in an extraordinary letter, that Lasseter demanded Johns' arrest for 'violent assault'. Conceivably he was not investigated as there were no witnesses to verify the allegations. Johns was the last white man to see Lasseter alive.[3]

In Sydney, the company became concerned about Lasseter's whereabouts and ordered an air search. On 20 December 1930, the *Golden Quest II* flew from Alice Springs to Ilbilba to deliver instructions to its employee, Phillip Taylor. Captain Leslie Pittendrigh, formerly of the RFC, was accompanied by geologist SJ Hamre. As recounted in Pittendrigh's diary, after flying for four hours he could not find Ilbilba so decided to return to Alice Springs. The aircraft was blown off course by heavy winds and, after running out of fuel, Pittendrigh was forced to land in one of the most desolate parts of Australia. The country was timbered with light mulga scrub and devoid of any permanent water. At that time of year, temperatures often reached 110° F and sometimes climbed to 120° F (49° C). They found it impossible to identify their exact position but, aided by the plane's compass, started to walk towards Mount Zeil and the Dashwood Soak, hoping to find water. Their provisions were five tins of Rex pies, two cans of sheep's tongues, sausages, malted milk tablets, two packets of biscuits and four water bags. They trekked about 10 miles before camping.[4]

The next morning they walked south-east in temperatures of 120° F, only to find a waterless river. They had only one remaining water bag, which Hamre suggested they drink before it evaporated. The two men were in a perilous situation, knowing they would perish in another 24 hours without water. Suddenly Hamre *'staggered to the centre of a clearing with his hands in front of him'*.

A few drops of rain fell, and then the heavens burst! Both men stripped naked and collected as much rain as their containers could hold. Pittendrigh wrote, '*This is nothing short of a miracle.*' Revived, they pushed on until sunset, when they reached Dashwood Creek and a water pool. They continued at 3 am next morning and walked until 11 am, when it was too hot to continue. It rained again that evening, but they found no standing water. Opting to return to Dashwood Creek, they were delighted to find two substantial water pools and decided to camp until help arrived; they enjoyed a Christmas dinner of two milk tablets each. Charles later estimated the two had managed to walk at least 30 miles, a brave effort considering the heat, rough conditions and Hamre's age.

The lost men did not know exactly where they were and their feet were so bad that further walking was impossible. They built a rough shed, nicknamed 'Hamreville', from dead mulga saplings. Some nights were so hot they slept under the stars, but they froze on other nights. Both suffered from bites from the hordes of flies and ants. They saw only a few dingoes, birds and fresh camel tracks. With such low rations, they foraged for natural foods including a wild mint weed. Because of the 'miracle' rains, desert frogs were breeding so they supplemented their diet with hatched tadpoles. On New Year's Day they discovered they had more sausages than they had thought so celebrated the first day of the year by eating six for dinner. Next day the remaining sausages smelled, so they devoured them all. The two then lived from day to day hoping a search party was looking for them. They were not to know that trackers and two of Australia's newest aircraft were doing just that.

When the message that the *Golden Quest II* was overdue was relayed from Alice Springs to the expedition's directors in Sydney, they lost no time informing Canberra. The Minister of Defence, sensitive to public criticism after the slow response to the *Southern Cross* affair, acted immediately. Eric Coote wrote in his book *Hell's Kitchen*: '*As a result, the hero of the Anderson–Hitchcock search Flight Lieutenant Charles Eaton, accompanied by another competent flyer, 'Gerry' Gerrand, left Point Cook for Alice Springs at dawn on*

Suddenly Hamre 'staggered to the centre of a clearing with his hands in front of him'.

Both men stripped naked and collected as much rain as their containers could hold. Pittendrigh wrote, 'This is nothing short of a miracle.'

New Year's Day, 1931.' The two Gipsy Moths, A7-34 and A7-37, reached Maree at nightfall after an 11-hour flight and battle with 50 mph head winds.

After the planes were serviced and extra fuel tanks fitted the next morning, they flew to Alice Springs, arriving at noon. Initial investigations found that 'Archie' Giles, owner of a station near Mount Giles, had reported sighting an aircraft flying due west at 10 am on 20 December. Desert tribesmen to the west of Ilbilba had seen a plane flying in a north-eastern direction. Early the following morning, 3 January, the two RAAF pilots flew to Hermannsburg, arriving at 4.30. Charles learned from 'Rolf', an Aboriginal bushman, that he had seen *'when the sun was immediately overhead'*, a black aeroplane flying towards Mount Peculiar and Haasts Bluff.

Charles called on German missionary, Friedrich Wilhelm Albrecht, to enlist Aboriginal trackers for land support. With his previous experience of Aboriginal help in 1929, Charles was keen to use their immeasurable bush craft. Two Aboriginal men from Hermannsburg Mission were employed and sent by camel to contact desert tribes for information that may lead to the *Golden Quest II*. They were armed with a series of signals to let the pilots know if the aircraft had been found. Gerrand and Charles found the desert people cooperative despite few having ever seen white men or aeroplanes, which they called *Walawurru,* the 'Giant Eaglehawk', in the Pintupi language.[5]

Charles considered it was important to immediately fly to Ilbilba to interview Phillip Taylor. They arrived mid-morning, but Taylor could add nothing to solve the whereabouts of the *Golden Quest II* except to confirm the authenticity of the tribesmen's sightings of the plane on 20 December. Little did Charles know at the time, but his planes had been spotted by Pittendrigh as they flew to Ilbilba.

Charles described his impressions of Ilbilba and its 'aerodrome':

> Ilbilba is probably one of the most out of the way and outback places in the continent. A small tribe of about 30–50 Aborigines live in the nearby Ehrenberg Range which is surrounded by desert country for

'As a result, the hero of the Anderson–Hitchcock search Flight Lieutenant Charles Eaton, accompanied by another competent flyer, 'Gerry' Gerrand, left Point Cook for Alice Springs at dawn on New Year's Day, 1931.'

Charles learned from 'Rolf', an Aboriginal bushman, that he had seen 'when the sun was immediately overhead', a black aeroplane flying towards Mount Peculiar and Haasts Bluff.

A small tribe of about 30–50 Aborigines ... had never seen a white man before and certainly not an aeroplane.

miles. The majority had never seen a white man before and certainly not an aeroplane. Of course, no proper landing ground existed at Ilbilba and we landed on a small portion of flat ground covered in fairly long grass.

Charles decided it would be more practical to base the search from Hermannsburg, which had a wireless set and fuel supplies. Next morning, he and Gerrand searched the country around the Giles, Hay and Chappel mountains and north of the MacDonnell Ranges but failed to find any trace of the missing pair. After refuelling they flew around Mt Sonder and Mt Zeil.

The search continued the following day. Again, Pittendrigh and Hamre saw the planes but remained unseen. This prompted Pittendrigh to create a large 'T' from ash to attract attention and to place a flag on a small hill a mile from 'Hamreville', an excursion that totally exhausted the already weakened pilot.

The nation's media reported the difficulties the RAAF faced:

> Great difficulties have to be surmounted by the relief party. Uninhabited country containing red sand ridges, spare vegetation, and practically no natural water, affords few land marks, and except for the aerodromes at Hermannsburg and Ilbilba there are practically no emergency landing grounds. These factors also intensify the danger facing the missing men,

Tribal support watering RAAF Moths at Ilbilba, January 1931.

and if they are still alive somewhere in the desert after 16 days, they must be in a terrible plight.[6]

Charles and Gerrand return to Ilbilba on 6 January to ask Taylor if the Aboriginals had found either the *Golden Quest II* or had any further helpful information. Unfortunately, Gerrand's plane hit a tree stump and lost its starboard lower wing. Charles returned to Hermannsburg alone to wire the Air Board for spare parts and was advised two more Gipsy Moths would be sent to support him, piloted by Flying Officer 'Bob' Dalton and Flying Officer Andrew Evans. The spare wing was sent by overland transport from Victoria.

Charles broke his own rules and continued to search for the *Golden Quest II* by himself until Dalton and Evans arrived on 9 January. The next morning, they began searching at daybreak. All three Gipsy Moths flew in parallel formation and in sight of each other. When they landed at Ilbilba at 10 am, Dalton reported seeing a white 'T' ground marker near Dashwood Creek, 140 miles north-west of Alice Springs. Dalton thought it may have been a signal from one of the Aboriginal scouts but, after some discussion, they decided it was an aviation signal for landing directions. The three Gipsy Moths took off to investigate the sign and, on arrival, dropped a message, '*If you are Captain Pittendrigh lie flat on the ground.*' Pittendrigh did this immediately but was so

The three Gipsy Moths took off to investigate the sign and, on arrival, dropped a message, 'If you are Captain Pittendrigh lie flat on the ground.'

F/O Gerrand and scout watering camels, January 1931.

weak he could hardly get to his feet again. The relieved airmen parachuted water and food with instructions they should not move until motor transport arrived. Pittendrigh wrote in his diary:

> Saturday Jan. 10. Planes at last! They passed right over us, and went towards Ilbilba again. We enlarged the 'T'. Heat and flies awful. At 3 pm, the planes came back and saw us, and dropped a message ... Light fires to guide cars to you tonight. Eaton R.A.A.F.

A month after getting lost, the two men had been down to their last two malted milk tablets when the RAAF planes 'rained' biscuits, roast beef and cigarettes! They did not sleep much that night as they were so relieved and excited. The next morning they heard shrieks and yells as five delighted Aboriginal men appeared—there was '*much hand-shaking and thousands of questions*'. They told the stranded men that Charles had informed them the previous afternoon where they were. Meanwhile, Archie Giles was travelling 'post haste' with fresh meat for the lost pair.

Although the missing pilot and his passenger had been found, the *Golden Quest II* was still missing. It was finally spotted on 16 January by Dalton, Evans and Gerrand in his newly repaired aircraft. Now that the search was over, the Air Board instructed Eaton to inspect a possible aerodrome site seven miles south of Alice Springs[7] before returning to Point Cook.

Capt. Pittendrigh, his fiancée Alice Dunn and Charles Eaton at Spencer Street Station, Melbourne.

The next morning they heard shrieks and yells as five delighted Aboriginal men appeared—there was 'much hand-shaking and thousands of questions'.

'Hamreville Airport'. The bough shelter on the right served as 'terminal' and the ash 'T' the landing marker with a 'windsock' nearby. Dashwood Creek, January, 1931.

Golden Quest II *as found by the RAAF, January 1931.*

Before leaving Alice Springs, Charles offered to search for the still missing prospector, Possum Lasseter. Puzzled and disappointed that the Air Board did not order him to do so, Charles approached 'Bob' Buck of Middleton Ponds cattle station to look for Lasseter. Buck was one of the last colourful white cameleers of the Centre and followed in the footsteps of the explorer Ernest Giles as an outstanding bushman. Charles had such high regard for him that whenever visiting Alice Springs he made sure to always call on him.

Buck, accompanied by his Aboriginal stockmen, led his expedition to Lake Christopher and Giles Peak on the Western Australian border in what was described as '*a mammoth tracking feat*'. His party had no trouble following Lasseter's tracks although they were three months old. He eventually found the decomposing body of '*that dogged little man*' in a cave at Winters Glen, some 30 miles from Hull Creek. Buck calculated he must have died in the last days of January.

It was later learnt that after Johns departed for Alice Springs, Lasseter continued to Lake Christopher, where he planned to join Johannsen, a miner from Boulder in West Australia. Unfortunately, Johannsen and his companion were speared by desert tribesmen *en route* to their rendezvous, with their bodies subsequently found and recovered by mounted police.

Lasseter's two camels bolted and his scanty supply of food was soon eaten. He managed to find a cave and water at Hull Creek in the Petermann Ranges. His diary and letters to his wife, later found in the cave, revealed he was suffering from dysentery and sandy blight (conjunctivitis) and that *'flies and ants were gradually eating my face away'*. A band of Eumos tribal people cared for him for some time, after which an old man and his wife remained with him near the cave. He died believing he had found his reef.

The syndicate mounted yet another expedition for the lost reef, this time with Bob Buck as leader. They left Alice Springs in September 1931 and travelled via Ayers Rock to 'Lasseter Country' but dissension again broke out. This, coupled with a food shortage, resulted in the expedition breaking into two groups. Before the two parties returned to Alice Springs independently, they came across yet another expedition looking for the reef.

Over the years, even as late as 1951, fossickers still searched unsuccessfully for 'Lasseter's Reef' and rumours abounded that Lasseter himself was still alive and living in America. However, in December 1957 his skeleton was found. The brave, determined man was finally laid to rest in the Alice Springs Memorial Cemetery in June 1958.

Pioneer commercial aviators Keone Dirk Parmentier (left) and Jan Moll (right) of the Netherlands who won second place in the London to Melbourne Centenary Race, 1934. They flew a DC 2 aircraft that carried three paying passengers.

His diary and letters to his wife, later found in the cave, revealed he was suffering from dysentery and sandy blight and that 'flies and ants were gradually eating my face away'.

17 Intermezzo, 1931–1939

The young airman's work during the search for Anderson and Hitchcock is well known. His most recent exploit places him amongst our super-airmen, and Australia will be delighted to honour him. The search revealed tenacity and a genius for organisation, which has made Eaton one of Australia's greatest cross-country fliers.

The Melbourne Age, 1931

Only six years after joining the RAAF in 1925, Charles was recognised as one of Australia's most experienced cross-country aviators and was awarded the Air Force Cross for his services in Central Australia.[1] It must have seemed all the more precious given that Charlie Napier's father wrote from England congratulating Charles on his award. Napier had been Charles' close friend and mentor in WWI (Vignette 1).

After commanding the successful search for the *Golden Quest II* over New Year in 1930, the Melbourne media dubbed Charles a modern 'knight errant'. For the next eight years, until the outbreak of World War II, Charles held administration posts, sought lost aircraft, acted as a race marshal for the

London–Melbourne Centenary Air Race, participated in air pageants and was appointed commander of the City of Melbourne Squadron. In February 1939 he formed a new general-purpose squadron, based in Darwin, that was to provide air defence for the north-west coastline of Australia.

The Government recognised Charles' experience and called on his advice to try to prevent aircraft accidents and misadventures. By the late 1920s, ambitious aviators were attempting to break records and fly from country to country. Because many crashed or became lost, resulting in costly and fruitless air and ground searches, some governments made it obligatory to obtain permits for long ocean flights. The Australian Government instructed Charles to check out two New Zealanders, Captain George Hood and Lieutenant John Moncrieff, who planned to fly from Sydney to New Zealand. Both aviators were WWI veterans, Hood having lost his left leg in action. After a series of cables between the Australian and New Zealand governments over the suitability of their Ryan-B1 Brougham aircraft, Charles reported that the two pilots were competent, but their new gyro-compass was suspect. Nevertheless, the two aviators were allowed to proceed, taking off from Sydney just before 3 am on 10 January 1928 in their aircraft, *Aotearoa*. They were never seen again, although engine noise heard near the Marlborough Sounds may have been their aircraft. The disappearance of the *Aotearoa* and its crew remains New Zealand's equivalent of Australia's *Southern Cloud* tragedy that occurred just three years later.

Southern Cloud, an Avro tri-motor, disappeared on a commercial flight from Sydney to Melbourne. The whereabouts of the aircraft and its crew and passengers became the most baffling mystery in Australian aviation history— and another mystery involving Charles Kingsford Smith and, to a lesser extent, Charles. Kingsford Smith and Charles Ulm had established Australian National Airlines (ANA) to be an interstate air service. ANA's first flight, captained by the newly-knighted Sir Charles with co-pilot 'Scotty' Allen in the *Southern Cloud*, had flown from Brisbane to Sydney on New Year's Day 1930. The airline's routes had soon extended to Melbourne and Tasmania.

This rare photo of Charles in dress uniform was taken after receiving the Air Force Cross in 1931.

The disappearance of the Aotearoa *and its crew remains New Zealand's equivalent of Australia's* Southern Cloud *tragedy that occurred just three years later.*

Unfortunately, at 8.15 am on 21 March 1931, the *Southern Cloud* left Mascot Airport in Sydney but never reached Melbourne. The pilot, Captain Travis 'Shorty' Shortridge, an RFC veteran and former RAAF flying instructor with a good reputation as a pilot, co-pilot CW 'Charlie' Dunnell and six passengers flew in the face of cyclonic conditions. After the alarm was given that the *Southern Cloud* was missing, 12 RAAF and 18 civil aircraft from Victoria and NSW searched many thousands of square miles from Wilsons Promontory in Victoria to north of the NSW border. Special attention centred on the uninhabited, forested bush country of the Australian Alps given the police at Holbrook in NSW had reported that residents of Tintaldra saw a fire toward Kiandra that afternoon that continued intermittently until 10 pm that evening.

Charles was one of the RAAF's 16 pilots and 28 observers involved in the search, which continued for weeks. Two months after the *Southern Cloud* and its passengers disappeared, the chances of finding the plane and any survivors appeared remote. Defence Minister Chifley wrote to Prime Minister Scullin on 20 May stating that any further search by air would be costly and further searches should be carried out by the police. In a macabre twist to the story, the Attorney General received a telephone call from a C Farrall in Melbourne; the caller identified himself as a brother of a missing passenger. He said he had received a letter stating three survivors from the *Southern Cloud* were stranded near the Cotter River, some 25 miles from Canberra. The allegation proved unfounded and the writer was recognised as '*mentally unbalanced*' and '*unnecessarily harrowed the feelings of Mr Farrall's family in a very painful fashion*'.[2]

Charles wrote nothing about this search and only ever mentioned the affair in passing. Given that he knew Shortridge well from Point Cook days, his silence was perhaps further evidence of his habit of removing the deceased from his mind. The cost of the search, combined with the world economic depression, forced Kingsford Smith's airline into liquidation.

On 21 March 1931, the Southern Cloud *left Mascot Airport in Sydney but never reached Melbourne.*

For 27 years there were many theories but no evidence of the *Southern Cloud's* fate. Then, in October 1958, carpenter Thomas Sonter found the wreckage while filming the scenic Tooma River Gorge near Kosciusko National Park. A gold watch found at the site had stopped at 1.15 pm. Another two watches, cufflinks and a key ring marked 'Clyde Hood Capital Theatre' were also found. Apparently Shortridge had got lost in the bad weather and the Southern Cloud had suddenly banked and crashed into the Tooma Range. It was unlikely anyone survived the initial impact and their deaths must have been mercifully instantaneous. The fire seen at Tintaldra may possibly have been the crash of the missing aircraft. The skeletal remains of the crew and passengers now share a common grave under a row of pines in the Cooma Cemetery where a memorial to their memory has been placed.

For 27 years there were many theories but no evidence of the Southern Cloud's *fate.*

RAAF officers were also called upon to give demonstrations at air pageants. Melbourne's Moonee Valley Race Course hosted one aerial display that included many well-known flyers; 48 aircraft took part in the pageant and 26 in the Victorian Aerial Derby, a race at the same event. The pageant particularly highlighted the popularity of the De Havilland Moth aircraft; 18 entered the derby, including one piloted by Horrie Miller, the winner of the 1929 Sydney to Perth air race. Squadron Leader Johnny Summers won the derby in his Bristol Bulldog fighter, which the newspapers termed the '*fastest bus in the pageant*'. The air extravaganza ended in a dog-fight between two good friends, Hereward de Havilland and Charles Eaton, both piloting Moths. The fight ended with Eaton being '*shot down in flames*'.

'Aerobatics.' Flight Lieutenant Charles Eaton left and Major Hereward de Havilland in the front cockpit. Circa 1934.

The Melbourne *Herald* reported:

> The most effective exhibition during the day was the fight between Major de Havilland and Flight Lieutenant Eaton in two Moths representing scout planes with Vickers guns firing through the propellers. Flight Lieutenant Eaton, while waiting for his foe in the air, executed a glittering series of loops, rolls and half-rolls and other aerobatics just to show how easy it all is.

In Sydney, Eaton and celebrated aviator Captain 'Bill' Lancaster flew together in air shows during the early 1930s. However, in an episode reminiscent of the 1929 *Kookaburra* saga, Lancaster disappeared in the Sahara in April 1933; the French Foreign Legion found his body beside his aircraft, *Southern Cross Minor*, 29 years later.

There have been some comments that the pre-WWII air force was an 'Aero Club' with its pageants, air displays and weekend excursions to Bass Strait islands for part-time Citizens Air Force (CAF) personnel.[3] Family members were taken for flights regularly; Peter Eaton remembers how, when a teenager, one of his father's younger pilots, 'Johnny' Lerew, told him to '*jump in the old Wapiti*'. After a hedge-hopping joy ride, buzzing farm houses at tree height, they flew to Geelong where Lerew dive-bombed a friend's home. Years later, when Peter himself was in the RAAF, he reminded Lerew of the episode. Lerew, by then a Wing Commander, replied, '*Shush ... I'm now the Director of Flying Safety.*' Charles dubbed Lerew 'The Hero of Rabaul'. Early in the Pacific War, Lerew led his obsolete Wirraways against the high-speed manoeuvrable Japanese Zeros. Before taking off from Rabaul in New Guinea to an almost certain death, he telegrammed the Air Board the Roman Gladiators' Imperial Salute, '*Nos morituri te salutamus*—We who are about to die salute you'. Johnny Lerew was one of his squadron's few survivors; his salutation to the hierarchy is now firmly entrenched in RAAF legend.

To mark Melbourne's centenary in 1934, the chocolate millionaire, Sir MacPherson Robertson, offered £10,000 to the winner of a London to Melbourne air race. He stipulated: '*Make it the greatest race yet conducted in the world, make as few conditions as possible consistent with reducing risks to the minimum.*' The Smithsonian Institute wrote in its history of aviation that Robertson never dreamed how his race would transform world commercial aviation. Charles participated in this momentous event as a race marshal. Wing Commander Adrian Cole was the handicapper.

The race was won by Britons Charles Scott and 'Tom' Campbell-Black in a DH-88 Comet in 70 hours and 59 minutes. Second place went to a

'Make it the greatest race yet conducted in the world, make as few conditions as possible consistent with reducing risks to the minimum.'

Dutch DC-2 KLM airliner, piloted by pioneer aviators Keone Parmentier and Jan Moll, on a commercial flight with three paying passengers! Third place went to well-known American aviators Roscoe Turner and Clyde Pangborn in a Boeing-247; Pangborn was the first to fly from Japan to Alaska while Turner was considered America's leading racing pilot of the time. One Dutch race participant, Dirk Asjes, was later to play a senior role in Charles' 79 Wing during WWII (Vignette 23).

At the time, many believed the race was the greatest sporting event in the history of aviation. Coming at a time when the world was recovering from economic depression, the 11,000-mile race provided an impetus to commercial and military aviation beyond the promoters' wildest expectations. The winner, the DH-88 Comet, evolved into the Mosquito fighter-bomber. KLM's DC-2 became the forerunner of the famous DC-3, the work-horse of WWII. The Boeing-247, sponsored by Warner Brothers of Hollywood, became the ancestor of the now famous Boeings. As race officials, Adrian Cole and Charles Eaton had the rare opportunity to entertain this assembly of the world's most renowned aviators on their home turf.

As Squadron Leader (Air), it was Charles' responsibility to organise and coordinate all RAAF units at Laverton, manage air pageants and represent the service at civic functions. He flew to Nhill in western Victoria for the 1937 Armistice Day to address ex-servicemen and relatives.

Winner of the 1934 Centenary Air Race, the DH-88 Comet, piloted by Charles Scott and Thomas Campbell-Black.

Centenary Race third place-getters, Warner Brothers' Boeing-247 piloted by Roscoe Turner and Clyde Pangborn..

The *Nhill Free Press* reported:

Squadron Leader Eaton, wearing the navy blue and gold uniform and silver wings of the R.A.A.F. said he felt embarrassed at the reception from such a large audience. It was now 19 years since the original Armistice Day, and although the years were rolling past, all of them who took part in creating Armistice Day remembered it as if were only yesterday, because it was the day they had striven for and longed for since the beginning of the war. When he said all of them who remembered and helped to create Armistice Day, he meant not only the returned men and women who actually took part in the war, but those who were at the back of them and who gave them encouragement to carry on in the years of war—the wives, mothers, sweethearts, and those who remained behind whose lot was often harder than those who went away. To those people it meant time set apart to pay reverence and tribute to those who helped to create this Armistice Day, this day of peace, many of whom did not come back, but who's remembrance of husbands, brothers, and 'cobbers' who were gone, and whose courage and fortitude would always be an ideal to be attained. Squadron Leader Eaton said that the first Armistice Day meant 'actual' liberty for at the time; he was a prisoner of war.

The value of your celebration is greater than you really imagine, not only to yourselves for your personal reasons, but by example, you are leading your section of the community on the only road to peace. Squadron Leader Eaton claimed his profession was the finest in the world. It was not an aggressive force and was trained for defensive measures only; indiscriminate bombing did not come into the question. There were many fine young men in the service who were the 'salt of the earth' and who could, if called upon, carry on the traditions of the A.I.F.

Charles initiated a chain of events, perhaps unique in the then British Empire, when he recommended a bravery decoration for ACI McAloney in 1937. After an aerial display at the Hamilton Agricultural Show, three Hawker Demons of 1 Squadron prepared to return to their home base. Historian Clark describes what happened:

> The first Demon got away safely, but as the second machine (flown by Flying Officer Ken McKenzie and Sergeant Norm Torrens-Witherow in the observer's seat) took off minutes later, the pilot attempted a climbing turn. With the loss of speed entailed by this manoeuvre, the plane stalled and dived to earth again from a height of 200 feet, in full view of a horrified crowd.

The third Demon was just preparing to take off when new recruit 'Billy' McAloney, in the observer's cockpit, saw McKenzie's Demon hit the ground and burst into flames. McAloney immediately sprinted to the burning aircraft and tried to free the two men, unfortunately without success. He later wrote:

> I saw the aircraft do a stall turn and knew it would not clear the ground: I had to run a quarter of a mile, and Verey cartridges were exploding. The main fuel tank had burst. I went in to rescue the two occupants. I knew I had to be quick to get even one; I didn't know whether they were still alive or not.

McAloney tried to pull McKenzie out but the pilot was on fire and his leg was caught in the plane's fabric. While McAloney was trying to release McKenzie the fuel tanks exploded, which *'finished me off'*. Both crew members died and McAloney himself had to be pulled away from the burning crash by spectators. McAloney's heroic but futile effort resulted in his hospitalisation with severe burns.

Charles presided over the court of inquiry into the crash. He recommended that McAloney receive the Air Force Medal (AFM) for his

Bristol Bulldogs of 21 (City of Melbourne) Squadron at Laverton being reviewed by the Governor General Lord Gowrie VC (left middle-ground) with Squadron Leader Eaton AFC (front right) in 1937.

bravery but McAloney's commander thought the British Empire Medal (BEM) was more appropriate. Civil authorities also sought recognition from the Royal Humane Society. Eventually, McAloney was awarded the Albert Medal, which was warranted by Queen Victoria for 'Gallantry for Saving Life on Land'. He had the unique distinction of being the RAAF's first and only recipient of this award. King George VI instituted a new order for heroism not in the presence of an enemy, the George Cross. The Albert Medal was superseded by this decoration so McAloney became an automatic recipient of the George Cross, Australia's first. McAloney's unique Albert Medal is now displayed at the RAAF Museum at Point Cook.

On 3 May 1937 Charles realised his long-held ambition to be appointed commander of a fully-operational squadron. Based at Laverton, 21 (Cadre) Squadron had been formed on 20 April 1936 with Squadron Leader Johnnie Summers its inaugural commander. The squadron was renamed 21 (City of Melbourne) soon after. The squadron was a Citizen Air Force (CAF) unit comprising seven officers and 43 permanent air force airmen and 20 officers and 106 part-time, weekend personnel. The first aircraft were four Demons, two Wapitis and three DH-60s; the following year the squadron acquired Avro-Ansons, a light reconnaissance bomber, and from 1937, four Bristol Bulldog fighters.

Eaton described his appointment:

> Early in 1937, I was appointed to Command No. 21 Squadron, the City of Melbourne Squadron. In those days, with war looming, considerable work was carried out, particularly when doubling the size of the C.A.F, training pilots and cooperating with the Navy on joint exercises. Yanakie, King Island, and Flinders Island aerodromes were established and many well-known exercises in conjunction with our naval forces were carried out.
>
> Great interest in the Squadron was taken by the Governor of Victoria, Lord Huntingfield who was the Honorary Air Commodore of the Squadron. Many of the pilots and ground personnel of those days proved their worth during the war and many reached high ranks. Unfortunately, too many paid the supreme sacrifice of winning the war.

The squadron's duties included the wide range of flying training activities the CAF air crews would need to form the core of a wartime air force, just as Charles' Territorial regiment had done for the British Army in WWI in its preparation for a ground war. Activities included bombing, gunnery, night flying, formation flying, signals, reconnaissance, air navigation and instrument flying. In addition, 21 Squadron carried out the important work of meteorological flights and bushfire control. Charles must have felt at home on reconnaissance duty as he had been doing reconnaissance on the ground and in the air since early 1915.

Charles' reconnaissance flights included the far eastern coast of Victoria and as far north as Bega in southern NSW. The RAAF was particularly interested in the country around Maffra, Sale, Lake Wellington and Bairnsdale as potential emergency landing grounds. During summer the squadron undertook bushfire patrols. In November 1937 Charles and Forestry Commission staff spent five days surveying Victoria's forests. In January 1938 the squadron's fire patrol reported 90 bushfires. Air force

Many of the pilots and ground personnel of those days proved their worth during the war and many reached high ranks. Unfortunately, too many paid the supreme sacrifice of winning the war.

In January 1938 the squadron's fire patrol reported 90 bushfires. Air force legend has it that Charles told his pilots 'to keep their eyes skinned' for possible trout streams.

Visiting old friends in Alice Springs, 1937. Charles with legendry bushman and cameleer Bob Buck and Alf Butler.

legend has it that Charles told his pilots '*to keep their eyes skinned*' for possible trout streams. An avid fisherman, he scouted new locations for his trout fishing companions, Frank Lukis (later Air Commodore), Lionel Lemaire (later Brigadier) and Thomas Blamey (later Field Marshal). The four eventually leased a small trout fishing lodge at Taggety, north-east of Melbourne, which was used on many a weekend.

Australian-born Lord Huntingfield, Governor of Victoria, was a keen supporter of 21 Squadron. As its honorary Air Commodore, he arranged for the squadron to be formally affiliated to 600 (City of London) Squadron RAF in 1938. Four London class flying boats visited Melbourne in February 1938. Charles commanded five Avro Ansons in an interception exercise with the visiting flying boats over Western Port Bay. On completion of the manoeuvres, the RAF and RAAF planes flew in formation over Melbourne City, but one of the flying boats suddenly dropped in altitude directly above Flinders Street Railway Station. Smoke came from one engine and a propeller blade fell directly towards the platforms.

The squadron's history elaborated:

An elderly man called out it's a bomb, and everyone ran from its path. A split second later, there was a loud crash as the falling blade and boss tore through the galvanized roof and buried itself three feet deep in the platform. The nearest person was eight feet away when the blade struck.

The plane's second propeller blade just missed an electrician in nearby Collins Street. The flying boat, using its remaining engine, managed to land on Port Phillip Bay and taxied more than a mile to a Williamstown jetty. It was amazing no one was killed or injured.

In early 1938, the RAAF appointed Wing Commander George Jones and Squadron Leader Charles Eaton as a two-man committee to 'consider plans and all other matters connected with the establishment of a RAAF station at Darwin'. On 16 May, Charles piloted Jones and his son Peter in an Anson (A 4-1) to Darwin. The next day he flew with three other aircraft to search for a lost plane; a DH-83 Fox Moth piloted by Anthony Curdy and carrying Dr King, a flying doctor. The plane was found next to the Victoria River within 24 hours. Two days later, accompanied by Colonel (later General) Sturdee, Charles carried out an aerial survey for the army of the country between Darwin and the Adelaide River. After ten busy days in the Northern Territory, the airmen returned to Laverton to submit their recommendations for a RAAF Darwin base.

Peter later recalled that while in Darwin, his father went missing for some days with no explanation. His official RAAF record states: '... *proc. Darwin 16.5.38. ret. 26.5.38 SRO 76/38 proc. to N.E.I.*'. Apart from that brief entry in his record of service, no other mention or report of his obviously highly sensitive visit has ever been located. Charles never mentioned this clandestine mission to the Netherlands East Indies, though many years later he did admit, '*I was placed under house arrest by Dutch officials for a few days.*'

On 30 October 1938, Charles commanded a fly-past of six Ansons at the opening of the WWI Australian Flying Corps Memorial at Point Cook by the Governor General, Lord Gowrie. More than 7000 people attended the event in perfect weather. Other pilots in the fly-past were

'Freddie' Thomas, who later became Lord Mayor of Melbourne, Dallas Scott, who was tragically executed by the Japanese on Ambon, and Robert Hitchcock, the son of Bobby Hitchcock who died with Keith Anderson in the Tanami.

As the world situation deteriorated, the squadron participated in war games with the Royal Australian Navy (RAN) locating and destroying a possible enemy cruiser and intercepting two cruisers and four destroyers that were approaching Port Phillip Bay from eastern Bass Strait. To carry out the operational exercises, the squadron moved to temporary bases on King Island in Bass Strait and Wilsons Promontory.

Because of the tension in Europe, the Australian Government, acting on the decade old Salmond report, gave the RAAF funds to expand. Charles was appointed as commander of the new 12 (General Purpose) Squadron and transferred his command of 21 Squadron to Squadron Leader 'Paddy' Heffernan. Once established, 12 Squadron—with its 14 officers, 120 airmen, four Avro Anson bombers and four Hawker Demon fighter aircraft—was to be stationed at Darwin, Australia's gateway to Asia. Once the new RAAF Darwin airport was built, Wing Commander Jones was to be station commander.

Charles wrote with obvious pride of his new appointment:

> On 6 February, 1939, I was appointed to command the new Squadron, No. 12, which was to proceed to Darwin at the first opportunity. The Squadron consisted of 2 flights of twin-engine aircraft, Ansons and 1 flight of Demons, later to be replaced by Wirraways. The Squadron was formed into what I considered to be the finest Squadron at that time in the air force.

Charles proposed the squadron's motto be *Ngillimurr Marachina Makarrda*, which originated from a language of the Northern Territory and translated as 'We go upwards with peaceful negotiations after conflict'.[4] The motto changed in 1943, much to Charles' displeasure, to *Irramus et Impugnamus*, translated as 'We roam we charge'.

'We go upwards with peaceful negotiations after conflict'.

A wet Victorian winter, RAAF Laverton, 1939

The first six months were not comfortable for the new unit. Being only temporarily at Laverton until moving to Darwin, little priority was given to accommodation for the personnel, aircraft and equipment. The men were quartered in temporary huts and, later, in the middle of a cold Victorian winter, under canvas. The aircraft were housed in one old, uncomfortable WWI Besseneau hangar, with offices made from discarded packing cases from imported Seagull sea planes. Nevertheless, all ranks pulled their weight to get the squadron operational. Its first operational flight was on 2 March when 'Jock' Whyte flew an Anson in an interception and shadowing exercise with HMAS *Vampire*.

Charles wrote that *'after some hard training and quite a bit of battling'* the advance party was ready to leave for Darwin. The morning after their farewell party at Melbourne's Alexander Hotel on 30 June, the party left *'with sore heads'* on the SS *Marella* under Flight Lieutenant Arthur Hocking. Charles arranged for a fly-past to see them off into Port Phillip Bay. On arrival in Sydney, the party transferred to the SS *Montoro* then sailed to Darwin, docking on 24 July. Led by Charles, the first flight of three Ansons touched down at Darwin's civil aerodrome the same day and were welcomed by the Administrator, Charles Abbott. After four days familiarising themselves with the tropical environment, the three flight crews, including Charles, returned to Laverton.

The serious international situation in September necessitated the mobilisation of Australia's armed forces. This meant the hurried departure of the remainder of 12 Squadron from Laverton to Darwin, leaving behind their, as yet undelivered, Wirraway fighter aircraft.

Fifty years later, 'Cec' Fisher wrote on the first days of the new unit:

> S/L Eaton, he was my first C.O. when No.12 Squadron was formed at Laverton in February 1939. I cannot express how highly we regarded him for, to us, very young men at the time, he was a real father figure and like all fine men; he led 'from the front'. In those early Darwin and Laverton days, with limited numbers, most of us got to know him closely.
>
> I will never forget that week, when 'Moth' called us together to tell us we were the pick of the air force. We believed him, and he went on to tell us that most likely in the future we could be called on to rough it until our modern luxurious tropical station in Darwin was complete. 'Moth' could have no idea (nor did we) how true his words were.

The official history of 12 Squadron summed up its first commander:

> Called 'Moth' by his men (but obviously not to his face) he was a well liked and highly respected Commanding Officer who gave a high priority to the welfare and morale of those under his command, and was not afraid to lead by example. The Air Force had chosen well in appointing Squadron Leader Charles Eaton as the first Commanding Officer of No 12 Squadron.

Just days before WWII began, a partly-equipped squadron, two flights of 'Aggie' Anson reconnaissance bombers, arrived in Darwin to provide the air defence for the entire north-west coast and hinterland of Australia.

*'Moth Eaton's Flying Circus'
concert at RAAF Darwin*

The three Avro-Ansons of 12 Squadron taking off from Victoria to defend northern Australia, August 1939.

18 Moth Eaton's Flying Circus, 1939–1940

The members of 12 Squadron were pioneering RAAF operations in the tropical, northern Australian environment and their success did not come easily. There were many hardships to overcome.[1]

The original Darwin aerodrome site, selected by the founder of Qantas, Sir Hudson Fysh, was on the Parap police horse paddock. It gained a place in Australia's aviation history as the terminus for the £10,000 England to Australia Air Race, when brothers Keith and Ross Smith touched down in a Vickers Vimy, a WWI bomber, on 10 December 1919 after the first flight between the two countries. By the 1930s Darwin was a regular staging point for commercial aircraft carrying passengers and mail between Australia and Europe. In 1937 Amelia Earhart left Parap on her ill-fated trans-Pacific flight. Amy Johnson and Bert Hinkler both used Darwin as a staging point on their historic flights.

On arriving in Darwin, the RAAF's Avro Ansons were stationed at Parap and the airmen accommodated in Vestey's abandoned meat works at Bullocky Point. Just three days after the squadron arrived, Hitler's armies launched their *'blitzkrieg'* against Poland. Radio Operator Ron Hargraves recorded Wing Commander Eaton's words when addressing the Squadron: *'Well, the balloon has gone up and we are now at war with Germany.'*

'Well, the balloon has gone up and we are now at war with Germany.'

Charles described that day:

> I well remember when war was declared, going with the officers to the Airmen's and Sergeants' Messes, the reception of the news and the wonderful spirit of all. The day war broke out, we carried out the first patrols, really to keep an eye on the Japanese luggers[2] which were then quite prolific in the Darwin area. The first patrol of the war was carried out by F/O Les Collings who later, unfortunately, became a prisoner-of-war in Germany. The Japanese lugger question was always uppermost and their movements continuously watched. Every week a search was made from Darwin to Broome spotting and placing the lugger fleets.
>
> The usual scares occurred and on one occasion a line ahead patrol was carried out from Darwin to Timor and return by Ansons, refuelling at Bathurst Island to search for Italian submarines which had set out from Massawa in the Red Sea to make for Japan. This was one of the first actual operations of the R.A.A.F from Australia in the war. Again, on another occasion, a continuous search was made for a German surface raider.

This was one of the first actual operations of the R.A.A.F from Australia in the war.

Although Japan was not yet involved in the war, the squadron also carried out surveillance patrols against Japanese shipping. The mint-new fighter-bomber Wirraways, which had left Victoria for Darwin on the day Germany invaded Poland, arrived on 5 September. Unfortunately, A 20-5 stalled coming into land and crashed, killing Flying Officer Arnold Dolphin and Corporal Harold Johnson instantly. A misunderstood wireless message while in flight caused Dolphin to miss a refuelling stop; the Wirraway simply ran out of fuel as it was about to land. Dolphin and Johnson may have been Australia's first casualties of the war.

By mid-September the whole squadron was billeted at the Vestey meat works. The adjoining cemetery had a somewhat ominous sign stating '*Abandon All Hope Ye That Enter Here*'. The Vestey complex was a huge, rambling set of buildings that the air force shared with the army's mobile force.

Charles wrote:

> This accommodation we shared with the Darwin mobile force under Major 'Bandy' McDonald was perhaps one of the happiest times we had in the service. We messed and lived with the Army in a most co-operative spirit and at the same time built our own camp and hangars at the civil aerodrome. Although times were hard and difficult there was not a grouse and all personnel put their backs into the work.

Armourer Corporal Cec Fisher wrote that the view over the Darwin Harbour from '*our airy Bayview Mansions was excellent*'. While the airmen of the lower ranks who were quartered in the upstairs pavilions were satisfied with their scenic views and cool breezes, the sergeants on the bottom level were not so fortunate. James Truscott remarked, 'The sergeants were quartered on the ground floor immediately below us, till they realised the moisture falling on them at night from up top wasn't water. They then moved to a safer area.'

All non-essential flying was halted as all ranks were organised to erect 'Tin City Parap'. Fisher continued:

> Now you can picture the scene, the area piled high with this material, concrete stumps already erected and gazed upon with complete bewilderment by well over a hundred personnel, for 'Moth' had said that everyone from pilots to cooks, observers to mess hands, maintenance blokes to orderly room types would be on the job 'without exception'.
>
> The first buildings up were the toilet blocks (no septic), ablution block, kitchen, airman's canteen (used by all ranks—and a wet canteen at that) followed by the two hangars. The Sergeants' and Officers' Messes (also tin huts) were to be last. They were too. Everything commenced enthusiastically and smoothly with the medical tent well occupied in tending to skinned knuckles, mashed fingers and sundry cuts from inexpert workmen but the spirit was there and the morale was high under 'Moth's' example. The wet canteen helped a lot.[3]

The adjoining cemetery had a somewhat ominous sign stating 'Abandon All Hope Ye That Enter Here'.

The wet canteen helped a lot.

*'Tin City Parap ... we built it ourselves.'
1 RAAF Darwin, 1939–1940.*

Truscott wrote that the cooks were wonderful, there was no serious outbreak of disease and '*at the first sign of trouble we often paraded and had our throats painted*'. Fresh vegetables proved difficult to obtain due to the long distances from suppliers. Historian Myriam Amar admired the men's initiative to construct makeshift ice boxes, as there was no refrigeration. She said there was '*a real consciousness of the need for self-help ... units grew vegetables and bred their livestock for consumption*'.

There was 'a real consciousness of the need for self-help ... units grew vegetables and bred their livestock for consumption'.

Charles' challenging task was to prepare the aeroplanes and keep them, and the base personnel, supplied with the necessary equipment and provisions. He deemed it essential to fit the Ansons with extra petrol tanks so they could extend their patrols over the Arafura Sea while searching for the German raider *Admiral Graf Spee* and to escort both commercial and navy shipping. Spare parts were in short supply so maintenance crews improvised; when the Ansons' exhaust assemblies corroded, they flew with flattened roofing iron patched over their exhausts. Charles complained that the air force's equipment and supply staff in the south had little comprehension of what was required for Darwin. Ironically, after the Ansons returned south for training purposes, a shipload of Anson spare parts arrived; an annoyed Charles promptly had them '*about face and sent aback south*'.

When Squadron Leader Valston 'Val' Hancock from HQ in Melbourne arrived in Darwin after a three-day flight in a Demon to report on equipment allocated to the northern base, he proudly reported to Charles. However, he was taken back when met with *'a cold steely eye'*. Charles got straight to the point that most of the furniture and fittings were totally unsuitable and unnecessarily expensive. Charles gave the young officer a piece of his mind: *'Hancock, never take anything for granted and hearsay, go first and see for yourself.'* Hancock, later a post-war Chief of the Air Staff, never forgot *'the best lesson he ever received whilst serving in the RAAF'.*[4]

'Hancock, never take anything for granted and hearsay, go first and see for yourself.'

Gunnery and bombing exercises were carried out at a remote area near Lee Point, a few miles west of Parap. Fisher commented that the only cover for the observer party recording the bombing results was a large sand dune. The observers also carried rifles to ward off inquisitive crocodiles, angry buffalo and wild pigs. Charles told the observers to return with the odd duck, goose or pig for the messes. In one exercise, Flying Officer John Hickey, looking for excitement, flew his aircraft so low that his propeller hit sand near Rapid Creek, bending it back nine inches. He managed to fly back at tree level and, once he lowered the undercarriage, the aircraft just dropped onto 'the deck': *The CO had to get tough with Wirraway pilots who were coming home with salt spray on their wingtips and John Hickey spent a prolonged period as Orderly Officer.*'[5]

Together with army commander Colonel Robertson, Charles organised shooting parties to relieve boredom and to supply duck and geese for all three services. Corporal Fisher reported that Christmas 1939 was celebrated by parties, concerts and drinking contests:

> It was a magnificent Christmas/New Year. At the Christmas concert one hula dancer's grass skirt suddenly caught fire much to the amusement of the wives and invited ladies.

Charles later recorded his judgement of Darwin and the people of the 'Top End':

Celebrating Christmas at RAAF Parap, (Charles is third from left), Darwin, 1939.

Darwin, which is often very much maligned, is worthy of description. Usually the visitor to Darwin has been someone used to life in suburbia of southern cities and even the sunshine does not meet with their approval. Darwin is really a very fine township and one can easily visualise that after the war it will really become a pleasure resort.

The men and women of Darwin can only be described as magnificent and certainly different to those of the southern cities. They are used to the sunshine, open air life and are broadminded in comparison with the ordinary southern city dweller. Many of the houses are very comfortable to live in and life in this city is pleasant for all. Tennis and golf are available and football and cricket are played throughout the appropriate season.

The RAAF guards still had to be vigilant as many tons of bombs and large quantities of ammunition and petrol were stored within the base. One senior officer, who Charles had taught to fly, was disparagingly amused by Charles' order to double the guards on the outbreak of war; however, his commander had learnt the lessons of alertness as a frontline soldier and left nothing to chance. His caution was justified on the night of 4 May 1940, as reported by the duty officer:

Shots fired at unknown intruder at Civil Aerodrome, DARWIN. At approximately 22.30 hours an airman whilst on beat as a roving piquet along the petrol and bomb dumps had to challenge two unknown persons for trespassing. On the order 'halt that goes there' no reply was given and the two persons concerned ran away. The sentry again gave the order, 'Halt' but they kept on running, the sentry then fired three shots at them, with no result.

Meanwhile, the new base at Six Miles[6], which George Jones and Charles had recommended in 1938, became operational on 1 July 1940. RAAF Darwin sat on almost 4000 acres.[7] Charles was promoted to Group Captain Eaton and appointed commanding officer of the new base, thereby relinquishing command of 12 Squadron after almost 18 months. To recognise the traditional owners, Charles proposed to HQ that the base be named *Lelare*, meaning roosting place for birds, but his request was refused. Charles' great grand-daughter, born in Darwin on 18 October 2005, was named Lelare.[8]

13 (City of Darwin) Squadron, which had been formed the previous month from two flights of Ansons from 12 Squadron, was transferred to the new base. Almost the entire administration staff of 12 Squadron now formed the core of Darwin's new HQ. At the end of November the strength of the base had increased to 47 officers and 536 NCOs and airmen.

Charles later wrote:

> From the time of our first arrival at Darwin, work commenced on the new R.A.A.F aerodrome which now can be considered the finest aerodrome in Australia. After many difficulties our camp was completed and we settled down to the phoney war period that was before the Japanese declared war. Aerodromes were constructed from Port Hedland to Groote Eylandt and inland at Bachelor.
>
> My headquarters and No 13 Squadron moved to this new 'drome about the middle of 1940 and No 12 Squadron remained in our temporary hutted camp on the civil aerodrome. In 1940 a change took place and No. 12 Squadron was split, the two Anson Flights which had done thousands of hours of flying with no casualties whatsoever, were returned

South and replaced by Hudson aircraft, which in addition to another Hudson Flight, returned to Darwin to become the famous No 13 Squadron. At the same time the remaining Flight of Wirraways was reinforced by two other Wirraway Flights and No 12 Squadron became a fully equipped Wirraway Squadron and was to remain as such until after the outbreak of the Japanese (Pacific) War.

As the war in Europe continued, most of the pilots of the two Squadrons were a little bit concerned at not being in action although it was obvious that sooner or later they would be at war with Japan. However, many of them were posted, which included the two Squadron Commanders, S/L Glascock of No 12, and S/L Balmer of No 13. Both unfortunately, lost their lives later in the war. Apart from that, not being in the war and with their occasional patrols and general training, the morale of all personnel was always at a very high standard; I think it was over 18 months before I had an Orderly Room case before me at Darwin. The officers and, in particular S/L Moffat-Pender, the administrative officer, organised bush shooting trips and sport in general for all.

Sports activities were supervised by Ian Moffat-Pender, with 'The Eaton Cup' awarded for the unit with the best all-round sports ability.[9] An administrative officer, Moffat-Pender was a wealthy Scot who had played rugby for Scotland, served in both the Black Watch and the RFC during WWI and joined the RAAF at the outbreak of WWII. He was dedicated to the welfare of the airmen and donated his entire war-time salary to the Red Cross. All airmen respected him despite thinking him 'completely troppo'; the aging Scot jogged every morning quite oblivious of the heat.

The inaugural commander of 13 Squadron was a 30-year-old regular officer, Squadron Leader John Raeburn 'Sam' Balmer, whom Charles considered a born leader. Later in the war, Balmer commanded 100 Squadron, composed of Beaufort torpedo bombers. Balmer took this squadron to New Guinea and was then transferred to Bomber Command in the United Kingdom to become commanding officer of 467 (Lancaster) Squadron. He was awarded the Distinguished Flying Cross (DFC) for *'great skill and devotion to duty'*

Presentation of the Eaton Cup for sports, won by 12 Squadron, 1941.

but was killed in action on 11 May 1944 while flying a bombing mission over Belgium. Squadron Leader Clarence Glasscock, another capable commander who had joined the RAAF in 1932, was appointed the second commander of 12 Squadron. He was later transferred to New Guinea as commanding officer of a Beaufighter squadron and awarded the DFC for gallantry. He lost his life on a mission near Cape Hoskins, New Britain, in September 1943.

July 1940 saw an official visit by the Minister for Air, the Hon. James Fairbairn. A former WWI pilot, Fairbairn piloted his own aircraft and was greeted in the air by an escort of four Wirraways. This distinguished and energetic Minister held frank discussions with Charles, who listed 14 major issues including promotions, the base's defence requirements and the problem of the lack of spares and equipment.

Just three weeks after his Darwin inspection, James Fairbairn was flying in a Hudson bomber that crashed near Canberra with no survivors. Cabinet ministers Sir Henry Gullet and Brigadier Geoffrey Street and the Chief of the General Staff, General Sir Cyril Brudenell White, were killed with him.

The pilot was Robert Hitchcock, previously of 21 Squadron and the son of Bobby Hitchcock, who Charles had buried in the Tanami in 1929. The accident changed Australia's political history. In the election that followed this tragic crash, Prime Minister Menzies lost his majority in Parliament, making way for John Curtin to be eventually elected Prime Minister.

The RAAF Darwin Record Book states for 13 August: *'The death of Mr Fairbairn is keenly felt by all personnel. His cheerful presence and vigorous optimism were an encouragement and inspiration to all.'* Charles considered that, had Fairbairn lived and remained as Minister, the RAAF may not have had the complex and confusing command structure the service experienced for the rest of the war.[10] Just two days before setting out on what was to be his final flight, Fairbairn's office had transmitted a message to Darwin:

> The Minister for Air has requested Group Captain C Eaton AFC be informed that he was particularly pleased with the keen-ness and efficiency of all ranks of the station Darwin. The Minister added that the very high morale was particularly praiseworthy in view of the definitely difficult conditions under which all have been living and working since the establishment of the station.

In August 1940, the two squadrons flew 749 hours on coastal surveillance and security patrols for shipping. Many of the pilots later held high command in the RAAF, including John Hampshire, John 'Ginty' Lush and Ian Campbell.

First control tower, RAAF Darwin. (Courtesy CAHS Collection)

Forever the reconnaissance man, on 28 August Charles ordered Sam Balmer to fly him over Cartier Island and Ashmore Reef in the Timor Sea. He wanted to ascertain the possibility of landing an aircraft on these ribbons of sand in an emergency. Three years later, a damaged Beaufighter from his 79 Wing made it to Ashmore and the crew were taken off by Catalina flying boat (Vignette 24).

Charles complained to the Air Board about the lack of sufficient armaments for the aerodrome's perimeter defence. As the base had only 204 rifles, 12 revolvers, and a small number of Lewis guns, he placed an order for 7 Vickers guns, 266 rifles and a further 316 revolvers. It is unknown if all the rifles were received, but by the following March only one Vickers machine gun had arrived and no Lewis guns.

In an interview in 1984, 'Ron' Hargraves, an original member of the advance party of July 1939, summed up the squadron's *esprit de corps* and sense of achievement when establishing RAAF Darwin. When asked if the early years in Darwin were *'boring, happy, interesting or exciting?'* Hargraves answered:

> All of those things, delete boring. All of those that you said, yes; it was interesting, exciting, happy, never boring really. ... I think it was the work challenge, it started out almost as though it was a boy scout mission, you know, you're going to achieve something, to build something, where nothing was before. Every time we built something, we did it the hard way; you know. We built the camp on the old civil drome with these prefabricated

Wirraways of 12 Squadron, RAAF Darwin 1939–1940.

things with our own bare hands. We moved in and the whole squadron had a tremendous pride of achievement. We didn't hire professionals to build the camp, we did it ourselves. When we wanted to set up our workshops, we did it ourselves; when we wanted to set up our communications centres and so on, we did it ourselves ...

'The arrest and court martial of Dr Clyde Fenton', December 1939.

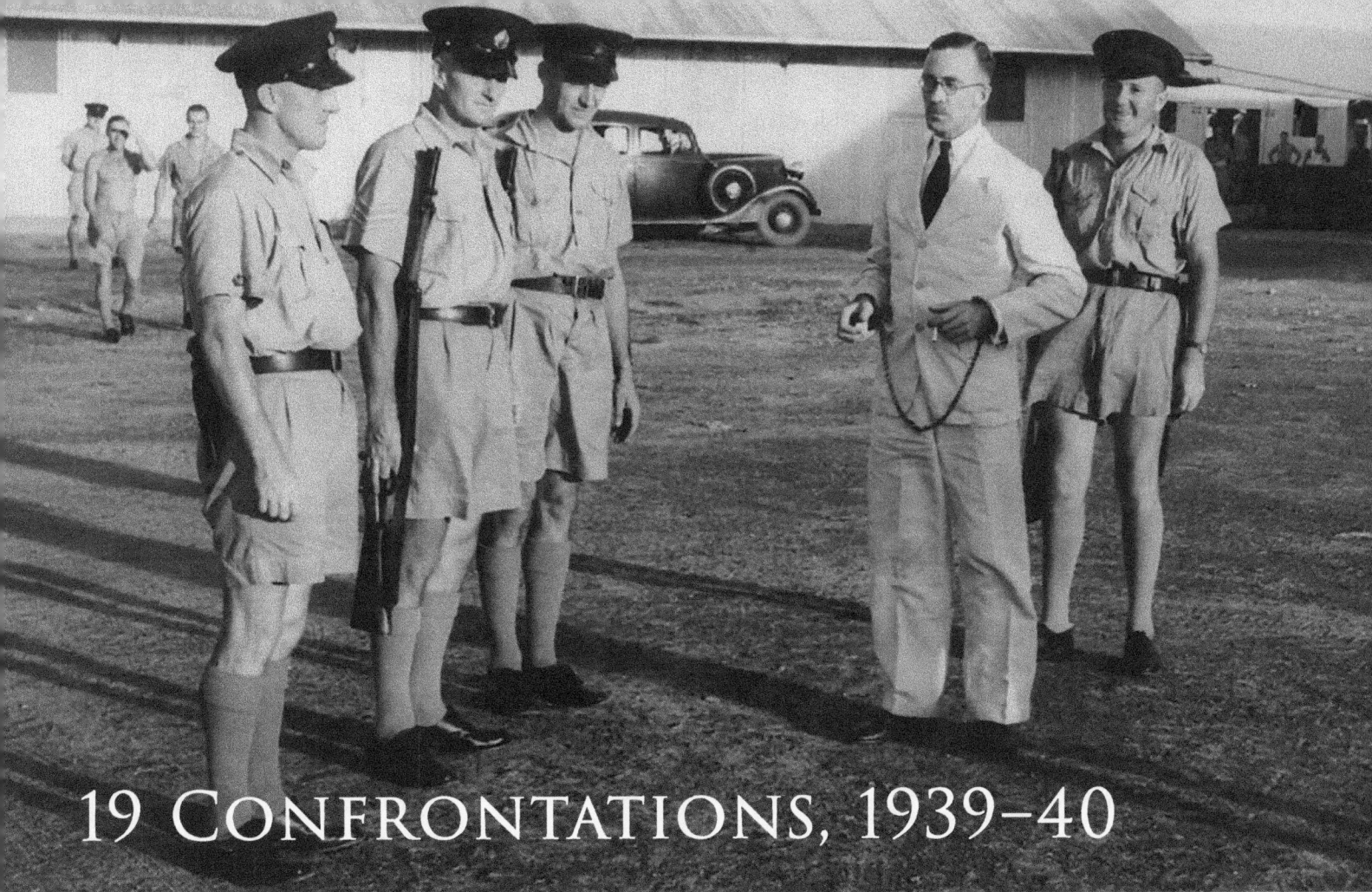

19 CONFRONTATIONS, 1939–40

Prosecutor: *Can you tell the court why you think LAC Smith is mad?*

Defence: *Well, only the other day I see 'im in town. 'E pulls up at a bowser and asks for a couple of gallons o' petrol. Mad all right!*

Prosecutor: *Why what's wrong with that?*

Defence: *'E was on a bloody horse!*[1]

The two squadrons settled into Darwin and the training regime necessary to prepare them for the looming war. Base life was a time for developing skills, discipline and camaraderie—all equally important as it appeared inevitable that Japan would attack Australia from the north. However, in true 'Aussie' style, there was always time for a bit of fun along the way, particularly at the expense of the bureaucracy and civilians.

One such incident occurred after the government approached Charles to intercede and apprehend a flying doctor, Dr Clyde Fenton, who was a colourful legend in Australia's aviation history. After gaining his medical degree, Fenton learnt to fly and joined the RAF in England. His RAF career came to an abrupt end following a confrontation with a senior officer, so he became a flying doctor with the Northern Territory's medical service. When Fenton continually flouted regulations by landing on main roads, sometimes in front of motor traffic, the government asked Charles to intercede. Charles's attitude was that Fenton's breaches of road traffic laws were civil misdemeanours and, unless there was a threat to national security, he was reluctant to intervene. But then, in December 1939, Fenton breached security at the air force's base at Parap in an incident that tested both the fortitude of the sentry involved and the empathy of his commander.

Fenton left his Tiger Moth at the temporary Parap base and went to fetch his friend, 'Bill' Short, so they could fly to a good duck shooting location. When they arrived back at Parap's gate, the RAAF sentry demanded the doctor give the official password. Fenton claimed he had no knowledge that the RAAF were in control of the base and, after complaining, *'When did this rot start?',* requested the sentry call the commanding officer. The sentry politely told the doctor he would not under any circumstance leave his post.

Fenton later wrote:
> It was a ticklish decision to make, but I was relying on the effect of surprise. Without warning, I let the clutch out and trod hard on the accelerator. We went in like a rocket through the gate and around the corner on two wheels. To this day, I do not know what the sentry's reactions were—I was too busy to look back. There were some dreadful moments of suspense during which I expected to hear (or feel) a shot, and then around a second corner and safe behind a building.

The men took off in the Moth and flew on their merry way, shot ducks, and returned to Darwin. The next day, two RAAF sergeants called on Fenton with instructions from Charles that a court martial for the doctor would be held at RAAF Parap to *'teach him a lesson'* and that he would be formally arrested at 6 pm at the Club Hotel. The public arrest of Fenton, a well-known and popular identity, was a shock to all. Resisting detention, Fenton shouted for

'There were some dreadful moments of suspense during which I expected to hear (or feel) a shot, and then around a second corner and safe behind a building.'

all to hear, *'I'm a civilian and you can't interfere with me!'* Fenton was handcuffed and hustled into a Black Maria and taken to Tin City.

The court martial was conducted in front of more than 100 airmen. Charles selected his three most notorious and recalcitrant airmen as president, defending council and prosecuting officer. After the prosecutor issued the charge that Dr Fenton had broken the barrier gate without the password, the defence intervened by stating that the guard, Leading Aircraftsman Smith, was *'off his rocker'*. The prosecuting officer cross-examined the defence about this allegation. The RAAF's doctor, Charles Leleu, confirmed that Smith was being treated for craziness. The defence demanded that the case be dismissed. The judge intervened and said the defence witnesses were probably crazy also. Finally, Fenton called his star witness, Bill Short, who claimed the guard had shot him. The prosecutor ordered Short to show the court his wound; he replied, *'In front of all these men? I'm too shy.'* Following an uproar from the gallery, the president ordered Short be publicly debagged.

Fenton explained:

> Half a dozen tough-looking airmen bounded down and seized the unfortunate witness; in a twinkling, they had torn off his trousers, and revealed to the interested assembly a plump and rosy posterior. In addition, there, on the off side cheek, grotesque and monstrous, was a mass of adhesive plaster in the shape of a gigantic swastika. It brought the house down!

The court found the doctor guilty and fined him a keg of beer. The sentence proved popular, as both officers and the ranks had already begun imbibing. In his autobiography, Fenton wrote that he was shocked to learn the keg had been tapped well before the court martial had started. Charles received no more complaints from the government about the doctor's behaviour.

The RAAF was soon to assist the administration in a more serious matter. Charles felt that *'12 Squadron had an obligation to support the town and its people as much as possible, particularly in times of crisis.'*

The prosecutor ordered Short to show the court his wound; he replied, 'In front of all these men? I'm too shy.'

'12 Squadron had an obligation to support the town and its people as much as possible, particularly in times of crisis.'

Darwin Defence Co-ordination Committee, Darwin 1940. Central three from left: Group Captain Eaton RAAF, Captain Thomas RN and Colonel Robertson AIF.

The defence of north-west Australia was entrusted to the Darwin Defence Co-ordination Committee (DDCC). In 1940 the three-member Committee comprised the Chairman, Captain EP Thomas RN, known as 'God' because of his reputation as a martinet with a touch of humanity; the army member, Colonel 'Red Robbie' Robertson, who later became a well-respected general; and Charles, who held the junior rank of the three members.[2] Their responsibilities included defence strategies, interactions with the administration, the detention of aliens living near military establishments and joint training exercises. The DDCC also considered the appointment of suitable chaplains:

> It is also desired to stress the extreme importance of spiritual supervision of the right calibre for the members of the Defence Forces in view of the numerous opportunities for mental and moral guidance which obtain (sic) under the somewhat crude and unusual conditions of living at Darwin.[3]

In April 1940, the DDCC was confronted by a strike on Darwin's waterfront. Airman Wilson-Smith reported that the Darwin wharf labourers caused a lot of trouble in 1940, the first year of the war. His mother sent him a box of canned food by sea *'but the wharfies controlled all goods from the ship to the shore—my case "fell off" the wharf into a dingy and of course wasn't seen again!'.* Amar, in her study of RAAF Darwin, wrote of robbery on the wharfs:

> Reports indicate evidence of pillage of liquor, tinned goods, and foodstuffs, in short, anything readily saleable or usable. Pilfering of items in transit appears to have been accepted as a matter of course.

The SS *Montoro* had docked in Darwin with 800 tons of coal for the town's power station and the navy. After unloading half the cargo, the wharf labourers went on strike for dirt money after arbitration refused an additional award. As the strikers refused to work, the DDCC decided that service personnel would be employed to unload the remaining 420 tons. Charles paraded all RAAF personnel, spoke on the critical coal shortage at the power station and called for volunteers to unload the ship. Fisher wrote that they were all fed up with the wharfies and the airmen volunteered *'almost to the man'*. Working in 20-man shifts, the airmen unloaded the *Montoro* in record time, the navy manning the davits and the army driving the trucks. Charles and Dr Leleu shovelled coal down in the hold with the men. Fisher wrote, *'Yes, he led by example. A great man. With that infernal pipe in his mouth!'* Charles, having led the airmen openly against the unions, earned himself *'the eternal hostility of Socialist Left'*.[4]

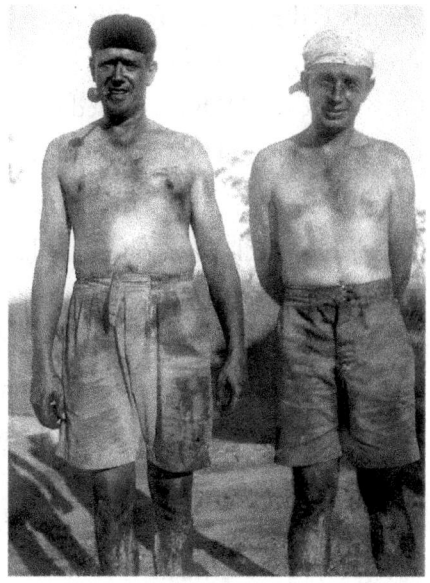

Charles (with pipe) and Dr Charles Leleu after their shift unloading coal from the SS Montoro, *April 1940.*

The DDCC also had a confrontation with the Northern Territory's Administrator, Charles Abbott, over the employment of Aboriginal people within the armed services. Charles had not forgotten the valuable contribution of his tracker companions on the long trek into the Tanami in 1929 and the help of desert tribesmen when searching for the *Golden Quest II* 19 months later. The RAAF contingent in Darwin had increased and, with the construction of the new base, Charles had engaged Aboriginal workers for primary jobs as gardeners and to maintain the bomb bays. This allowed trained airmen to be released for more skilled duties. Abbott wrote to the DDCC on 29 April 1940 that he was *'against any system of recruiting native labour from Aboriginal areas along the Northern Territory Coast or from Bathurst and Melville Islands'*.

He also threatened to withdraw the Aboriginal workers Charles had already employed on a small but regular wage with sustenance rations. On 6 May, the DDCC replied curtly to Abbott that every able-bodied man would be required immediately for 'Service with the Colours'.

Charles, in an effort to landscape the new base, arranged with prison authorities to allow prisoners to plant trees. Street names were given arboreal names that reflected Charles' forester days in India. His son Peter remembers how convicted murderers happily gathered coconuts for planting by climbing the palms and kicking the nuts down with their feet. In his submission to the Air Board, Charles stressed that the RAAF would need at least 30 Aboriginal workers when 12 Squadron moved to the new base. He recommended an alteration to previous policies to cater for *'changing times and the present emergency'*. He eventually got his way. One working Tiwi family from Melville even adopted the Eaton name and added it to their tribal ones.

The first United States Army Air Corps unit to visit Australia under command of Major (later General) Emmett 'Rosie' O'Donnell: Boeing-B17 bomber of 14 Bombardment Squadron under RAAF guard, September 1941.

Daisy (of the Tiwi Islands) and Charles Stuart, Darwin 1941.

20 War Games, 1941

With the war drawing near in 1941, apart from general exercises, full scale manoeuvres were held by the Darwin Defence Committee which consisted of the Navy, an A.I.F. Brigade and the RAAF. The direction of these operations was placed under me and although it is easy to say so now, what happened during the exercises was a lesson to be learned and what actually did happen to Darwin when the Japanese came into the war.

Charles Eaton, 1973

As 1941 unfolded, the Darwin-based squadrons continued their coastal patrols and reconnaissance over the Timor Sea and Arafura Sea. The Australian military presumed that all Japanese fishing boats had a naval reserve officer aboard. Wing Commander Sam Balmer located a Japanese lugger hiding in the island-studded Buccaneer Archipelago off Western Australia. He flew so low over the lugger that his aircraft's slipstream severely rocked the boat, causing the crew to shake their fists at the aircraft. Was this perhaps the first, even if inconsequential, act of aggression between Australia and Japan?

Many of 12 Squadron's original members had been promoted and transferred south to help train Australia's expanding air force. Cec Fisher boarded a ship with the first batch to be transferred south. He wrote: *'Moth came down to see us off, and with tears in his eyes, thanked each and every one of us for a job well done.'*

In late February, Charles was instructed to head a reconnaissance of Timor, Ambon, Dutch New Guinea and the Tanimbar Islands in what is now eastern Indonesia. On the reconnaissance, Charles and Wing Commander Bill Hely posed as civilians to try to bamboozle Japanese agents. The Station's diary recorded, *'Acting on most secret instructions from the Air Board, Group Captain C. Eaton A.F.C. left by flying boat for the DUTCH EAST INDIES.'* While he was away, 13 Squadron had the task of seeking the German battleship, *Scharnhorst*. Six new Lockheed Hudson bombers searched the Indian Ocean for four days to no avail. Charles said later that his pilots' main worry was that they may miss the war altogether!

With the Sino-Japanese war escalating, the political situation deteriorating in Asia and The Netherlands at war with Germany, the two RAAF officers were warmly welcomed by the Netherland East Indies (NEI) authorities. This was in sharp contrast with Charles' mysterious visit to Dutch-controlled West Timor in 1938 where he was allegedly placed under house arrest before being told to leave the NEI by the Dutch authorities.

Charles and Hely considered an enemy invasion of West Timor through Portuguese territory (now Timor-Leste) was unlikely because of the mountainous terrain and poor ground communications. The Atambua Airfield in the north was defended by six officers and soldiers armed with rifles and cutlasses. The Penfoei Airfield near Kupang in the south was defended by four Dutch officers and 100 local soldiers. The Australians thought the airfield limited because of short runways and limited facilities. However, Kupang had a flying boat base and room for further expansion.

Charles decided to select potential targets sooner rather than later:

> When I was in Timor, I took some 130 odd photographs of probable targets in Timor should the Japanese ever occupy that Island. One of the targets which impressed me most was the Mina River Bridge—a bridge some 29 miles from Kupang, connecting the Hinterland of West Timor to its capital. The bridge was supported by very strong concrete pillars and was fairly narrow.

Exactly three years after he photographed the bridge, Charles witnessed its destruction by squadrons under his command. It was one of his many '*excitements*' in life (Vignette 22).

Charles and Hely then flew in a Dutch Dornier-DO24K flying boat to Ambon, 600 miles north-west of Darwin. They considered Ambon's Laha Airstrip to be strategically important but in need of lengthening and resurfacing. Laha's location commanded a strategic arc between the Celebes, Halmahera, Dutch New Guinea and Australia's north-western approaches. They reported that Laha would be vital as a forward base for the defence of Australia and that it was already defended by anti-aircraft guns and soldiers armed with automatic weapons. At Buru, 70 miles north-west of Ambon, the Dutch had an emergency landing ground at Namlea. The airmen recommended to the Dutch authorities that Namlea's runway be lengthened and facilities developed before RAAF bombers could land.

In Baro, Dutch New Guinea, the Australians inspected the aerodrome and flying boat facilities. They found a reasonably well-developed and equipped base which they considered '*of strategic interest as an advanced refuelling base for landplanes and flying boats operating to the north of New Guinea*'. Finally, they went to the Tanimbar Islands, some 300 miles north of Darwin. The islands had no airstrip but Charles proposed that a refuelling stop would be essential if RAAF aircraft were to reinforce Ambon in any emergency. They inspected possible landing grounds near Saumlaki on the island of Jamdina.

'When I was in Timor, I took some 130 odd photographs of probable targets in Timor should the Japanese ever occupy that Island.'

Charles wrote:

> A possible site for a landing ground was investigated. The site lies on a ridge approximately ¼ mile from the village of Saumlaki. The site is overgrown with dense scrub and tall grass and cannot be improved without cutting strips. It appears that a strip approximately 700 x 100 metres may be possible. On departure from Saumlaki, two other sites were inspected from the air. These lie on small islands S E and S W of Saumlaki and from the air appear to be good natural sites but may be swampy.[1]

Returning to Darwin, Charles confirmed to headquarters that an understanding had been reached with the Netherlands East Indies Air Force (NEIAF) to lengthen the runways at Penfoei and Laha and to extend existing buildings to accommodate at least two RAAF squadrons. The NEIAF was also expected to provide bomb and ammunition storage and build up reserve food supplies and hospital facilities for Australian military forces. He reported that he had stressed to the Dutch officers the need to examine the three possible airstrip sites in the Tanimbar Islands. His report stated:

> (i) We should press for permission to use Koepang and Ambon now. The use of Koepang would materially assist our reconnaissance and trade protection in the north-west area and occasional landings at Ambon would familiarise personnel of No 13 Squadron with the conditions of operations at Ambon and help promote effective liaison. Unless we can do this now, we cannot expect efficient operations immediately on landing at these points in time of emergency.
>
> (ii) It is apparent that if we are to provide support for Army forces at Koepang and Ambon, then this must be done before an emergency arises. Australian forces in Malaya are still in the process of settling in, although it is some time since they landed in Malaya.

The outcome of their mission was significant; it promoted strategic policies for Australia's defence and initiated contacts between the RAAF and the NEIAF. Charles concluded, *'The visit proved most interesting and instructive and after a special report was made, some steps were taken to obtain co-operation*

'The visit proved most interesting and instructive and after a special report was made, some steps were taken to obtain co-operation with the Dutch Forces.'

with the Dutch Forces.' One immediate outcome of the new relationship was the arrival on 16 May 1941 of three Dutch Dornier flying boats on Darwin Harbour under the command of Captain of Boats, Baron van Lawick, and three NEIAF Glenn Martin-166 bombers at the Six Mile base under Captain G Roos. Charles handed each Dutch aircraft a message of welcome from the Secretary of the Air Board:

> The Minister of Air and the Chief of the Air Staff extend (a) hearty welcome and cordial greetings to yourself and air crews under your command on the important occasion of (the) first visit to Australia by Netherlands East Indies Military aircraft. Your visit and personnel contacts during your stay at Darwin cannot but strengthen the bonds of friendship between our two countries and result in mutual benefits to both air forces.

The visitors were accommodated and entertained by Australia's air force. The two forces carried out flying exercises during the next two days, with flight crews being interchanged for mutual experience. On 17 May the RAAF officers mess entertained 86 for dinner including Northern Territory Administrator Abbott, Brigadier Steele and Captain Thomas. A man for occasions, Charles ordered a black-out drill:

> Immediately after the dinner a practice black-out took place, and was very successfully conducted. Officers and men of the R.A.A.F. reported to their allotted posts with alacrity. Such aircraft that were detailed took off, and the proceedings were carried out impressively and without a hitch.

Visit of NEIAF Glenn Martin aircraft from Dutch Timor, May 1941

Official inspection of 13 Squadron by Governor General, Lord Gowrie, in Darwin, July 1941. Sam Balmer is being introduced to the Governor General by Charles Eaton.

When the NEIAF's aircraft returned to Kupang three days later, they were accompanied by five RAAF Hudsons led by Wing Commander Sam Balmer. The RAAF flight flew on to Laha and Namlea in the Molucca Islands, returning to Darwin on 24 May. Charles was gratified his recommendations for regular visits to Ambon had made a start. Shortly after, Charles and Sam Balmer attended a conference in Melbourne with the Chief of the Air Staff to discuss advanced operation bases in the NEI. Despite Charles having proposed an immediate presence in the NEI following his tour in March, no RAAF squadrons were deployed to Timor or Ambon until six months later—6 December—when 2 Squadron was dispatched to Timor and 13 Squadron to Laha in support of the AIF's Gull Force and the NEI army. The Japanese attacked Pearl Harbour the following day.

It was considered likely that America would declare war if the British Empire was attacked in the Far East. In preparation for this, in July 1941 two United States Navy (USN) Catalina-PBY flying boats from Hawai'i made an inaugural visit to Darwin to undertake a preliminary survey for an alternative route to the US-controlled Philippines from Honolulu. The American officers were ordered to liaise with their Australian counterparts, take note of their war strategies, inspect the air force's infrastructure and assess the performance of its aircraft. The two Catalinas carried a representative of the Marine Corps, Lieutenant Colonel WJ Wallace, and two United States Army Air Corps (USAAC) officers, Major A Muelenberg and Captain B Hubbard. The latter disembarked at Port Moresby, leaving Major Muelenberg to become the first member of USAAC to visit Australia in an official capacity. The two Catalinas were piloted by Lieutenant Commander F O'Beirne USN and Lieutenant TH Moorer USN.[2] On his return to Hawai'i, O'Beirne commented on the excellent cooperation the RAAF gave his flight team and said no confidential information was withheld. He added that most of the information was obtained from '*Group Captain Charles Eaton, his Operations Officer, Wing Commander J.R. Balmer, and Wing Commander W.H. Garing*'.

The American officers were ordered to liaise with their Australian counterparts, take note of their war strategies, inspect the air force's infrastructure and assess the performance of its aircraft.

O'Beirne noted that after his crew's stay-over at the Darwin base:

> The officers' mess treasurer, acting on instructions from the Commanding Officer, would accept no payment for the services provided during our two day stop-over ... The morale of the R.A.A.F appears to be excellent. The officers are unanimous in their desire for overseas service. These same feelings were noticed in the lower ranks and in the Royal Australian Army stationed at Rabaul.

As the war came closer, Charles initiated joint exercises with the other services; he appeared to relish directing such 'war games'. In one drill, the RAAF attacked an 'enemy invasion convoy' led by the corvette HMAS *Bendigo*, which acted as an aircraft carrier. Sam Balmer commanded the defending bombers based at the auxiliary airstrip at Daly Waters, south of Darwin, while Charles remained overall controller at Darwin. The second day saw a RAAF hanger 'blown up' and, at sea, the *Bendigo* was strafed by Hudsons flying at 600 feet. The RAN seamen watched in admiration as the practice bombs landed barely 60 feet abeam of the vessel while RAAF observers on the corvette ran for cover. The exercise had its lighter moments; on the final day of the exercise one pilot, 'Bill' Ross, was apprehended when found smoking on the tarmac. After being told that the base was under attack Ross was ordered to explain his behaviour to Charles: *I'm sorry Sir, but I was shot down on the first day and don't exist. The hanger was bombed out of existence yesterday and doesn't exist. I wouldn't have thought either of us were visible.*

The air force continued live exercises when a passing Royal Navy County-class cruiser was hijacked to provide yet another opportunity for the RAAF to practise precision bombing. Eaton also organised a combined operation with HMAS *Westralia,* with three Wirraways of 12 Squadron as the attacking force. Between 5–7 August 1941 a substantial day–night exercise took place to test an 'Appreciation and Plan for Defence for Darwin'. Naval ships, three army battalions of 23 Infantry Brigade and the two squadrons were involved. Charles was appointed director with Major Wheeler as his assistant. The combatants were designated 'Blue Force' as the defenders and 'Red Force' as the attacking enemy. The entire town of Darwin was designated as a battle zone and all civilians were expected to cooperate by obeying sirens and black-outs. Hotels were closed and military sentries, in conjunction with the local police, were on duty in the town throughout the three-day operation.

As director, Charles made the exercise as realistic as possible despite the shortage of training ammunition and fireworks; otherwise, he wrote, the value would be negligible. More than 20,000 blank .303 cartridges, thunder flashes and smoke generators were issued to provide some authenticity. Incendiary bombs were made by soaking bagging in kerosene. Fire-fighting teams were allocated to particular localities; umpires were appointed to ensure the rules of the game were upheld and to report structural damage and casualties to the wardens. Lessons learnt during the exercise prompted one army officer to recommend: '*It is suggested that a lecture be given in Darwin to civilian officials on the methods used by the Nazi 5th Column in France and Poland ... and also give them an outline of what we are fighting for and what we are fighting against.*'

'I'm sorry Sir, but I was shot down on the first day and don't exist. The hanger was bombed out of existence yesterday and doesn't exist. I wouldn't have thought either of us were visible.'

'It is suggested that a lecture be given in Darwin to civilian officials on the methods used by the Nazi 5th Column in France and Poland ... and also give them an outline of what we are fighting for and what we are fighting against.'

In the same month, Washington directed the USAAC in Hawaii to form a squadron under the command of Major, later General, Emmett 'Rosie' O'Donnell. The new 14 Bombardment Squadron of nine unmarked Boeing-B17 Flying Fortresses flew from Hawai'i to Darwin, arriving on 10 September, and continued to the Philippines two days later—becoming the first flight of land-based bombers to cross the Pacific. The squadron flew over the Japanese-occupied Caroline Islands without navigation lights and radio contact to avoid an international incident. The mint-new B17 American aircraft created a positive impression on the Australian airmen.

Charles observed:

> Of great interest, too, was the visit of a Squadron of American Flying Fortresses to Darwin in September 1941. These aircraft were preceded by 2 American Catalinas who flew out to Darwin from Honolulu to ascertain the state of the Darwin aerodrome for these big aircraft.
>
> I was very disappointed that after being offered by the Americans to return with them in their Catalinas to Honolulu and come back with the Squadron of Fortresses that a 'Not Repeat Not Approved' came back from higher authority. Also, when the American aircraft left for the Philippines, another 'Not Repeat Not Approved' came to go on with them and then return via Singapore. However, full co-operation in those days was not always realised. Also, in the middle of 1941, we had a visit from a Dutch Squadron. I think I can safely say that both the Dutch and Americans were very impressed with the standard of our war preparation and training and our general ideas.

American navigator, Lieutenant FR Cappelletti, recalled in retrospect: *'We could consider ourselves as pioneers in view of the fact that navigation aids across the Pacific were non-existent.'*

Lieutenant EJ Sponable added:

> Port Moresby was our first contact with the RAAF personnel. They were extremely helpful in assisting us, getting our airplane serviced and taking care of all our needs. I must say I have a very lasting and vivid impression of Darwin...The RAAF base there was very good and well-equipped, people were absolutely marvellous to us and everyone had a very good time.

In fact, when we landed, RAAF people escorted us to their club for cold beer. It was the best I have ever tasted, either before or since. On departure, to the last man, all of us had fond and lasting memories of the gracious hospitality we received from the Australians. Little did any of us realise that in a few short months we would be back on Australian soil, each engaged in a war of survival.

'Little did any of us realise that in a few short months we would be back on Australian soil, each engaged in a war of survival.'

Owen Griffiths RAN, wrote that the Americans were feted at their *'palatial'* RAAF Headquarters. The American crews were too respectful to state formally that the only military planes they saw were a few Lockheed Hudsons and Wirraways. The USAAC thought the capacity of the RAAF base would prove inadequate if war broke out and they would need alternative bases inland. Captain Colin Kelly, a B17 pilot, presented his shoulder epaulettes to Bea Eaton, who kept them as a memento for many years. Kelly, who was killed after attacking the battleship *Haruna* during the Japanese invasion of The Philippines, was posthumously awarded the American Distinguished Service Cross and became a national hero.

After the Japanese attack on Pearl Harbor on 7 December 1941, Australia provided important bases in the Northern Territory for American fighter and bomber aircraft. USAAC aircraft were the backbone of the counter-offensive against the first Japanese bombing of Darwin on 19 February 1942. Of the 11 American Curtiss-P40 fighters involved, only one survived. The American pilots who lost their lives included their commander, Major Floyd Pell. The now abandoned airstrips of Pell, Livingstone and Strauss, all close to Darwin, are permanent memorials to those American pilots who gave their lives in Australia's defence.

Ambon was over-run by Japanese forces in late January 1942 and Timor three weeks later. After a hopeless and out-gunned attempt to defend both islands, the RAAF units were withdrawn to Australia. Many fine pilots were lost, including Wing Commander Dallas Scott DFC, a well-respected officer formerly of pre-war 21 Squadron. As officer-in-charge of the advance base, he had remained at Laha Airport to destroy ciphers and equipment and ensure as many RAAF airmen as possible were evacuated. He was captured after attempting to escape and, with Flight Lieutenant Vyner White of 13 Squadron, executed by the Japanese military on 6 February. Vyner White was the first air force officer to be awarded the DFC in the Pacific war. Although Charles did not have a resentful nature (as his time as a PoW in WWI attested), the summary executions in Ambon left a bitter taste. In 1947, while Australian Consul-General to the NEI, Charles visited the graves of those executed RAAF officers to pay homage to his former comrades.

However, under somewhat controversial circumstances, Charles was to miss the arrival of the USAAC P-40 aircraft and the bombing of Darwin. Charles and Group Captain Scherger, commander of No. 2 Flying Training School at Forrest Hill near Wagga Wagga in southern NSW, were ordered to exchange commands during the first week of October 1941. There is speculation the transfer was linked to the friction, as noted by historian Alan Powell, between the RAN's Captain Thomas and Charles over joint staff accommodation and a lack of communication over sea searches. Powell noted that Captain Thomas had complained to the navy about Charles' alleged shortcomings, saying Charles '*had many admirable quantities but experience has shown that in emergencies, his judgement is not invariably well balanced due, to a very severe Inferiority Complex.*

The service backgrounds of the two Englishmen, Thomas and Eaton, were of marked contrast. Thomas, the product of a traditional and rigid Royal Navy officer training regime, was on secondment to a dominion navy. Eaton, who after 16 years in the country had become a declared Australian, had risen from the ranks though a series of situations where physical survival was required, at times almost on a daily basis; no doubt the lessons learnt during this time moulded his temperament. Evidence of his morph from an Englishman to an Australian may be linked to the fact that few who served with him knew much of his service in WWI and India.

Professor Powell said that although Charles was well regarded he was *'not a disciplinarian'* when compared with the Darwin Fortress' naval and army commanders. Conversely, in his book *The Shadow's Edge,* Powell wrote that the original 12 and 13 Squadrons in Darwin were *'well trained and disciplined'*. Both units were formed under Charles' direction and control. One aspect of Charles' character was beyond doubt—his determination and tenacity. He was well known to confront his superiors if he thought they were wrong and inefficient. He fought RAAF high command for Darwin to have its own command structure. He arbitrarily instituted a wet canteen for non-commissioned airmen, which was contrary to practice at that time.

Airmen Wilson-Smith and Cec Fisher wrote that the efficiency of the RAAF and *'our late intrusion into Darwin'* resulted in an envious response. They pointed out the air force had a fully operational squadron that provided *'a bit of glamour'* for the township while the navy had only a wireless station. They added cheekily that the RAN had *'no ships, not even a canoe'*. They suggested the difficulties between Charles and Thomas may have been triggered by the coal strike, claiming the RAN had *'procrastinated over petty things'* while Charles got on with the job of unloading the SS *Montoro*. This was not the last time Charles received a broadside from the sea; in 1945 he had another confrontation with a navy, this time the Royal Navy's Pacific Fleet (Vignette 24).

Sergeant Truscott said Eaton hand-picked his airmen for Darwin. When asked if he knew Eaton well, Truscott said, *'Old Charles Eaton, yes, very well ... I got on well with him ... Yes, he was a good man for the job up there.'*

Fisher, writing in 1995 about Eaton not being a strict disciplinarian, said:
> He did not need to be because leading from the front, he inspired by example ... he inspired self-discipline and squadron pride among all ... he had a most distinguished reputation in air force circles and in aviation generally. He had real experience in aviation in tropical conditions and was widely respected for his achievements ... he displayed great qualities of organisation and leadership in establishing the bases at Parap and at the

Five Mile [sic], and set the pattern for air force operations along the entire Northern Territory and Kimberly coastlines.

Perhaps it was time for Charles to leave as he had already served two years in Darwin, a long period for a tropical posting. The citation for the decoration he received on transfer from Darwin read:

> This officer has carried out his duties at Darwin with marked success, and it is due to his untiring energy and example that the operational units there have obtained a high degree of efficiency, especially in view of the fact that for a considerable time it was necessary for the unit under his control to work from two separate stations and under improvised conditions. This officer has, on all occasions, set a high standard of flying. His example, energy, cheerful outlook and tact in handling men at Darwin, have done much to maintain the standard and morale of airmen at this isolated station.

Perhaps the most definite acknowledgement or decoration Charles received was from a young cattle station mechanic. Early in 1940, 18-year-old Ron Barker from Tennant Creek arrived in Darwin to join '*Moth Eaton's Air Force ... that old bastard ... he really led us from the front.*'[3]

At Charles' official farewell concert the men sang:

We want to go home
We want to leave this aerodrome
I don't want to live in Darwin no more

Where Harry Best's boots
Cover half the mess floor
Down south where I want to be
Where there's plenty of sheilas for free—

Group Captain Eaton
Around the bush don't be beating
And please send us home.

Charles' own views on the reasons for his transfer are unknown, but he indicated his disappointment at being given what he considered a non-active role in the war. Charles explained:

'Moth Eaton's Air Force ... that old bastard ... he really led us from the front.'

It seemed at one time that the Darwin area was well prepared for war, but unfortunately even although combined options exercises had been held a lesson should have been learned. When war came, Darwin was hit fairly badly, but not quite as badly as most people imagined. Until the middle of 1941, the defence of the Darwin area was the direct responsibility of the commanders on the spot to their various service boards, but unfortunately towards the end of 1941, the Air Force for instance, was placed under a Northern Command with Headquarters at Townsville and this Headquarters also looked after various bases as far east as the Solomon Islands. Although a fight was made, there was no alteration in this set-up and it was not for a week or so before war was declared against Japan that Darwin was again put under its own command.

However, with a new Area (Command) forming there, it was too late, and, with a change of personnel unfamiliar to Darwin conditions or requirements, assisted to make the debacle which eventually occurred. However, this was soon got over and Darwin became the main base in Australia for hitting back at the Japanese and eventually stopping enemy shipping to all eastern islands of the Netherlands Indies. Darwin will certainly come again after the war and, I think, will come again in a very big way, particularly as an air base for civil aircraft from overseas and the main bulwark for Australia.

6,500 RAAF personnel parading to celebrate the Battle of Britain, Flemington Racecourse, Melbourne, 1942. Charles Eaton, on the dais, taking the salute.

'Darwin will certainly come again after the war and, I think, will come again in a very big way, particularly as an air base for civil aircraft from overseas and the main bulwark for Australia.'

21 Training the Empire, 1942

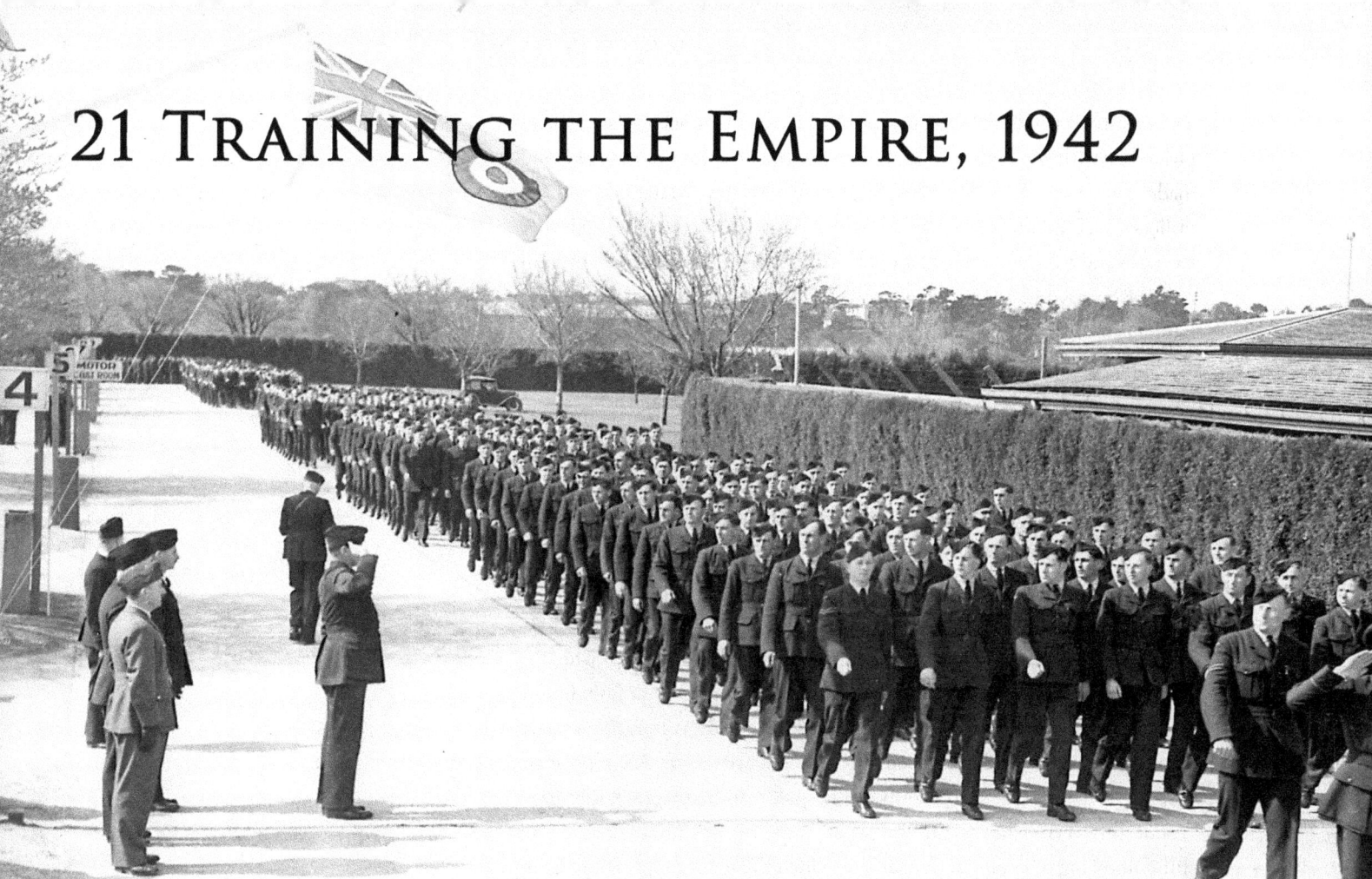

The grand and apparently simple concept of the Empire Training Scheme was so enthusiastically received in all quarters that many of its practical difficulties remained hidden during the strenuous months devoted to establishing schools in Canada, Australia and New Zealand. [1]

Normally in wartime, officers of Charles' age and rank were either assigned to administration, training or a station command; they were rarely operational. Charles was disappointed at being transferred to a training command after being in an independent operational role; however, his original appointment in 1925 had been to train air force pilots.

Describing his departure from Darwin, Charles wrote:

> It was on 10 October 1941 that I left my command and proceeded south by road ... I felt at the time that I was leaving a country I knew very well with most of my great friends and that certainly proved true.

The new road from Alice Springs to Darwin was then being planned and pushed on with and I was very anxious to see the preparations for war being made. The road had not been completed from Darwin to Mataranka and in a utility truck I did the journey along the old north–south track through very tortuous and tedious terrain. I had a break of a few days to visit Elsey Station on the Roper River. A lot has been written about the Elsey by Mrs Gunn, and her *We of the Never Never* gives a very fine description of Elsey Station and its surroundings. There is no question that the Station is a most delightful place and it was really in the 'Never Never' as described in Mrs Gunn's book.

The manager of the station and his wife, Mr and Mrs Giles, were pleased to see me and gave me a good break for three or four days. The homestead, situated on the Roper River is most picturesque and a few miles from the station, the lily lagoon is probably one of the most famous swamps in Australia. It is very different now, but at that time, turkey, geese and duck were just there for the shooting and I thoroughly enjoyed my few days stay at the Elsey.

From there I proceeded back to Mataranka and then to Birdum which is the end of the railway to Darwin, a distance of some 330 miles where I met the new road to Alice Springs. After passing Daly Waters, Newcastle Waters, Tennant Creek, I arrived amongst old friends at Alice Springs. The highway was good—certainly, a fine piece of engineering, and gave wonderful service during the war when shipping was unobtainable and difficult owing to enemy action, and provided the main supply route from the south to Darwin.

Meanwhile Bea and seven-year-old Charles Stuart stayed behind in Darwin to await evacuation to southern Australia. Peter was at boarding school in Victoria and Aileen was waiting to join the air force's nursing service. Charles Stuart clearly remembers the upheaval and being most disappointed he was not allowed to stay to see any bombs that 'may be dropped' in the future. They were eventually evacuated out of the Northern Territory by ship to Queensland via the Torres Strait. He will never forget the poignant farewells at their departure with Gracie Field's song *Wish me good luck as you wave me goodbye* playing from the Darwin dock. They disembarked in Brisbane before joining Charles in Wagga Wagga.

Conditions on at least one of the evacuee ships, HMAT *Zealandia*, were hellish due to overcrowding with Darwin evacuees, sick soldiers returning from Singapore and 100 Japanese internees. Janet Dickinson wrote that the *Zealandia* had not been debugged or cleaned for nine months and, as one female evacuee stated, '*the smells from the bowels of the ship ... made my morning sickness worse*'; she never left her cabin. Another 200 Japanese embarked at Thursday Island, adding to the confusion and increasing the number of passengers to 1349. The *Zealandia* received yet another name, 'a floating brothel', as some female evacuees formed relationships with the crew and sick soldiers. Dickinson observed that some of '*their activities took place on the top deck, often in full view of children and adults alike*'.[2] The soldiers guarding the Japanese went on strike as they did not receive a beer ration. There were too many people on board and too few lifeboats, but the children thought the lifeboat drills fun. The *Zealandia* returned to Darwin just in time to be sunk by Japanese aircraft on 19 February 1942. Charles Stuart cannot remember what ship he was evacuated on but thought it may be the SS *Montoro*.

The idea for a Commonwealth aircrew training scheme had come from a series of meetings of senior Empire leaders. Initially, some 20,000 pilots and 30,000 aircrew—including navigators, observers, and wireless/air gunners—were to be trained in the United Kingdom, Canada, Australia and then Rhodesia under the Empire Air Training Scheme (EATS). Even small island colonies in the West Indies mustered contingents and Fiji sent 31 volunteers. Once trained, the aircrews were expected to serve in their respective air forces or in composite RAF squadrons. In December 1941, Australia was training some 8300 crews in 35 establishments, including the Wagga base, which was classified as No. 2 Service Flying Training School.

After only six months at Wagga, Charles was transferred to Ascot Vale in Melbourne as commander of the RAAF's Engineering School. He wrote his impressions of the training scheme:

'Some of their activities took place on the top deck, often in full view of children and adults alike'.

I took over command of the Wagga Training School on 24th October and there I had my first insight into the Empire Air Training Scheme, which had then been in progress for nearly two years. I was amazed at the progress that had been made and there is no question that the R.A.A.F. effort was a very worthy one to supply the aircrews that evidently were to take such a tremendous part in winning the war. After being concerned with operations I did not relish my job, but it had to be done and I soon found the work most interesting.

I was at Wagga when war broke out against Japan and formed 2 reserve squadrons, which were to be used in the event of any great emergency. I had a week of operations trying to get the Squadron into operational shape ... It was a great interest to all air and ground crew and what might have taken place if the Japanese had landed in Australia.

After I had been at Wagga for about six months, the station closed down as a Flying Training School and become an Aircraft Depot, and I, much against my will, was posted to Ascot Vale in charge of the Engineering School. Again, I found the Engineering School a wonderful effort on the part of the RAAF for the training of ground staff, and at one time, I had over 10,000 officers and airmen at Ascot Vale under going training of some description. I well remember the day when we were commanded by the King to hold throughout Australia a Thanksgiving Service for the successful ending of the Battle for Britain. 6500 officers and airmen marched past me to the stand at the Flemington Race course for a wonderful combined church service.

'At one time, I had over 10,000 officers and airmen at Ascot Vale undergoing training of some description.'

At the Battle of Britain parade, an incident occurred that completely circumvented all military protocols. When passing abreast of the saluting dais, a non-commissioned officer suddenly bellowed, *'Jeez Christ ... Moth Eaton.'* Charles allegedly replied, *'The latter ... CONTINUE.'* Evidently, the airman had served with Charles on one of the desert searches and the shock of seeing Charles in such an exalted position completely overrode his composure and disciplinary training.

In April 1943, Charles' prayers to return to operations were answered:

Although the appointment of C.O. of the Engineering School at Ascot Vale was again full of interest I was most pleased at the beginning of 1943 to once more be posted North to form No 72 Wing which was to go in and establish an air base at Merauke to prevent the Japanese from coming down the south coast of New Guinea to Port Moresby. At Townsville I formed 72 Wing Headquarters with the help of a grand officer, F/Lt. Janes, and on 28 April 1943 I left Townsville with my Wing Headquarters by Empire flying boat for Merauke.

'The River War'. AIF and RAAF personnel with Kaja Kaja boatmen en route to Boepol on the Merauke River, West Papua, 6–9 May 1943. (Photograph by Charles Eaton from the bow.)

22 'The River War'—West Papua, 1943

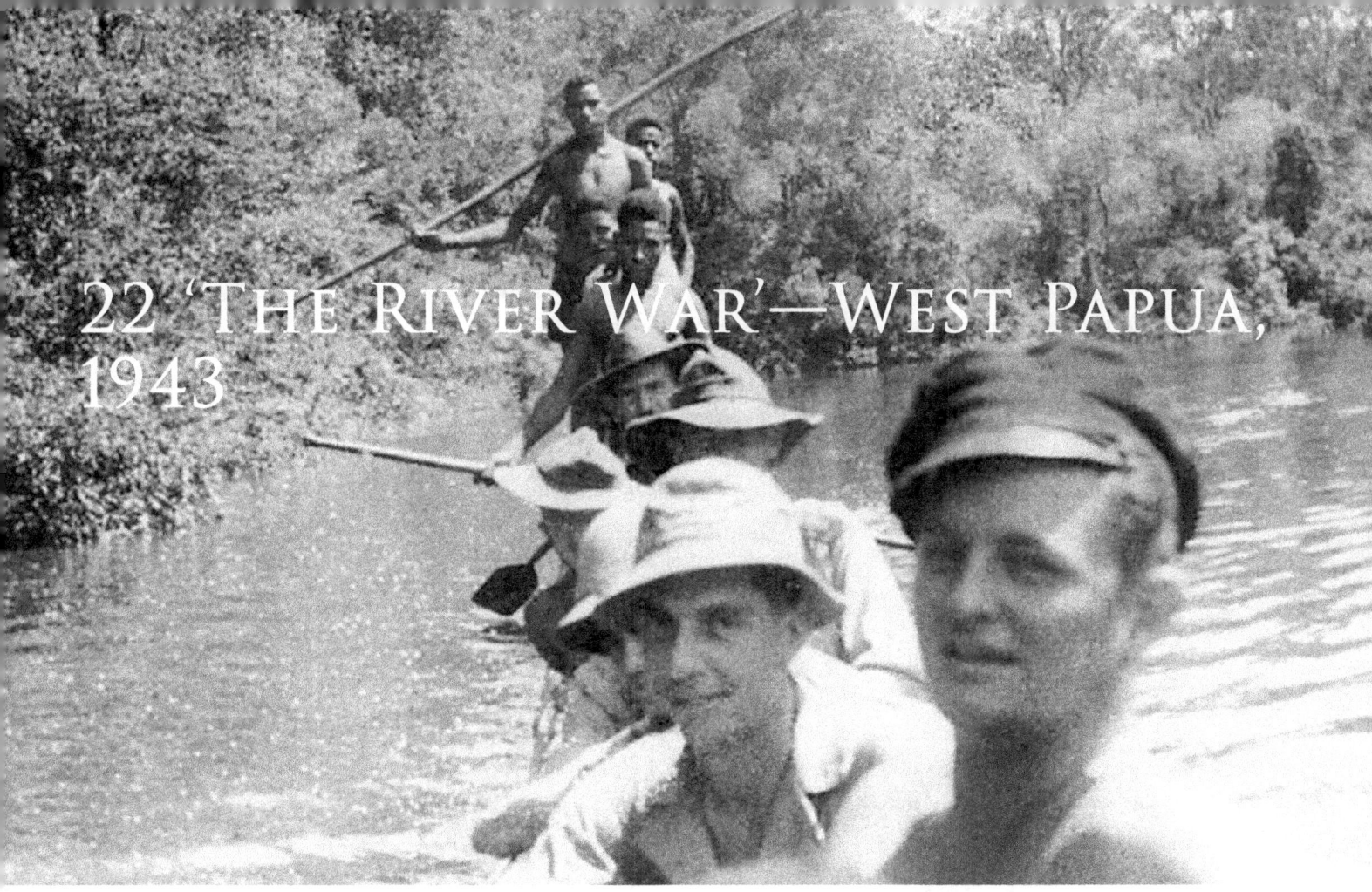

Recent enemy activity in the vicinity of Merauke has led to a reconsideration of plans.

General Douglas MacArthur, 1943

In early 1943 the Allied Commander, General Douglas MacArthur, initiated limited offences in both the Solomon Islands and New Guinea. Intelligence reports from China indicated the Japanese might try to invade Darwin from Australia's weaker left flank. In the islands north of Australia, the Japanese were constructing airfields that could handle up to 1500 aircraft. The only part of the NEI not occupied by the Japanese was Merauke and the small township of Tannah Merah in south-east Dutch New Guinea. With only a token force of Dutch soldiers stationed at Merauke, there was the possibility the Japanese might overrun the area. MacArthur ordered the strengthening of the town's defences as a priority. He requested a full AIF brigade be transferred there and that the small airstrip be upgraded for a RAAF fighter wing.

Charles' responsibility was to form 72 Wing in Townsville to defend the Allies' dangerously exposed left flank. Until the Merauke airstrip was completed by American army engineers of the 96 Engineer General Service Regiment, the new wing's aircraft were based at Horn Island off the tip of the Australian mainland. Charles went to Merauke to join the Merauke Force Commander, Brigadier Stevenson, Major Thomas of 96 Engineer General Service Regiment and the Dutch Resident, Colonel Vanderburgh.

Charles later wrote:

> We got together and made certain that the requirements of the Commander in Chief would be met; there would be a real force command, and co-operation was to be 100%. I don't think better co-operation could have existed than between the Army, Navy, Air Force and American Engineers. It was a great show and the strip that was built was a monument to Major Thomas (96th USA Engineers). The outline of the country was such that the highest point for hundreds of miles was only a few feet above sea-water level, and the difficulties that were encountered in building the strip, roads and jetties can well be imagined. When we first went there, no jetty was available and a ship coming in with supplies had to be tied to the shore and unloaded with the help of pontoons.
>
> Merauke was really a strip of land, a slight ridge a few feet high, two miles long and about ½ a mile wide, and on this land the entire defence had to be built, including the airstrip. At the time we went there, the defences consisted of a few Bofors guns; Japanese aeroplanes flying at a height of over 8000 feet had an open go on a concentrated small target. As can be imagined on the small amount of land available, dumps were everywhere and any bomb placed within the area could do damage. Once the equipment came ashore, we selected the site for the strip which, by the way, was not the site that had been selected previously to our arrival. Once sufficient equipment was available we commenced work. Within a week from the time we pushed over the first coconut tree, a squadron of P 40s [Curtiss-P40E Kittyhawks] were on stand-by as a deterrent to Japanese interference. Within fourteen days from the start, as the steel mat was laid for 6000 feet, our position could then be considered safe.

Merauke was only eight degrees south of the Equator and the whole area was described by an American survey team as a *'vast swamp interlaced with vegetation'*. Transport by road was impossible; all travel was by small boats or local canoes. The indigenous people, the Kaja Kaja, practised head-hunting, were spirit worshippers and had no fear of foreigners. Nevertheless, Charles found them friendly and cooperative in support roles and building the airstrip, writing, *'They were extremely helpful, willing and keen workers.'* In the jungles of India, in the Central Australian desert and when introducing Aboriginal men for RAAF duties in 1940, Charles had learnt it was essential to involve and cooperate with local people.

Soon after his arrival, three enemy Mitsubishi-G4M 'Betty' bombers were intercepted and repelled, but one of the defending fighter's guns failed. Charles realised his fighter aircraft needed sufficient time to 'scramble' from Horn Island so ordered a daylight standing patrol of two fighters over the airstrip while it was under construction. He also planned radar listening posts north and west of Merauke, which would give at least 15 minutes warning that enemy bombers were on their way. Six days after arriving in Merauke, together with AIF soldiers and RAAF radar personnel, Charles embarked on a four-day reconnaissance by canoe to the village of Bopul, north of Merauke. As they paddled in local canoes through nearly impenetrable swamps the party were more worried by mosquitoes *'larger than fighter-bombers'* than by Japanese ambushes.

Charles described the objectives of their 'Sanders of the River'[1] expedition in some of the most inhospitable terrain on earth:

> From this point we went further afield and after an interesting trip up the Merauke River we found the site and placed a radar station at Bopul in a direct air line some eighty miles north of Merauke. By flying boat we went inland to the old Dutch civil station at Tanna Merah, where another radar site was established and also a small strip site surveyed.

Two days after Charles' party returned to Merauke, on 11 May, the deployment of radar sites was justified when a radar listening post spotted 10 enemy aircraft approximately 106 miles from the town. Nine Japanese

Commanding the River War. Merauke Force Commander Brigadier Stevenson and Major Thomas, USA Engineers, on the Merauke River, May 1943

The village of Moffa, near Merauke, bombed by 23 Japanese Air Flotilla on 11 May 1943, killing two Kaja Kaja tribesmen.

bombers dropped an estimated 72 bombs in three clusters. The village of Moffa was seriously damaged; two villagers were killed and four wounded. Three Australian soldiers were injured and an ammunition store and small fuel dump destroyed. Charles was dismayed that he had no aircraft to counterattack the enemy on site and that his air defence was 18 Australian-built Boomerang fighters based at Horn Island, 130 miles away.

Charles now had an HQ, radar stations, limited accommodation and messes, but no resident squadrons. The airstrip was not finished and there were logistical problems. Compounding these difficulties was that direct control of the RAAF at Merauke was based in Townsville—a similar and complex situation that Charles had faced in Darwin—yet the combined force was nominally under the control of the competent Brigadier Stevenson. Despite his dissatisfaction with the divided command, Charles initiated a combined mess with the army and navy and built a squash court that could be used as an emergency surgery. Messing was a problem as supplies came from army stores and, at times, only a couple of days' food stocks were on hand. When an officer objected to the combined mess idea, Charles stated that if he did not like it, he would send him home.

72 Wing officers with a Kittyhawk at Merauke, May 1943

At 11.20 am on 16 May, the radar units reported that hostile aircraft were approaching from the north-west at a distance of 100 miles. The yellow then red warning signals were sounded well before eight Japanese aircraft appeared, only to be chased away by fighters from Horn Island. From 19 May, the overhead air defence of Merauke was carried out by three flights of Boomerangs, four aircraft per flight, in staggered rotation through daylight hours. By mid-afternoon the last flight would return to Horn Island. It was only in late June that Kittyhawks of 86 (Fighter) Squadron of 72 Wing were able to land at the new airstrip. By then there were more than 3700 AIF, 700 RAAF and the 96 American Engineering Regiment personnel stationed at the base despite a lack of accommodation and messing facilities. In July, a lone Japanese bomber accompanied by three fighters raided the new airstrip but was chased away by 16 Kittyhawks.

Charles applauded the efforts of the American engineers and the general efficiency of the USAAC. Whereas he had to account for any expenditure or damage over £A20 to RAAF HQ in Melbourne, his American counterpart had '*a bag with thousands of pounds to spend as he wished*'. The Americans floated the idea of offering to equip and service all RAAF squadrons, which would then be amalgamated into a joint allied air force under American administrative command and logistic support while the Australians retained their own individual fighting units. Charles voiced strong support for this proposal, as did the previous RAAF Chief of Staff, Sir Charles Burnett, but the proposal was rejected by the Australian War Cabinet and the RAAF hierarchy.

Meanwhile a young radio operator, 'Jack' Dawson, wrote with some apprehension of the new base's location:

> ... which was virtually across the Merauke River from the Japanese, and the difficulty of getting in and out of this base many of the original party had expressed views relating to the dangers associated with its location, but after a few months they settled down and it became a strong forward base with a sound aerodrome.

Dawson's anxiety may have been unnecessary. General MacArthur, when visiting the base in July, thought the vast swamp surrounding Merauke a sound defensive barrier and considered the chances of an overland invasion by Japanese ground troops to be remote. Despite this protection, Charles instigated a defence perimeter for the airmen to support the AIF's Defence Plan A in case of a Japanese attack; the airmen were issued with rifles, Tommy guns and revolvers. On the lighter side, Dawson remembered his regular squash games with Charles: *'The excellent times we spent playing Squash Racquets with 'Moth' ... it was a real privilege for me to have been invited to play with him.'*

As with the rest of the RAAF, Charles had to work within what the official RAAF historian Odgers described as a *'division of responsibility which was endemic throughout Australia's air force during WWII'*. There were two commanders at the top echelon; Air Vice-Marshal Jones was responsible for administration, and Air Vice-Marshal Bostock controlled active air operations against the enemy. The two rival camps within the air force, one for Bostock and the other for Jones, did nothing to help service morale. In April 1943 even General MacArthur commented on the unsatisfactory situation of RAAF's command: *'It is still in somewhat of turmoil.'* This situation, comprehensively described in Air Commodore Ashworth's *How Not to Run an Air Force*,

Whereas he had to account for any expenditure or damage over £A20 to RAAF HQ in Melbourne, his American counterpart had 'a bag with thousands of pounds to spend as he wished'.

'The excellent times we spent playing Squash Racquets with 'Moth' ... it was a real privilege for me to have been invited to play with him.'

impaired the service's effectiveness. Bostock and Jones' ongoing vendetta caused bitter friction that extended beyond the end of WWII. Charles was known to be impartial; he never voiced or wrote of his opinion either way except to state: *'The RAAF would have done far better if they fought the Japanese as hard as they fought amongst themselves.'*

The Area Commander, based in Townsville, was Air Commodore Harry Cobby, Australia's renowned fighter ace of WWI who flew with 4 Squadron AFC as part of 11 Wing in mid-1918. Charles had also flown with 11 Wing as a reconnaissance pilot (Vignette 5). A series of cryptic signals between Charles and Cobby appeared to reflect on the RAAF's inability to service its Merauke base and Charles' self-acknowledged impatience to get things done. Cobby's staff officer, Wing Commander 'Tom' Curnow, confirmed 72 Wing was handicapped by supply shortages and emphasised the communication problem. He added that the wing's morale was good and confirmed Charles' opinion *'that Army and Air Force Co-operation is 100%'*.

In early July 1943, for some unexplained reason, Cobby sent a junior officer to issue orders directly to a newly arrived squadron, thus bypassing Charles' authority. Charles, a stickler for correct chain of command procedures, took umbrage at Air Commodore Cobby's action and demanded a court-martial. Air Vice-Marshal Jones decided a court of inquiry would be more appropriate. The two antagonists were duly summoned to Townsville, where Jones presided. Jones was in an awkward position; judging two of his most senior and experienced officers. He decided they should be separated as it was obvious they could not continue to work together. Charles, the junior officer, was transferred to No. 2 Bombing and Gunnery School at Port Pirie in South Australia. In the formal conclusions of the inquiry, no adverse comment was officially recorded on either of their personal files but Jones did remark on the poor communications and the irregular chain of command procedure.

Charles briefly summed up his own view of the episode and his departure from Merauke:

> *'The RAAF would have done far better if they fought the Japanese as hard as they fought amongst themselves.'*

Although a combined force, the air defence was placed under the Headquarters at Townville and without question the problems of Merauke were not understood from there and difficulties arose, mountains were made out of mole hills, and after one or two fairly cryptic signals, I left Merauke to be posted to the Bombing and Air Gunnery School at Port Pirie.

Although 72 Wing saw relatively little action compared with other RAAF units in the New Guinea–Papua theatre, the unit did strengthen and guard the Allies' exposed left flank. Included in this limited action were clashes between Allied patrols servicing the radar stations and their Japanese counterparts in a mini-version of Churchill's 'River War' in the Sudan.[2]

After a couple of months in Port Pirie in South Australia as commander of the Bombing and Air Gunnery School, he was transferred back to the Northern Territory to assume *'the best appointment of my service life'*.

Later in the war, Air Commodore Cobby was relieved of his command of the RAAF's Tactical Air Force when its morale fell to *'a dangerously low level'*, resulting in an unfortunate incident that would forever be known as the 'Moratai Mutiny'.

B-25 Mitchell bombers of the NEIAF over the Timor Sea, 1944.

23 One Wing, a Broken Pipe and a Prayer, 1943–44

Bombers continued to hit the island from bases in Northern Australia. The Commander of the Japanese Forces in Timor later stated 'that after April 1944 Allied air attacks in Dutch Timor were so skilful and heavy that vehicles could not move by day and coastal shipping could only travel at night'. By autumn 1944 the combination of air raids and United States submarine activity had isolated Timor, and strict fuel economies had to be instituted.[1]

In July 1943, Air Vice-Marshal Adrian 'King' Cole was appointed to command the RAAF's North West Area (NWA), based in Darwin. King Cole had distinguished himself in WWI as a fighter pilot and been wounded in 1942 during the failed Dieppe raid. He took over a well-organised command, but had only nine Australian, British, American and Dutch squadrons to carry out attacks on Timor and central and eastern NEI and to maintain the air defence of north-western Australia—the same air defence that Charles had established in 1939 with only a handful of Anson bombers. Cole pulled no punches when confronting what he thought was inefficiency and questionable tactics within his own service and those of the Dutch and Americans. Through his

Charles at Batchelor, 1943.

initiatives, the strength of the NWA increased to 13 squadrons by early 1944. He considered the Allies should take the offensive and weaken the Japanese, particularly if the Allies attacked the nearby Tanimbar and Kai Islands.

Cole differed from the Americans in attack strategy; he complained that his USAAC units were given instructions '*not to attack near enemy fighters in daylight*' so circumventing his authority. He claimed this affected his control and was inconsistent with the RAAF's tactics. With the NEIAF he faced the problem of allegedly low morale and poor administration. In October 1943, Cole reported to the RAAF high command that 18 (NEIAF) Squadron's morale had resulted in '*the lack of offensive spirit and the general outlook of the NEIAF men*'. Historian Alan Powell wrote that the NEIAF was known as the '*fishing fleet*' because aircrews had the habit of jettisoning bombs in the Timor Sea well before reaching their target. Cole recommended that unless the RAAF had full control of the Dutch units '*all NEIAF Squadrons be replaced on this front*'. Conversely, Dutch historian Mozes Weers claimed that faults lay with the Australians due to '*injudicious tactical utilisation*'.

Only weeks after Cole's damning report, Charles was appointed to reorganise 79 (Light Bomber) Wing as part of NWA Command. The wing was a formation of five squadrons with its HQ at Batchelor, 60 miles south of Darwin. One air force wit commented that Batchelor was a place '*God made on a wet Monday morning while suffering from a hangover and a sore head'*. The wing included the controversial 18 (NEIAF) Squadron. The command's heavy Australian and American B-24 Liberator bombers were to attack long-range targets in the NEI leaving Timor, West Papua and islands in the Arafura Sea and Banda Sea to 79 Wing. In October 1943, the five squadrons of 79 Wing and their commanders were:

- RAAF 1 Squadron (Loneragan)—Bristol Beaufort general-reconnaissance bombers based at Gould.
- RAAF 2 Squadron (Campbell)—Bristol Beaufort general-reconnaissance bombers based at Hughes.
- RAAF 13 Squadron (Kennan)—Lockheed Ventura general-reconnaissance bombers based at Gove.
- NEIAF 18 Squadron (Zomer)—North American B-25 Mitchell medium bombers based at Batchelor.
- RAAF 31 Squadron (Mann)—Bristol Beaufighter long-range fighter/bombers based at Coomalie Creek.

Batchelor was a place 'God made on a wet Monday morning while suffering from a hangover and a sore head'.

Squadron Commanders of 79 Wing 1944. Left to right, rear: W/C Darcy Wentworth (31 Sqn)[2] and W/C Charles Loneragan (1 Sqn). Left to right, front: W/C David Campbell (2 Sqn), G/C Charles Eaton (CO 79 Wing) and Col. Dirk Asjes (18 NEIAF Sqn).[3] W/C Kennan (13 Squadron) absent.

Charles (with pipe) briefing pilots of 2 Squadron, 1944.

Although relationships between the Dutch and Australian air force officers were reported to be cool, with some top-ranking RAAF officers being anti-Dutch, Charles' own relationship with the Dutch was positive and harmonious. He wrote in 1975:

> Towards the end of 1943 the North West Area was re-organised into three separate Wings all under the command of Air Vice Marshal A T COLE. These Wings comprised (i) a Fighter Wing (Spitfires), (ii) A Heavy Bomber Wing (Liberators) and a Light Bomber and General Service Wing—this later Wing was designated No 79 Wing. The HQ of No 79 Wing was located at Batchelor, NT. When the Wing was formed a most zealous Commanding Officer was appointed to command No. 18 Sqn.— Colonel ZOMER. Although the B 25s (Mitchells) were manned by Dutch personnel it must be remembered that the tail gunners were (small in stature) RAAF Air Gunners. Colonel ZOMER was followed by Colonel Eddie TE ROLLER, another fine commander, who unfortunately was soon to be lost in action, leading an attack on enemy shipping near ARU Islands. His loss was a great one to the whole Wing. Command of No. 18 Squadron was taken over by yet another outstanding officer and well known pilot, Colonel Dick ASJES, who survived so many ably led sorties.

Colonel 'Eddie' TE Roller, Commanding Officer of 18 (NEIAF) Squadron. Killed in action off Aru Islands, 23 June 1944.

Heavily camouflaged 30 metre oil barge after destruction by 79 Wing, Semau Island, West Timor, 6 April 1944.

During 1944 the Wing became a closely knit team with high efficiency and great esprit de corps operationally and socially. It practically cut off all supplies to the Japanese remaining on Timor and the other islands. Unfortunately several aircraft with their gallant crews were lost.

Another interesting strike by No 18 Squadron was against the WISSELL LAKES in northern New Guinea. These lakes are some 7,000 feet high and it had been reported that Japanese flying boats were there evacuating their personnel from Hollandia. We set off from Darwin in B 25s and landed the same day at Merauke. Early next morning, from Merauke to the WISSELL LAKES. We found no flying boats but strafed and sank several boats used by the Japanese ground defences for the Hollandia district. Finishing our strafing we climbed out of the valley and skirted the Kartenz Mountains some 17,000 feet high and an amazing sight. The mountains which have perpetual snow for 2,000 feet looked great and when we passed over the Kartenz peak, I spotted a new lake which was uncharted. Then with the few bombs we had left we bombed the Japanese aerodrome at Timuka, returned to Merauke to refuel, and then back to Darwin.

Nowhere in his writings did Charles mention anything negative about the Dutch airmen or their performance. On the contrary, he states that the Dutch gave good support. When asked by an interviewer in the 1970s whether there had been trouble with the Dutch air force, his reply was short and to the point: *'Yes, a little ... but that was soon fixed,'* and he immediately switched to another subject. To the Dutch officers and airmen he was known as '*Oom* Charles' or Uncle Charles.

Historian Odgers reported that by early 1944, 79 Wing was bombing Timor daily. Flight Lieutenant Lugg, a staff officer with NWA's HQ, noted, *'With his peculiar and extensive knowledge of the region as a whole, G/C Eaton proved an ideal co-ordinator and CO, being able to supply specific local knowledge to all officers working under him.'*

Charles continues:

> Somehow or other, with W/Cdr. Lampe as my second in Command, we formed the Wing into a real team, and although it is difficult to mention individuals, officers and airmen, the co-operation with the Wing and between the Squadrons was very good and many friendships made which will be lifelong. Many of our strikes took place from advanced bases as far apart as from Broome to Merauke.
>
> There are many strikes and sorties which I feel inclined to write about but I think a few only can be described. No. 1 Squadron's strike at Kiang will well be remembered by many as it was their first strike in that tour of duty. They hit Koepang [Kupang] well at night time but unfortunately lost two aircraft, either to ack-ack or Japanese night flying aircraft, and in this strike we lost their second in command, S/L Roxburgh. The other Squadrons were very upset about it and we planned a 'hate bash' on Koepang. This time other Squadrons took part, and with No.1 Squadron, we practically completely wiped out the Japanese Barracks there.
>
> Night and day bombing was carried out by all Squadrons and was very interesting. The pretty bombing of the Soe Township in Timor was an example of how to bomb, but, of course, the bombing could not be compared to bombing which occurs in Europe, but the ack-ack defences

'With his peculiar and extensive knowledge of the region as a whole, G/C Eaton proved an ideal co-ordinator and CO, being able to supply specific local knowledge to all officers working under him.'

The 'pretty' bombing of the Japanese Army barracks, Soe, West Timor, 19 April 1944.

of the Japanese could not be ignored. I think pilots of the wing mostly liked the various shipping searches and strikes. Aeroplanes, usually four together, kept up a ceaseless patrol of the Arafura Sea and any ships met, were usually attacked from mast height by 500-pound bombs. In the end shipping closed up completely and barge traffic was resorted to only at night by the Japanese.[4]

Charles was anxious that his five squadrons participate in combined actions. One strike—scoped by Charles three years earlier—gave him an opportunity to weld 79 Wing together and to personally observe the target's destruction: *'I think the first strike which got the Squadrons together occurred on 19 February, 1944.'* His target was the Mina River Bridge, which he had photographed in 1941 when on a clandestine mission to West Timor. Eaton called

'I think the first strike which got the Squadrons together occurred on 19 February, 1944.'

the crews of 18 and 31 squadrons together and outlined a plan of action. Eight Beaufighters of 31 Squadron under Wing Commander 'Bill' Mann were to act as fighter cover for six 18 Squadron B-25 bombers. The formation was to fly across the Timor Sea from their bases at 3000 feet and, once over the target, four Beaufighters were to strafe the anti-aircraft gun defences at 'zero' feet. The other Beaufighters were to fly overhead above the bombers. When the ack-ack was neutralised, the Dutch B-25s were to bomb the bridge at 6000 feet.

Charles described the raid:

> On the day in question, we set out from Darwin with Beaufighters and B 25s. I went in low with W/C Mann to strafe the bridge with cannon and to put out any defences. As we passed through, the Mitchells bombed from 6,000 feet and, on top of the Mitchells, again more Beaufighters as air cover. The plan worked well. We got three direct hits with 600 pounders on the bridge and returned without casualties. A year afterwards the bridge was still under repair.

After the strike, Eaton requested Mann to break formation and fly back over the bridge for him to photograph the results. The central span had been hit by three bombs and wooden sentry huts on the east bank destroyed. The strike force then crossed Timor's south coast for their long journey home.

Mina River Bridge, West Timor. Photographed by Charles, March 1941.

The Mina River Bridge under attack, 19 February 1944.

In 1994, Bill Mann wrote of the raid:

> On 19 February the attack was mounted as planned with perfect timing essential as wireless silence was maintained until the target area was reached to keep as much as possible the element of surprise. Last minute timing was coordinated using wireless R/T between the two Squadrons so that the Beaufighters would be through the target and clear before the actual bomb drop. In actual fact that is what occurred and the Beaufighters having strafed and taken out the ack-ack were clear by several seconds as the bombs badly damaged the bridge.
>
> Group Captain Eaton insisted that he wanted to see and be a part of the raid so he flew with me in Beaufighter A19-140 and as this aircraft was crewed by a pilot and navigator only this meant that G/C Eaton had to stand in an exit well behind the pilot for the whole trip and watch the action over the pilot's shoulder. This was no mean feat as the trip was 5½ hours flight time and there was no seat or harness. With the 'G' forces involved in sometimes violent turns during the action, to keep standing upright required considerable effort. Not the

most comfortable experience for the 'Grouper'. This discomfort and the excitement probably caused G/C Eaton to snap the stem of his ever present pipe which, if it was not fuming away in his mouth, was invariably clutched in his hand. While this distressed him somewhat it had the reverse effect on my navigator Flying Officer RS Harber and myself as we were spared the discomfort of acrid smoke and running eyes during the two and a half hour run home to base.

Notwithstanding the loss of his pipe, Charles must have felt gratified with the result. He had identified and photographed the target in 1941 and witnessed the bombing of the Mina bridge when in the leading aircraft during the strike. In 1947, he photographed the bridge's damaged central span at ground level when on a diplomatic visit to Dutch-held West Timor (Vignette 26). A unique multi-reconnaissance mission indeed.

Despite Charles' perpetual screen of *'acrid smoke'*, Bill Mann wrote that Charles was a concerned and compassionate leader and was well thought of by 31 Squadron because of his personal interest in the squadron's welfare. Charles must have had the leadership style that moulded 18 NEIAF Squadron into an effective fighting unit. He was a good social mixer, was known to put the NEI contingent at ease and placed morale as a priority with all his commands. Since his 1941 visit to the NEI, he wore an Indonesian *sarong* at nights, but not in the mess.

The NEIAF recorded that Charles flew on 50 missions with 18 Squadron, though this appears excessive for a senior commander. He definitely participated in a sortie with 18 Squadron on 6 June 1944; he was in a Mitchell (N5-164) aircraft when it sank an enemy ship off Timor then bombed Dili's runway. Although not averse to excitement, Charles would perhaps have preferred to have missed one close encounter. Leading another raid, he flew with Squadron Leader 'Pat' Boyd[5] and navigator Flying Officer 'Fred' Anderson. Passing over Viqueque in central Timor, the aircraft received a direct hit to the starboard engine.

'While this distressed him somewhat it had the reverse effect on my navigator Flying Officer RS Harber and myself as we were spared the discomfort of acrid smoke and running eyes during the two and a half hour run home to base.'

Charles explains:

In a Beaufighter, with S/L Pat Boyd, together with other Beaufighter fighters, we set out to do some ground strafing at a camp near Dili; I had rather an amazing and exciting experience. After crossing the coast at Timor low down, looking for targets, we were in a valley, when an odd .5 [mm] bullet from the Japanese hit our starboard engine. It went right through the front housing then hot oil enveloping the engine in smoke. The propeller was immediately feathered and we climbed out of the valley and headed for home some 400 miles away. As a protection one of the other Beaufighters was ordered to accompany us and the other six to carry on with the job. Over Timor, with one engine, was not very pleasant, but once the coast was reached we seemed fairly safe. Our predicament was to wireless back to Darwin and a Catalina was sent out to pull us out of the drink if necessary. About 50 miles off the coast of Timor the port engine started to give trouble and developed a tremendous vibration. It seemed the only thing to do was to ditch and so down we went to ditch. Boyd let the ditching hatch go and I opened my parachute to rest my head against it to take the bump. At that time I lost my Army slouch hat. When only about 100 feet above the sea, the port engine came good again so on we went towards the coast of Australia.

About half way across, Boyd endeavoured to pump the petrol from the starboard tanks to the port engine, but unfortunately the pipes were blocked and the petrol could not get through. There was nothing to do but to dump the petrol on the starboard side into the Timor Sea and go on until

'Home after the Party'. Beaufort light bomber returning home after a raid to Batchelor airstrip, Northern Territory, 1944

we ran out of petrol. With great skill by Boyd in the use of his remaining engine, after what seemed a very long time, the north coast of Australia was sighted and we got down OK at Snake Bay at the top of Melville Island. 'On a Wing and a Prayer' was often sung to me after that show.

Charles must have been too embarrassed to mention in his notes that he had broken his pipe yet again but the navigator, Fred Anderson, recalled that Charles ordered him to wireless HQ Darwin *'for a new pipe and a car'* in that order. Anderson wrote that the 'Groupie' would have had more to worry about beside his broken pipe had he known that their aircraft had only five minutes of fuel and the rubber dinghy was shot to ribbons. Charles, when flying Beaufighters himself, was reputed to have his pipe clenched firmly in his mouth. At a mess night a few weeks later, the pilots of 31 Squadron presented him with a replica slouch hat signed by the squadron's air crews.

79 Wing RAAF: Area of Operations, south-west Pacific 1943–44

After a strafing mission, the flight climbed out of the valley and skirted the Kartenz Glaciers of West Papua, an amazing sight.

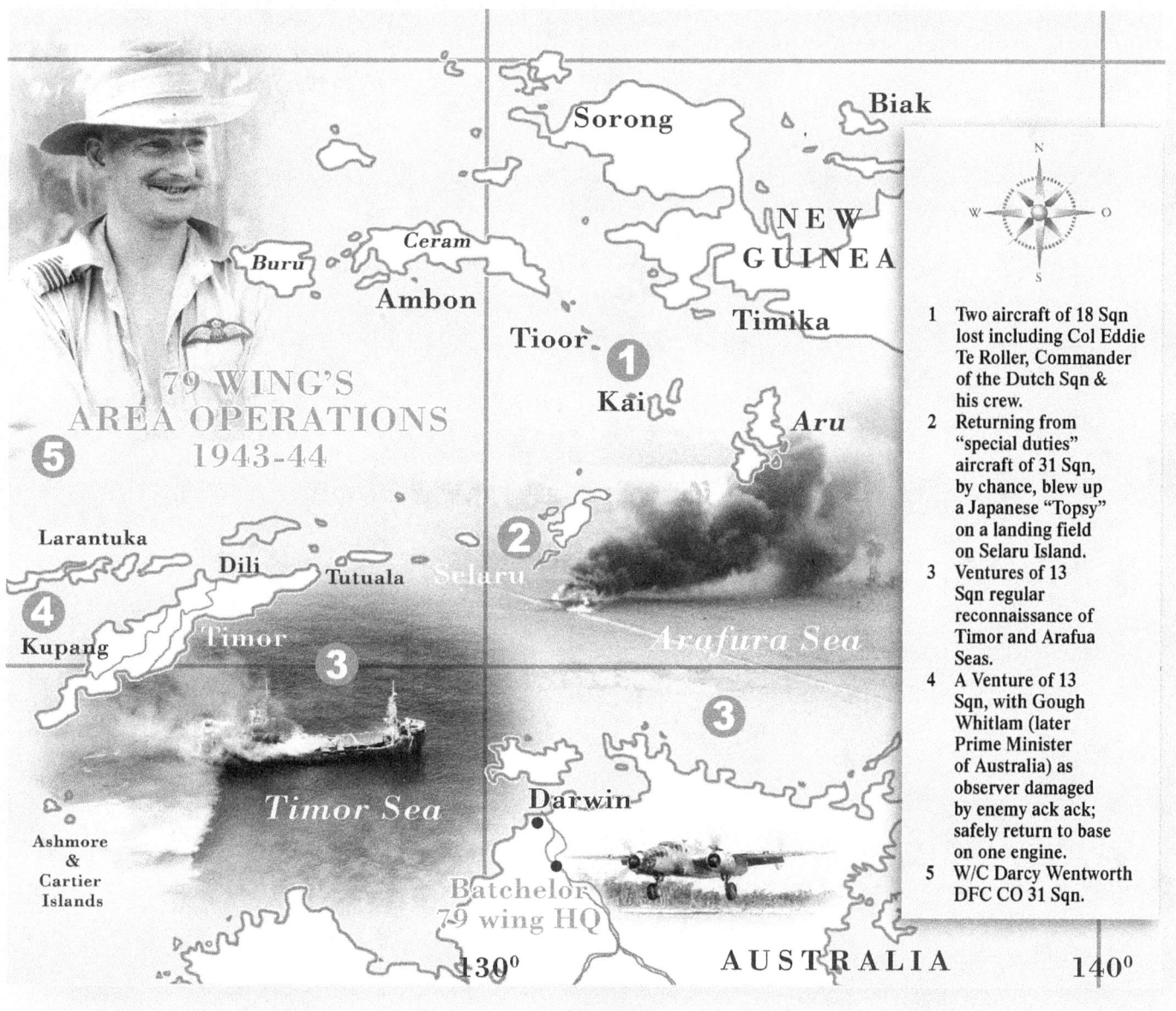

Beaufighter of 31 Squadron attacks a Japanese 'Betty' bomber Mitsubishi Ki-57/L4M at Selaru airstrip, Tanimbar Island, 22 July 1944.

24 A Knight with Swords, 1944

They did not fear the summer's sun
In whose hot centre lie
A hundred hissing cannon shells

And when on Dobadura's field
We landed, each man raised
His thumb towards the open sky

David Campbell DFC,
Commander 2 Squadron, 79 Wing

As the war played out, a few incidents stood out that showed Charles' experience as a leader in precarious situations. One such incident was 'Operation Potshot'. Although only an insignificant footnote in Australia's history, Operation Potshot showed what Charles' men were capable of and provided some excitement for 79 Wing; *'bizarre'* as the NEIAF reported.

In March 1944, Japanese aircraft carriers had arrived in Singapore Harbour and battle cruisers were reported in the Indian Ocean. Seventeen suspected Japanese informers masquerading as ethnic Chinese from Japanese-occupied Java were picked up on the *Bandoeng Maru* only three miles off the coast of Western Australia. As Japan had suffered a series of defeats elsewhere, it was considered they might try a face-saving attack on either the air bases around Exmouth Gulf or on Fremantle. The Japanese must have been fully aware of the airstrip at Potshot and other airstrips on the west coast, some of which had been bombed from bases in Timor.[1]

The Australian high command decided on a sudden redeployment of RAAF units to defend Western Australia in case of a surprise Japanese attack. Charles was ordered to transfer his HQ, two squadrons and the Dutch 120 (Kittyhawk) Squadron to Exmouth Gulf 'post haste'. The order was given at 7.30 am, 8 March; by 10 am the squadrons left their Batchelor and Coomalie Creek base, landing at Potshot that afternoon. Eighteen transport aircraft were employed to transfer equipment and ground personnel. The squadrons arrived in the middle of a tropical cyclone, but as urgency was essential in what was thought to be a serious threat to Australia's security, the weather factor was disregarded. On landing, all aircraft were confined to the airstrip's apron—moving off the tarmac would result in bogging. The cyclone had *'converted the airfield and camp into a swamp.'*

One RAAF crew member, Clive Diggelman, noted vivid impressions of Operation Potshot:

Operation Potshot showed what Charles' men were capable of and provided some excitement for 79 Wing.

79 Wing HQ defensive perimeter, Potshot, March 1944

Well, what a panic there is today, they have given us about two hours to get ready to move, we don't know where we are going, but F/O Curtis says he does not like it at all, and that we are going to a very hot spot and the whole Squadron is going by plane ... so things don't look too good ... I have written to Mum and told her not to worry about me. We left at about 10 am ... one of the crew told me he had no idea where we were going. We landed at Wyndham, the weather was very rough on the way over ... the plane was wallowing all over the sky ... I have never seen so many close shaves in my life.

'We landed at Wyndham, the weather was very rough on the way over ... the plane was wallowing all over the sky ... I have never seen so many close shaves in my life.'

Once established in Potshot, Charles immediately drew up an elaborate network of defences for the command's temporary base. Perhaps his experiences when helping defend Vimy Ridge in 1916 helped his planning; his trench layout and machine gun deployment strategies were pure WWI army. Charles' defence orders were outlined as:

> Hostile Forces may be expected to make attacks on this Base in the near future by means of low flying aircraft, airborne troops or a naval force. These attacks may be heavy and might be simultaneous ... Defence equipment available consists of 14 .50 cal M.G.s [Machine guns], two Bren guns, and all personnel armed with, in the case of Officers with pistols, and other ranks with Tommy guns and rifles and bayonets. There is an adequate

Charles in jeep with his senior NEIAF officers, Potshot, March 1944

supply of ammunition for all weapons, the .50 M.G. are sited to cover the runways and dispersal areas, the Bren Guns are in a position to cover the Camp Area. Of the personnel of 18 Sqn there are two fully equipped and trained Security Guard sections, totalling 23 men ... This base will offer the most strenuous resistance to any form of attack.

Including himself, Charles had 369 men of all ranks to defend Potshot Airstrip. He strengthened his defence network by strategically deploying anti-aircraft and machine guns with their respective arcs of fire, organising perimeter and beach patrols 24 hours a day, providing adequate ammunition, food supplies and back-up medical services with first aid posts. Mobile teams were appointed in case of enemy breakthroughs, trenches dug, and all ranks issued with pistols or Tommy guns, emergency rations and full water bottles. Charles ordered that a week's provisions and water for 370 men be kept in a central and well-guarded storage area. In his demolition and evacuation orders, which prepared the base for worst-case scenario, Charles listed 26 eventualities and the action each section leader should take in each. His 25 months with the Lambs on the Western Front from 1915 to 1917 had served him well.

31 Squadron Beaufighters at Potshot, March 1944

Airmen of 79 Wing relaxing, Potshot, March 1944

79 Wing HQ Potshot

In spite of the weather, 79 Wing managed sea reconnaissance flights, but no Japanese ships or aircraft were sighted. Ten days later, after what was described as *'a very tough ten days'*, Operation Potshot was called off. Charles gave his officers and airmen time for rest and recreation, including trawling off the fish-rich coastline of Exmouth Gulf. After returning north, the airmen thought Batchelor was a welcome sight. According to Diggelman, *'Our humble tent camp seemed like Paradise in comparison to Potshot.'*

Soon after Operation Potshot, Charles led a successful mission on the Japanese military barracks at Soe, West Timor on 19 April. The coordinated attack involved 18 Squadron and 2 Squadron with the Beaufighters of 31 Squadron overhead as protective cover. King Cole signalled: *'I wish to congratulate all concerned in the excellent day of operation, and reconnaissance ... The record number of sorties reflects great credit on ground staff and maintenance crews.'*

June 1944 was a typical month for 79 Wing; it flew 3542 hours on 387 operations that included seaward air reconnaissance, bombing and escort duties. Charles reported:

'Our humble tent camp seemed like Paradise in comparison to Potshot.'

'I wish to congratulate all concerned in the excellent day of operation, and reconnaissance ... The record number of sorties reflects great credit on ground staff and maintenance crews.'

Kittyhawk of 120 NEIAF Squadron, Potshot, March 1944

During the month of JUNE, anti-shipping sweeps were intensified, and the results achieved were of a high order. The most outstanding operations was NEI 18 on the 23 JUNE '44; two Sugar Charlies of approximately 150 tons were attacked, and left smoking, and one Fox Tare Dog of 1,500 tons was left enveloped in flames. Duty No 5 carrying Lt Colonel te Roller Commanding Officer No 18 NEI Squadron was hit by anti-aircraft fire, and was last seen to crash into the sea off TIMOR ISLAND, no survivors were seen. CAPE CHATER and LAUTEM WEST strips were successfully bombed and numerous attacks carried out by No 2 Squadron and 18 NEI Squadron. Ten Beaufighters of No 31 Squadron operated from an advanced base carrying out special operations. The operation was successfully completed, and the aeroplanes returned to base on 25 JUNE '44. Photographic reconnaissance of enemy territory was carried out on an increased scale and the results achieved were excellent.

Some air crews had amazing stories of lucky escapes. Navigator Patrick Delaney deserved the title of 'Luck of the Irish' when his Beaufighter, flown by Pilot Officer Garner, made a forced landing in a minefield near Darwin. By a miracle, no mines detonated and the crew were rescued without injury.

Termites had built nests in the mines' triggering mechanisms, rendering them harmless. After an attack on an oil barge off Semau Island on 6 April, a Beaufighter was hit by anti-aircraft fire and the starboard engine ceased. Losing height, the pilot, Strachan, knew he could not make it back to base so headed for Cartier Island, about 120 nautical miles south. This was the island Charles had selected on a reconnaissance flight in March 1941 for emergency landings. Strachan pancaked his aircraft on the beach of this microscopic island. With navigator 'Jack' Brassil he walked a mile over the sharp reef then *'fell into the sea'*. They eventually climbed, with difficulty, onto a Catalina of 43 Squadron.

A Ventura of 13 Squadron lost an engine over the Sunda Sea; with great skill, the pilot nursed it to the mainland. Charles recommended a citation for the pilot, little knowing he had perhaps saved the life of Australia's future, most effervescent prime minister—his young navigator, Edward Gough Whitlam. On 22 July three Beaufighters of 31 Squadron intercepted a message that an enemy 'Topsy' aircraft was about to take off from Selaru Island. The Beaufighters attacked and destroyed the aircraft as it taxied for takeoff. The squadron's diary described the action:

> Landfall was made at the SOUTHERN tip of SELARU ISLAND at 220720z and duties Eight & Nine proceeded straight to target area. 15 to 20 Jap personnel standing about were caught unawares and a short burst was fired at them and six of their number were killed. A twin engine "TOPSY" standing on WESTERN end of runway facing into the wind, i.e. facing EAST, was then raked by cannon and machine gun fire. The transport caught fire and was completely destroyed. One Jap who had been standing near the aeroplane was seen to fall and is considered to have been killed. The Beaufighters then joined up and making one further circuit set course for base leaving the island at BOKAT VILLAGE.

This was the island Charles had recommended to the Dutch and the RAAF for construction of a staging airstrip in March 1941, but the Japanese had beaten them to it!

On 27 September, while returning from duty after shepherding two Catalinas, two Beaufighters, A19-208 with Wackett and Noble and A19-193 with Richie and Warner, got lost due to thick smoke from bushfires. Despite radio calls, search lights and the discharge of Verey pistols, both aircraft missed their base and disappeared off the radar. Next morning their commander, Wing Commander Darcy Wentworth, flew several of the navigational tracks the missing aircraft may have taken, but to no avail. Later that day, Warner arrived on foot at the nearby railway line. When his Beaufighter had run out of fuel, the pilot told him to parachute first. Warner was almost hit by the spiralling aircraft but managed to land safely and found an old track, which led him to safety. A ground search party found the wreck of his aircraft in a creek bed, but no trace of Richie or the other two missing airmen and their aircraft. Charles, distressed at the possible loss of life, wrote to Wilbur Wackett's father, aircraft designer Sir Lawrence Wackett, explaining that everything possible was being done to find his son and the other missing airmen. Air and ground searches continued for another week but Wackett's Beaufighter was not found until 1946 by Mounted Constable 'Ted' Morey. Parachutes were hanging on trees and open tins of food were found nearby. Clearly there had been at least one

Two Beaufighters of 31 Squadron attack a Japanese 'Betty' bomber (Mitsubishi Ki-57/L4M at Selaru airstrip Tanimbar Islands, 22 July 1944.

survivor but their fate and what really happened remains unknown. Charles was of the opinion they had jumped too late and were injured on landing.

By October 1944, the pressure on 79 Wing was easing as targets were becoming harder to find. No Japanese military or naval ordnance could be seen by day on land or water. Charles reported on 6 October:

> Towards the end of the month, it was necessary to practically cease operational flights in No 2 and 18 Squadrons ... Targets for the month have been limited, probably on account of the previous six months' work of the Wing Squadrons on Japanese occupied areas in TIMOR. No targets worthy of note remain, and even then, shipping of the small Sugar Dog Charlie or Sugar Dog class are practically non-existent, enemy aircraft nil, townships and camps of any size have been destroyed and the Japanese have now resorted to pony supply trains for transport in the interior of TIMOR.

Charles had been pressing to have air-to-ground rockets introduced to the wing. Rockets had been used in Europe and elsewhere and he thought it unfair his units should be excluded. In his normal manner, he badgered his seniors for the missiles and, in due course, rockets were provided. He describes what proved to be the '*grand finale*' of his active war service, which had commenced in France on 14 March 1915:

> Another exciting strike was the first rocket strike in the South West Pacific Area. I had been battling to get rockets for Beaufighters for some time. When all was ready, we set off to an old Monastery which, from information received, was used as a Japanese Headquarters, probably a signal headquarters. It could be described as a very cushy target. It had never been attacked before. It was in a valley, hard to bomb, and six of us went on the strike. Machine guns started firing at us, but soon ceased as the first rockets went in or near the building. We formed a circle and went around one after the other watching the rockets go in eventually to demolish the target.
>
> The rockets had 60-pound heads and one was very tempted, on firing, to the watch rockets go into the target. As the range was only short, if you did not turn away soon enough, the rocket explosion was felt and a piece of the rocket could easily hit you. In fact, in our case, we actually did get too close and a chunk of the rocket was found in our wing after we landed.

'Another exciting strike was the first rocket strike in the South West Pacific Area. I had been battling to get rockets for Beaufighters for some time.'

The media of the day reported the rocket attack in more detail, stating that *'a huge stone building'* in the Japanese garrison town of Hatolia in Portuguese Timor disintegrated in seconds after the Beaufighters *'unleashed their thunderbolts'*. Not to be left out, the Mitchells dived down and strafed what was left of the devastated building. As Hatolia had not been previously attacked, it came as a shattering blow to the Japanese.

During his time at Batchelor, Charles found there was little time for recreation; all units were fully occupied taking the war to the Japanese. As at Merauke, he had a mess erected to cater for the air crews and support staff during off hours. If the celebrations got too boisterous, particularly after a spectacular strike, he had all ranks partake of an hour's morning exercise with the medicine ball to sweat it all out. Moth Eaton was known to parade young pilots suspected of being intoxicated the night before operations and dry them out in a most unusual manner. He would take them on 'a joy ride' in a Beaufighter, put the aircraft into a power dive then do a sudden half loop. From all accounts, this tactic sobered the offender in time for his next mission.

NWA's fighter wings were also running out of targets. Charles explains:

> The wing in nine months completed some 30,000 operational hours and sank 107 vessels of all descriptions, from 4,000 tonners to sea-going barges, completed about 3,630 sorties and dropped nearly 1,200 tons of bombs. In addition, continuous reconnaissance of the Timor, Arafura and Banda Seas were carried out. I built a little hut at Batchelor and an Officers' Mess which seemed to be the home of nearly all the members of the Squadrons when off duty which I am certain will be remembered by many.
>
> The poor Spitfire boys at Darwin, in the end, had very little to do. In order to give them a go, targets were selected as near as possible to an advanced base to give the boys a chance of some ground strafing. Usually it was my job to navigate the Spitfires direct to the target, so as not to waste any of their time on account of their short fuel range and then hang around and see them directly back to the advance base. But I am afraid we also used to take a formation, usually of B 25s, with us and to start the fight in the

The media of the day reported the rocket attack in more detail, stating that 'a huge stone building' in the Japanese garrison town of Hatolia in Portuguese Timor disintegrated in seconds after the Beaufighters 'unleashed their thunderbolts'.

'The wing in nine months completed some 30,000 operational hours and sank 107 vessels of all descriptions, from 4,000 tonners to sea-going barges, completed about 3,630 sorties and dropped nearly 1,200 tons of bombs.'

messes afterwards, we used to knock down the target when they were strafing it. I remember this did occur to the strike on the radar station at Cape Lore, on the eastern tip of Timor. It was very good to see the boys in the Spitfires shooting up the place when actually after they completed their job, our bombs knocked down the radar masts. Anyway, it was a cause of great discussion in messes afterwards.

Very good work was done by One Squadron in dropping supplies to the various posts we had in Timor. It was a difficult job and usually had to be done under bad weather conditions, and some fine flights and missions were completed by this Squadron. The Venturas of No 13 Squadron carried out great work in their sea searches, not a very interesting job, but a most important one. In December 1944, my tour was considered completed and I was again posted south to take over Southern Area, where, unfortunately, I was when the surrender terms were signed.

By early 1945, the Allied victory was assured. Douglas Hurst noted:

This quick victory for the allies owed much to their aerial dominance ... it also owed a debt to 79 Wing operations that blocked potential Japanese reinforcements from Timor and surrounds during the allied landings at Hollandia and Aitape.

Dr Helsen's research into the RAAF's campaign in the South West Pacific Area, *The Forgotten Air Force,* concluded that it was '*neither a sideshow nor a misuse of air power*'. Instead it was '*vital to the overall allied Pacific war strategy and deserves greater recognition in contemporary and subsequent accounts of the war*' and '*an appropriate use of air power and was very important to the allied victory in the SWPA.*'

On Christmas Eve 1944, 15 months after joining 79 Wing, Charles was transferred as Officer Commanding Southern Area, one of the RAAF's five operational areas. His superiors may have thought Charles had done his duty in the firing line having spent almost three and a half years on operations. On handing over to Group Captain John Ryland, Charles said 79 Wing would be in good hands. He was now aged 50. Colonel Dirk Asjes, Commanding Officer of 18 Squadron, commented on his transfer:

'This quick victory for the allies owed much to their aerial dominance ... it also owed a debt to 79 Wing operations that blocked potential Japanese reinforcements from Timor and surrounds during the allied landings at Hollandia and Aitape.'

> In him we have a true friend, a fine brother-in-arms and a brave, well-balanced Commander. But after having done his best and given himself entirely during two world wars is supposed to have done more than his share, I would say.[2]

Although his new responsibilities entailed the supervision of all RAAF units and bases in Victoria, southern New South Wales, Tasmania and South Australia, it was an administration role and one he did not really relish. However, it did not stop him from confronting the British Pacific Fleet. In his 'Tactical Appreciation for April 1945' he reported that the Royal Navy did not inform his staff when their ships altered their course. On occasions, their ships were sighted by Southern Area's reconnaissance planes *'up to 260 miles ahead of datum. This was the main reason for the forces not being met and also a great wasting of aircraft hours.'* Charles emphasised that it was disconcerting for his aircrews to search for warships that were not there.

As the war gradually wound down, he dismantled units and even ceased air patrols a week before the Japanese surrender. During the last quarter of 1945 he organised the demobilisation of thousands of airmen and their rehabilitation to civilian life. Many of the pilots and airmen of 79 Wing called in to Southern Area HQ when on leave in Melbourne. A young Dutch visitor, Jan Staal, challenged Charles to a game of squash. Thinking it would be a walk-over, *'I got soundly and hopelessly beaten because the old Group Captain turned out to be an agile wizard on the squash court. We had a good laugh about that one when I said ... to witness the old fighter you had to see him on the squash court.'*[3] Another Dutch officer, Herman Arens, was at a function in Melbourne when abused by an Australian officer because of his nationality. According to Arens, Charles intervened and said that he *'didn't mind a scrap, but would not stand abusive behaviour'.*

After almost 30 months' separation from Bea, they now enjoyed a small flat in Punt Road, South Yarra. They could see their three children more often. Aileen was in the Royal Australian Air Force Nursing Service and Charles Stuart was at boarding school. Peter, now aged 18, had been working on a sheep station west of Charleville in Queensland but in December 1944 had ridden a bicycle

'We had a good laugh about that one when I said ... to witness the old fighter you had to see him on the squash court.'

A Knight with Swords, 1944

Charles at Southern Command HQ, 1945.

to Melbourne to join the air force. Although station hands were a restricted occupation, his three-week journey had circumvented that regulation; Charles senior was proud of his elder son's effort to join the 'Colours'.

Charles was honoured when Queen Wilhelmina of the Netherlands bestowed on him the decoration of Knight Commander of the Order of the Orange Nassau with Swords.[4]

In December 1945, after 20 years of service, Charles, along with many airmen of WWI vintage, was retired from the RAAF. In uniform on 1 August 1914 as a private soldier with the Royal West Surreys, he had served throughout the entirety of both world wars.

Air Commodore Mark Lax summed up Charles' career in 2001:

> Charles 'Moth' Eaton was one of the RAAF's true unsung heroes. Described by a superior as 'a hard working commander who had the confidence of all his subordinates' and 'keen to fly' his long periods of remote and tropical service remain largely unrecognised by present day servicemen and women. Despite his personal efforts and a love for the

Bea (bottom right) and Charles (top, second from right) celebrating the end of WWII with staff of HQ Southern Command, Melbourne, August 1945.

RAAF, he never attained high rank as so many other pre-war RAAF did. Perhaps it was his British birth; perhaps his preference for flying and the Territory to a comfortable desk job in Southern Command that stopped him achieving greater recognition. His contribution to Australia both in the air and as a diplomat should never be under-estimated. Our association with the North really began with him.

Charles (left) and Peter Eaton, Melbourne, 1945.

Australia's first Consul to Portuguese Timor, Charles Eaton, and his younger son arriving at Dili's 'wharf' by lighter from HMS Camperdown, *January 1946.*

25 'The Hitch-Hiking Consul': Our Man in Timor, 1946

The Right Man: Group Captain Charles 'Moth' Eaton, last heard of in Darwin thumbing his way to Portuguese Timor, where he is to reign as Consul, is the most appropriate appointment we have made since the war. Wasn't he the Eaton I remember leading our Beaufighter squadrons from Batchelor in 1943–4 to bomb the daylights out of Timor? It was terrific. Not a worthwhile centre in Timor remained intact. It will be Group Captain Eaton's job to help, I suppose, in the rebuilding. I am sure it will be a pleasure.[1]

Charles' first introduction to the island of Timor was in mid-1938. In January of that year, the British Consul-General in Batavia warned Australia *'to consider seriously the adoption of a definite policy to establish an interest in Timor to counter-balance Japanese activities'*. The warning continued by saying that it was time to *'take a leaf out of the Japanese book and acquire a footing [in Timor] even if bears no financial promise'.*[2]

In May of 1938, Charles reputedly visited West Timor on a surveillance mission to assess Japanese influence in eastern Netherlands East Indies (Vignette 17). Three years later, he was sent to Kupang in Dutch-controlled West Timor, Dutch New Guinea and the Molucca islands by the Australian

Government on a fact-finding mission directly related to Australia's defence (Vignette 20).

Although neutral in the conflict, Portuguese Timor was in the frontline throughout the Pacific war. Australia unilaterally sent troops to the Portuguese colony in late 1941 to forestall a possible Japanese occupation, which was technically an 'act of aggression' against a neutral country. The Japanese then invaded in February 1942. More than 40,000 East Timorese may have died as a result of conflict and starvation.

Former diplomat James Dunn wrote in 1964:

> In most parts of the colony the war had a devastating effect on the livelihood of the Timorese. Many farms were abandoned, especially in fighting zones, and most of what little food production there was went in forced deliveries to the Japanese. In addition to the destruction caused by the war and by the looting of the occupiers, the Timorese had to endure devastating bombing raids by Allied aircraft operating out of Darwin.

In addition to the destruction caused by the war and by the looting of the occupiers, the Timorese had to endure devastating bombing raids by Allied aircraft operating out of Darwin.

By the end of the war in 1945, Australia acknowledged the strategic importance of Timor and agreed with Portugal's proposal that diplomatic links be formalised. A few weeks before his retirement from the RAAF, Charles read an advertisement for a consular appointment to Dili; he remarked, *'Yes, I know it well ... bombed it from one end to the other,'* and applied for the position. Although Charles had visited Dutch Timor, he had not been to the Portuguese colony. Selected as the only applicant with any knowledge of the region, he was tasked to create a diplomatic mission from scratch. He was provided with a construction team, a jeep and an army 'blitz-buggy' truck. Eleven builders, the vehicles, building materials and Charles' personal effects were to be ferried to Dili from Darwin on the SS *Quanza*. The initial, temporary consulate was to include two staff houses; ancillary buildings were to include a shower house, latrines and a garage *'of the simplest design'*.

A few weeks before his retirement from the RAAF, Charles read an advertisement for a consular appointment to Dili; he remarked, 'Yes, I know it well ... bombed it from one end to the other,' and applied for the position.'

The jeep and truck were driven by Charles and army drivers overland from Alice Springs to Darwin to await the SS *Quanza*. Charles wanted to get to Dili without delay to arrange his diplomatic accreditation and organise the logistics for the construction team. On arriving in Darwin, he found the *Quanza* delayed and no transport heading in the right direction. Son Charles Stuart, who accompanied him, knew the impatient man his father was and thought he was like 'a cat on a hot tin roof' seeking any possible way to get to Timor. Journalist Douglas Lockwood learnt of Charles' predicament and splashed the story in the national media that, *Charles Eaton is stranded in Darwin and must be the only hitch-hiking Consul in the world.* After some delay, Charles flagged down a ride on a passing British destroyer, the HMS *Camperdown,* under the command of Lieutenant Commander James Yorke, DSC.

'Charles Eaton is stranded in Darwin and must be the only hitch-hiking Consul in the world.'

On reaching Dili, the *Camperdown* anchored offshore and the consul-designate and his son were rowed ashore to Dili's temporary wharf—all that remained since 79 Wing had obliterated the original wharf leaving it hardly able to handle a canoe, let alone a destroyer. In fact, as a later consul, James Dunn, wrote, Dili had been *'almost bombed out of existence'.* The new acting Governor of Portuguese Timor, Captain Oscar Freire de Vasconcelos Ruas, accommodated the Eatons at his residence, a substantial Baroque building on the outskirts of Dili. Shortly after Charles' arrival, Ruas asked him to arrange for an estimation of costs for a new Dili jetty.

Dili had been 'almost bombed out of existence'.

Dili's Cathedral, destroyed by 79 Wing, 1943–44.

Charles soon cemented contacts with Portuguese officials and visited Timor's interior to meet those Timorese who had supported Australian soldiers during the war and to assess the state of the colony's food supply. The Governor also requested that Charles examine the proposed site of an international airport at Baucau and visit Nova Dili, a planned new township just eight miles inland from Dili. After three weeks, father and son returned to Australia and were reunited with Bea in Melbourne; Charles senior returned to Dili at the end of April. He reported in May: *'The position of the Timorese seems to be one of general improvement. Food requirements have improved and the natives are regaining their strength although many are still suffering the general privations of Japanese occupation.'*

Consul Eaton first focused on the rehabilitation of the colony, conscious that his own squadrons had inflicted the greater part of the damage throughout the whole of Timor. He suggested to Bea and his son that it would be indiscreet to emphasise that his command was responsible for the destruction of Dili's cathedral and churches in Baucau, Ermera, Venilale, Ainaro and the large building at Hatolia, even though Allied intelligence had identified the holy places as munitions dumps and Hatolia as a Japanese Army HQ.

Charles noted that 250 Timorese who had collaborated with the Japanese during the war had been deported to Atauro Island. Atauro was also the depository of 'left-wing' dissidents from Portugal who, when released, were allowed to remain in the colony as *deportados*. Many *deportados* had helped the Australian soldiers in the mountains during the Japanese occupation and a number had lost their lives. Despite Charles forming a close relationship with Governor Ruas and his staff, he was never allowed to visit the island or know who was interned. He dubbed Atauro 'The Island of the Unknown'. Charles believed that the numbers of Portuguese and Timorese who allegedly collaborated with the Japanese were exaggerated. Many remained neutral and a substantial number supported Australian commandos in 1942.

He reported in May: 'The position of the Timorese seems to be one of general improvement. Food requirements have improved and the natives are regaining their strength although many are still suffering the general privations of Japanese occupation.'

The Câmara Municipal de Dili, *destroyed by 79 Wing, 1943–44.*

Construction of the consulate progressed well, apart from delays in the supply of building materials due to spasmodic shipping. Charles recommended that the Australian tradesmen building the consulate be allowed to remain in Timor if they so desired. Some had formed personal relationships and were enjoying the easy 'simpatico Latino' lifestyle. This suited Charles, who was anxious to build up and strengthen an Australian presence in Timor. Although few in number, the Australian workmen had pushed the black-market value of the local currency, the pataca, up 25 per cent.

The general economic situation in Timor on Charles' arrival was poor. He wrote that there was much rehabilitation work to be done but the lack of equipment and machinery was a great handicap, adding that *'Sawmills brought in from Australia are electrically driven,* [but] *without power, are useless at the present time.'* Most of the rebuilding and the construction of Baucau airport was carried out manually.

'Sawmills brought in from Australia are electrically driven, [but] without power, are useless at the present time.'

Charles was often seen touring with Governor Ruas, so much so that locals dubbed him *'Grande Carlos de Deputado Governador'* to everybody's amusement, including the governor's.[3] Ruas would commandeer the

Portuguese Air Force's only DH-82 Tiger Moth in Timor and request Charles to fly him around his domain. Apparently, the consul's superiors in Canberra never learnt of his extra-consular duties as the governor's honorary pilot. Charles started to teach his Timorese driver, Ernesto Simões, the fundamentals of flying then applied to purchase a Tiger Moth for the consulate. Perhaps wisely, Canberra declined Charles' request, which left Ernesto a disappointed man.

Many Portuguese, Timorese and Chinese attended the consulate's opening ceremony on 2 July 1946, witnessing the raising of a composite Australian flag made from a gifted Mercantile Marine flag and locally made blue jean denim material. A fortnight later Charles was present at the confirmation of Captain Ruas as governor. He wrote:

> At the Palace I witnessed quite an imposing display of welcome from the natives. Parade, march past and general order was good and the dress and bearing, although unorthodox to our standards, was both original and interesting and without doubt strong loyalty was displayed.

Charles also made a courtesy call on the Chinese community in July. Their leader, Chung Hean Chung, spoke of the strong ties the community had with

Liurai (Chiefs) of Fatu-Maca de Cima, who met Charles in July 1946.

the Portuguese, who had been *'the earliest discoverers so figuring in the History of the Evolution of Man'*. Chung continued:

> Thanks to the Victory of the Allied Nations, for today, I am very glad to state that we are happy and free of the god-forsaken and barbarous Japanese occupation. Before the outbreak of the South Pacific War, your Country showed a great interest to link this Colony with commerce and various products of Portuguese Timor were exported to Australia and products imported there-from. Now, we presume the same or even better goodwill exists between the two Nations, therefore it is our ardent desire that soon may arrive the day to mark the beginning of the progress with regular commercial communications established. This, as businessmen, we are earnestly looking for.
>
> Viva Portugal! Viva Australia! Viva China!

Bea Eaton joined her husband in late July. They drove into the hinterland, where they were particularly impressed with the beautiful countryside of Ossu and the 'Lost World of Mundo Perdido', which they toured on Timor ponies. The Eatons were impressed with the agriculture of the area and visited experimental plantations of cocoa, sandalwood and rubber. In August they visited the *postos*[4] of Aileu, Maubisse and Ainaro.

Unfortunately, the vehicle of Vassalo da Silva, a former acting governor who was travelling ahead of the consular party, ran off the tortuous road to Ainaro. Charles arrived just a few minutes afterwards, applied first aid to the seriously injured da Silva and took him the 44 miles to Aileu and a doctor. Fortunately, Senor da Silva made a full recovery.

By October the lack of shipping resulted in the consulate having to cut back on its tours because petrol had run out. Charles wrote that his generator hardly had enough fuel for a few hours of electricity at night. In his despatches, Charles noted the first evidence of apathy and discontent among the Portuguese officials. The fact that he knew this reflected the confidence and respect the Governor Ruas and his staff must have had in him. Charles wrote:

'Thanks to the Victory of the Allied Nations, for today, I am very glad to state that we are happy and free of the god-forsaken and barbarous Japanese occupation.'

'From general conversation with various new officials I am of the opinion that most of them are not very keen on their appointments in Timor mainly on account of lack of personal facilities, climatic conditions and general rehabilitation difficulties.'

Governor Ruas told Charles in confidence that he was in difficulties over a new budget and *'must do practically all the work himself'* because of incompetent staff. Charles noted, *'His Excellency was suffering from overwork, overstrain and worry.'* Ruas pressed him to go to Darwin, on behalf of his administration, to negotiate matters regarding the reconstruction of Timor. Charles was reluctant to go as it was outside the ambit of his responsibilities, but when pressured by the governor he agreed to cable Canberra for permission to do so. His request was refused.

Director of Portuguese Timor Air Services, Lieutenant Solano d'Almeida, and the Secretary of Cabinet, Ruy Cinatti, made many informal calls on the Eatons. Perhaps they just wanted to practise their English or join with Charles in his six o'clock sundowners. Charles became an insider to the internal intrigues and manipulations of Portuguese colonial politics. He wrote to Canberra:

> Senor Solano [d'Almeida] often asks for some particular advice from me regarding air matters generally. Senor Solano informed me in general conversation, but confidentially, that it is probable that His Excellency may again pay a visit to Lisbon; he did not indicate the reasons for the visit but personally I feel the visit would probably be connected with the finances of Timor. Until just recently, in fact until money was available from the collection of taxes from the natives, civil officials had not been paid their salaries for about six weeks.

Later, in March 1947, Governor Ruas confided in Charles how disappointed and frustrated he was in the progress of the post-war rehabilitation of Timor. Charles wrote of Ruas that *'difficulties beset him on all sides'* including the non-arrival of essential materials from Portugal. Charles considered Ruas a conscientious man who took his responsibilities seriously but who was *'very tired'*. Shipping from Portugal was irregular, at times once in every eight months,

'His Excellency was suffering from overwork, overstrain and worry.'

and in April the colony ran out of both flour and sugar. Used to acting on his own initiative, Charles was astounded to find the governor had to refer trivial matters to Lisbon, such as approval for the right air routes to mail the post. He commented that local officials were *'timorous'* towards their metropolitan government. At one stage, when export coffee was to be shipped on a visiting ship, the *Comet*, Charles found *'the Portuguese Authorities were not capable at such short notice of arranging to load the coffee'* so he organised it himself.

In November 1946, the consul went on another inspection tour, accompanied by Bea and driver Ernesto. They visited the *postos* of Lautem, Lospalos and Cape Lore, about which he reported that the civil administration in the *postos* was still unsettled and confused. Many of the officials were new to Timor, not happy with conditions and wished to be sent back to either Portugal or Africa. The Eatons stayed with the *chefe de posto* of Los Palos; although kind and hospitable towards the couple, Charles found his manner of dealing with the Timorese *'most severe ... he drives them considerably and without doubt the natives of the district are frightened of him'*. The secretary of the *posto* complained to Charles about his superior's methods, confirming the consul's own assessment. The secretary continued to question the *'proposed plans of the Governor who, he considers, is only a talker and dreamer'*. He told Charles that he wanted to return to Portugal at the first opportunity and was prepared to pay his own way. Similar attitudes were later confirmed by Consul Dunn, who wrote that appointments to Timor were considered *'a kind of penance'*.

It was in Los Palos that Charles found the first indications of Timorese unrest. Although there had been initial enthusiasm among the native Timorese for the return to Portuguese rule after the Japanese, this attitude was waning. The imposition of a head tax of 16 patacas per year caused *'shock and grumblings'*, but Charles found no evidence of organised opposition.

The visit to Los Palos enabled Charles to show Bea the damage caused to the Japanese radar installations by his 79 Wing two years previously:

'The Portuguese Authorities were not capable at such short notice of arranging to load the coffee'.

During my last visit to the interior I was particularly interested to see the Japanese defences of Lautem-Cape Lore areas. I do not know if the full facts are known to our military authorities but at one time some 25,000 Japanese soldiers occupied these areas. The Japanese camps and defence works along the road between Lautem and Fuilore were considerable and the camouflage almost perfect. The Cape Lore beach-head was the best defence work I have seen in Timor; the earth and wire works were extensive.

I also visited the Japanese Cape Lore radar station. This station is actually on the top of a mountain at the rear of Cape Lore. I was very interested in this station as I personally took part in an attack on this work in December 1944. The attack was an interesting one as it was the first time that diaphragm bomb-heads were used in Timor. The Radar Station had been hit but the extent of the bomb damage was difficult to ascertain as after the attack the Japanese dismantled the remains. Without doubt the main building was severely damaged by the diaphragm bombs.

Travelling in Timor was not without its dangers. In January 1947, the Eatons had a real scare when travelling back to Dili after visiting the western districts. While crossing the Comoro River, a sudden surge of monsoonal water stranded their jeep mid-stream. Within seconds Bea was sucked out of the car and began floating downstream. Ernesto and Charles quickly jumped into the turbulent waters and managed to drag her to the river bank. Meanwhile, Charles Stuart, who was on school holidays, ran a few miles back to the nearest village to obtain help. Eventually the jeep was retrieved. While Charles and Ernesto extracted water from the engine, Bea and Charles Stuart were taken to the village where they spent the night as welcome guests of hospitable Timorese villagers.

The Eatons enjoyed their time in Timor, which reminded them of their India days. Charles, who had begun collecting orchids in Orissa's jungles, particularly relished his tours to the interior of Timor, where he collected many other orchid varieties. The consulate was soon festooned with ex-Japanese Army rice containers displaying a wide selection of the island's orchids.

The Governor of Portuguese Timor's visit to Australia 1947. From left, Consul Charles Eaton, Guinea Airways Air Hostess, Senhora Ruas, Captain Oscar Ruas and Senor Ruy Cinatti.

'I was very interested in this station as I personally took part in an attack on this work in December 1944.'

26 Oil on Troubled Waters, 1947

Communications here are the great difficulty. Since our arrival, we have had practically no supplies and no mail has been received since 23 November 1946. The Catalina service is not good and I feel there is certain apathy to do it from Service Circles at Darwin. The visit which I really did want to come off of Civil Aviation authorities has also been postponed.

Charles Eaton, 1946

While in Timor, Charles became closely involved with the nation's development, in particular the nation's oil reserves, the opening of the country to air travel and incipient political agitation. Immediately before WWII, Japan and Australia had vied for oil concessions in Timor; various companies including Timor Oil and Oil Search had negotiated for leases. The Japanese occupation of the island halted all exploration, but after the Australian Consulate opened in 1946, companies visited Timor to reactivate lapsed leases and search for new areas.

In July 1946 Charles inspected Laclubar district, 4000 feet (1220 metres) in altitude, and was impressed with its temperate climate, fertile soils and the condition of its livestock. He learnt that oil at the village of Pualaca was being *'ladled out of the well by hand'* at a rate of 400 gallons (1515 litres) a month. After a four-hour journey on horseback to Pualaca he found that the oil fields consisted of three wells just 30 feet deep. The Japanese had constructed a crude refinery that was still operating. After being refined, the oil was poured by hand into 45-gallon barrels that were carried on poles by a team of 20 Timorese to Laclubar, 10 miles (16 kilometres) away—a full day's journey.

Charles extracted oil samples and photographed the oil fields, mailing both photographs and samples to Canberra after his return journey to Dili, during which he was kicked in the leg by a pony and laid low for some time. Eventually, production at Paulaca increased to 5500 gallons (25,000 litres) of 'kerosene' a month, destined for the local market and retailing at 40 cents a litre or 3/4d Australian a gallon.

The subject of oil concessions occupied much of Charles' time in early 1947; in May, he inspected Timor Oil's assets at Aliambata, but dismissed their infrastructure as *'junk.'* He thought the oil wells in Suai were the most encouraging. A European geologist suggested to Charles that substantial oil fields would be discovered offshore. Charles found out that American companies were to be allocated oil concessions by the Portuguese authorities west of 125° 50' and Portuguese companies to the east of this longitude.

Charles suggested to Governor Ruas that he could arrange for the RAAF to conduct an aerial survey in June and August, when the least cloud is present over the islands. Charles wrote in one despatch: *'It seems to me that the position (of oil concessions) is both obscure here and at Lisbon.'* Unfortunately, the survey did not eventuate.

Charles arranged for Governor Ruas and himself to visit Australia to *'particularly help in the matter of the intricacies of Timor oil'*. The Governor and Senhora Ruas were guests of Australia's Governor-General for three days, entertained by Dr Evatt at a state reception then taken to inspect the Newcastle steel works. During his visit, from 10 June to 5 July,

He learnt that oil at the village of Pualaca was being 'ladled out of the well by hand' at a rate of 400 gallons (1515 litres) a month.

East Timor's oil industry in its infancy. Hand-ladling oil, Pualaca village, November 1946.

Charles arranged for Governor Ruas and himself to visit Australia to 'particularly help in the matter of the intricacies of Timor oil'.

Governor Ruas also discussed with officials and private interests the need for increased commerce between Timor and Australia. The Portuguese media reported:

> In Melbourne, Adelaide, Darwin and other cities the Governor of Timor was the centre of highest respect on part of the Australian authorities, who see in Timor a reborn colony and in Portugal, a friend and ally whom Australia can count upon.

Charles' concern about the need for better communications between Timor and Darwin had featured in despatches from early 1946 and led to a twice weekly RAAF Catalina flying-boat service. Charles regularly reported on airport matters in his despatches; for example, he noted that in the absence of any mechanical aids, many thousands of Timorese were preparing the Baucau Airport runways by hand. Charles relished his role as the unofficial advisor for Timor's civil aviation. He advised on improvement to the airstrips at Dili and Lautem, adamant they be improved to Australian standards for safety reasons. Lautem aerodrome was still damaged from WWII bombing but Charles commented that '*except for a few bomb craters, which were flagged, it is suitable for landings*'. He facilitated the visits of two young Portuguese pilots to Australia to procure light aircraft and, when in Australia, personally approached the RAAF's Chief of Air Staff and Director of Aviation to ensure Baucau airport was equipped with the best technology available. He also recommended

Lautem aerodrome was still damaged from WWII bombing but Charles commented that 'except for a few bomb craters, which were flagged, it is suitable for landings'.

Darwin–Dili RAAF Catalina service Dili Airport, 1947.

that, for safety and convenience, a radio transmitting station be installed near Dili to enable direct communication with Darwin.

Unfortunately, the RAAF Catalina service proved unreliable; Charles was annoyed that his workmen therefore did not receive their promised beer ration. In July 1946 he finally admitted the Catalina service had been a failure; it had arrived on schedule on only three occasions. He recommended that a commercial aircraft company take over responsibility and invited Australian aviation administrators to Dili to assess the situation. After months of promises, no Australian aviation experts appeared. Charles fumed; he wrote to Canberra on a wide agenda of aviation issues and voiced his disappointment: *'I am particularly sorry that the visit of the Australian Aviation officers has not taken place as I consider there are many matters regarding aviation and technical information that are keenly desired by the Portuguese authorities.'*

By 15 January 1947 no Catalina had arrived since late November, despite a message stating that *'a Catalina might arrive in the New Year with Civil Aviation Officials'.* Charles blasted the RAAF: *'The position is still obscure ... I am of the opinion that the service is not favoured by the RAAF,'* adding that the Darwin–Timor service should be operated by a civilian company. Finally, after a two-month lapse of the service, an Australian aviation delegation arrived on 24 January 1947. The visitors were wined and dined by the Portuguese and shown Baucau and Lautem aerodromes, but left early the next morning. Charles wrote to Canberra that the Australian party had failed to meet its objective. Everyone, including Governor Ruas, was disappointed. Charles was furious as the RAAF *'could not give any definite indications regarding the future of the Catalina service'.*

At the same time, political tensions were increasing. Timorese from both sides of the border clashed in February 1947; one Portuguese African soldier was killed and five West Timorese were wounded. Charles reported that Javanese nationalists probably influenced the West Timorese to incite such incidents for political purposes. A month later, a Portuguese patrol crossed

'I am particularly sorry that the visit of the Australian Aviation officers has not taken place as I consider there are many matters regarding aviation and technical information that are keenly desired by the Portuguese authorities.'

Portuguese African soldiers on duty, November 1946.

into Dutch territory in mufti. A rifle fight with Dutch troops eventuated and, although no one was killed, there were wounded on both sides and one Portuguese African soldier was captured by the Dutch. The motive for the patrol was thought to be revenge for the death of an African soldier the month before. This second clash resulted in intense ill feeling on both sides. Although some border incidents were a result of cattle stealing and inter-tribal animosities, Charles warned: *'Such infiltration, however, underlines the need for interest by Australia in this island.'*

Charles also kept busy touring Timor as much as practical. He departed on an extended tour of the *fronteira postos* that bordered Dutch Timor: Ermera, Fatu-Bessi, Hatolia, Lete-Foho, Bobonaro and Suai. He was informed there were '*a few minor frontier incidents*'. Governor Ruas, however, confided in Charles his concern that Indonesian political agitation could filter into Portuguese territory from the Dutch side.

Charles reported to Canberra:

> The Fronteira Province seems to be causing the Government little concern. This was the Province where most collaboration with the Japanese occurred, and according to the Portuguese, was caused by infiltration from Dutch Timor. Two companies of West African soldiers have been sent to the Fronteira Province with their Headquarters at Bobonaro.
>
> The village of Lete-Foho has been completely destroyed during the war but, in this case, it is admitted that the village was destroyed by hostile Timorese. Practically all main buildings in all townships visited had been destroyed during the war.

On this tour, Charles witnessed first-hand the reluctance by the Timorese to pay their head-tax. He estimated half the Timorese in the *fronteira* districts were refusing to pay and many had *'gone bush'* to avoid payment. He said many of the border's population had cooperated with the Japanese during WWII, especially around Hatolia. This was the only occasion he saw the *chefe de posto's* home guarded at nights. Hatolia was the target of 79 Wing's successful rocket attack in November 1944 and where Charles' Beaufighter returned to base with a piece of rocket embedded in one wing.

On one of his *fronteira* tours, Charles found that the rubber and coffee estates of the *Sociedade Agricola Patria e Trabalho* (SAPT) had begun rehabilitating their plantations. He again took the opportunity to push Australia's interests in Timor:

> The SAPT plantations at Fatu-Besi consist of about 12,000 acres of probably the best country in Timor and as stated in previous dispatches were 40% owned by the Japanese prior to the last war. Attached to my dispatch No 8 dated 13 August, 1946 was an annex of a decree of the Portuguese Authorities and in paragraph 42 of this decree it stated that all Japanese interests in Timor were to be confiscated and taken over by the Portuguese Government.
>
> In view of the efforts of our own country during the war towards the defeat of Japan generally and the Japanese occupation of Timor in particular, I think consideration may be worthwhile for Australia to take over the previous

'The village of Lete-Foho has been completely destroyed during the war but, in this case, it is admitted that the village was destroyed by hostile Timorese. Practically all main buildings in all townships visited had been destroyed during the war.'

Japanese interest in the SAPT and thus give Australia a permanent [and] practical interest in Timor. However, I realise this matter is a very delicate one in view of the present Portuguese outlook on their colonies.

He described an incursion into the Portuguese enclave of Oecussi by escaped Japanese prisoners-of-war and Javanese nationalists who asked Portuguese African soldiers for their machine guns. Heavily armed soldiers were immediately flown into Oecussi but the intruders returned to Dutch territory without incident. Not only was Charles concerned with Portuguese Timor affairs, he was also charged by Canberra to investigate the situation in Dutch-controlled Timor. Canberra viewed the Indonesian nationalist intrusion into the eastern islands of Indonesia to be of the greatest importance and in need of close monitoring.

Charles visited Kupang in Dutch Timor in May and July of 1947. He reported to Canberra that there was confusion as Dutch Timor was now part of the new Dutch-sponsored 'State of East Indonesia', with its capital in Macassar. The Dutch Resident had to report not only to local councils headed by traditional rulers, but to Lieutenant Governor-General van Mook in Batavia. Charles continued: '*The administration* [of Dutch Timor] *is in a state of flux and the administration of other islands is being handed over to the local councils. The Resident told me he was in a most unenviable position. There is no actual outward political trouble in Timor itself but I was told that political trouble has extended to Sumbawa.*'

Charles tried to explore if the Dutch would lease part of their territory to Australia. Dr Steven Farram wrote in 2010 that Charles had '*noted the importance of the territory to Australia for defence purposes and its potential economic capabilities*'. He had, in fact, suggested that the Dutch were likely to relinquish their Timor holdings in the future as the gradual shift to local Indonesian administration had left most Dutch officials with little desire to remain in the territory. Charles was later proved correct. His personal view was that the whole island should be an interim protectorate of Australia '*for the protection of the Timorese people and the defence of Australia*'.

His personal view was that the whole island should be an interim protectorate of Australia 'for the protection of the Timorese people and the defence of Australia'.

During these visits Charles took the opportunity to inspect some of the damage inflicted by 76 Wing during WWII; of particular interest were the dock areas of Kupang and the Japanese barracks nearby. Charles drove to the Mina River and visited the bridge to the north-east of Kupang that Beaufighters and Mitchell bombers of 79 Wing had destroyed.

In late August Charles was suddenly transferred to Batavia as the Consul-General to the Netherlands East Indies (NEI). He summarised his prime responsibilities while in Dili: *Reported on the political and economic development of the territory with emphasis on the 'Australian Defence Policy' for the area immediately north of Darwin. Liaison with all local and foreign officials, private business people and trade enquiries from all sources.*

Six weeks after Charles' departure, Secretary Cinetti wrote to Canberra on the Governor's behalf thanking Australia for the attention Portuguese Timor had received since the war. He concluded: '*Concerning Mr Charles Eaton, if on one hand His Excellency the Governor received with great satisfaction his promotion to Consul General, on the other hand it is with sadness that he sees him leaving Timor, where he has only friends.*'[1]

The Portuguese Government offered to award Charles the decoration, Commander in the Military Order of the Cross of Christ, '*in recognition of his useful co-operation in securing all necessary facilities in connection with reconstruction and development of Timor*'. The Australian Government declined permission for him to accept the decoration. Nevertheless, Charles must have been gratified to be formally recognised for his contribution to the territory's post-war reconstruction in addition to an order of chivalry from The Netherlands, a citation from George VI for his participation in Timor's liberation, and acknowledgement by the Japanese Commander in Timor that the attacks he directed '*were so skilful and heavy*'.

Postscript

Charles' vision of industrial-scale onshore oil production has yet to be realised in Timor-Leste, the independent state that Portuguese Timor finally transitioned into on 20 May 2002 after a failed decolonisation process and a civil war. The Timor Sea has since yielded billions of dollars' worth of gas that has contributed to the buoyancy of the modern Timor-Leste economy and caused friction between Timor-Leste and Australia concerning which state should receive the lion's share of royalties.

The transmitting station that Charles recommended be built in 1946, which became known as the Marconi Building, played a critical role in the 1975 civil war prior to the Indonesian intervention.

Charles Eaton heading the UN's first investigation to monitor conflict. Central figures from left: The Sultan of Yogyakarta, His Highness Hamengkoe Boewono, C Eaton, E Raux. Eaton's Dakota of 85 Wing RAAF in the background. Yogyakarta, Central Java, 3 September 1947.

27 The Pathfinder, 1947

The end of WWII not only hastened the demise of western colonialism, it challenged Australia's response to dramatic political changes in the countries of South East Asia.

The Secretary for External Affairs, Dr John Burton wrote:

I was worried about developments in Indonesia. I needed someone who could take initiatives in a difficult and even dangerous situation. No available diplomat or officer in the Department was appropriate. I can recall being relieved that [Eaton] was available. I knew little of him but was impressed immediately with his objectivity and willingness to cope with a new situation. He was to be on his own to do what he could, and not many people can be given such tasks.

The end of WWII not only hastened the demise of western colonialism, it challenged Australia's response to dramatic political changes in the countries of

South East Asia. Philip Dorling wrote in 1994 that *'Indonesian independence was an early and critical test of Australia's capacity to respond positively to change in Asia ... Australia was the Indonesian Republic's most active and effective diplomatic ally.'*[1]

The Japanese had occupied the whole of NEI since 1942, except the region surrounding Merauke in Dutch New Guinea where Charles had commanded a composite RAAF fighter–bomber wing in 1943. On 17 August 1945, just two days after the Japanese capitulation, Indonesian nationalist leaders unilaterally declared independence from Dutch colonial rule, starting a war for independence. The new Republic of Indonesia was led by President Sukarno and Vice-President Mohammad Hatta.

The NEI administration, exiled in Australia during WWII, returned to find large areas of Java and Sumatra were Republican-controlled. British forces, which had initially landed in Indonesia to accept the Japanese surrender and to protect Dutch civilian and military prisoners of war, then endeavoured to impose civic order after fighting broke out between mainly ethnic Indonesian and non-Indonesian factions, including the Battle of Surabaya. Adrian Vickers identified the violence as 'The Bersiap Period' with killings reported as *'nearly 20,000 individuals were indiscriminately killed between August 1945 and December 1946.'*[2] The Allied Commander in South East Asia, Lord Louis Mountbatten ordered that Japanese Army troops be kept under arms to help control the chaotic situation. Arriving in Sumatra early in 1946, he was never-the-less *'astonished'* to see hundreds of armed Japanese soldiers guarding the road from the airport.[3]

The Dutch military began returning to NEI in significant numbers in early 1946. Dutch and Indonesian representatives reached a *status quo* accord, the Linggadjati Agreement, in December 1946. British troops withdrew from Indonesia at the same time. The agreement gave the Indonesian Republic *de facto* recognition in parts of Sumatra, Java and Madura and stipulated that the Netherlands and the Republic would cooperate to create a federated United States of Indonesia. The new state would include Kalimantan and the eastern islands of Indonesia, many of which were well-disposed towards Dutch influence.

However, by July 1947 relations between the antagonists had deteriorated to the extent that the Dutch launched an armed action, dubbed 'Operatie Product', against the Republic. The Indonesian Premier, Amir Sjarifuddin, appealed to Australia to intervene on his nation's behalf; Dr Herbert Vere Evatt, Australia's Minister for External Affairs, offered Australia's support for the Republic. Indonesia's overseas representative, Soetan Sjahrir, petitioned the newly formed United Nations Security Council to take direct action to halt the Dutch aggression *'because we have no faith in the honesty and goodwill of the Netherlands Government'.*

Australia and India put separate resolutions forward to the Security Council on 30 July calling for a ceasefire. Australia's proposal was approved on 1 August after an amendment by the USA. The Dutch finally bowed to international pressure and ceased hostilities on 4 August. The Dutch forces had resumed control of half of Java and extended their foothold in resource-rich Sumatra.

The UN Security Council was then urged to initiate a supervisory body as soon as possible to assess the situation. Australia called for an immediate report by a 'Commission of Investigation' as the situation was confused, with reports of violations of the ceasefire agreement. [4]

Dr Steven Farram summarises:

> On 25 August 1947, the UN Security Council passed two resolutions relating to the security situation in Indonesia. Both resolutions were the result of a draft resolution put to the Council by Australia on 30 July, calling for the armed forces of the Netherlands and those of the Republic of Indonesia to cease hostilities immediately and for both sides to submit their dispute to arbitration ... This was the very first UN ceasefire order, but hostilities were not ended and all attempts to bring the two parties together to resolve their dispute were unsuccessful. Australia and other countries continued to raise the matter in the Security Council, resulting in the two resolutions passed on 25 August.

Of these two resolutions, Australia and China proposed the resolution calling for a Consular Commission (the Commission) to be created to investigate breaches of the ceasefire and to report on the military, social and economic situation on both sides of the ceasefire line. The Commission was to comprise the consuls resident in Batavia; those of Australia, Belgium, China, France, the United Kingdom and the United States.

Australia also proposed an arbitration mechanism, but this was rejected by the USA, which instead proposed a mediation mechanism. The subsequent resolution approved a United Nations Good Offices Committee (GOC) to negotiate a political settlement for Indonesia's future as a nation. The GOC first met in October 1947.

Charles, as the newly appointed Consul-General designate to NEI, was appointed as Australia's representative on the Commission. As was his practice, Charles left no personal reminiscences of his participation in the Commission and subsequent events, which laid the foundations of Australia's future relations with Indonesia. He arrived in Batavia to take up this next challenge on 30 August 1947. Through his RAAF connections he had organised a fully-crewed DC-3 Dakota aircraft to be based in Batavia with him and had Australian flags painted on the aircraft. He later reminisced that his Dakota transported the representatives of four permanent members of the Security Council—the United States, China, the United Kingdom and France—around Indonesia as they lacked their own transport.

Charles, as the newly appointed Consul-General designate to NEI, was appointed as Australia's representative on the Commission.

Charles was instructed by Canberra to report the authenticity of alleged breaches of the ceasefire and was urged to use his discretion to obtain details of the Dutch position regarding the future of Indonesia. He was to act decisively so Indonesia would nominate Australia as its representative on the GOC.[5] On arrival in Batavia, Charles learnt that the proposed Commission had not yet met. However, he began his task by interviewing Dutch officials and liaising with resident consuls in Batavia. He was unable to see the Lieutenant Governor-General of the NEI, Hubertus van Mook, and because

Charles was instructed by Canberra to report the authenticity of alleged breaches of the ceasefire and was urged to use his discretion to obtain details of the Dutch position regarding the future of Indonesia. He was to act decisively so Indonesia would nominate Australia as its representative on the GOC.

the Dutch officials forbade individual investigations, was prevented from flying immediately to Yogyakarta, the Republican-held city in central Java.

In seeking to meet all sides, Charles pre-empted the monitoring of the military stand-off days before it was formally sanctioned by the yet-to-meet Commission. Having trained as a reconnaissance soldier and aviator in WWI, his instinct was to seek to observe and report as soon as practical on the other side of The Line;[6] this time, The Line was the ceasefire line that separated Dutch and Indonesian forces. But his reconnaissance was not to wage war, but to observe the military and political situation from the Republic's perspective to balance the view from Batavia. His impatience to see the other side of the conflict incurred the wrath of the Dutch representative in Canberra, Petrus Ephrem Teppema, who complained of Charles' *tactless approach* and added that *'Eaton should refrain from any activity until recognition of his appointment was confirmed.'*[7] In Batavia, Dutch official Schuurman cabled the Minister for Foreign Affairs in The Hague stating that *'Eaton is an unusual character'* who would go to Yogyakarta regardless. He added that *'Australia was trying to bluff us and to play first violin,'* and that *'Eaton had no understanding of the Dutch standpoint.'* The Dutch view was that if Charles acted arbitrarily and without their approval, formal recognition of his diplomatic status would be withheld.

His impatience to see the other side of the conflict incurred the wrath of the Dutch representative in Canberra.

The Commission's inaugural meeting was held in Batavia on 1 September and chaired by the American, Dr Foote, following his nomination by Charles. The consuls of the United States, Australia, Belgium and France attended; the Chinese Consul failed to turn up and the United Kingdom representative sat in as an observer only. The meeting concluded that direct contacts were to be sought with Indonesian and Dutch officials, that both sides list all danger points along the ceasefire line and military observers be recruited by their respective consuls. Professor Peter Londey wrote in *Sixty Years of Keeping the Peace* that *'Eaton suggested that the Consular Commission needed military assistants to monitor the situation as a matter of priority.'* As a result, the first major decision of the meeting was that the boundaries between the conflicting parties be policed by impartial observers stationed along the line. Charles requested Canberra to appoint four Australian military officers on attachment to the Commission without delay. Stressing the Commission's resolution, he added:

> Recommendations by all members to their governments for [a] total of 24 military officers to be attached as observers to either side for observance of 'ceasefire' order and to obtain any other relevant information.

Supporting Charles' impatience to visit the Republican-controlled areas, the Commission authorised him to proceed to Yogyakarta with the French Consul, Etienne Raux. They were to establish contacts with the Republicans, identify dangerous situations, verify allegations of violations of the ceasefire and obtain assurances for the Commission's freedom of movement. Late in the afternoon of 2 September, Dutch officials finally agreed for Charles to visit Yogyakarta the next morning. Two American journalists, Briggs of the *Christian Science Monitor* and Scheffer of the *New Rotterdam Courant*, were banned by the Dutch from going despite having Charles' permission to do so. On the same day, Australia agreed to Charles' request that four officers be attached to the Commission as a matter of urgency.

On arrival in Yogyakarta, the consuls were met by His Highness Hamengkoe Boewono IX, the Sultan of Yogyakarta and traditional ruler of Central Java. Over the next three days the consuls inspected as much of the region as possible, held discussions with President Sukarno, members of the Indonesian Cabinet and military commanders. Their talks centred on the ceasefire, the economic situation within territory controlled by the Republic and the structure of the National Army of Indonesia, the *Tentara Nasional Indonesia* (TNI). They visited hospitals, where they found Dutch prisoners were being treated well. They observed that many Chinese were fleeing the Republican-held areas due to harassment by Indonesian guerrillas. They also assessed the stability of the ceasefire. The Republicans showed the consuls maps defining the boundaries before and after the Dutch police action. The Indonesians admitted that 60 renegade Japanese soldiers were instructing the

TNI and British Indian Army deserters were in their ranks, but no Germans. There were, however, some German teachers in the Republican-held area. They confirmed that all non-Indonesian soldiers were to be returned to their respective countries once transport became available; this repatriation subsequently occurred.

On the stability of the ceasefire the consuls reported:

> We were informed that the approximate weekly casualty rate since the ceasefire was 150 Indonesians, of whom 80 per cent were civilians killed by artillery or mortar fire. They expected the present rate to continue or even increase. Their estimate of Dutch casualties was twenty killed each week.
>
> It is our considered opinion that, in view of the present situation regarding the Netherlands demarcation lines and the present positions of both Netherlands and Indonesian troops, the cease-fire order cannot be observed, and that incidents and guerrilla fighting will continue and probably increase.

Describing his reception in Central Java, Charles reported: '*I received all facilities and kindness from the Indonesians*' and was impressed with the genuineness of Sukarno and Sjarifuddin. Rather prophetically, he observed

From left, Sjarifuddin, Raux, Sukarno and Eaton meeting in Yogyakarta, 3 September 1947.

that in the future '*what* [the Indonesians] *expect from Australia is going to be most difficult for Australia*'. He emphasised that without an international military force to police the ceasefire, the only alternative was for the Dutch to return to their original territory because, in his opinion, if no military observers were in place immediately, non-observance of the ceasefire would intensify.

The consuls returned to Batavia on 7 September and prepared a report on the military, economic and political situation in Republican-held Central Java. Charles summarised his findings to Canberra in a cable marked 'Top Secret':[8]

> 1) **Political**. The Republic will not agree to the 'Van Mook' ceasefire line. The Republicans will resist any attempt by the Dutch military if they move from 'stand-fast' positions. The Indonesians expressed intense bitterness against the Dutch for the police action and their attitude is fanatical. The Republic places full reliance on the UN to solve the conflict.
>
> 2) **Military.** In comparison to the Dutch military the organisation and equipment of the Republic is hopeless and pitiful. Some pockets of Republican troops are within the Dutch area. Organised resistance by the Indonesians is impossible: only guerrilla and *franc tireur* actions can be carried out. There is no possibility of the ceasefire being observed in East Java. It is impossible to ascertain which side initiated non-observance of the ceasefire order. It would be a waste of time to attempt to do so.
>
> 3) **General.** The Republicans are cut off from all communications except for radio broadcasts and aeroplane arrivals at Yogyakarta and then only with Dutch permission. The civil administration, public utilities and agriculture are normal. There are shortages of materials, clothing and medical supplies but not food. Imports are impossible. The morale of the population is high and people extended public greetings en route on our travels. Attempts to provide social welfare were evident. Freedom of religion is permitted.

Their five-day visit was the UN's first direct intervention to evaluate a conflict and a precursor for the four Australian military observers, who were *in situ* by mid-September—the UN's first military observers to prevent and monitor conflict. The genesis for the UN's future role and *modus operandi* for global peacekeeping may be attributed to that nine-day period, 30 August to

Their five-day visit was the UN's first direct intervention to evaluate a conflict and a precursor for the four Australian military observers, who were in situ by mid-September—the UN's first military observers to prevent and monitor conflict.

From left, Etienne Raux, President Sukarno and Charles Eaton at a dinner hosted by the President in Yogyakarta, 3 September 1947.

7 September 1947. Unfortunately, and following his normal practice, Charles never wrote a personal account of what must have been the most significant reconnaissance and far-reaching achievement of his life.

Republican Premier Sjarifuddin cabled Australian Prime Minister Chifley on 7 September formally requesting that Australia represent Indonesia on the UN-proposed GOC based in Batavia to broker a permanent solution to the conflict. Chifley replied that Australia would accept Indonesia's request, which he hoped would find a lasting solution. The GOC was formed in October 1947 in Batavia with Australia, the United States and Belgium as members.

Australia informed the Dutch that Charles' actions, described by the Dutch as '*impetuous*', had their full support. However, Charles' superior in Canberra, Dr Burton, warned him that while his general report was most satisfactory, other members on the Commission would not necessarily concur with '*your facts, as they will be only interested in obtaining support for their political theories already formulated*'. [9]

Dr Burton advised Charles to use discretion to ensure the Dutch withdrew its troops, under the auspices of the Commission's military observers, to the agreed ceasefire line. Charles replied that, in his opinion, the Dutch would not withdraw unless ordered to by the UN Security Council. Furthermore, he considered a Dutch withdrawal could only be carried out without casualties if Republican guarantees were obtained first.

Meanwhile, Dr Burton cabled Dr Evatt in New York that van Mook was pressuring the United States and the United Kingdom to support the Netherlands by making accusations against Australia:

> The need for Dutch haste is now greater, because the Consuls, on Eaton's initiative, are penetrating into areas previously closed by the Dutch from observation. Eaton's first report is in my immediately following telegram. It gives a totally different picture of the position and the strength of the Republican movement than that given by the Dutch.

Because of the abrupt ceasefire of 4 August, the Dutch were caught between 'Cossack and Cannon'; either they advance or withdraw. Unless an agreement was reached, Charles' prediction of a fanatical and bloody reaction by the Indonesians would be realised. Charles wrote that he had positive collaborators in the British and French delegates; the Belgian *'was pro-Dutch'*, the Chinese *'was sitting on the fence'* and the American was *'a master of ceremonies'*. He reported that the Dutch attitude towards

Charles acknowledging the Indonesian Army's guard of honour, Central Java, 3 September 1947.

Australia and Australians in general was cold. However, the Dutch military he contacted were personally friendly; in fact, he found that some Dutch officers voiced opposition to van Mook's policies. Charles was well known to them and they were aware that he had been decorated by their Queen for his war services.

The newly appointed United Kingdom Consul, Sir Francis Shepherd, who arrived after the first meeting of the Commission, was critical of the Commission. Reporting to London he wrote:[10]

> The Consular Commission is going into action in a rather a wavering manner. The first meeting I attended was completely chaotic but a little order has now been introduced into the proceedings. It was unfortunate that the Commission decided at the first meeting to appoint the American Consul General as its first Chairman ... [he] is a very autocratic person with strong views and apparently a complete inability to delegate functions or to share information with anybody ... In the meanwhile various members of the Commission have been making more-or-less preliminary investigations the most energetic member being undoubtedly the Australian, Eaton, who has been provided an aircraft by his government and seems determined to observe as fast [and] as often as he can manage. He and the Frenchman already have spent several days in the Indonesian sector east-wards from Djocjakarta and Lambert has gone with him this week to Sourabaya to see the corresponding area from the Dutch side.

Three days later Shepherd reiterated his opinion of the Commission:

> Apart from Eaton, the Australian, who is a very energetic person and arrived with a full briefing and a Dakota aircraft, the only expression I can find to describe my colleagues, if you can excuse the cattiness, is suet puddings.

'Various members of the Commission have been making more-or-less preliminary investigations the most energetic member being undoubtedly the Australian, Eaton, who has been provided an aircraft by his government and seems determined to observe as fast [and] as often as he can manage.'

An Indonesian crowd welcoming members of the Consular Commission. Eaton (third from left foreground) talking to Indonesian delegate, Bukittinggi, Sumatra, 16 September 1947.

28 In the Line of Fire, 1947

One redeeming feature, there are some lovely orchids in Java.
Charles Eaton 1947

Ever the impatient man, Charles returned to Batavia for only two days before making his second reconnaissance, this time to the Dutch-controlled areas of East Java. British Deputy Consul-General, 'Teddy' Lambert, and Charles flew together to east Java in the RAAF Dakota on 9 September. Before leaving Batavia, he cabled Dr Burton that the '*seedy*' Australian Consulate in Batavia needed to be renovated to give the place the '*dignity*' of a Consulate'.

Secretary John Burton's prediction that a dangerous situation might occur proved correct when the consuls' motorcade was ambushed near Malang by unidentified vigilante machine-gunners on the second day of their visit.

Charles blandly reported that the shooting was normal in view of the many military convoys travelling throughout the area. The local media, *Keng Po*, reported that *'Eaton appeared fearless.'*[1] *The Canberra Times* reported the ambush more dramatically:

> CONSUL WAS NOT AFRAID
>
> Batavia, Friday. AAP-Reuters. When a machine-gun opened fire on a Dutch convoy escorting the British Consul-General (Mr ET Lambert) and the Australian Consul-General (Mr C Eaton) all took cover except for Mr Eaton who strolled around behind his car saying: 'they are not firing at me'. The Dutch declared that the machine-gun fire was by Republicans. The incident occurred on Wednesday near Singosari, Java, after the consuls investigated the ceasefire in the Malang area.

'They are not firing at me'

How Charles knew the bullets were not directed at him remains unclear. After reading the account of the ambush in the Australian press, an old friend and Gallipoli veteran, Hector McWhae, suggested that after the Somme, being attacked by German fighter aircraft, being targeted by angry prison guards at *Festung Neun* and braving Japanese ack ack, *'Moth must have learnt which bullets were meant for him.'*

A cloak and dagger situation arose while they were still in the Malang area; a police informant, Soedjono, was kidnapped by unknown perpetrators. This caused a flurry of telegrams between the Commission and the conflicting parties as Soedjono was under suspicion of having given information to Charles and Lambert. Soedjono's wife was also kidnapped. Dr Adan Kapau Gani, the Indonesian minister in Batavia, cabled his government in Yogyakarta:

> On 25 September the Consular Commission requested me in a note immediately to investigate the case of SOEDJONO of the State Police Force at Malang. Soedjono was in the possession of a report for EATON and LAMBERT at Malang but was kidnapped on September 16 or 17. We do not know by whom. Please settle this matter as soon as possible, for this makes a very bad impression.

The National Army of Indonesia, Tentara Nasional Indonesia (TNI), Guard of Honour for Charles Eaton, East Java, 1947. As usual, his camera and pipe were at hand.

The implications of the kidnapping indicated a pro-Dutch report by an Indonesian, an act the Republicans wished to suppress. Charles continued to move around East Java freely, visiting the port city of Surabaya. He cabled Canberra:

> I seem to have been rushing around a bit here but I am pleased that I feel I have been able to initiate a real commencement of the investigation. I have had minor opposition which I have taken no notice of, and now all is going as well as I can expect.

He did not clarify if the minor opposition was van Mook's hostility towards him, the bullets of the unknown gunmen or from his fellow members of the Commission. Dr Burton wrote to Dr Evatt that Charles had made a favourable impression on the Indonesians, his relationship with the Dutch had improved and that *'Eaton's suggestion that a permanent representative of Australia be stationed in Yogyakarta was well received.'*

Meanwhile, prompted by Charles' recommendations, Canberra moved quickly to send the four military observers. The honour of being the first ever

'I am pleased that I feel I have been able to initiate a real commencement of the investigation.'

'Eaton's suggestion that a permanent representative of Australia be stationed in Yogyakarta was well received.'

UN-sponsored appointed military observers fell to four Australians on 14 September 1947. Brigadier LGH Dyke and Squadron Leader LT Spence[2] took up their positions in Yogyakarta in Indonesian-held central Java; Commander HS Chesterman and Major DL Campbell went to Dutch-controlled Surabaya. The four were initially seconded to the Australian Consulate and supervised by Charles, who in turn passed their findings to the Commission and the Australian Government.

On 16 September consuls Raux, Lambert and Eaton began a hectic five-day visit to both Republican and Dutch areas of Sumatra, including the large centres of Palembang, Padang, Bukittinggi and Medan. Large crowds greeted the consuls in the Republican-held areas, many carrying welcome banners and requesting international support for the Indonesian Republic. Charles cabled Canberra that the Dutch military would find it difficult to maintain control within their demarcation line, armed clashes were continuing and irregular bandits, some under the command of Japanese deserters, were operating against both the Indonesians and the Dutch. This chaotic situation again highlighted the urgency to implement his proposal for independent joint peacekeepers.

The three consuls returned to Batavia on 21 September to make recommendations to the Commission and their respective governments. They confirmed that the ceasefire in both Java and Sumatra was *'not fully effective and that casualties and damage continue'*, including spasmodic guerrilla activity, looting and the killing of Chinese.

Charles stressed to his superiors in Australia that Dutch forces may not be able to maintain law and order within their territory as defined by the Van Mook Line except in *'occupied towns and immediately adjacent areas'*.[3] He confirmed he was *'pressing for early completion of* [the] *joint report'* that the Commission was to forward to the Security Council in New York. Given that only the four Australian observers were in the field, an obviously frustrated Charles proposed a joint Dutch–Indonesian police force take on the responsibilities of maintaining law and order. He wrote, *'It must be understood that except for the Australian efforts and*

The honour of being the first ever UN-sponsored appointed military observers fell to four Australians on 14 September 1947.

United Kingdom and French colleagues accompanying me, very little has been done by the other members to date. This also applies to Military observers.[4]

The Australian observers presented their initial findings to Charles in Batavia on 23 September before moving on to other districts bordering the ceasefire line. Charles reiterated his proposal to Canberra that a joint Dutch–Indonesian police force be formed to supervise law and order before any Dutch withdrawal.

Now officially Australia's Consul-General, Charles opted to stay in Batavia to focus on van Mook's reluctance to approve Australian representation in Yogyakarta and to lobby for his joint police force. He reported to Canberra that the Dutch would use delaying tactics to prevent a quick and impartial outcome of the Commission's mission. Dr Burton reported to Dr Evatt that it was anticipated the Commission would recommend troop withdrawals which, in Charles' opinion, would result in inevitable clashes unless supervised. Canberra cabled Charles on 29 September supporting him:

> You have every right to maintain a leading position in the drafting of the report as the Australian observers are the only ones who turned up in time and the only ones who are in a position to make a full report ... One matter which should be included is a firm recommendation regarding troop withdrawals. You have paved the way for this in the previous report by stating that no immediate solution could be suggested and implying that nothing but withdrawal could be effective.

As the Commission's mission drew to a close, Charles became more agitated with the Belgians, the Americans and the Dutch. He wrote that the Belgian Consul considered the Commission's report was '*NOT urgently required by the Security Council*', that the '*American officers have NOT arrived*' and the Dutch army commander, General Spoor, '*has no suggestion regarding any method of avoiding casualties on both sides*'. The ceasefire situation was critical and Australia considered any delay by the Americans and the Belgians in producing the Commission's report would enable the Dutch to dictate Indonesia's future. Dr Burton supported Charles' concerns, cabling

'*It must be understood that except for the Australian efforts and United Kingdom and French colleagues accompanying me, very little has been done by the other members to date.*'

'*You have every right to maintain a leading position in the drafting of the report as the Australian observers are the only ones who turned up in time and the only ones who are in a position to make a full report.*'

Dr Evatt in New York, '*If they succeed, it would make a farce of all Australia has done and a farce also of the one United Nations action which has been effective.*'

On 29 September Charles chaired a meeting of the Commission with Dutch officials in Batavia; the American and Belgium members stated that they would not sign the report as there was no urgency in submitting it. The topics discussed at the meeting included the definition of what was a ceasefire, why the Dutch were arming Chinese militias, the attitude towards the Indonesians within the Dutch-controlled areas and policing the ceasefire line. Each consul was preparing his own submission that would inform the final submission. Charles' submission was tabled and accepted by quorum. He predicted that if no immediate resolution to the Indonesian–Netherlands dispute was found there would be further military action by the Dutch. He wrote to Canberra that his view, and those of the Australian observers, had the full sympathy of the British, Chinese and French consuls, but France may be reluctant to act.

In commenting on the different consuls' reports to the Commission, Dr Steven Farram wrote that they revealed many things, including the fact that the three investigative tours undertaken by Charles were easily the most comprehensive and thorough report of the six tours that provided much of the information used to write the main, final report.

'*If they succeed, it would make a farce of all Australia has done and a farce also of the one United Nations action which has been effective.*'

The UN Security Council's Consular Commission meeting with Dutch officials with Charles (centre with pipe) presiding as chairman, Batavia, 29 September 1947.

In what is now considered an historically significant event, Charles cabled the Australian observers' first comprehensive joint report to Canberra on 1 October 1947, with his observations attached. Among other things, the report addressed interpretations of the Security Council's resolutions and the general conditions of the Indonesian and Dutch areas, including:

> The term 'ceasefire' used in the Security Council's resolution of 1 August 1947 caused both sides to interpret the order as they wished, rather than the broader and more comprehensive term 'ceasefire of hostilities'. The report concluded that breaches of the ceasefire were inevitable taking into consideration the mutual antagonism of both parties. Armed clashes were common since the ceasefire of 4 August.

Australia's military observers had confirmed Charles' previous judgment of the high morale of Indonesian civilians and the determination of the population to resist the Dutch to their utmost. The populations of Republican cities grew as refugees, caught along the ceasefire line, filtered in from No Man's Land. The observers found it very difficult to identify which side initiated breaches of the ceasefire agreement. In the Indonesian areas, civil administration and defence forces had been organised and villagers were prepared to defend themselves with bamboo spears. The Australians found that the Indonesians would refuse to cooperate with the Dutch if overrun. There was a shortage of medical supplies but schools were functioning except in No Man's Land. The observers found that in the Dutch-held areas the Indonesian population appeared to be treated with understanding, justice and tolerance, however infiltrations by Indonesian guerrillas were damaging telephone lines, bridges and roads.

The delay of the Commission's final report disappointed Charles and his despatch to Canberra lambasted the American and Belgium consuls for being too pro-Dutch and added that the former would only submit a minority submission. He could not understand the attitude of the Americans; their military observers had just arrived and had instructions to report directly to their consul and not to the Commission. Charles found this most

Armed clashes were common since the ceasefire of 4 August.

disconcerting. He doubted if a truly joint military assessment of the situation was possible, saying '*This point now seems rather hopeless.*'

In his contemporary analysis, Dr Farram summarised the complexity of the Commission's reporting procedure and confirmed Charles' frustration.

> Furthermore, both Foote [American Consul] and Vanderstichelen [Belgium Consul] declared that they knew that the US had not yet officially appointed its member to the GOC and there was thus no urgency in submitting the report. Eaton felt that waiting for the US observers to submit their report would 'detract all value' from the Commission's report, which was otherwise complete. Burton was in total agreement, believing the US and the Belgians were causing a delay so that the Dutch could consolidate their position before the arrival of the GOC.

> On 3 October, Eaton was advised that Frank Graham had been appointed as US representative on the GOC, so that reason for delaying the report had been removed. Eaton replied by stating that the delays were 'disappointing', but he had no hesitation in apportioning blame to Foote and Vanderstichelen, especially the former. The Americans had undermined the unity of the Commission, said Eaton, as the long-awaited US observers would not be reporting directly to the Commission and there was much doubt that Foote would share any of their conclusions. Furthermore, they would not be taking part in the proposed joint military report, and it was believed that Foote might lodge a minority report.

In the meantime, more armed clashes were reported, for example:

> In Abulu a school-teacher and an Indonesian family were murdered. In the night of 4–5 September an attempt was made to set fire to the nunnery. A Ngiri godown was looted. West Java: The Mosque at Bayongbong was set on fire. Approximately 100 Chinese were kidnapped by the TNI in Sukareja; their fate is unknown.

In an effort to force the Commission to act, the British member, Sir Francis Shepherd and Charles despatched a joint telegram to their respective governments. They stated that the Commission proposed a demarcation line between the Dutch and Republican troops and the cessation of mopping up operations by the Dutch and guerrilla attacks by the Republicans. Charles' opinion was that the actual demarcation would take too much time and that it would entail sacrifices for the Indonesians only. He considered the existing ceasefire boundaries were absurd; both he and his military observers were emphatic there would be no solution unless a realistic boundary was drawn and troops on both sides withdrew under supervision. Obviously frustrated, he highlighted that the Commission's terms of reference were to report on the situation and not to make recommendations; a fact that must have disappointed him.

He considered the existing ceasefire boundaries were absurd; both he and his military observers were emphatic there would be no solution unless a realistic boundary was drawn and troops on both sides withdrew under supervision.

A joint report was produced on 11 October. Even then, the report was unsigned by some consuls, particularly the French, who wished to make amendments that were possibly influenced by events in Indo-China. Charles expressed his doubts that either side would stop random breaches of the August ceasefire by stressing different interpretations of the ceasefire agreement, writing:

> Apart from actions involving regular forces, a considerable amount of banditry including murder, arson and looting, is still being carried on to some extent by irregular bands. The population suffered considerably even before police action from banditry and scorched earth policy. This intensified during and after the police action. The Chinese were a special target.

Now that he had spent over a month in the country, Charles was forming an opinion on the social and political atmosphere of Java and Sumatra. He considered that the influential and western-educated Indonesians were practically all nationalists who sought some kind of independence, but not all supported the policies of the Republic. He found, perhaps to his surprise, there was little personal animosity toward the Dutch as individuals and their expertise in helping to run the country was not only recognised by Indonesians but considered essential. But he found in East Java '*a strong feeling of hatred*' of the Dutch military and colonial administrators.

But he found in East Java 'a strong feeling of hatred' of the Dutch military and colonial administrators.

Charles returned to Timor to pack up his Dili household, but received instructions from Canberra to return to Java immediately to supervise his four military observers and monitor the ceasefire. On his return, Charles found that the Commission's final report had been signed by all consuls and was factual and impartial; however, he said it should be read with the individual reports. The final report, signed by Charles as Chairman, was presented to the Security Council on 14 October 1947.

On 17 October the Dutch began what they termed *'mopping up operations'* of Republican troops that had been cut off by the August police action. Charles cabled Canberra that the situation would develop into a full-scale war unless the Dutch military forces were stopped. He continued to badger Canberra on the importance of the Dutch and Indonesians ceasing hostilities and withdrawing from disputed territory and the need to form a joint police force to monitor The Line. He said this must be the first consideration of the UN Good Offices Committee (GOC). Canberra did not agree and replied rather bluntly:

> We note with some surprise your emphasis on the need for a Joint Police Force and would like to know your reasons for this conclusion. Our impression has been that establishment of a Joint Police Force is not only impractical now that matters have gone so far, but might also provide the Dutch in future to extend their influence at the expense of Indonesians in contravention of whatever settlement may ultimately be reached.

Charles' immediate response was, *'A Police Force would be necessary to safeguard* [the] *interests of either side and maintain law and order with strict neutrality. Such a Police Force could be controlled internationally.'* He considered such a force would safeguard against the danger of the Dutch extending their influence. Once again, these suggestions were not in the ambit of Charles' responsibilities but, being persistent by nature, he badgered Canberra and his fellow members on the Commission for such a force. He was convinced that if both sides withdrew from disputed districts, a joint force acting with strict neutrality would safeguard law and order:

> Such a Police Force could be controlled internationally or jointly [by] Republican and Dutch and be composed of Foreign Police or of Indonesians who were members of the Field Police before the war and the Dutch. These are questions which only can be decided after discussions between Dutch

'We note with some surprise your emphasis on the need for a Joint Police Force and would like to know your reasons for this conclusion.'

'Such a Police Force could be controlled internationally or jointly [by] Republican and Dutch and be composed of Foreign Police or of Indonesians who were members of the Field Police before the war and the Dutch.'

and Republicans arranged and sponsored by the [GOC]. A Police Force constituted as above should not provide the Dutch with the opportunity to extend their influence at the expense of Republican resistance.

Charles also touted his plan to Vice Premier Gani, who was in complete agreement. However, Charles' concept for joint policing was not accepted by the UN until a decade later.

As rotating chairman of the Commission, Charles recommended on 10 November that military observers' reports should go to the GOC and not to the Commission. Firstly, *'the [GOC] Committee must appreciate the delicate position of career Consuls who were accredited to foreign countries who at the same time were being called upon to implement the order of an international body'.* The members of the Commission agreed as the observers were expected to soon number more than 50.

However, Charles reported to Canberra that the British, Chinese and French members of the Commission were wary of committing more military peacekeepers. They first wanted to know the outcome of the GOC; Charles, having a long military background, knew that armed conflict may not wait for any man or nation. At the same time the question of military observers and a joint peace force was being discussed, the Dutch air force, in what was termed 'retaliatory action', bombed Bandjarnegara in Central Java, killing seven civilians. Charles was concerned the Dutch may attempt a *fait accompli* and try to create a unilateral federated United States of Indonesia by combining the various regional governments they had created, particularly in eastern Indonesia. He stressed that Dutch policies to create separate states in West Java and coastal enclaves in Sumatra and Madura would confuse the total issue, particularly for the GOC.

The Commission's work was complete and the negotiations for a just settlement of the dispute were to be in the hands of the GOC. Elizabeth Scott, researching Australian–Indonesian relations during the period, summed up the *raison d'être* of Charles's *'robust initiatives'* when acting as Australia's representative on the Commission:

> 'The [GOC] Committee must appreciate the delicate position of career Consuls who were accredited to foreign countries who at the same time were being called upon to implement the order of an international body.'

Eaton was well known for his ability to bolster and maintain morale amongst 'his men'. He had the task of integrating the informal relationship to the political goals of the organisation. Eaton was able to bridge the semi-communal ties between the members on the one hand, and those between the members and the hierarchy (or those in authority) on the other. This ability is of strategic importance in establishing the kind of communications necessary for institutionalising social ties and political loyalties within an organisation or culture.

Furthermore, through his army and air force years Eaton had been totally immersed in the machinations of military protocol and the tactful judicious command of servicemen from diverse backgrounds and nationalities (British, Indian, Australian, Dutch, American and Indonesians with the NEIAF). As a result of his First and Second World War exploits he was able to draw on these experiences and be socially adept with his counterparts in both the Dutch and Republican military forces.

The GOC was formed to act as the conduit to conclude a satisfactory solution to the NEI–Indonesian conflict. The first formal GOC meeting was held in Sydney on 20 October 1947 and meetings moved to Indonesia later that month. Justice Richard Kirby of Australia was appointed to the GOC and later became its Chairperson. Thomas Critchley, a fellow countryman, became a committee member. Charles, now permanently based in Batavia as the Australian Consul-General to the NEI, was given the brief to support the GOC and liaise with the Indonesians and the Dutch in any way he could to ensure the committee's objectives were achieved.

These few months in 1947 had presented Charles with an opportunity to take a pioneering and leading role in launching world peacekeeping. Perhaps his life-long involvement in reconnaissance, search and rescue missions provided him with the necessary aptitude to carry out such a challenge. At the same time, Charles found the time to study the country's orchids, a life-long passion. He remarked how beautiful the orchids were in his official despatches; a digression that perhaps masked his frustrations.

'The Pathfinder' with three of Australia's military observers. From left, Commander HS Chesterman, Group Captain C Eaton, Brigadier LGH Dyke and Major DL Campbell.

*The Australian Consulate, Pegangsaan Oost,
Batavia (now Menteng, Jakarta), 1948*

29 A Diplomatic Missionary, 1948–51

It was the people themselves that I found so interesting and so pleasant—the Dutch, Indonesians, English, Americans and many other foreign nationalities; most of whom were charming with a high sense of integrity. Yet I was in the midst of tragic and vicious happenings.

Bea Eaton, 1947

Bea Eaton sailed from Timor for England in August 1947 for her first return visit since leaving her London home for India in 1920. On learning her husband had been posted at short notice to Batavia, she cut short her stay in England and sailed for Singapore. Charles met her in Singapore on 22 December and they flew to Batavia, which was to be their home for nearly three years.

Bea described her life in Batavia:

> Batavia, or Jakarta as it is now known, I liked very much. I had a nice home, living conditions were good, particularly after Timor, and, being used to the tropics, I did not find the climate oppressive.

A large colonial-style bungalow with extensive grounds in the leafy suburb of Menteng served as the Australian Consul-General's home and office in Batavia. Early in his tenure Charles had complained to Canberra that the condition of the consulate was not suitable to entertain and accommodate visitors and that his household supplies, including a case of prized whiskey, had still not arrived! That Scottish beverage was almost unobtainable in the austere post-WWII era and any diplomatic mission that procured it became popular overnight. Once the consulate was refurbished and Bea arrived, the Eatons settled into a routine of diplomatic meetings and seemingly endless parties; indeed, it reminded them of their glory days in *gay Paree* immediately following WWI.

In October 1947, with the Commission's objective complete, attention turned to the GOC, which had been formed to act as the conduit to a satisfactory solution to the Dutch–Indonesian conflict. The military observers of all Commission countries (Australia, France, Belgium, the United Kingdom, the United States and China) were eventually attached to the GOC. As Charles later pointed out, at that time, '*The military observers were strictly speaking, still attached to the Consular Commission.*'

Charles' brief was to support the GOC and liaise with the Indonesians and the Dutch in any way he could to ensure the GOC's objectives were achieved. He was to monitor the interactions between the Dutch colonial administrators, Indonesian Republicans, those Indonesians allied to the Dutch, and foreign diplomats accredited to the NEI. He provided the GOC's Justice Kirby with current political and economic information, much of it based on first-hand information from his extensive travel to both the Dutch and Republican controlled regions. Kirby reported to Secretary Burton, '*Of course Eaton is co-operating with me very well and is eminently satisfactory in every way.*'

Charles also mediated at an informal level between the two adversaries and foreign representatives, all with their own agendas. Some Dutch military officers, acknowledging his reputation within their own military, sought his confidence to voice their displeasure at their own government's strategies. Elizabeth Scott, in her analysis of the period said:

> Charles Eaton, as Australia's Consul General, occupied the role of *dalang* or puppeteer in the Javanese *wayang* (shadow puppet) performances. Eaton had to untangle people from policies and prejudices from pride in order to assist in the weaving of a new chapter in Southeast Asian relationships. In a sense, Eaton was the *dalang* ... In brief, he was an extraordinary person with exceptional networking skills probably best described as a 'change agent.'

Under the auspices of the GOC, direct negotiations between the Republicans and the Dutch commenced in November 1947 in a neutral venue, the cruiser USS *Renville*, anchored in Batavia Bay.

On 1 November the UN Security Council had made a further resolution that required, among other things, that the opponents '*consult with each other, either directly or through the GOC, as to the means to be employed to give effect to the cease-fire order*' and to refrain from gaining any territory that they had not occupied on 4 August 1947. Kirby, on USS *Renville* for the negotiations, wrote to Secretary Burton on 8 December on the complicated situation that arose from the resolution. Charles cabled Evatt on the same day agreeing with Kirby's opinion that the GOC '*was sitting on dynamite*'. He displayed his characteristic persistence by reiterating his hobby-horse proposal for a joint police force.

In his final despatch of 1947, Charles stressed to Dr Evatt the stubbornness of the Dutch, asserting they would '*not give up an inch of ground*'. He emphasised his fears of a divided Indonesia:

> This is obviously unfair ... It appears, therefore, that the talks on the cease fire will break down at an early date, but that the Dutch will keep them going until they are ready to give effect to the cease fire order and announce their future plan for Indonesia ... their solution will be a Federal Government for a United States of Indonesia, embracing those States already formed and others they are pushing hard to form immediately, such as West Java.

'*Charles Eaton, as Australia's Consul General, occupied the role of dalang or puppeteer in the Javanese wayang (shadow puppet) performances.*'

'*Charles cabled Evatt on the same day agreeing with Kirby's opinion that the GOC 'was sitting on dynamite'.*'

The *Renville* negotiations were riddled with accusations and differences. The Dutch delegation told the GOC that unless the Republic accepted its proposals the Netherlands might initiate their own freedom of action; in short, another act of aggression like Operatie Product. A truce was finally accepted by both the Netherlands and Republic governments on 19 January 1948.

The Renville Agreement confirmed Dutch territorial gains and granted the Dutch *de jure* sovereignty until the formation of the United States of Indonesia was completed. The Republic was promised a plebiscite in the Dutch-occupied parts of Java, Sumatra and Madura to decide whether they would become separate states or join the Republic. The two warring parties agreed to withdraw to The Line of 4 August.

Charles cabled Dr Evatt on 21 January that the Agreement suggested *'what is going to happen next rather than any great relief and jubilation'*. In Charles' assessment, later confirmed by historian Margaret George, it was only a temporary arrangement between the two adversaries that had not solved the major issues. Charles was concerned the Republic would end up a state within a United States of Indonesia. However, in February 1948 he was able to report the satisfactory withdrawal of 11,000 Republican troops from Dutch controlled areas of Java and the withdrawal of Dutch soldiers to their line of control as agreed in the Renville Agreement. However, sporadic violence continued.

Charles informed both Canberra and Justice Kirby of the constantly changing state of affairs and his general concerns of the unsatisfactory situation regarding the question of sovereignty, which he said, *'remains very much in the air'* adding:

> The Indonesian political situation, in my opinion, with its present ramifications will remain a 'hornet's nest' for a very long time to come, unless some drastic international pressure is exerted on the parties concerned. Unless some reasonable settlement is made at an early date I feel in the future, Indonesia, particularly the Republican element, will look towards the Asian countries for support, rather than rely on other powers.

Charles cabled Dr Evatt on 21 January that the Agreement suggested 'what is going to happen next rather than any great relief and jubilation'.

In April 1948 Charles launched another initiative, writing to Dr Burton:

> In order to avoid well known difficulties of liaison, co-operation, confusion which was so evident and existed in spite of Australian efforts up to and during the last war regarding mutual defence of the Netherlands East Indies and Australia, I suggest that consideration, of the necessity for active Australian defence co-operation with the future United States of Indonesia on the account of the geographical and economic position for both world peace and defence be brought forward to the [*Renville*] conference as a special point, particularly as regards the future political sovereignty of Indonesia and the Dutch home defence requirements in Europe.

Charles' submission for an Australian co-operative defence agreement with Indonesia at that time was surprising as the Republic's future as a sovereign nation that encompassed all provinces in the archipelago was still uncertain. In short, he was proposing a security treaty with a future, and potentially powerful, neighbour. Having established Australian northern air defences and having first-hand knowledge of eastern Indonesia, West Papua and both East Timor and West Timor since 1938, he must have appreciated the importance of Australia's northern security. He had experienced the horrors of war and was familiar with the evolution of political control from a colonial power to those being governed. When serving in India in the early 1920s, Charles was influenced by the philosophies of the then Governor of Orissa, Lord Satyendra Sinha, whose approach to self-government and independence had been pragmatic and based on legal constitutional progression. However, it was not until 1995, 47 years after Charles' proposal, that Australia eventually signed its first bi-lateral Agreement on the Maintaining of Security with Indonesia.

However, it was not until 1995, 47 years after Charles' proposal, that Australia eventually signed its first bi-lateral Agreement on the Maintaining of Security with Indonesia.

As the year progressed, Charles tempered his concern about a possible second Dutch police action; he considered '*cooler heads*' would prevail and further military opportunism by the Dutch would prove disastrous for any Dutch-sponsored federation. He misjudged his first presumption regarding cooler heads, but just nine months later, he was right about the second.

He misjudged his first presumption regarding cooler heads, but just nine months later, he was right about the second.

Charles wrote to Dr Evatt in early June stressing that the Dutch would not be so foolish as to reopen hostilities against the Republic, but to safeguard against that possibility, he recommended to Evatt that the dormant Commission be revived. He didn't say anything to his fellow consuls as he needed Canberra's support first. However, the Chinese Consul, Tsiang Chia Tung, approached Charles to encourage the Commission to take some action due to the gravity of the situation. For example, guerrilla war was increasing within the Dutch-controlled areas and, if nothing was done, there would soon be chaos. Despite their advice, the Commission was not revived.

By mid-1948, Charles' responsibilities shifted from the political scene to the educational and social requirements of the emerging nation. Charles recommended to Dr Evatt that an Australian Information Bureau and Trade Commissioner be appointed to Indonesia at an early date. He identified Indonesian students for scholarships to Australia and recommended AU $320,000 worth of clothing and supplies be delivered to civilians who had suffered as a result of the civil and military disturbances.

Charles travelled extensively in eastern Indonesia, including a visit to the Ambon war cemetery where some of his former air force comrades were buried; they had been killed in action, died in captivity or been summarily

Charles and Bea Eaton and friends attended seemingly endless parties in 1948.

executed by the Japanese. He informed Canberra in September that he planned to tour Republican areas of Java and would be accompanied by his wife. Many in Batavia tried to persuade him not to undertake this risky venture because of intermittent violence but he persisted. Once approvals were granted by the respective Dutch and Indonesian authorities the couple left Batavia on 26 September for an eight-day tour.

Bea watched from the side-lines and wondered why there was not a peaceful and equitable solution. She wrote: '*Conference had followed conference, commission followed commission, and still no satisfactory solution had been found*.' At the many functions she attended, the representatives of the opposing sides met freely, without any outward sign of animosity, and in fact indulged in pleasantries with each other. However, she thought there was an undercurrent of deep ill-feeling. When the opportunity arose, Bea accompanied Charles on his tours.

On a trip from Batavia to Republican Java with their driver, Joel, and an air force wing commander, Bea wrote:

> The first part of our journey was to Bandung via Buitenzorg (now Bogor). The road took us through beautiful scenery and many interesting villages. The entire countryside was cultivated and the picturesque rice fields are right up to the edge of the road. The roadways, too, were lined in many places by Kapok trees with their rather weird horizontal branches. Along the road there was an unending movement of villagers, passing in a jogging gait, with a pole over their shoulders, carrying bundles of rice in the ear. Every village was full of bustle with its own market lining the road.

At Bogor, still in the Dutch-controlled area, they paused to admire the Governor-General's summer headquarters, where a herd of tame deer were grazing in the spacious, park-like surroundings. They visited the world-famous botanical gardens founded by Sir Stamford Raffles. She described as '*magnificent*' the gardens and lake, with its huge and wondrous water lilies, *Victoria regis*, which had floating leaves up to four feet in diameter with a vertical edge. The road then descended to Bandung, where a number of fatal ambushes had been reported and was now patrolled by Dutch soldiers.

Bea watched from the side-lines and wondered why there was not a peaceful and equitable solution.

The Eatons thought Bandung a beautiful town, well laid out, with fine buildings and excellent hotels; it was also a Dutch military headquarters. The whole region was unsettled and populated with many Republican sympathisers, whose sabotage was a great source of annoyance to the Dutch. The area they passed through was troubled; devastation to buildings, factories and bridges carried out by Republicans in their scorched earth policy gave the country a haunted appearance. To Bea, it was accentuated by their escort of armed vehicles with machine guns that she felt *'were always pointing at me'*. When they reached The Line at Gombing, with a Dutch officer carrying a white flag, a Republican officer came from the other side carrying a similar banner. Once in the centre of the bridge, Charles and Bea were *'ceremoniously handed over'* to the Indonesians and continued their journey.

When visiting Republican hospitals, the Eatons received pleas to obtain Red Cross assistance; all had serious shortages of medical supplies, clothing and staff. Charles and Bea then dispensed with their armed escort for the remaining journey to Yogyakarta, retaining only a Republican army officer as escort. Every few miles there was a tank on the road, some cunningly hidden and others quite obvious, and many other obstacles; all prepared to delay a Dutch advance should hostilities recommence. They were told that all large buildings and structures were prepared for destruction. Their Australian flag attracted attention and much excitement; there were no demonstrations but frequent cries of *'merdeka'* or 'freedom'. The Indonesian red and white flag was flying in all villages. The villagers appeared in good spirits but undoubtedly had suffered as a result of the recent conflict. Two things struck the Eatons more than anything else; the total absence of westerners and the poorly-clad villagers, often dressed in hessian.

On their arrival in Yogyakarta they were surprised to find traffic lights operating normally. The next morning Charles conferred with Indonesian leaders while their wives accompanied Bea on a tour of the city and its bazaars. Many shops were either virtually empty or closed but Bea found the food bazaars and the silversmiths' street intriguing. She was amazed by the creation of beautiful pieces of silver by age-old methods and infinite patience. Their next highlight was lunch with President and Madam Sukarno at their residence. Although the Javanese dishes served were delicious, Bea said apologies were made for '*the paucity of the food*'. She thought a lot of trouble had been taken on their behalf. She also thought the ladies '*charming in every way*'.

A house at Kaliurang, near the slopes of the famous Merapi volcano, was placed at their disposal. Bea continues:

> Approaching Kaliurang, it was becoming dark, and ahead of us, great flashes of light appeared in the sky, it seemed as if the mountain was on fire; it was too! We stopped the car and got out to watch. Merapi, the ten-thousand-foot peak ahead of us, was in eruption. The sight was wonderful and awe inspiring. With considerable timidity, I continued the journey and on arrival at Kaliurang, which was only a short distance further on, I was assured, at least to a degree of half conviction, that all was quite safe.
>
> It was not until after I had had dinner, and we were visited by that great Indonesian character and elder statesman, Haji Agus Salim, who, with his wife was also staying at Kaliurang, that I became completely reassured that all was well and safe. His talking qualities put me at rest.
>
> At that time Haji Salim was the Republican Foreign Minister. His appearance, dress and manner were just something different, that, apart from his experience and ability, made him an outstanding character. He was well respected, in both Indonesian and European circles. A great linguist, he had a fund of amazing stories that he could tell, in an inimitable manner in many languages. With his crooked shepherd's walking stick, that he always carried, he looked most colourful; Haji Salim was both a clever and shrewd statesman and a most influential Moslem leader.

Haji Salim and his family formed personal links with the Eatons. They spent many hours discussing Indonesia's history, its future and what role the Dutch might play in the country's development. Haji Salem was fluent in English, Dutch and Arabic in addition to Indonesia's regional languages. He told Bea, '*If a young child could learn a language why not a mature person.*'

The Cross in the Sky

The next day the Eatons returned to Yogyakarta for a banquet given by the Sultan of Yogyakarta in their honour. His Highness, Hamengkoe Boewono, was a well-respected leader of millions of Javanese and was, at that time, considered to be divorced from political bias. The Eatons were received with colourful, unforgettable ceremonies at his palace. They were seated on a large open portico where an Indonesian orchestra played traditional music. The setting was entirely apart from the western world, with Bea describing the music and chanting as giving an atmosphere that *'only the potentate eastern world can give'*. In between the many food courses, young Indonesians performed their famed dances. The wonderful technique of the dancers, who expressed their art from their toes to their fingers, took up to seven years of training. Although extraordinarily artistic, the dances could only be understood if the legends upon which they were founded were known. These were explained to Bea as the dances progressed. The finale came with the celebrated Monkey-God dance, which was as exciting as it was strenuous.

On the return journey to Batavia, they visited the imposing Buddhist temple, Borobudur. Bea said *'seeing is believing'* and *'unless one has seen Borobudur, no description can possibly make a realistic picture of this immense temple'*. Its base covered nearly three acres, with recessed terraces rising up in great tiers and adorned with large sculptured heads; the walls were covered with ornate carvings and masterpieces of sculpture. Large images of The Buddha can be seen in tomb-like recesses of the terraces. Bea wrote that the short visit *'left me with further wonder of eastern culture and religion. I felt very puny with Borobudur standing high above me in its magnificence, and towering in the distance was Merapi, still belching forth smoke.'*

Although they took care to avoid road blocks and disguised tank traps on the return trip, an armed escort was not necessary. Everyone on both sides of The Line made the couple welcome. They could see the beginning of the gradual reconstruction of the countryside. Charles wrote, however, of a general feeling of growing animosity toward the Dutch. He commented that the Indonesians would rather have complete chaos than surrender

'Unless one has seen Borobudur, no description can possibly make a realistic picture of this immense temple'.

to the Dutch, who in turn would not compromise under any circumstance. He considered those attitudes nullified any benefits for future Indonesia and Netherlands cooperation.

In November 1948 Charles and Bea travelled to Melbourne for long leave, Charles' first since the beginning of 1939 and the first time since then that the family had been united. Aileen had just returned from Japan, where she was stationed with the Allied occupation forces. Peter was on semester break from agricultural college and Charles Stuart was home from boarding school. It was their first Christmas together since 1938 and Charles Stuart remembers 19 December 1948 vividly. As the ABC announced the commencement of the second Dutch Police Action in Java and Sumatra, Charles rose bolt upright from his chair declaring, 'The fools, the fools, that's the finish for the Dutch.' His worst fears had been realised.

The Dutch were militarily successful but, in the political sense, their action heralded their ultimate demise. Yogyakarta was captured; the Republic's leaders—Sukarno, Hatta, Sjahrir and the Eatons' friend Haji Salim—imprisoned. After some delay, a USA–Colombia–Syrian resolution was passed in the UN on 24 December calling for an immediate ceasefire. Australia's delegate, Colonel Hodgson, was annoyed at this *weak and ineffective resolution* and demanded the Netherlands be expelled from the United Nations.

The Eatons returned to Indonesia in January 1949 to find the country in a political limbo and the economy still struggling. Although the imprisoned Indonesian leaders were released by April, and the Dutch agreed that Yogyakarta be re-established as the Republic's capital as long as the Indonesians stopped all guerrilla warfare, the tension remained unresolved until the Round Table Conference held in The Hague from 23 August to 2 November 1949. Australian Thomas Critchley formally represented the GOC at the conference, which agreed that a united and federal state, to be known as the United States of Indonesia, would be created by December 1949.[1]

He considered those attitudes nullified any benefits for future Indonesia and Netherlands cooperation.

As the ABC announced the commencement of the second Dutch Police Action in Java and Sumatra, Charles rose bolt upright from his chair declaring, 'The fools, the fools, that's the finish for the Dutch.'

While Critchley was focussing on political matters, Charles was occupied with delivering supplies of medicine as part of Australia's contribution to the UN's relief fund. He continued in his diplomatic missionary role by identifying areas where Australia could help, particularly in economic development and the training of Indonesian military officers and technicians. The organisation and training of an efficient civil aviation service was a subject close to his heart and included Australian participation in airlines. Charles also communicated to Canberra that *'The future of West Papua must be settled as soon as possible,'* and stressed:

> Australian diplomacy, up to the present time, with regard to Indonesia has placed her in the position of being considered an outstanding friendly country and future cooperation and assistance is looked for a greater degree than Australia realises and moreover is able to give. However, as Indonesia will probably be the last bastion in the East against communism, it seems that it would be a fatal mistake not to give the utmost assistance particularly as Australia stands in such a high regard with practically all Indonesian political and military leaders.

The transfer of sovereignty took place on 27 December 1949. In The Hague, Queen Juliana of the Netherlands signed the Act of Transfer of Sovereignty that formally proclaimed Dutch recognition of a free and independent Indonesia with both countries united as a Netherlands–Indonesia Union. The Queen delivered a speech; Republican Vice-President Mohammed Hatta responded, stressing the need for the two countries to cooperate. In a poignant act of reconciliation, the Dutch-educated and judicious Mohammad Hatta laid a wreath at the Dutch National War Memorial. At the same time, a parallel ceremony was held in the newly-named capital, Jakarta, with LR McIntyre of the Department of External Affairs in Canberra and Charles representing Australia.

The next morning, President Sukarno made a triumphant entry into Jakarta, where he addressed an enormous and enthusiastic crowd. McIntyre, Charles and Charles Stuart were seated on the official dais; the latter at the President's personal invitation.

As peace settled the new nation, the Eatons continued their diplomatic life. On one of Charles Stuart's visits from boarding school, he was involved in an incident that exposed his mother in rather a different light. Before flying to Indonesia, Bea had arranged with a mutual friend in Melbourne to give young Charles AU£20, a carton of Benson and Hedges cigarettes and a bottle of Scotch. On arrival at the consulate Bea challenged him rather sharply, *'Have you got it? The parcel Auntie Eleanor gave you ... and if you tell your father I will kill you.'* Her son was shocked to the core and is convinced to this day she meant it. The next day mother and son travelled to Pasar Baru, a rather seedy Jakarta suburb, where Bea told the driver, Joel, to drop them at a particular junction and return in two hours. They walked at least three blocks before entering a murky narrow side-street and then a small dingy shop where the owner greeted Bea like a long-lost cousin; they certainly had had previous transactions. The cigarettes and £20 note were passed over for many times higher than the official exchange rate. After wandering around this fascinating quarter of Jakarta, Bea, followed by her apprehensive son, retraced her steps to rendezvous with the presumably unsuspecting Joel. Although traumatised into silence for decades, Charles Stuart thought at the time that Al Capone of Chicago would have approved of his mother's strategy. He regretted never having had the courage to ask his father about the contraband brandy Charles senior had stored under Lloyd George's seat when flying the Prime Minister back to London from the Paris Peace Conference.

Unfortunately, peace was not widespread. In early 1950 Charles, Bea and Charles Stuart were travelling to Bandung in central Java when their motorcade was turned back at a road block manned by Indonesian soldiers due to an insurgency by irregular armed bandits. This outbreak of violence was led by Istanbul-born Raymond 'Turk' Westerling, a Dutch–Greek soldier-of-fortune with a colourful past. Westerling had fought with Australian troops in North Africa and later with the underground in the Netherlands during the German occupation. Following WWII, Westerling commanded a special Dutch force that was accused of the random killing of Indonesian nationalists in Sulawesi. Cashiered from the NEI forces, he formed a private army in Central Java composed of religious extremists and deserters from the Dutch Army. Westerling's freebooters had entered Bandung, killing some Republican soldiers and taking control of the city. While thousands of Dutch troops were still garrisoned in Bandung, they did not intervene; later their commander ordered Westerling and his followers to abandon the city. A few nights after his failed *coup d'état,* an armed but harassed Westerling woke Charles around midnight demanding an instant visa to Australia. Charles refused, then immediately notified the Indonesian military, but the 'buccaneer' had melted into the night and eventually turned up in the Netherlands.

> *Charles refused, then immediately notified the Indonesian military, but the 'buccaneer' had melted into the night and eventually turned up in the Netherlands.*

President Sukarno invited Charles and the GOC's Thomas Critchley to accompany Vice-President Hatta on a goodwill visit to Pontianak in Kalimantan. Although Charles had to decline due to pressing commitments, Sukarno offered that Charles Stuart, whom he had entertained in his home, go instead. For more than a week the 14-year-old toured with Dr Hatta, Thomas Critchley and the Sultan of Pontianak, thus experiencing the euphoria of a newly-independent nation. His most vivid memory was that the former Dutch colonialists and the post-independence Indonesians appeared to be on amicable terms at the social level.

Charles and Bea remained in Indonesia until mid-1950. During that time, Charles became *Chargé d'Affairs* of Australia's mission when it was upgraded to an embassy. Although requested by President Sukarno to remain in Indonesia, Charles was not qualified to nominate himself to the position and was keen to return to Australia to be closer to his children. He had been separated from his family since 1939, meeting them only on rare, fleeting occasions. The Eatons last few months in Indonesia were taken up with farewells with all sections of Indonesian and expatriate communities.

Dr Margaret George wrote that Australia's pre-WWII indifference to the NEI was consistent with its general lack of interest towards South East Asia and was influenced by a dependency on the British to represent

Australia's affairs. In 1947 Australia's Department of External Affairs was still at the embryonic stage; Dr George emphasised that Australia's foreign policies at the time *'lacked both consistency and co-ordination'*. This was partly due to Dr Evatt's *'schizophrenic volte-faces between spreading disaffection and displaying effusive goodwill'.* She continues:

> At the Department level Evatt's lack of operational responsibility in his relationship to the Department of External Affairs meant that the presentation of official policy was diffuse, and at times contradictory. A combination of historical circumstances, a lack of official direction and of operational constraints also meant individual diplomats, notably Brooks [in Singapore] and Eaton in Batavia, were able individually to affect the shape of Australia's policies.

Despite Australia's relative inexperience, its foray into the complexities of the Dutch–Indonesian conflict was the first time the country had assumed a major role in global diplomacy. By successfully supporting Indonesia in its quest for independence, and its decisive action when positioning military observers, Australia earned the respect of its new neighbour. Indeed, Indonesia's selection of Australia as its representative on the GOC, with Justice Kirby's appointment as its Chairman, and the warm rapport Indonesian political leaders had with Richard Kirby, Thomas Critchley and Charles Eaton, was a direct result of that support.

Charles' relations with the NEI administration, particularly with the Governor General van Mook, had been problematical. His insistence to cross The Line between the Republic and Dutch forces before the Commission was formed and before he gained diplomatic recognition raised van Mook's ire. He accused Charles of *'being weak'* and *'drinking too much'*. Since 1918, Charles had experienced an extraordinary roller-coaster relationship with the Netherlands, where he was interned, quite legally, for four weeks (Vignette 6). In May 1938 he was reputedly expelled from West Timor by NEI authorities as a suspected military undercover agent. Conversely, when heading another reconnaissance mission in March 1941, he was offered full cooperation and a Dornier flying boat by NEI officials to report on Dutch defences in West Papua and eastern NEI (Vignette 20). In 1943 he commanded the only operational airfield in West Papua still in Allied hands and subsequently, 18 NEI Squadron as part of his bomber 79 Wing (Vignettes 22–24). The Queen of the Netherlands recognised his wartime efforts by bestowing upon him an elevated decoration for chivalry.

The year 1950 brought Charles Eaton's years of active service to a *finale*. His journey of adventures had begun in early 1915 as a teenage soldier with The Lambs at the battles for Festuburt, Givenchy and Loos. He never wrote a word of a personal nature about those three actions nor, 32 years later, about his *sortie* into conflict at an international level.

Charles, now retired, and Bea, East Gippsland in the 1950s

Memorial parade of 18 NEIAF Squadron, Java 1950
Aircraft: Mitchell B 25 NS-246

30 Twilight: Moth's Last Flight, 1952–81

As soon as I started the car's engine a sudden calm crossed my father's face as if someone had drawn a mask over it. My father realised that his time had come and it was as if he was recalling the faces of his comrades dying in their thousands at Festubert, Loos, Vimy Ridge and on the Somme. His anger and frustration at being incapacitated and taken to hospital suddenly evaporated.

Charles Stuart Eaton

On returning to Australia in 1950 after his extraordinary role in Indonesia's independence, Charles was posted to Canberra to fly a desk; a job he did not relish. He was reputedly nominated to head a new legation in Rio de Janeiro that was to provide Australian diplomatic representation throughout South America; however, for the first time in his life he acknowledged health problems. In 1951, Eaton was hospitalised in Heidelberg Military Hospital with kidney stones and later diagnosed with dermatitis resulting from tropical service. Although he fully recovered, he forfeited the Brazil appointment.

Charles retired at the age of 57. He and Bea joined Peter on his farm adjacent to Gippsland Lakes in eastern Victoria. *The Bluff* had a mile frontage to the lakes so swimming and fishing for flounder became a common routine throughout summer. Perhaps not as exciting as stalking tigers in India, Charles did his best to eradicate the burgeoning vermin rabbit population. On one bracken-covered hill, the *'entire mountain'* appeared to move with the grey creatures.

The property, with its two lagoons complete with water lilies, various species of duck, black swans and water fowl, was declared a nature reserve. The Eatons, who had been avid conservationists since living in India, restricted their shooting to rabbit control.

Other newcomers to the area included Robert and Florence Jubb, who purchased a farm nearby and became close friends of the family. 'Jubby' had captained a Halifax over Düsseldorf and, after his aircraft was hit, parachuted *'down into a blazing inferno'*. He managed to escape safely to American lines.[1]

Charles and Bea sailed to England in 1953; the first time Charles had visited his country of birth since November 1919. His mother, Maude, had died but his father, William Walpole, was in his 80s. William died just a few months after seeing his only son following 33 years of separation. On their return journey, they toured southern Africa with John Alston Wallace, a grazier friend from the New South Wales Riverina. Bea recorded their visit to the Transvaal and Mozambique:

> Years before, I had lived in India and it was a thrill to be in animal country again. The Kruger National Park is not a park as we know one, but a huge reservation of country where all animal and bird life are protected, the animals living in their natural state.

Back at *The Bluff* Charles began to write his biographical notes. He wrote two stories about the jungles of India and another on the search for the *Kookaburra*. These notes and articles were never published or given to historians. The only article he ever published was titled *Central Australia*, which was a general description of that region and the indigenous people whom he found *'friendly, cooperative and peaceful'*. The article did not touch on his aviation activities except to recommend procedures for aircraft that had force landed. Unfortunately, his biographical notes were sparse and ended in 1945. His times in both East Timor and during The Netherlands–Indonesian conflict were never mentioned apart from official documents.

In 1956 *The Bluff* was the venue for the wedding of Charles and Bea's only surviving daughter, Aileen Beatrice, to William 'Bill' Warner of the RAF. Aileen resigned from the RAAF and sailed to England with her husband.

The Eatons then purchased a small but comfortable two-bedroom cottage with a large garden on Victoria's Mornington Peninsula. From his superannuation, supplemented by a modest inheritance from two aunts in England, Charles was able to pay cash for their home. He stubbornly refused to apply for a returned serviceman's home loan. When challenged by his sons for not accepting the generous war service loan, he stated bluntly, *'It was an honour to serve my King and country'* and thought it presumptuous of them for raising the subject. Bea named their home *Sonning* after Sonning-on-Thames, where they had spent their honeymoon in January 1919. *Sonning* was to be their home for the next 18 years, their longest stay in a house throughout their married life.

Although content with their lifestyle, they were a long way from their children: Aileen in England; Peter, who had relocated to Western Australia; and Charles Stuart in Africa and, later, the South Pacific. The large garden gave Charles the chance to create a meticulously maintained mini-botanical garden and concentrate his energy on his orchid hothouse. They had a modest but active social life, either entertaining or going out for dinners at least once a week. Former Beaufighter pilot, Dave 'Horse' Hitchens and Keith Dober, ex-Bomber Command, often dropped by for a sundowner and to 'chew the cud'.

Meticulously, every Friday afternoon Charles would front up at the Frankston Returned Servicemen's League (RSL) for a few ales with his cronies. These included Keith Hatfield, who had served as a soldier in Burma and an army aviator in Korea, Alex 'Spud' Murphy, a former prisoner of war who had been an able seaman on HMAS *Perth*, and Doug Foden, who had been a tail-gunner in Bomber Command at age 19. Doug's aircraft had been shot down on his first mission over France. After bailing out, only he and one other crew member managed to evade capture. Doug informed Charles Stuart that he had become a guerrilla with the French *Maquis* and ended his war by capturing *'a couple of hundred German soldiers and twenty odd Americans'*; the Americans had themselves been captured by the Germans a few days previously. Doug considered fighting with the *Maquis* had been much safer than being a Lancaster tail-gunner, where the remains of gunners were often washed out with fire-hoses. At exactly 6.30 pm, Moth would leave the RSL for home. Sometimes a passenger, Spud noted that Charles, after filling petrol *'would not move until the fuel indicator was fully static'*. Nothing was left to chance even decades after his flying training.

Doug was a fellow-member with Charles of the Royal Air Forces' Escape Society and drove the WWI veteran to their meetings; he said there were some *'very tall stories'* told during their long dinners. Charles emphasised that his Pacific war *'was a picnic'* compared with Bomber Command's efforts over Europe.

Visiting Fiji with Doug Foden, Charles sailed for a week through the stunningly beautiful Yasawa Islands in an open Fijian 25 foot cutter; staying in villages overnight, drinking *kava*[2] and eating the local fare. In the villages they visited, Charles was provided with a personal maid to attend to his food and laundry, much to Doug's chagrin. The cutter's captain, Petero Ului, explained to an envious Doug that it was local protocol to give older dignitaries such service and that Doug was far too young to warrant his own maid. Captain Petero thought the old pilot *'had the makings of a good sailor'*.

Meanwhile, in 1965 in England, Aileen was diagnosed with cancer and underwent a series of operations. Herself a nurse, she knew the consequences of her illness and bore them with courage. In spite of the best medical care available, she passed away in February 1968. Charles and Bea were devastated at losing their only living daughter at the relatively young age of 49. She left behind her husband and three children under ten.

In 1969, Charles and Bea celebrated their golden wedding anniversary. On a bright sunny January day more than 50 people came to wish the couple well; their garden was in full bloom and as meticulous as ever. Charles was delighted when guests showed interest in his *Cymbidium* collection. A notorious early riser, Charles' personal advice for a long, happy marriage was to never have breakfast with one's wife.

Charles could not escape the *Kookaburra* drama. The ABC interviewed him in 1972 for a documentary on the disappearances of both the *Southern Cross* and the *Kookaburra*. He informed the interviewer that, apart from the small hole dug under the starboard wing, there was no indication Anderson and Hitchcock had dug for water. If they had dug in the dense bush, it was not noticed by his ground expedition. He added, *'without water in that country one cannot last longer than 48 hours'*. He said that apart from Anderson's diary on the tail plane and the papers found near his body, there was no evidence that the two airmen left any alleged messages in the aircraft or elsewhere in the vicinity. Charles stressed that their time at the landing site was limited due to the urgent need to get the horses to water.

Counteracting criticism of Kingsford Smith and the crew of the *Southern Cross*, Charles said he believed that when the aircraft's crew dropped messages to two different missions, they received conflicting directions. They purposely landed in an area near the Glenelg River where they could be easily seen from the air. He thanked the ABC for the offer to take him back to the site of the *Kookaburra* but declined as he was caring for Bea and, at 74, felt he *'would not be able to pull my weight'*.

In 1974, Joyce Batty of Adelaide wrote to Charles stating that she was researching the Westland Widgeon *Kookaburra*. She wanted details of the location of the aircraft so she could mount an expedition to recover its remains. In his reply Charles reiterated his confidence in Indigenous Australians:

> I have had many inquiries from South Australia and NSW as to the exact location of the Kookaburra and this is impossible to give. A rough position would be no good at all. I do know that the CO of the RAAF Darwin, Group Capt D Hitchens AFC has endeavoured to find it but I do not know if he has been successful. I doubt with the recent season in North Australia and subsequent growth, if anything can be seen at all from the air. However the Aborigines in the vicinity of Wave Hill would probably be the answer in guiding a ground party to the site.

The two maintained a regular correspondence over the next six months. Miss Batty wrote on 6 September to say her expedition to find the *Kookaburra's* remains failed, possibly due to the excessive vegetation in the desert after heavy rains. She added that her four-vehicle expedition experienced 34 punctures in four days.

In another twist to the on-going 45-year controversy, correspondence released from the then Attorney-General of Australia revealed that the Government Resident in Darwin had telegrammed him on or about 13 June 1929: *'That three of my friends saw on the body of Anderson a contract between* [Kingsford] *Smith and Anderson signed before* Southern Cross *left Sydney to the effect that Anderson was to discover* [the] *Southern Cross ... '.* In reply the Attorney-General suggested that Home Affairs instruct the Police investigation branch to interview Flt Lt Charles Eaton and that any findings would be confidential. The next day an Inspector of Police reported:

> I have to report that I have this morning interviewed Flight Lieutenant Eaton. He states positively signed by himself, and certified correct by Mr Moray [Lawrence], comprised everything found on the body of Anderson, and nothing whatever was left. Flight Lieutenant Eaton is satisfied that the copy contract, referred to in the telegram from the Government Resident, Darwin, is that entered between Anderson and Cantor, a copy of which was left with you yesterday. I share the opinion of Flight Lieutenant Eaton that further inquiry by the Government Resident at Darwin or Mr Moray will make it clear that no reference to contract, other than that between Anderson and Cantor, has been made by Mr Moray.[3]

In 1975, the ABC produced a documentary of the *Kookaburra* saga as a part of their *Big Country* programme. In the documentary, a member of the Thornycroft expedition that exhumed the bodies of Anderson and Hitchcock stated Anderson had committed suicide by shooting himself; a used Verey pistol was found nearby. Also, the allegation prevailed that the 'Coffee Royal' affair had been a stunt to promote Kingsford Smith's circumnavigation of the globe. Charles saw red. He had avoided media publicity throughout his life but demanded an interview with Rodger Sanders of the Melbourne press:

> GROUP-CAPT. Charles Eaton, 80, is not one to get angry. Normally he is happy to enjoy the peace of the large garden of his Frankston home and reminisce on a busy life. But this normally placid, family-loving ex-serviceman is indignant and hurt. His hurt is the deeply personal kind felt for a respected late colleague whose name, he says has been wronged. It is so strong that it has forced him to break a 46-year silence on one of Australia's most tragic and unusual aviation stories.

Charles considered the suicide allegation was a cowardly attack on Anderson's honour. To support Charles's findings both Sgt Eric Douglas and Alex Moray, who were present at the burials, never wrote or commented to the contrary. Charles explained to Saunders that most aircraft carried a Verey pistol, to be used to attract attention; either Anderson or Hitchcock had fired the gun to start a fire, which was the correct procedure. During WWI Lance Corporal Eaton had buried hundreds of his fellow soldiers and would have noticed any wound or injury. He stated that a wound from a Verey pistol would make *'a bloody mess'*—and he wasn't swearing. Charles concluded, '*This is the third day I have wasted on the* Kookaburra *and I have so much to do from 6 am every morning.*' On 19 September 1975, Charles wrote to the program's producer, David Poynter:

> I must admit I was very disappointed in the TV production ... in my mind and many others too ... it only showed some mud-raking of a gallant Australian airman ... known worldwide. To Miss Falvey I particularly stressed the document I found near Anderson's body, afterwards handed over to the Commission of Inquiry, and completely cleared all the airmen

concerned of any stunt for publicity purposes. I and the Aviation Historical Society sincerely trust that as these concern the finding and burial of Anderson and Hitchcock it is included in your documentary so that any mud-slinging will be obliterated.

To be able to assist in the making of an official Government record is a pleasure and no gain or reward is sought although I would appreciate if my part in the searches be played down. The whole affair was a team effort.

In 1976 Dick Smith, aviator and adventurer, contacted Charles regarding the location of the *Kookaburra*. Dick's story on how he found the elusive aircraft was described in Vignette 14—Aftermath and the publication, *Kookaburra: The Most Compelling Story in Australia's Aviation History*.

By 1975, the Eatons could no longer physically travel to visit their sons in Fiji and Perth; age was catching up and Bea needed periodic blood transfusions to counter-balance anaemia. Charles became a part-time carer to Bea and was utterly devoted to her wellbeing. He even gave up his pipe, which had been a permanent fixture in his mouth since he was a teenager. When Charles had a serious stroke in late 1978, he refused to be taken to hospital. To make it worse, Bea could not drive. After a call to Fiji from a mutual friend, Charles Stuart flew to Melbourne immediately and was horrified at his father's condition. After a confrontation about being hospitalised, Charles Stuart managed to get his father into the passenger seat of his car. Always the fighter, Charles growled at his son, *'You have no right to take me anywhere ... and anyway, you don't know how to drive my car.'* As soon as Charles Stuart started the car, he became uncommunicative, perhaps realising that he would not be returning home.

Charles was admitted to a nursing home while Bea still resided at *Sonning*. While mobile, she was in no condition to stay on her own. Charles Stuart's wife's niece flew from Fiji to look after Bea. This arrangement worked perfectly for nine months until Bea, reaching for her evening brandy, slipped and broke her hip. She was admitted to the same nursing home as her husband. A short time after, on 11 January 1979, Bea and Charles celebrated their diamond wedding anniversary together. The management and staff arranged quite a party. After receiving the traditional telegram from the Queen, Charles, the ever-loyal subject, was overcome with emotion.

Although Charles had difficulty in distinguishing the identity of his two sons, he could recite the engine number of his DH-9 aircraft that crashed in the German trench 60 years previously. He detested being looked after and, when depressed and despondent, told Charles Stuart he wanted to go quickly and please would he give him *'something'*. Before his return to Fiji in mid-1979 Charles Stuart unknowingly bade his last farewell to his father.

On the morning of 11 November 1979, Charles was watching the Remembrance Day service on television. Perhaps his emotions became too intense after seeing the veterans on parade; he had a massive stroke in his chair. He passed away that evening, nine days short of his 84th birthday. Peter and Charles Stuart arrived to comfort their mother and make arrangements for a private funeral. At their father's request, there was no obituary announcement.

A simple service was held in a Frankston funeral parlour. Bea could not attend but about a dozen close friends came including Dene and Geri James, Keith and Elsa Hatfield and Jack and Bettine Millar. Spud Murphy played the Last Post and *Reveille* as Charles' flag-draped casket left for the crematorium. Surprisingly, the retired Chief of the Air Staff, Sir George Jones, appeared to farewell his colleague of many years; how he learned of the event remains a mystery.

Charles died with the understanding that he would be seen off only by his immediate family, quietly and privately according to his wishes and nature. He was not to know that in 1981 and 1995 two public memorial services were to be held in his honour and that he would return to the region he loved, northern Australia.

Despite Charles' desire for anonymity, the RAAF and the Tennant Creek Shire Council gave the old aviator a final farewell and dedicated a National Trust Memorial to his memory. In the afternoon of 15 April 1981, a RAAF Caribou aircraft took off with Peter, Group Captain AJ Simmonds and a chaplain. After a mid-air service, Charles' ashes were dispersed over the Tanami Desert. On the aircraft's return to Tennant Creek, Group Captain Simmonds unveiled the historic engine of DH-9A A1-1, which Charles had crashed landed in April 1929. Mayor Alf Chittock, Town Clerk Bruce McRae and the President of the local National Trust, Fred Kittle, attended. The inscription plaque reads:

In Memory of Pioneer Aviator Group Captain Charles 'Moth' Eaton OBE AFC MID, Commander-Knight of the Orange Nassau with Swords

Peter Eaton spoke about how proud the Eaton family were that his father was so honoured and said that he now realised how difficult the conditions were for the airmen when searching for the *Kookaburra* and later the *Golden Quest II*. Landing grounds and communications in the late 1920s were non-existent and the aircraft were themselves relics of WWI. The next morning, the *Eaton Apartments* in the township were formally opened and named.

Bea bore her loss bravely. Charles Stuart remembers how his mother secretly stored her bottle of Remy Martin among her night dresses so she could enjoy an evening tot. Beatrice Rose Elizabeth, named after Victoria's youngest granddaughter, died quietly in her sleep in May 1981, aged 88. As a young girl, she and her brother Harry had been patted on the head by the Queen's regal hand. Family lore suggested they both *'never recovered'*. Bea had been a loyal and supportive wife for 60 years in a life that had not been easy as they had been constantly on the move. Her quiet dexterity and tact maintained the marriage on an even equilibrium throughout their long lives.

Charles was again honoured on 15 August 1995, when a memorial display was unveiled in Parliament House Darwin as part of *Australia Remembers* celebrations marking the 50th anniversary of the ending of WWII. More than 350 guests and visitors attended and the Last Post was played; the eulogy was given by Colonel Keith Hatfield and speeches made by Charles' grandson, Charles Warner, and Brendon Doran on behalf of the Minister of Foreign Affairs, Senator Gareth Evans. The Eaton family present will never forget the words of Group Captain Brian Kavanagh who spoke for the RAAF:

Twilight: Moth's Last Flight, 1952–81

In its 74 years of existence the RAAF has had its ups and downs. During that time a number of heroes emerged; 'Moth' Eaton was one of those heroes.

The caption heading the display simply stated:

Soldier – Pioneer Aviator – Diplomat

Charles Eaton, aged 80, being interviewed by the ABC in 1975.

Charles Eaton, Commanding Officer, RAAF Darwin, 1939–1941.

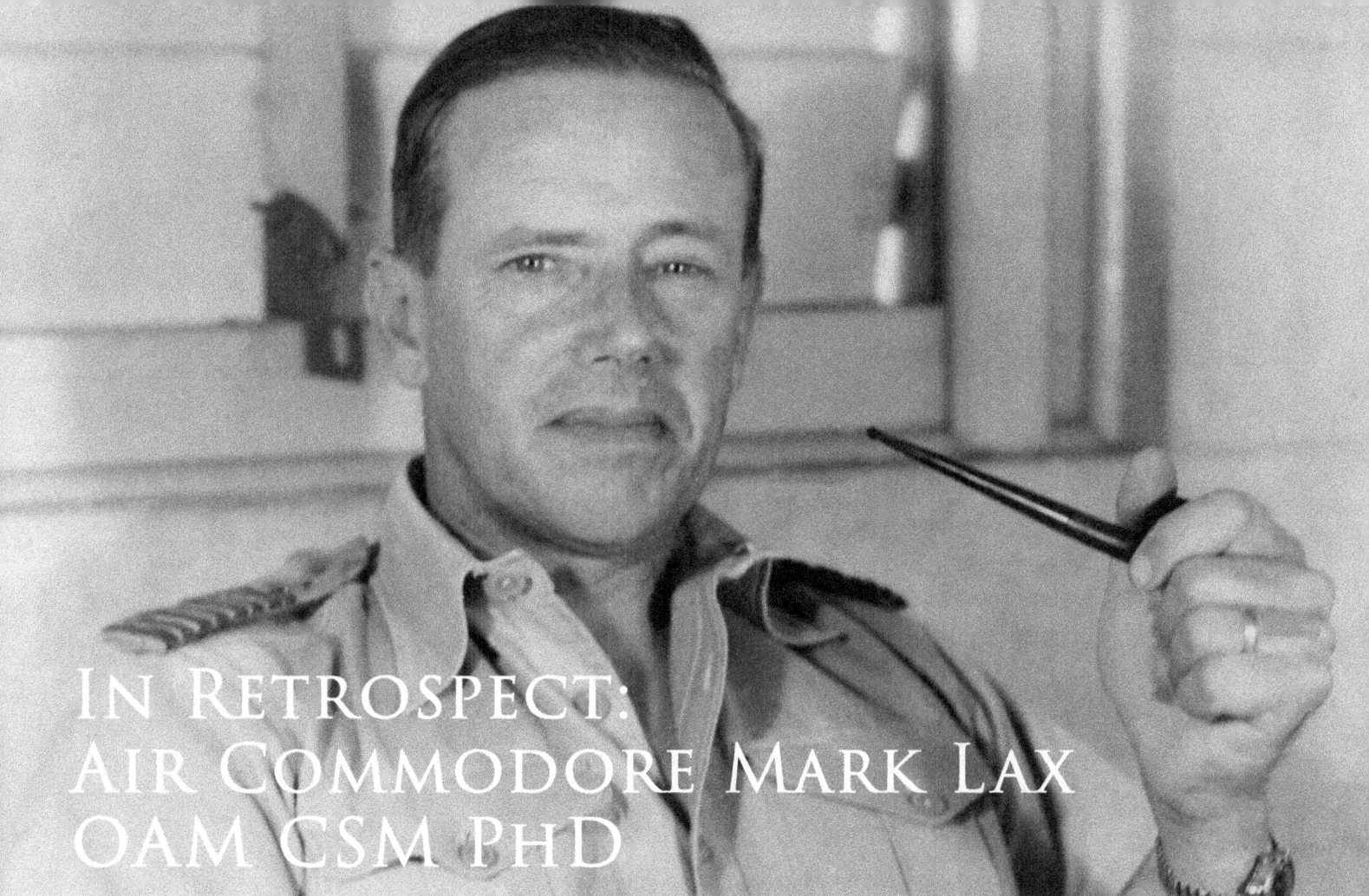

In Retrospect:
Air Commodore Mark Lax
OAM CSM PhD

Private soldier, reconnaissance pilot, prisoner of war escapee, adventurer, commander, diplomat and orchid-lover. These titles were all used to describe the man who affectionately became known in air force circles as 'Moth'—an endearment allegedly coined because of the unkempt state of his uniform or his association with the Gipsy Moth aircraft. He wore that nickname as a badge of honour and the name Moth Eaton is still recognised today. Not one for pomp, ceremony or pretentiousness, he may have been pushed to the sidelines throughout most of his air force career, but history now records he made more of a mark on contemporary Australian affairs than many of his peers. I am sure *The Cross in the Sky* has done him the justice he so richly deserves.

I was never fortunate enough to meet Moth Eaton, one of the Royal Australian Air Force's true pioneers. I first encountered him through reading of his exploits in preparing a presentation on Australian aviation personalities of the Great War, delivered in 2001. I chose him amongst the dozen or so 'well-knowns' because, although of British birth and from a Royal Flying Corps background, his exploits in the Northern Territory in the 1930s and after more than justified his inclusion.

Moth had several characteristics that shaped his life. First and foremost might be said was luck—he was a survivor, when many of his generation weren't. To come through the trenches of the Somme, to fight in the bloody skies over the Western Front, and to be forced down and taken prisoner by the Germans, who court-martialled him (not once, but twice) might be reason enough to claim this title—but not for this man. He escaped at least twice and eventually found his way to the harsh outback of the Australia's Northern Territory. Here, he spent time searching for lost airmen, all in intense heat, low on rations and water and yet not giving up. This too might be valid reason to lay claim to being lucky. But perhaps his walking away from an air crash and subsequent fire, which incidentally claimed the RAAF's first aircraft A1-1, might suggest such luck does come in threes.

Second, he was a quiet achiever who did not seek the limelight. Described by a superior as '*a hard working commander who had the confidence of all his subordinates*', his long periods of remote and tropical service remain largely unrecognised by present day RAAF men and women. Yet he helped open up Northern Australia's air routes and established the airport in Darwin as World War Two was breaking. Despite his personal efforts and a love for the air force, he never attained high rank, as so many other pre-war RAAF officers did. Perhaps it was his British birth, perhaps his breaking of the dockers' strike in Darwin in 1940, or perhaps it was his preference for flying and the Northern Territory over a comfortable desk job 'down south' in HQ that prevented him from rising higher, but his contribution to Australia both in the air and on the ground as a diplomat should never be forgotten.

Third, he was loyal to both his fellow man and his adopted country, best illustrated by his life post-RAAF. Turning his hand to external affairs, his appointments as Australian Consul in Portuguese Timor, to the United Nations Consular Commission in NEI, as Consul-General in the Netherlands East Indies then as Charge de Affairs to the newly independent Indonesia gave him the extraordinary opportunity to personally shape Australian foreign policy—a prospect few have the opportunity for today. His personal drive for what he felt was best for the country was his greatest legacy. Events in South East Asia today would come as no surprise to him. Australia's post-war association with Indonesia and East Timor really began with him and he foresaw the troubles ahead; in particular, West Papua. Arguably, it was Moth Eaton who set us on the road to UN peacekeeping missions, so common around the globe today.

Charles Stuart Eaton, Moth's younger son, has done a commendable job in bringing to life the story of this remarkable man. Starting with just a few pages of Moth's original biographical notes, his many years of painstaking research has brought to us the fullness of Moth's life that might otherwise have been lost with the passage of time. Moth may have thought a life such as his *'uninteresting and dull'*, but the younger Charles' work has proven Moth wrong.

To conclude, I am delighted that as a tribute to Moth, the Northern Territory Government decided to name a new Darwin suburb 'Eaton' in Moth Eaton's honour as the one who selected the site of the airfield now shared between the air force and commercial operators. In recognition of his close connection to, and admiration for the Northern Territory and its people, the Tennant Creek Shire Council and RAAF combined to disperse his ashes from the air north-west of the township.

'An Edwardian Family': From left: Margery, Charles, Maude, William Walpole and Constance Eaton, London 1914.

Family Background

I Recommend to the Earth to be buried in decent Christian burial ... in a brick Grave with a drain from it to lay it dry and my Coffin set upon some Bricks some distance from the Floor with room for my Wife to lye by me. And no more Writing upon my Grave Stone than my Name Day of the Month Date and Age.[1]

The origins of Charles Eaton's paternal ancestors, the Eatons and Walpoles, were the villages of Kelmarsh and Winwick in Northamptonshire in England's midlands. The Anglo-Saxon name 'Eaton' was recorded in those villages well before the 18th Century.

Edward Eaton married Elizabeth Walpole at St Michael's Church, Winwick in 1796. Two years later his sister, Anne Eaton, married his brother-in-law, John Walpole, in Kelmarsh but John died the following year aged 26. The will of Elizabeth's brother, William Walpole (1778-1800), the last survivor of his immediate family, bequeathed the Winwick Mill, lands and hereditary entitlements to his brother-in-law, Edward Eaton. In 1796 Edward was appointed 'Overseer of the Poor'. Edward and Elizabeth's eldest son, William Walpole Eaton (born in 1802), migrated to London and entered into the butchery trade. William's youngest son, Charles Samuel Eaton, eventually controlled a number of butcher stalls in London's Smithfield market. He reputedly was one of the first importers of chilled beef from The Argentine. In the 1881 United Kingdom National Census Charles Samuel, aged 42, lived in 76 Kennington Road Lambeth with his wife Harriett *née* Evans. Living in the household were his three children, William Walpole, Edith and Harriett and three domestic servants, Sarah Prior, Fredrick Hall and a Charles Chaplin.[2]

Charles and Marjory as children

Charles Samuel Eaton died in 1887, aged 48, leaving a large cash settlement to his two daughters and the butchery business to his son, William Walpole, then aged 21. William married Grace Maude Martin, the daughter of William and Hephzibah Martin of *Bourne Farm in* Wrotham, Kent. The Martins, Beadles and Batts were long-established farming families from 'The Pilgrim's Way'.

William and Maude had three living children—Margery, Charles and Constance—with two other children dying in infancy. Charles was born on 21 December 1895 and baptised on 16 January the following year at St Philip Church, Kennington Road. Due to inexperience and a penchant for gambling, William forfeited the butchery business and the substantial house in Kennington Road and the family moved to a modest semi-detached residence at 5 Gayville Road, Battersea, where Margery, Charles and Constance attended the Honeywell Road School.

Young Charles' introduction to the new mode of transport, 'the flying machine', was in 1911 when the Circular Air Race of England was held. Looking with awe at these new machines, he pleaded with his maternal grandmother to witness this historic event. The aged lady retorted, '*If God meant people to fly, He would have given them wings.*' Little did Hephzibah Martin and her young grandson realise that these new-fangled machines would provide him a calling that would span three continents for three decades!

Charles, far left centre row: Honeywell Road School, Battersea

By 1909 Charles' father was virtually bankrupt. Aged 14, Charles left school to financially support his family. He maintained this support for the rest of his parents' lives, his mother dying during WWII and his father in 1952. His first employment was at the Southwark Borough Council as a message boy to George Rose of the accounting department. An older family friend, Charles George Napier, encouraged him to join a Territorial unit of the British Army in 1912. For the next eight years, Charles Napier was to have a guiding and protective influence on his younger namesake.

George Rose's wife, Francis, had four cousins—Harry, Florence, Beatrice and Albert Godfrey. Their father, Edwin Godfrey, was a caterer at Buckingham Palace and a member of the Vintners Guild, who claimed descent from Huguenot stock. Harry Godfrey, later an architect, wrote that Francis Rose introduced Charles to his sister, Beatrice, at the Bohemian Tennis Club, Shepherds Bush. Known as 'Beattie' or 'Bea', she *'had lots of admirers'* but within a short time of their meeting, Harry remarked that Charles was *'determined to have her for keeps'*. On 1 August 1914, Harry was surprised to see Charles at the Club dressed in the uniform of the Queens West Surrey Regiment,

Beatrice Godfrey as a young woman

commonly known as 'The Lambs'.³ The British Army had mobilised due to the probability of war with Germany.

Like so many homes during WWI, the Eaton household was always apprehensive, particularly as by March 1915 their only son was fighting in France and the casualty lists were mounting in their thousands. Many of Maude Eaton's soldier nephews, the Martins from Canada⁴, visited the Eaton house on their home leave, as did Australians on recuperation leave. Some left a memento of their visit; on 11 January 1917, Private SR Fleming of 60 Battalion Australian Imperial Forces, penned:

> *There's a certain darned nuisance called 'Beachy'*
> *Whose shells are exceedingly screechy*
> *But we're keeping the score*
> *And we're after your gore*
> *So lookout, 'Beachy Bill' when we meet ye.*
> *They've given us all respirators*
> *And we've bundles of ancient spectators*
> *But we'd give up the two*
> *For a good oyster stew*
> *Or a dixie of chipped potaters*

In May 1917, after just over two years as frontline soldiers in France, Sergeant Charles Napier and Lance Corporal Charles Eaton transferred from IV Corps Cyclist Battalion to the Royal Flying Corps. Charles was to remain in England until May 1918 when he returned to France as a reconnaissance pilot. In early July, the Eaton family received the dreaded telegram stating that their only son was missing in action and, a month later, that he had died in captivity on 3 August 1918.

Following a four-year courtship by army mail, personal contact in England and postcards from prisoner-of-war camps, Bea and Charles were married by the Reverend Small at St Thomas' Church, Shepherds Bush, on 11 January 1919. Lieutenant Warren 'Patchy' Waterson RFC of Vancouver Island, Canada, was best man and some 50 friends and relatives attended the wedding breakfast at the Godfrey residence at 26 Ingersoll Road. Patchy later married

Charles' elder sister Marjory and they returned to live in Canada, where he died in 1931. Beatrice and Charles had five children—Aileen Beatrice (1919-1968), Irene (1924), Peter Charles Godfrey (1925), Brian John (1930) and Charles Stuart (1934); Irene and Brian both died in infancy.

Last Word: Author's Notation and Acknowledgements

An autobiography is usually uninteresting and dull. But at the same time, the story of a life of the generation which has seen two major wars, with the interval between of time and space occupied by travel and adventure, can be of interest to both young and old. In this story the dull periods are omitted, and in accordance with the old slogan that truth may be stranger than fiction, my intention is to give an outline, particularly to the younger generation, of what can happen to all who have inherited a spirit of travel and adventure.

Charles Eaton, 1953

The Cross in the Sky is the journey of a man who exemplified his generation in war and peace. Charles Eaton played many diverse roles and participated in some of the most momentous events of the 20th Century. The 30 vignettes presented in this book were intervals of space in his life, with portrayals of the units and personalities with whom he served.

Initially, I considered it would be difficult to write his biography as he left only 58 pages of miserly notes, with each page raising more questions than answers. He wrote virtually nothing of a personal nature on his roles in carrying out the first aerial survey of India or on vindicating Australia's hero, Charles Kingsford Smith, of misdemeanour. Nor did he write on his contribution to the post-war rehabilitation of East Timor or his role in the first UN investigation into conflict. Yet, when playing 'hide and seek' in and out of German prisons, he wrote with subtle humour. And on India's forest people and wildlife, he opened up in detail and with compassion.

I remember the few occasions he did mention his army service; he stressed the '*dirt, the filth and the mud*' and that '*one could never keep clean*'. On one occasion, when the Battle of Loos was mentioned on television, he suddenly stared into the ceiling and said *'Looooooooz'* like the name had no ending. I did receive a few tit-bits of his army life from my mother, particularly his participation in the actions at Givenchy and Loos. My brother Peter told me that our father had such an abhorrence of barbed wire that, when fencing on his farm in the 1950s, he simply dropped his tools and walked home without comment. The memories of his comrades 'hanging on the wire' were still too strong. The subject of death was taboo; he never mentioned the deaths of his friend Charlie Napier, his comrades-in-arms and his own two infant children, Irene and Brian. Oddly, he had an almost boyish awe of a number of diverse characters. These included Leefe Robinson VC, his 'cellmate' in Germany, the aviator Herewood de Havilland, bushman and cameleer Bob Buck of Central Australia, Johnny Lerew 'The Hero of Rabaul' and his *major domo* in India, Pathan Din. Their names were mentioned randomly and 'out of thin air'.

When asked about his WWII, he said, *'It was a picnic.'* He was presumably comparing his participation in the bloodbath of Loos, burying the dead, that 'Minenwerfer Hour' and mining salt when a prisoner; all in WWI.

Charles wrote three short, unpublished stories: 'The Bear Hunt' and 'Fear', which described life in the jungles of India and are amalgamated as Vignette 8, and 'The Cross in the Sky', which I have adopted as this book's title as it marked an extraordinary occurrence at a defining moment of his life (Vignette 12). He never kept a diary. Unfortunately, the whereabouts of his log books remains a mystery, but a wide range of official reports, published literature and correspondence helped provide authenticity for all vignettes. One blessing; he bequeathed an extensive photograph collection, a legacy of his time as a reconnaissance soldier and pilot.

Charles, verbally and in his notes, praised many but rarely criticised; if he disapproved of anybody, they were damned by silence. A conformist Edwardian by character, his only expletive was 'damn'. His vice was 'The Pipe', which was fixed to his face from the age of about 16. Habitually, his sundowner Scotch was rarely before 6 pm; perhaps the only mannerism I have inherited.

In recording his life, it would be his wish to focus on the activities of the units and the personalities with whom he served. I was apprehensive of involving personal emotions and making biased judgments of his character and actions of which I had no first-hand knowledge. I have therefore focused on historical facts and avoided any appraisal of his service and diplomatic life except when quoted by a third party. From the age of seven, I saw my parents only on intermittently due to his war service and diplomatic postings from 1941 to 1950, and my own departure for overseas employment. The chance to investigate my parents' lives gave me a unique opportunity to discover the conditions they and their compatriots experienced.

The Cross in the Sky commemorates Charles' comrades in war and peace. Initially in 1915–1917, his fellow soldiers of the Royal West Surreys, many of whom died in their thousands in France's sodden, bloody fields, and the nine teenage boys of 206 Squadron RAF who lost their lives in a few weeks in the spring of 1918. In peace, the members of 28 Squadron during the first aerial survey of India in 1920 and *'those good people'* the Khond forest-dwellers of Orissa. In addition, *'those wizards of the desert'*, the Central Australian tribesmen who guided Charles and his party in their rescue missions in 1929 and 1931. The Australian, Dutch, Indonesian and American airmen with whom he served in the Pacific during WWII. Finally, in 1947, Charles' fellow members of the UN Consular Commission in Indonesia who initiated UN international peacekeeping.

As the youngest child, I gave my parents many anxieties, as verified by Sargeant Kennedy in Darwin: *'That snowy-headed kid, mischievous little devil, gave us no end of trouble.'* This opportunity has given me the chance to repay the debt I owe my parents. They migrated to Australia from India with just twenty pounds; yet my father, with my mother's support, was able to contribute to Australia's aviation history and diplomatic integrity in South-East Asia. For more than 60 years, Charles was blessed to have the lifelong love and support of Beatrice Rose Godfrey. In a most elusive and discreet manner, Bea usually had the 'last word'.

I must first acknowledge Mitchell Williamson, who suggested that I research my father's life and gave me the confidence to persevere. The late Edward Gough Whitlam QC, my gratitude for his encouragement and forwarding of specific archival material. The major contribution of Dr Steven Farram for his publications relating to my father's air force and diplomatic service, in particular the Consular Commission of 1947. Gavin Bromlow, Ian Tankard, Alastair McGregor and the late Ian Rolls who all offered sound advice on manuscript preparation. Dr Dick Watling for his long-time moral support. Dr Peter Stanley for his advice to reduce my original unwieldy script and to Professor Peter Londey and Dr Christopher Clark for their suggestions and amendments. My indebtedness to Sally Douglas, Group Captain Eric Douglas' daughter, who provided access to her father's dairies and images that reinforced vignettes 11 and 12. Penny Gibson of Canberra for her exacting editorial inputs and friendship for the past 35 years, without which this publication would never have been completed.

Professor Dennis Rumley in Perth, who managed to teach me 'structure' when writing social geography studies. Dr Silvano Jung for his support and co-authorship of *Operation Potshot* (Eaton, CS. & Jung, S: 2016). Michael Raafa of the Bull Creek Aviation Museum for his help and long-time custodianship of the Charles Eaton Collection. Major General Ian Gordon for accepting *The Cross in the Sky* for publication and Dr Rodney Nixon for his introduction to Echo Publications. Dr Tim Coyle for his valuable contribution on the RAAF's role in the search for the *Kookaburra* in 1929; also John Haslett, Charles Schaedel, Ian Law, Dr Christopher Griffin and Air Commodore Norman Ashworth for their inputs and encouragement. A special thanks to Lorraine Williams for her translation of the Yolngu Matha language, north-east Arnhem Land.

My cousins in England, Brian and David Eaton, who provided information on the origins of the Eaton and Godfrey families. My friends, particularly Ian Law, Jack Ellis and David Tough, who forced me to the Last Word. My nephew, Charles Warner, for his keen interest in the project and his contribution for the presentation of the images. My sincere gratitude to my dear wife Vani and children, Phillip, Godfrey and Karoline, for their encouragement and patience. Lisa Buchanan of Darwin for assistance with graphic design of the maps in vignettes 11 and 16.

Finally, and most significantly, the contributions of Dick Smith, entrepreneur–philanthropist of Sydney and Air Commodore Mark Lax of Canberra, aviation historian, are sincerely appreciated.

ENDNOTES

Dedication

1. Sun Tze, 200 BC
2. Respect is acknowledged for all deceased people named through this publication.

Vignette 1

1. The badge of the Regiment depicts a solitary Paschal Lamb with the Cross of St George. This symbol originated from the flag of the Portuguese princess, Catherine of Braganza's bodyguard. Catherine was betrothed to Charles II. Hence the title 'The Queen's Regiment' and the sobriquet 'The Lambs.'
2. The Line. The normally static front line dividing the opposing armies; at times only a few hundred metres apart.
3. War Medals Index (UK National Archives) records that 63 men with the name Charles Eaton served in the British Army during WWI. Eaton was identified by his Regiment and service number.
4. Charles penned a short rider on the company's history describing Festubert: 'no rifles' and 'first casualties'.
5. Sepoy: Urdu sapah—Private soldier
6. Cyclist Company, 47 (TF) Division. In the Line 1915–1918: Pip Squeaks from the Past:.A Record in Short Bursts.
7. Eaton, B: personal communication
8. Keyworth's full citation states that 17 bombers survived out of 75, which corroborates

Endnotes

the battalion commander's and Beatrice Eaton's number.

Vignette 2

1 Charles' elder son, Peter, presumed that the 'third wave' event was on the first day of the Somme offensive, 1 July 1916. This is highly unlikely as Charles's company was transferred to IV Corps on that day. IV Corps was not involved on the first day of the Somme attacks.
2 Poilu—French soldier. Literally, hairy, reputably due to their unkempt attire.

Vignette 3

1 47 Division Cyclist Company: In the Line 1915–1918
2 Edmunds, Sir J: 1922
3 Correspondence from Osmet P: Guards Division (in Warner, P: 1976)
4 Uhlans—Light cavalry
5 Jägers—Light infantry; in this case, mounted
6 Maude, A: 1922

Vignette 4

1 A flight is a group of three aircraft
2 Zeppelins in the Silent Raid were: LZ 41, LZ 44, LZ 45, LZ 46, LZ 47, LZ 49, LZ 50, LZ 52, LZ 53, LZ 54 and LZ 55.
3 The original photographs of The Charles Eaton Collection are permanently deposited at the Bull Creek Aviation Museum, Bull Creek, Western Australia. Access to the collection is free of charge.

Vignette 5

1 Both Bishop and Mannock were awarded the Victoria Cross. Bishop survived WWI to become an Air Vice Marshal, Mannock was killed in action on 26 July 1918. Cobby served with the RAAF as an Air Commodore in the south-west Pacific during WWII.
2 Captain E Marrow: 12/8/1918
3 Tournay was just inside the Belgian border. Charles, at the time, was probably not concerned about what country he was over, but rather anxious to get his observer, himself and the DH 9 Tractor home in one piece.

Vignette 6

1 Mitze, Katja: 1999
2 There were two camps: one, in the grounds of the Karlsruher Schloss, contained naval and, later, aviation officers; the other, the former Europäischer Hof, was known as 'The Listening Hotel', and was an interrogation centre. Charles was interned in the latter. https://en.wikipedia.org/wiki/List_of_prisoner-of-war_camps_in_Germany
3 Charles was permitted by his German captors to mail photographs and letters, but this had not been permitted while he had been serving in The Line with the BEF.
4 R V Jubb DFC RAAF of the Royal Air Forces Escape Society mentioned that, at reunion meetings of the Society, Charles wasn't expansive on his prison experiences, except to recall that labouring in a German salt mine was 'not his cup of tea'.

Vignette 7

1 Armitage, M: 1999
2 A squadron of 86 Wing, RAF.

3   Ernest Bevin, member of the British War Cabinet during WWII.
4   The Army in India and its Evolution: 1924
5   28 Sqn RAF was equipped with Bristol F2b fighters.
6   Raj—Hindustani for rule.

Vignette 9

1   *Madhula longifolia*—in the Aryan Oriya language, Mahula. In Khond mythology the Mohul tree relates to alcohol. Charles firmly believed that bears discovered alcohol long before humans.

Vignette 10

1   Later Sir Richard Kingsland. A number of graduates of Point Cook transferred to the RAF in the United Kingdom. These included Donald Bennett, Sir Wallace Kyle and Sir Hughie Edwards VC, who all became famous names in the RAF.
2   Later, Sir George Jones, Chief of the Air Staff WWII.
3   Later, Sir Valston Hancock, Chief of the Air Staff post-WWII.
4   Later, Sir Reginald Ansett, founder of Ansett Airways.

Vignette 11

1   Australia Home page www.ourpacificocean.com

Vignette 12

1   Damper—a dough of flour and water baked in wood ashes.
2   Billabong—an Aboriginal term for an ox-bow waterhole.
3   The rudder diary is now in the Western Australian Museum in Perth.

Vignette 13

1   Berg, W: 1929
2   Wixted EP: 1985
3   Berg, W: 1929
4   The crew rotated one of the aircraft's wheels in an unsuccessful effort to generate sufficient power for the wireless.

Vignette 14

1   AFC—Air Force Cross

Vignette 15

1   Bill Baker, no relation to the entrant Harry Baker flying the Klemm L25 VH-ULU.
2   *The Age*. 7 October 1929
3   Zekulich, M. in Western Australian, November 20 1979

Vignette 16

1   *The Melbourne Herald*: 12 January 1931
2   Coote, E: 1982

3   Blakely, F: 1972
4   Pittendrigh, W L. Personal Diary 20 December 1930 to 12 January 1931
5   Burg, W: 1931
6   *The Argus*, 6 January 1931
7   The Alice Springs Airport was developed on this site in 1940.

Vignette 17

1   Clarke, C: 1996
2   *The Sun, Melbourne*, 29 October 1958
3   Eaton, P: personal communication
4   Motto of 12 Squadron, Royal Australian Air Force, Darwin 1939. The motto was selected by Charles Eaton and an unknown Aboriginal informant. It was later confirmed as being from the Yolngu Matha language group of north-east Arnhem Land, Northern Australia as 'Ngilimurru Marrtjina Makarrata' (Lorraine Williams, 2018).

Vignette 18

1   12 Squadron, RAAF, May 1990.
2   Lugger boats, using four-cornered lug sails, were popular for pearl diving.
3   Wet canteen—A canteen where liquor was served. This was the RAAF's first airmen's mess that allowed liquor; Charles may have circumvented RAAF standing orders to justify this because of the tropical conditions. Nevertheless, he later had to send two men south for 'alcoholic inebriation'.
4   V Hancock, personal communication, 1992.
5   S Grantham: 1991
6   Named Six Miles because it was six miles from Darwin's city centre.
7   The base became Darwin International Airport after WWII. The area encompassing the airport and the RAAF base was formally designated as the suburb of Eaton by the Government of the Northern Territory in 2007.
8   Translation of Lelare by N McKenzie, personal communication.
9   An observant survivor of the Darwin bombing in February 1942 discovered a slightly dented but intact Eaton Cup from the debris.
10 N Ashworth: 1999

Vignette 19

1   C Fenton: 1947
2   A Powell: 1988
3   Royal Australian Air Force, unpublished manuscript, 1990.
4   C Fisher, personal communication, 1999.

Vignette 20

1   Japanese airstrip at Selaru. See Vignette 24.
2   Later, Admiral Thomas Moorer, Chairman of the United States Joint Chief of Staff.
3   J Haslett, personal communication.

Vignette 21

1. J Herington: 1954
2. J Dickinson: 1995

Vignette 22

1. 'Saunders of the River' is a classic story of conflict in the Nigerian river delta.
2. W Churchill: 1899

Vignette 23

1. C Wray: 1987
2. Later, Wing Commander Darcy Wentworth, DFC.
3. Later, Colonel Dirk Asjes, a general in the Royal Netherlands Air Force.
4. P Helsen: 1997
5. Squadron Leader P Boyd, DFC and Bar.

Vignette 24

1. https://www.defence.gov.au/sydneyii/COI/COI.005.0080_R.pdf
2. D Asjes, personal communication.
3. J Staal, personal communication.
4. R Williams: 2000

Vignette 25

1. M Lockwood, 30 January 1946.
2. C Archer, 1941
3. E Simões, personal communication.
4. Postos—an administrative district.

Vignette 26

1. R Cinetti: 1947

Vignette 27

1. P Dorling: 1994
2. The Indo Project, Bersiap, 2019.
3. Mountbatten, Lord Louis: 1945
4. S Farram: 2019
5. P Dorling: 1994. Docs 303 & 304
6. The Line: Refer Vignettes 1, 2 and 3—The front trench line between the Allied and German armies.
7. PJ Drooglever and MJB Schouten:1982
8. P Dorling: 1994. Doc 316. AA:A4355/2,7/1/7/3)
9. P Dorling: 1994. Doc 317

10 Sir F Shepherd, 12 & 26 September, 1947

Vignette 28

1 Keng Po, 13 September 1947

2 Squadron Leader L Spence later commanded 77 Squadron RAAF and was killed in action early in the Korean War.
3 P Dorling: 1994 Doc 344
4 P Dorling: 1994 Doc 346

Vignette 29

1 The Indonesian Government unilaterally cancelled this agreement in late 1950, thus dissolving the so-called Union.

Vignette 30

1 In 2010 'Jubby', aged 87, was still managing his 6000 acre cattle property at Warwick Queensland. He worked seven days a week apart for Wednesday afternoon's tennis.
2 A mildly sedative drink made from the dried and pulverised root of the Piper methysticum plant and drunk as a ritual at social gatherings. Also known as yaqona in Fiji.
3 Mr Moray, the Darwin Coroner, was no relation of Alex Moray Lawrence JP who accompanied Charles' desert expedition.

Family

1 John Underwood Eaton of Kelmarsh, Northamptonshire (1702–1771)
2 The 1881 National Census of the United Kingdom. In his autobiography, actor Charlie Chaplin, born in 1889 off Kennington Road, wrote that his father, also Charles Chaplin, lived in Kennington Road for a number of years.
3 The badge of the Regiment depicts a solitary *Paschal Lamb* with the Cross of St George. This symbol originated from the flag of the Portuguese princess, Catherine of Braganza's bodyguard. Catherine was betrothed to Charles II. Hence the title 'The Queen's Regiment' and the sobriquet 'The Lambs'.
4 From Orangeville and Kitchener, Ontario.

Abbreviations

ABC Australian Broadcasting Commission
ACI Air Craftsman Class 1
AFC (1) Australian Flying Corps
AFC (2) Air Force Cross
AFM Air Force Medal
AIF Australian Military Forces
AGPS Australian Government Publishing Service
AM Albert Medal
ANA Australian National Airways
ANU Australian National University
AWM Australian War Memorial
BEF British Expeditionary Force
BEM British Empire Medal
C Celsius
CAC Commonwealth Aircraft Corporation
CAF Citizen Air Force
CAS Chief of the Air Staff
DFAT Department of Foreign Affairs and Trade

DDCC Darwin Defence Co-ordination Committee
DCM Distinguish Conduct Medal
DFC Distinguish Flying Cross
DSC Distinguish Service Cross
EATS Empire Air Training Scheme
FTS Flying Training School
F Fahrenheit
GC George Cross
GOC United Nations Good Offices Committee
HMSO Her Majesty Service Office
Hon Honourable
HQ Head Quarters
IFS Imperial Forestry Service
ICS Indian Civil Service
IWM Imperial War Museum
KIA Killed in Action
LAC Leading Air Craftsman
MC Military Cross
MID Mentioned in Dispatches
MM Military Medal
MS Manuscript
NAA National Archives of Australia
NA (UK) National Archives of the United Kingdom
NEI Netherlands East Indies
NEIAF Netherlands East Indies Air Force
Per. comm Personal communication
NSW New South Wales
NTAS Northern Territory Archives Service
NT Northern Territory
NWA North-West Area
OBE Order of the British Empire

PRO (UK) Public Records Office (United Kingdom)
POW Prisoner of War
RAAF Royal Australian Air Force
RAF Royal Air Force
RAN Royal Australian Navy
RFC Royal Flying Corps
RNAS Royal Naval Air Service
RN Royal Navy
RSL Returned Servicemen's League
SWPA South West Pacific Area
TF Territorial Force
TNI Tentara Nasional Indonesia or National Army of Indonesia
UK United Kingdom
UN United Nations
USAAC United States Army Air Corps
USN United States Navy - **USS** United States Ship
Vol Volume
UWA University of Western Australia
VC Victoria Cross
WO War Office (UK)
WWI World War One
WWII World War Two

Bibliography

The Cross in the Sky is written as a true-life, human interest story and makes no attempt to evaluate the personalities and events in depth. The historical background of major incidents, i.e. France 1915–18, are primarily based on the Cyclist Company, 47th (TF) Division's unpublished manuscript, In the Line 1915–1918: Pip Squeaks from the Past: A Record in Short Bursts and the history of 206 Squadron, 1918. The three vignettes on India are mainly based on Charles' notes and his two unpublished short stories. The Central Australian desert searches of 1929 and 1931 are well summarised in the *Kookaburra* files in the National Archives of Australia including *Southern Cross Flight & Loss in Northern Australia*; the publication *Kookaburra: The Most Compelling Story in Australia's Aviation History* and Eric Douglas' dairies. In addition, Charles' official report in 1931, Operations in Connection with the Search for the Missing Airmen in Central Australia.

There is a wealth of literature on the RAAF activities in WWII, including *An Illustrated History of No 12 Squadron RAAF: 1939–1948*, *Whispering Death: A History of the RAAF's Beaufighter Squadrons* and *The Forgotten Air Force*, which relates to RAAF North-Western Area 1941–1945. Indonesia's war of independence and the outcomes of the United Nations Consular Commission are comprehensively covered in many publications including *Australia & Indonesia's Independence: The Renville Agreement* and *Indonesia, 1947: Australia and the first United Nations Cease-Fire Order.*

Significant references are included in endnotes and all citations are included in the References. Bibliographical publications are included for readers who may wish to extend their understanding of specific characters and incidents.

Agnew, I. Personal Papers of Lieutenant Ivo Agnew, 1893–1969. AWM Canberra.

Air Board (RAAF). Cable to Eaton, 19 April, 1929. A 705/1 153/1/645. NAA. Canberra.

Air Board (RAAF). Cable to Eaton, 20 April, 1929. A 705/1 153/1/645. NAA. Canberra.

Air Board (RAAF). Cable to Eaton, 21 April, 1929. A 705/1 153/1/645. NAA. Canberra.

Albrecht, F. 'Lasseter: Here is the Truth' in *Sunday Mail*, 1 April 1967.

Alford, R. Ed. 'Through the Eyes of a Young Airman: The Arrival of the RAAF—Allen, Darwin 1939' in *The Territory at War*. Australia Remembers Committee. Darwin.

Allen OE. *The Airline Builders*. Time-Life Books. Alexandria, Virginia. 1981.

Amar, M. *The Logistical Support of the RAAF & Associated Activities in the Northern Area of Operations during World War II—1939 to 1945*. Air Power Development Centre. Canberra. 1993.

Anderson, F. Per. comm.

Anon. 'Tragic Folly' in *Aircraft*, Vol. 7/8. 30 April 1929. Melbourne.

Anon. 'Flight Lieut. Eaton Again: RAAF Search Expedition Success' in *Aircraft*. 9 February 1931. Melbourne.

Arens, H. Per. comm. 16 December 1993.

Archer, CH. Report on Portuguese Timor, 1941. Unpublished MS. NAA Bar Code 181029. Canberra.

Armitage, M. *The Royal Air Force*. Cassell & Company, London. 1999.

Ashworth, N. *How Not to Run an Air Force—The Higher Command of the Royal Australian Air Force During the Second World War*. Air Power Development Centre, Canberra. 1999.

Asjes, General D. Per. comm. 1980.

Australia Home Page. www.ourpacificocean.com

Australian Military Forces. Plan for Combined Exercises. August 1941. AWM. Canberra.

Australian Military Forces. Report by Lt. Col. WW Ingram MC. Commander Red Force First Landing. August 1941. AWM. Canberra.

Australia Remembers 1945–1995 (NT) Committee. *The Territory at War*. Australia Remembers 1945–1995. Darwin.

Australian War Cabinet. Coal for Darwin. A 5954/69 455/3. NAA. 3 April 1940. Canberra.

Australian War Cabinet. Wharf Strike—Darwin. MP727/6/0 2/401/33. NAA. 28/8/1940. Canberra.

Australian War Museum. Statement made by Repatriated Prisoners of War. Lieutenant O. Flight. 27 December 1918. Canberra.

Australian War Museum. Operations Record RAAF Laverton. Micro Film 152 1934–39. Canberra.

Australian War Museum. 21 Squadron Operations Record. Micro Film 22 1934–48. Canberra.

Australian War Museum. 12 Squadron Operations Record. Micro Film 14 1939–48. Canberra.

Baker, B. 'The Great Transcontinental Air Race of 1929' in *Aviation Heritage*, Vol. 35/4, Melbourne. 2004.

Baldwin, H. *World War I: An Outline History*. Hutchinson & Co, London. 1962.

Batty, J. Per. comm. 30 May & 6 September 1974.

Beadon, RH. *Some Memories of the Peace Conference*. Lincoln Williams, London. 1933.

Berg, W. 'A Hoofprint in the Centre of a Continent' in *The Guardian*. 29 June, 1929. Northern Territory Library, Darwin. 1929.

Besenthal, P *et al*. 'Ingolstadt on the Danube' in *Tourist Information Altes Rathaus*. Ingolstadt. 2004. Bishop, P. *Fighter Boys: Saving Britain 1940*. Harper Perennial, London. 2004.

Blakely, F. *Dream Millions: New Light on Lasseter's Lost Reef*. Angus & Robertson, Sydney. 1972.

Blandford, JS. 'Sans Escourt: 206 Sqn. Reminiscences' in *Cross & Cockade*. Vol.7/4. London. 1976.

Blaxland, G. *Amiens 1918*. Star Books, London. 1981.

Blue, T. 'Horror of a Bygone Age' in *Weekend Australian Review*. 4–5 September 2004.

Boal, B. *The Khonds: Human Sacrifice & Religious Change*. Aris & Phillips, Warminster. 1982.

Brassil, J. Per. comm. 1994.

British Army Cyclist Corps Manual. IWM. London. 1914.

Brook, WH. *Demon to Vampire: The Story of No. 21 (City of Melbourne) Squadron*. Demonvamp Publication. Melbourne. 1986.

Brown, RS. Cable to Eaton A 705/1 153/1/645. 21 April, 1929. NAA. Canberra.

Brown, W. *Lasseter's Gold: The Mystery of Harold Lasseter and his Fabulously Rich Gold Reef in the Central Australian Desert*. Hachette, Sydney. 2015.

Bullock, A. *Hitler: A Study in Tyranny*. Oldham's Books, London.1964.

Burton, J. Per. comm. 12 September 1996.

Cadigan, N. *A Man Among Mavericks: Australia's Greatest Aviator*. ABC Books, Sydney. 2008.

Campbell, D. *Speak with the Sun*. Chatto & Windus, London. 1948.

Carthwright, M. *Lasseter's Gold*. Flinders University Press, Adelaide. 1997.

Central Australian Government. Resident's Annual Report. 1928/29 NT Archives. Darwin.

Centralian Advocate. 'Lasseter's Lost Reef.' 10 November 1950. Alice Springs.

Chaplin, C. *My Autobiography*. Penguin, London.1963.

Churchill, WS. *The River War: An Historical Account of the Reconquest of the Soudan*. By 2 vols. Longmans, Green and Co. London. 1899.

Clark, CD. *The Third Brother: The Royal Australian Air Force 1921–39*. Allen & Unwin, Sydney. 1991 (Also see Coultard-Clark)

Cinatti, R. Correspondence, Government of Portuguese Timor. 7 October 1947. NAA A/1838/283 Item 377/1/2 PT 1. Canberra.

Cobby, AH. *High Adventure*. Robertson & Mullins, Melbourne. 1948.

Cole, AT. Most Secret Report on No 18 Squadron. Report to CAS RAAF. 20 October, 1943. NAA A1757/100 Item P.C. 320-96 N 1-16. Canberra.

Cole, C. & Chessman EF. *Air Defence of Britain 1914–1918*. Putnam, London. 1984.

Cole, T. *Hell West & Crooked*. Angus & Robertson, Sydney. 1997.

Colebatch, H. Down the Memory-Hole: Strikes & Sabotage in Wartime Australia. Unpublished MS. 1996.

Colebatch, H. *Australia's Secret War*. Quadrant Books, Sydney. 2013.

Connellan, EJ. *Failure of Triumph: The Story of Connellan Airways*. Peter Donovan Ed., Paradigm Investments, Alice Springs. 1992.

Cook, J. *The Real Great Escape*. Vintage Books, Sydney. 2013.

Coote, E. *Hell's Kitchen*. Investigator Press, Sydney. 1982

Coultard-Clarke, C. Charles Eaton (1895–1979) in *Australian Dictionary of Biography*. Vol: 14. Melbourne University. 1996.

Coyle, T. Per. comm.

Cresswell, RC. Per. comm. 7 September 2005.

Crozier, B. *De Gaulle: The Warrior*. Eyre Methuen, London. 1973.

Cyclist Company, 47th (TF) Division. In the Line 1915-1918: Pip Squeaks from the Past: A Record in Short Bursts. Unpublished MS. NA (UK). London.

Dallas, G. *1918: War & Peace*. Pamlico, Bournemouth. 2002.

Darwin Defence Co-ordination Committee. Report Number 20 of 1 April 1940. NAA 15/501/157. Canberra.

Davis, P. *Charles Kingford Smith: Smithy, The World's Greatest Aviator*. Lansdowne Press, Sydney. 1985.

Davis, P & Smith, R. *Kookaburra: The Most Compelling Story in Australia's Aviation History*. Lansdowne Press, Sydney. 1980.

Dawson, J. Per. comm. 22 February, 2002.

Dennis, P. *The Territorial Army 1917–1940*. Royal Historical Society Studies in History 51. Boydell Press, London. 1987.

Department of Civil Aviation. Darwin Airport Provisional Master Plan. NQ 71178/4. NAA. Darwin. 1983.

Department of External Affairs. Report Portuguese Timor 'Relations with Australia: Political' A/1838/283 Item 3038/10/1 PT1. NAA. Canberra.

Department of External Affairs. 'Extract from press Lusitania'. A/1838/283 Item 3038/10/1 PT1. NAA. Canberra.

Department of External Affairs. Correspondence 'Temporary Consulate Timor'. A/1838/283 Item 3038/10/2 PT2. NAA. Canberra.

Department of External Affairs. Consul Report Dispatch No 8. 27 May, 1947. A/1838/283 Item 3038/10/2 PT2. NAA. Canberra.

Department of External Affairs. Report on the Activities of the Australian Consul at Dili Portuguese Timor. NAA. Canberra

Dermoundy, P. 'US Forces WWII Sites Survey & Memorials' in *Museums & Art Galleries of the NT*. Darwin. 1986.

Dickinson, J. Refugees in Our Own Country: The Story of Darwin's Wartime Evacuees. Historical Society of the NT. Darwin. 1995.

Diggleman, C in 18 Squadron (NEIAF) Newsletter. 1980.

Dodd, Nangari Molly. Interview with Miles Holmes, Kalkarindji. 9 March 2005.

Dorling, P. Ed. *Australia & Indonesia's Independence: Documents 1947.* Items 324, 304, 309, 316, 317, 321, 323, 324, 335, 336, 351, 356, 357, 358, 359, 360, 364, 366, 369, 372, 378, 380, 381, 382, 406, 407, 412, 416,421 & 477. AGPS. Canberra. 1994 & 1996.

Dorling, P & Lee, D. Eds. *Australia & Indonesia's Independence: The Renville Agreement.* Documents 28, 52, 120, 123, 138, 140, 160, 279, 509, 530, 545 & 546. AGPS. Canberra. 1996.

Douglas, E. Unpublished Diary entry. 28 April, 1929.

Douglas, E. Unpublished Flying Log.

Douglas, M. *Follow the Sun.* Rigby Ltd., Adelaide. 1978.

Drooglever, P. J. & Schouten M. J. B. *Officiele Bescheiden betreffende de Nederlands-Indonesische betrekkingen 1945–1950.* Rijks Geschiedkundige Publicatien Kleine Serie 52. s-Gravenhage Verrijbaarbij MARTINUS NIJHOFF, The Hauge. 1982.

Dunn, J. *East Timor: A Rough Passage to Independence.* Jacaranda Press, Sydney. 1983.

Dunn, J. *Timor: A People Betrayed.* ABC Books, Sydney. 1996.

Dunn, JC. *The War the Infantry Knew 1914–1919.* Cardinal Press (re-print), London. 1987.

Durnford, HG. *The Tunnellers of Holzmidden.* Cambridge University Press. Cambridge. 1930.

Eaton, B. Per. comm.

Eaton, B. My Journey. Unpublished MS. Eaton Collection. NTAS. Darwin.

Eaton, B. Via the Kruger National Park. Unpublished MS. Eaton Collection. NTAS. Darwin.

Eaton, BJ. Per. comm.

Eaton, C. Operations in Connection with the Search for & the Burial of Lieutenant Anderson & Mr Hitchcock. Official RAAF Report 1929. A 705/1 153/1/645. NAA. Canberra. 1929.

Eaton, C. 'Central Australia' in *Bomber.* August 1931. Melbourne.

Eaton, C. Unpublished biographic MS (1953). Eaton Collection. NTSA. Darwin.

Eaton, C. The Bear Fight. Unpublished MS. Eaton Collection. NTSA. Darwin.

Eaton, C. Fear. Unpublished MS. Eaton Collection. NTSA. Darwin.

Eaton, C. *The Cross in the Sky.* Unpublished MS. Eaton Collection. NTSA. Darwin.

Eaton, C. Per. comm. ABC. 20 May 1972.

Eaton, C. Per. comm Joyce Batty. 6 June 1974.

Eaton, C. Interview ABC, 19 September 1975.

Eaton, C. Per. comm David Poynter of the ABC. 19 September 1975.

Eaton, C. Unpublished Report. Operations in Connection with the Search for the Missing Airmen in Central Australia. January, 1931. NAA. Canberra.

Eaton, C. Correspondence to RAAF on Huts for Recreational Purposes Darwin. A 816/1 Item 37/301/25. 11 March 1940. NAA. Canberra.

Eaton, C. Correspondence to RAAF on employment of Aboriginals in the RAAF. A1196/6 Item 15/501/157. 28 April 1940. NAA. Canberra.

Eaton, C. Correspondence to RAAF on proposal to change name of RAAF Darwin. A 9300 171/6/150 23 April 1941. NAA. Canberra.

Eaton, C. 'General Summary of Contact with NEI Air Force.' *18 Squadron Newsletter*. April 1990.

Eaton, C. Dispatches 1946–1947. A1838 Item 377/3/1 Pts I & II. NAA. Canberra.

Eaton, C. Dispatch 14/47 9 June 1947. Baucau Aerodrome. A1838 Item 377/3/1 Pt 1. NAA. Canberra.

Eaton, C. Consular Series No. 63, Australian Consulate Dili, 12 May 1947. A1830, TS400/1/9/1/1. NAA. Canberra.

Eaton. C. Memorandum for the Secretary, Department of Defence, 23 May 1947. A1830, TS400/1/9/1/1. NAA. Canberra.

Eaton, CS. & Jung, S. 'Operation Potshot: Dutch Airmen in the defence of Western Australia, 1944'. In Peters, N. (Ed.) *A Touch of Dutch on the Western Third: Dutch maritime, military, migration, mercantile connections with Western Australia 1616–2016*. Carina Hoang, Perth. 2016.

Eaton, D. Per. comm.

Eaton, P. Per. comm.

Edmunds, Sir James, Ed. *History of the Great War*. Committee of Imperial Defence, London. 1922.

Elder, P. Charles Lydiard Aubrey Abbott: Countryman or Colonial Governor. Ph.D. Thesis, Northern Territory University. Darwin. 1998.

Elwin, Verrier. *Tribal Myths of Orissa*. Specimens of The Oral Literature of Middle India, Oxford University. Oxford. 1954.

Esher, Viscount in Maude, A. *The 47th (TF) London Division 1914-1919*. Amalgamated (1922) Press, London. 1922

Farram, S. *Charles 'Moth' Eaton: Pioneer Aviator of the Northern Territory*. CDU Press, Darwin. 2007.

Farram, S. *A Short-lived Enthusiasm: The Australian Consulate in Portuguese Timor*. CDU Press. Darwin. 2010.

Farram, S. *Indonesia, 1947: Australia and the first United Nations Cease-Fire Order*. Australian Scholarly Publishing, North Melbourne. 2019.

Fenton, C. *Flying Doctor*. Georgian House, Melbourne. 1947.

Fetherston, AB. *Towards a Theory of United Nations Peacekeepers*. St. Martin's, New York. 1995.

Fisher, C. Per. comm. 1998 &1999.

Foreign Office (UK). Report on visit to East Java area by Mr C Eaton, Consul-General of Australia & Mr E Raux, Consul-General of France, 7 September 1947. Consular Commission Report, 11 October 1947. FO 810/6. Appendix I. NA (UK). London.

Foreign Office (UK). Minutes of Informal Meeting Held between Committee of Good Officers & the Consular Commission, 10 November 1947. Ref Political FO 810/4. NA (UK). London.

Foreign Office (UK). Consular Commission Report, 11 October 1947. Ref FO 810/6. NA (UK). London.

Gani, AK. Telegram: Indonesian Republican Government. 2 October 1947. Ref: A 4355 2001/02955892 Item 7/1/7/10. NAA. Canberra.

George, M. *Australia & the Indonesian Revolution*. Melbourne University Press, Melbourne. 1980.

Gillison, D. *Australia in the War of 1939–45: The Royal Australian Air Force.* AWM, Canberra. 1962.

Godfrey, HV. Per. comm. 1965.

Grantham, S. *The 13 Squadron Story.* SR. Grantham, Sydney. 1991.

Graves, R. *Goodbye to All That.* Revised Edition. Cassell, London. 1957.

Greenwood JT. Ed. *Milestones of Aviation.* Smithsonian Institute National Air & Space Museum. Hugh Lauter & Levin, New York. 1989.

Griffiths O. *Darwin Drama.* Bloxham & Chambers, Sydney. 1947.

Grose, P. *An Awkward Truth.* Allen & Unwin, Sydney. 2009.

Gullet, J. 'Not as a Duty' in *The West Australian.* 6 July, 1994. Perth.

Gunn, GC with Lee, J. 'A Critical View of Western Journalism & Scholarship on East Timor' in *Journal of Contemporary Asia.* Manila. 1994.

Hackshall, R. Per. comm. 17 January 1996.

Hancock, Sir Valston. Per. comm. 7 July 1992.

Hanson, N. *Escape from Germany.* Transworld, London. 2011.

Hargraves, R. Oral History interview. 226 TS 61. NTAS. Darwin.

Hart, CA. *Air Photography Applied to Surveying.* Longmans, Green & Co, Harlow. 1955.

Haslett, John. The Search for the Kookaburra. Unpublished MS. NT Aviation History Preservation, Darwin. 1963.

Hatfield, K. Per. comm.

Haydon, J. Charles Eaton in *Dictionary of Biography of The Northern Territory.* Carment, D. *et al* Eds. Vol.1., NTU Press. Darwin. 1990.

Hayes, Grace. *World War One: A Compact History.* Hawthorn Book, New York. 1972.

Helson, Peter. The Forgotten Air Force. The Establishment and Employment of Australian Air Power in the North-Western Area, 1941–1945. MA Thesis, University of New South Wales, Sydney. 1997.

Henderson, D. & Warburton, I. *An Illustrated History of No 12 Squadron RAAF: 1939-1948.* Air Power Centre, Canberra. 1980.

Henshaw, T. *The Sky Their Battlefield.* Grubb Street, London. 1995.

Herington, J. *Air War Against Germany & Italy: 1939–1943.* AWM, Canberra. 1954.

Hinton, R in Warner, P. *World War One a Chronological Narrative.* Brockhampton Press, Leicester. 2000.

His Majesty's Stationary Office. Cyclist Training (Provisional), London. 1914.

His Majesty's Stationary Office. Cyclist Training (Provisional), London. 1917.

Holland, John. *Adolf Hitler.* Doubleday, New York. 1976.

Holmes, M. Per. comm. 2005.

http://en.wikipedia.org/wiki/List_of_prisoner-of-war_camps_in_Germany.

https://wikivisually.com/wiki/Japanese_occupation_of_the_Dutch_East_Indies

http://www.telegraph.co.uk/history/world-war-one/10849528/ in Pictures never before see photographs from World War One frontline.html. frame =2919231.

Hurst, D. *The Fourth Ally: The Dutch Forces in Australia in WWII*. D. Hurst, Canberra. 2001.

Imperial Forestry Service. Revenue Department, Orissa. File No. IIIF—19 of 1920. pp5. 1920. India House, London. 1920.

Indian Army. *The Army in India & its Evolution*. Government Printer, Calcutta. 1924.

Jackson, DJ. *Flying the Mail*. Life–Time Books. Alexandria, Virginia. 1982.

Jane's. *Fighting Aircraft of World War* I. Studio Editions, London. 1990.

Jones, Sir George. *From Private to Air Marshal: The Autobiography of Air Marshal Sir George Jones KBE CB DFC*. Greenhouse, Melbourne. 1988.

Jubb, RV. Per. comm.

Kelly, Kieran. *Tanami: on foot across Australia's desert heart*. Macmillan, Sydney. 2003.

Keng Po. Mirco film. Photo Science Studies n.d. Cornell University, 13 September, 1947. Ithaca, New York.

Kennedy, F. 'Bringing the Kookaburra Back'. *The Advertiser Saturday Review,* 7 December, 1974. Adelaide.

Kershaw, Ian. *Hitler*. Penguin, London. 2008.

Kimber, RG. 'Walawurru: The Giant Eaglehawk: Aboriginal Reminiscences of Aircraft in Central Australia'. *Aboriginal History*. Vol.6: 1-2. ANU Press, Canberra. 1982.

Kingford Smith, Rollo. Per. comm. 1996.

Kingsland, Sir Richard. Interview for RAAF Museum Point Cook. A8080679. D04. Point Cook. Victoria.

Kingsland, Sir Richard. Per. comm.

Kym@Cam.rcn.com. Per. comm. 31 August 2000.

Laffin, John. *British Butchers & Bunglers of World War One*. Macmillan, Sydney. 1998.

Lancaster, A. https://www.amazon.com/Lost-Aviator-Ewen-\Leslie/dp/B01NAU8ZV0. 2017.

Lax, M. 'The RAAF's First Mid--air Collision' in *Flying Safely Spotlight*, Department of Defence, 2nd Ed., Canberra. 1996.

Lax, M. 'The Albert Medal Crash' in *Flying Safely Spotlight*, Department of Defence, 2nd Ed., Canberra. 1996.

Lax, M. 'A Hint of Things to Come' in *Proceedings of Air Force History Conference*. RAAF Air Power Centre, Canberra. 2001.

Lee, D. Ed. *Australia & Indonesia's Independence: The Transfer of Sovereignty: Documents 1949*. AGPS, Canberra. 1998.

Lewis, C. *Sagittarius Rising*. Warner Books, London. 1998.

Lindall Hart, BH. *The Memoirs of Captain Liddell Hart: Volumes I and II*. Cassell, London.1965.

Lockwood, D in *The Herald*. 30 January 1946. Melbourne.

Londey, P. 'Sixty Years of Keeping the Peace' in *Wartime*. AWM, Canberra. 2001.

Londey, P. *Other People's Wars: A History of Australian Peacekeeping*. Allen & Unwin, Sydney. 2004.

Londey, P. 'Inventing Peacekeeping' in *Australian Peacekeeping: 60 Years in the Field*. Part 1 Chapter 1. Horner, P. Londey, P. Bou, J. Eds. Cambridge Press, Port Melbourne. 2009.

Long, Gavin. *The Six Years War: Australia in the 1939–45 War*. AWM, Canberra. 1974.

Lugg, R. Per. comm. 1994.

MacArthur, General Douglas. Correspondence to Admiral Coster USN. 5 January 1943. 503/528. NAA. Canberra.

MacDonald, L in *1914–1918: Voices & Images of the Great War*. Mac Gill, P. Ed., Penguin, London. 1991.

Mackersey, I. *Smithy: The Life of Sir Charles Kingsford Smith*. Little, Brown & Co., London. 1998.

Macksey, K. *Vimy Ridge 1914–1918*. Illustrated History of World War One No 6. Pan Books, London. 1972.

Madigan, CT. *Central Australia*. Oxford University Press, Melbourne. 1944.

Madigan, S. Oral History interview. 226 TS 274, NTAS. Darwin.

Makin, J. *The Big Run: The Story of Victoria River Downs Station*. Rigby, Adelaide. 1976.

Mann, IE. 'Bill'. Per. comm. 14 March, 1994.

Maude, Alan. *The 47th (TF) London Division 1914-1919*. Amalgamated (1922) Press, London. 1922.

McKenzie, N. Per. comm. 2018.

McGregor, A. *Frank Hurley: A Photographer's Life*. Penguin-Viking, Melbourne. 2004.

Mc Whae, H. Per. comm.

Mead, P. *The Eye in the Air: History of Air Observation & Reconnaissance for the Army 1785-1945*. HMSO. London. 1983.

Mitze, Katja. 'Das Kriegsgefangenenlager Ingolstart.' Ährend des Ersten Weltkriegs, Berlin. 2000.

Moffat, S. Per. comm. 1985.

Moran, CMW. *The Anatomy of Courage*. Constable, London. 1945.

Morris, DM. Per. comm. 5 May 1973.

Morris, Joseph. *The German Air Raids on Great Britain: 1914–1918*. H. Pordes, London. 1969.

Mountbatten, Lord Louis. Telegram from Lord Mountbatten on the situation in Indonesia, 21 November, 1945. 01/01.1945.CAB 119/193. NA (UK), London.

Mowat, C. *Britain Between the Wars 1918-1940*. The University of Chicago Press, Chicago. 1969. Moyse-Bartlett, H. *The Kings African Rifles*. Gale & Polden, Aldershot. 1956.

Nangari, Molly Dodd. Interview with Miles Holmes, Kalkarindji. 9 March 2005.

Nash, David. 'Aboriginal Knowledge of the Aeroplane Kookaburra' in *Aboriginal History*, Vol. 6. ANU Press, Canberra. 1982. National Archives of Australia. Kookaburra/Anderson & Hitchcock. A458/1 Y314/4/42. Canberra.

National Achieves of Australia. Southern Cross Flight & Loss in Northern Australia. Loss of Aeroplane 'Kookaburra' in Central Australia. Deaths of Anderson & Hitchcock. Series 741/3: Item 6410, Correspondence 13 June 1929. Canberra.

National Archives of Australia. The Kookaburra Files, A705/1 153/1/695. Canberra.

National Archives of Australia. Special Subject Kookaburra—Anderson & Hitchcock. A 3900 G10/A. Canberra. 1929.

National Archives of Australia. The Search for the Kookaburra. A 153/1/645. Canberra. 1929.

National Archives of Australia. Report on participation of Qantas in the Kookaburra search. A 705/1 153/1/645, Canberra. 1929.

National Archives of Australia. F 706/3 60/39. Darwin.

National Archives of Australia. F 742/0 1950/588 M. Darwin.

National Archives of Australia. The Southern Cloud Memorial. A5628/3 66/715. Canberra.

National Archives of Australia. The Southern Cloud Correspondence. A458/1 AG 314/1. Canberra.

National Archives of Australia. The Southern Cloud Correspondence. B741/3 V/8526. Canberra.

National Archives of Australia. Defence Orders Potshot Report. A A11243: ZI 17/3466677 17/3085362 & A1838 140062. Canberra

National Archives of Australia. Summary of Violations of the Crease Fire Order on 5 September 1947. A 4355. 2001/02955892 Item 7/1/7/10. Canberra.

National Archives of Australia. Royal Legation of the Netherlands to Department of External Affairs. Ref A1068 Item 1c47/15/2/2/1 C9/4369. Canberra.

National Library of Australia. Air Inquiry Committee Report on the Aircraft Southern Cross and the Aircraft Kookaburra. Canberra. 1929.

National Census (UK), 1881. NA (UK). London.

Neillands, R. *The Great War Generals: On the Western Front 1914–1918.* Magpie Books, London. 2004.

Norris, Geoffrey. *The Royal Flying Corps: A History.* Fredrick Muller, London. 1965.

Odgers, G. *Air War against Japan: 1943–1945.* AWM, Canberra. 1957.

Ortweiler, FJ. In Public Records Office. (UK). WO 161/96: O.408 pp 1128–1133. Experiences while in Germany of Lt. FJ. Ortweiler, RFC. London.

Osmet, P in Warner, P. *World War One a Chronological Narrative.* Brockhampton Press, Leicester. 2000.

Owers, C. *On Silver Wings.* Unpublished MS. CA Owers, PO 73 Boorowa. NSW.

Owers, C. 'De Havilland Aircraft of World War.' Vol. 2 DH 5-DH 15. Flying Machine Press, San Jose CA. 2001.

Parnell, NM. *Whispering Death: A History of the RAAF's Beaufighter Squadrons.* AH & AW Reed Pty. Ltd., Sydney. 1980.

Plenty, ED. 'Charles Eaton: Pioneer Aviator' in *Tennant Creek Times:* Tennant Creek, April Edition. 1981.

Pittendrigh, WL. Copy of Personal Diary. 20 December, 1930 to 12 January, 1931. In Eaton Collection, NTAS. Darwin.

Powell, A. *The Shadow's Edge: Australia's Northern War.* Melbourne University Press, Melbourne. 1988.

Public Records Office (UK). 95/7743 XC 6161 Operation Order 36, WO. 7 July 1916. London.

Public Records Office (UK). British Army Service Medals Record. WO. London.

Public Records Office (UK). 2744 OC 24 Battalion Narrative of Events 25–26 May 1915. WO. London.

Public Records Office (UK). 630 95/2740 7787 142 Infantry Brigade 'Operational Order'. WO 16 April 1915. London.

Public Records Office (UK). 95 2734 War Diary of the 22 (Queens) Battalion. 47 (TF) Division. WO. London.

Public Records Office (UK). 95 2717 War Diary of the 47 (TF) Division's Cyclist Company. 24 May 1916. WO. London.

Public Records Office (UK). 95 737 7787 War Diary of the IV Corps Cyclist Battalion. WO. London.

Public Records Office. (UK). Air/1/2396258/1 pp 159. RFC Casualty Reports. London.

Public Records Office. (UK). Air 1/610/18/15/276 xc 6602 Report on the Air Defences of London.

Public Records Office. (UK). Air 27/1221 Operations Record Book No 19 (G.R.) Squadron, 1917–18. London.

Public Records Office. (UK). Air 1/1826/204/7 xc 5889 Routine Orders 10 June 1918. London.

Public Records Office. (UK). Air 1/1826/204/7 xc 5889 Routine Orders 30 June 1918. London.

Public Records Office. (UK). Air 1/177/15/212/1 xc 7186 History of 206 Squadron. 1918. London.

Public Records Office. (UK) Air 1/1829/204/202/20 xc 5924. London.

Public Records Office. (UK). Air 1/1187/204/5/2595 xc 7186. London.

Public Records Office. (UK). Air 1/162 X C 5449, 12/04/1919. London.

Public Records Office. (UK). Air 1/2400/286/2/PL2 5449k 5/7/1919. London.

Rathbone, CEH. Experiences while in Germany of Colonel CEH Rathbone, Royal Marines. WO 161/96: O.373. pp1071-1072. PRO (UK). London.

Robinson, D. *The Zeppelin in Combat: A History of the German Naval Airship Division, 1912–1918.* Foulis, London. 1966.

Robertson, J. *Australia at War: 1939-45.* William Heinemann, Burwood NSW. 1981.

Rorrison, JD. *Nor the Years Condemn: Air War on the Australian Front: 1941–42.* Palomar, Sydney. 1992.

Rowe, Alan. '206 Squadron RAF: Some Australian Connections' in *Cross & Cockade*, Vol.28/1. London. 1997.

Rowe, Alan. 'Captain INC Clarke DSC & Bar. An experienced Australian bomber pilot with Nos. 5, 6 & 206 Squadron RAF' in *Cross & Cockade. Vol. 32/3, London.* 2001.

Royal Air Force. Service Record of Flt. Lt. Charles Eaton RFC/RAF 1917–1920. Eaton Collection, NTAS. Darwin.

Royal Australian Air Force. Operation Log Book 12 Squadron. 6 February 1939 to 30 June 1940. RAAF Historical Section. Canberra.

Royal Australian Air Force. Operation Log Book RAAF Darwin. 1 July 1940 to 10 October 1941. RAAF Historical Section. Canberra.

Royal Australian Air Force. Correspondence on proposal of name change, RAAF Darwin. 9300 171/6/150 6 May 1941. NAA. Canberra

Royal Australian Air Force. Brief History of R.AAF Darwin. Unpublished manuscript, RAAF Historical Section. Canberra. 1990.

Royal Australian Air Force. *Units of the Royal Australian Air Force. A Concise History* Vol. 1 RAAF Historical Section, Canberra. 1995.

Royal Australian Air Force. *Units of the Royal Australian Air Force: A Concise History.* Vol. 3 RAAF Historical Section, Canberra. 1995.

Royal Australian Air Force. Darwin Operation Record Book. 1941. RAAF Historical Section, Canberra.

Royal Australian Air Force. Operation Log Book RAAF Darwin. 1 July 1940 to10 October 1941. RAAF Historical Section, Canberra.

Royal Australian Air Force. Brief History of RAAF Darwin. Unpublished MS. RAAF Historical Section. Canberra. 1990.

Royal Australian Air Force. *Units of the Royal Australian Air Force. A Concise History Vol. 3 Bomber Units*. Compiled by the RAAF Historical Section. Canberra. 1995.

Royal Australian Air Force. Secret Report on the Reconnaissance of Koepang, Ambon, Namlea, Baro & Saumlaki by G/C C Eaton & W/C W Hely. March, 1941. RAAF Historical Section, Canberra.

Royal Australian Air Force. Operation Record Book 72 Wing. 26 April–10 May 1943. Air Power Centre. Canberra.

Royal Australian Air Force. Senior Staff Officer's Report, HQ North-Eastern Area. 25 May 1943. 19/129/AIR. NAA. Canberra.

Salmond, Sir John. Salmond Report. A5954 1285/10. NAA. Canberra. 1928. Salmond, Sir John. Salmond Report. A5945/69 1347/32. NAA. Canberra. 1928.

Saunders, R. Interview with Charles Eaton. 15 September 1975.

Schaedel, C. Unpublished Profiles of Pre-war WWII Australian Airmen. Adelaide. 2006.

Schaedel, C. Per. comm. 21 July & 28 August 2005. 17 January, 2006.

Schaedel, C. *Australian Air Ace: The Exploits of 'Jerry' Pentland & MC DFC AFC*. Rigby, Adelaide. 1979.

Scott, EC. Threads of Significance: Indonesia–Australia Relations 1945–1975. Unpublished Ph.D. Thesis, UWA. 2004.

Senapati, N. Chief Editor. *Orissa District Gazetteers*. Orissa Government Press, Cuttack. 1971.

Sheldrake, R. Per. comm. 9 May 2006.

Shepherd, Sir F. Correspondence to RHS Allen. 12 September 1947. NA (UK). Ref Political FO 810/4 1/331/47. London.

Shepherd, Sir F. Correspondence to RHS Allen. 16 September 1947. NA (UK). Ref Political FO 810/4 30/66/47. London.

Simões, E. Per. comm.

Sinclair, FR. Ministry of the Army Memorandum 46332. A/1066/4 Item S45/156. NAA. Canberra.

Skeet, M. 'RFC Pilot Training'. www.thearodrome.com/aces/training/index.html. 1999.

Slowe, P. & Woods, R. *Fields of Death: Battle Scenes of the First World War*. R Hale, London. 1990.

Staal, J. Per. comm. 23 December 1993.

Stevenson, B. *The Home Book of Quotations: Classical & Modern*. 10th Ed. Greenwich House, New York. 1958.

Sullivan, P. RAAF Report. A 705/1 153/1/645. 8 May 1929. NAA. Canberra.

Sun Tzu in *The Art of War*, Arcturus Publishing Ltd, London. 2018.

Taylor, AM. *Indonesian Independence & the United Nations*. Stevens & Sons, London. 1960.

Teppema, TE. Correspondence to Department of External Affairs. Ref A1068 Item 1c47/15/2/2/1 C9/4369. 2 September 1947. NAA. Canberra.

Terry, Michael. *Hidden Wealth & Hiding People*. Putnam, London. 1930.

The Advertiser. 'Long Trek for Lost Reef'. 2 February 1951. Adelaide.

The Age. April–May *1929*. Melbourne.

The Age. 1 October 1929. Melbourne.

The Age. 7 October 1929. Melbourne.

The Argus. 22 April *1927*. Melbourne.

The Argus. 'Missing Prospectors: Still No News'. 6 January 1931. Melbourne.

The Argus. 'Disastrous Attack by Rockets'. 20 November 1944. Melbourne.

The Canberra Times. 'Consul was not afraid'. Reuters Press Release. 10 September 1947. Canberra.

The Guardian Weekly. 'Anger at Blow to Rights of India's Forest People.' 22 February 2013. London.

The Herald. 'Modest Eaton: Gives Credit Another'. 12 January 1931. Melbourne.

The Herald. 'Air Pageant: Four State Contest Draws in Big Crowds.' 21 May 1931. Melbourne.

The Indo Project. https://theindoproject.org/resources/links/the-bersiap-2/. 2019.

The Nhill Free Press. 'Armistice Celebrations: Squadron-Leader Eaton Present.' 18 November 1937. Nhill.

The Sydney Truth. 'Expedition in Search of Lasseter's Fabulous Reef'. 21 January 1951.

The Sun. 'Cloud Hit the Mountain Flying the Wrong Way'. 29 October 1958. Melbourne.

The Tennant Creek Times. April Edition. Tennant Creek, NT. 1981.

The Victorian Truth. 'Lasseter Alive! Gold Reef Hoax.' 24 November 1956. Melbourne.

Thomas, EP. Correspondence to Navel Board on Combined Recreational Huts Darwin. 1 Feb 1940 A 816/1 Item 37/301/25. NAA. Canberra.

Trafford, F. Proposal to place Khond villages in the Banpur Mals under the Forest Department. Conservator of Forests Bihar & Orissa. File No IIIF-19 of 1920. India Office, NA (UK). London.

Trainor, J. 'Loos 1915' in *War Monthly.* Issue 47, Marshall & Cavendish, London. 1977.

Truscott, J. Per. comm. 27 October, 1993.

Truscott, J. Oral History Review. 226 TS 347. NTAS. Darwin.

Turner, D. Per. comm. 9 May 2006.

Tymms, F and Porri, C. *Flying for Air Survey Photography*. HMSO, London. 1927.

United States Army. Allied Geographical Section, SW Pacific Area; Study 44. 7 January 1943. Geology Library, UWA. Perth.

United States Navy. Report of Patrol Squadron 22 by Lieutenant Commander F. O'Beirne USN. VP22/A4. 9 September 1941. (C-073). Washington. van Beuge, H. Per. comm. 19 April 2002.

Vickers, A. *A History of Modern Indonesia*. Cambridge University Press, New York. 2005.

Warner, P. *The Battle of Loos.* William Kimber, London. 1976.

Watt, AS. Correspondence Department of External Affairs to Secretary Public Services. NAA A/1066/4 Item S45/156. Canberra. 1946.

Weers, Mozes. 'Military Affairs Abroad: Seventy Years of Netherlands Air Force History' in Air University Review. Maxwell Air Force Base, Alabama: Department of the Air Force. May–June 1985.

Wells, K. Pers. comm. 14 April 2005.

Whitehouse, A. *The Zeppelin Fighters*. Robert Hale, London. 1966.

Whitlam, EG Hon. Per. comm. 1996.

Williams, L. Per. comm. 2018.

Williams, RD. *Medals to Australians from 1858–1999 with Valuations*. 4th Ed. Downie's, Melbourne. 2000.

Williamson, M. 'From Trench to Sky' in *Cross & Cockade*. The First World War Aviation Historical Society. Vo.33:2. 2002. London.

Williamson, M. 'On a Wing & a Prayer: 'Moth' Eaton over Timor' in *Wartime*. Ed: 10. 2000. AWM. Canberra.

Wilson HW and Hammerton JA (Eds). *The Great War*. Vol. 9. The Amalgamated Press, London. 1917.

Wilson-Smith, W. Per. comm. 30 March 1994.

Wixted, EP. *The North West Aerial Frontier, 1919–1934*. Boolarong Publications, Brisbane. 1985.

Wray, CH. *Timor 1942: Australian Commandos at War with the Japanese*. Hutchinson, Hawthorn. 1987.

Young. AJ. 'The Royal Air Force in the North West Frontier India, 1915–1939' in *Journal of RUSI*. 1983. London.

Zekulich Michael. 'Death of Pioneer Aviator, Charles Eaton' in *The West Australian*. 20 Nov, 1979. Perth.

Photographs

The majority of the photographic images are from the Charles Eaton Collection (1914–1945) at the Aviation Museum, Bull Creek West Australia and the Charles Eaton Collection (1946–1950) at the Australian War Memorial in Canberra, unless otherwise cited in the text. The author appreciates the RAAF Air Power Canberra for allowing the publication of all official RAAF images, which form a significant segment of the Charles Eaton Collection. Also, Mr Dick Smith AC of Sydney for permission to include images from his publication *Kookaburra: The Most Compelling Story in Australia's Aviation History.*

www.ingramcontent.com/pod-product-compliance
Lightning Source LLC
Chambersburg PA
CBHW080222170426
43192CB00015B/2715